1ST EDITION

The Directory of Grant Making Trusts

FOCUS SERIES

Rural conservation and animal welfare

EDITORIAL TEAM
Johanna Davis
David Moncrieff
Joanna Wootton

© **1999 CAF**

Published by CAF (Charities Aid Foundation)
Kings Hill
West Malling
Kent ME19 4TA

Telephone
+44 (0) 1732 520000

Fax
+44 (0) 1732 520001

Website
http://www.charitynet.org

E-mail
cafpubs@caf.charitynet.org

Database management and typesetting
The Polestar Group (Whitefriars) Ltd

Design
Eugenie Dodd Typographics

Printed and bound in Great Britain by Bell & Bain Ltd, Glasgow

A catalogue record for this book is available from the British Library.

ISBN 1–85934–108–X

All rights reserved; no part of this work may be reproduced in any form, by mimeograph or any other means, without permission in writing from the publisher.

No responsibility for loss occasioned to any person acting or refraining from action as a result of the material in this publication can be accepted by the Charities Aid Foundation.

Contents

Introduction	v
The trusts we have listed	vi
The structure of the directory	vii
How to use the directory key steps	xi
About CAF	xv
Other publications from CAF	xvi
Trusts by geographical area	**2**
Trusts by field of interest	**18**
Trusts by grant type	**32**
Alphabetical register of grant making trusts	**49**

Introduction

It has been estimated that there are approximately 8,800 charitable grant makers in the UK. These are a major source of funding for the voluntary sector both in the UK and overseas. Figures published by CAF in the 1998 edition of *Dimensions of the Voluntary Sector* indicate that in 1997 the trust and foundation community had an income of approximately £2.1 billion and made grants of approximately £1.9 billion.

CAF published the first edition of *The Directory of Grant Making Trusts* (*DGMT*) in 1968. Since that time, the title has gained a notable reputation as a comprehensive guide to UK grant making trusts and their funding policies. Today it is hard to imagine the difficulties which must have been encountered in trying to obtain funds from trusts before the *DGMT* threw a spotlight on their existence.

Since the publication of the last edition of the *DGMT*, extensive research has been undertaken amongst both users of the directory, the grant seekers, and with the trusts themselves, the grant givers. One important message to come out of this research is that grant seekers want more information about trusts' policies. For their part trusts are desperate that applications should be targeted more accurately towards individual trusts' guidelines. It is the *DGMT*'s role to address these issues and bring the grant seekers and grant givers together to make the workload of both less onerous.

The *Directory of Grant Making Trusts Focus Series* was developed in response to demand from our readers. Many expressed the view that, while the main edition of the directory is extremely useful to larger organisations and reference libraries, smaller local bodies with a specialist interest could benefit from a publication containing a smaller, more focused selection of trusts.

Features new to the *Focus Series* include:

- an easier to read layout;
- clear headings in the trust entries;
- an index of trusts by grant type to further enhance the searching process;
- the top ten grants made by many trusts.

It is hoped that this book will provide grant seekers working in the fields of rural conservation and animal welfare with clear and accurate information on trusts most likely to be interested in funding their work.

The trusts we have listed

The details of trusts registered under the law of England and Wales are recorded on the public register at the Charity Commission and are consequently available for publication. As there is no register available in Scotland and Northern Ireland we have relied on either direct contact with the Scottish and Irish trusts listed or other published material in order to obtain the most up-to-date information.

Every trust in the directory was asked to update the information contained in its entry and to classify its grant-making activities for 1999–2000. Many of the trusts we contact are extremely helpful and provide us with comprehensive information on their funding policies.

However, not all trusts are so helpful and open. Where a trust did not respond to our request to amend its entry, the details have been updated using the information on its file at the Charity Commission. We have stated where we have been unable to find financial records on file for later than 1995. However, it should be noted that, in CAF's experience, records held by the Charity Commission in respect of accounts filed are not always accurate.

A new, more robust policy has been introduced to determine which trusts should be omitted from this listing. We believe that trust directories provide an invaluable bridge between the trust community and the rest of the voluntary sector, and that trusts in receipt of public funds through tax relief should not attempt to draw a veil of secrecy over their activities. Consequently, we have declined the majority of requests from trusts to be excluded from this directory.

In general we have included:

- trusts which make grants to charities and voluntary organisations (including the National Lottery boards and Arts Councils).

We have excluded:

- trusts which fund individuals only;
- trusts which fund one organisation exclusively;
- trusts whose funds are demonstrably fully committed for the life of the directory;
- trusts which have ceased to exist.

Frequent users of our directories will note a change of policy regarding trusts that do not respond to unsolicited applications. These trusts are now being included because we believe that this gives fundraisers a broader overview of the grant making community and because the information could be important in supporting relationship fundraising activity.

The structure of the directory

This directory contains three indexes:

- Trusts by geographical area;
- Trusts by field of interest;
- Trusts by grant type.

Using these indexes, users should end up with a shortlist of trusts whose funding policies match their needs. They can then look at the individual trust details in the Alphabetical register of grant making trusts

Trusts by geographical area

This index enables you to see which trusts will consider applications from a charity or project in a particular geographical area.

These pages contain two separate listings:

LIST OF GEOGRAPHICAL AREA HEADINGS

This is a complete list of all the geographical area headings used in the directory. The page numbers relate to the second listing.

LIST OF TRUSTS BY GEOGRAPHICAL AREA

These pages list trusts under the geographical areas from which they will consider applications for funding.

Trusts by field of interest

This index enables you to see which trusts are likely to fund projects doing a particular type of work. These pages list trusts according to:

- the type of activity or work they are willing to fund – their 'fields of interest'

These pages contain two separate listings:

CATEGORISATION OF FIELDS OF INTEREST

This lists all of the headings used in the directory to categorise fields of interest. This listing should help you match your project with one – or more – of the categories used. The page numbers relate to the second listing.

LIST OF TRUSTS BY FIELD OF INTEREST

These pages list trusts under the fields of interest they have indicated they might be willing to support.

Trusts were asked to indicate whether projects working in a field of interest:

- are a **funding priority**, ie the area is one which the trust is particularly interested in funding;
- **will be considered**, ie the trust may consider funding in the area but it is not one of their priorities.

vii

Trusts by grant type

This index enables you to see which trusts will consider making the types of grant you are looking for. Trusts are listed under the types of grant that they have indicated they are willing to make.

These pages contain two separate listings:

LIST OF GRANT TYPES

This lists all of the headings used in the directory to categorise grant types. Page numbers relate to the second listing.

LIST OF TRUSTS BY GRANT TYPE

These pages list trusts under the types of grant that they are willing to make.

Trusts were asked to indicate whether the grant types:

- are a **funding priority**, ie the type of grant the trust prefers to give;
- **will be considered**, ie the trust may consider making this type of grant.

Users should note that, although all trusts are listed under at least one geographical area and field of interest, not all trusts will be listed under grant type.

Alphabetical register of grant making trusts

The alphabetical register of grant making trusts contains the core data about the individual trusts held on the database.

In 1997 the Top 300 grant making trusts as defined by CAF gave away £1,132,877,000. In view of this total, we feel that it is important for these trusts to be covered in more detail than they have in previous directories.

For most of 1998 CAF's team undertook an extensive research exercise and personally contacted 300 major trusts in order to gain a greater understanding of their grant making policies. This information was then used to produce an in-depth commentary. The entries for these trusts are divided into two parts: the first part contains 'at a glance' details of the trusts' funding policies, and the second part contains the commentary. The number in brackets by the trust name indicates its position in the Top 300.

Each trust in the Top 300 was asked to send CAF a copy of their latest Annual Report and Accounts, which they are legally required to provide, upon request, to any person under section 47(2) of the Charities Act 1993. Fifty of these trusts did not send us a copy of their Annual Report and Accounts. As a result of this, we sent a team of researchers into the Charity Commission to find the most up-to-date information for these trusts. However, we were unable to find financial records later than 1995 on file for four trusts, and there was insufficient information to write a substantive commentary for a further 12 trusts.

A typical trust entry

A complete entry should contain information under the headings listed below. An explanation of the information which should appear in these fields appears alongside.

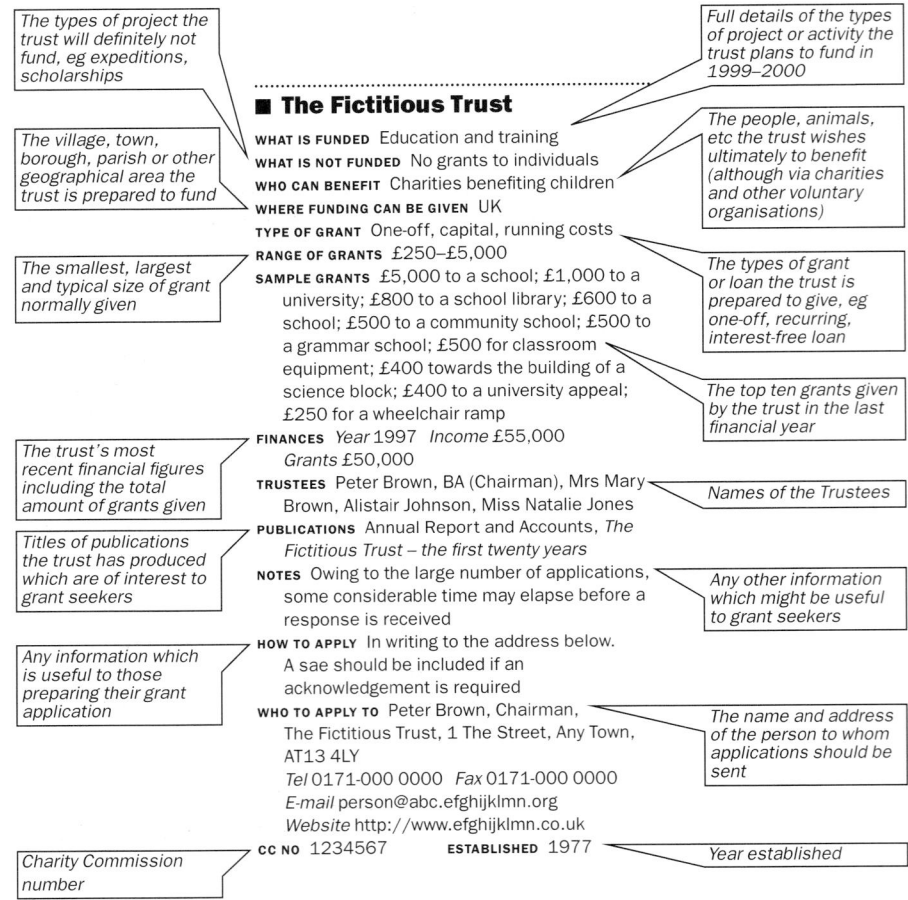

■ The Fictitious Trust

Full details of the types of project or activity the trust plans to fund in 1999–2000

WHAT IS FUNDED Education and training

The types of project the trust will definitely not fund, eg expeditions, scholarships

WHAT IS NOT FUNDED No grants to individuals

The people, animals, etc the trust wishes ultimately to benefit (although via charities and other voluntary organisations)

WHO CAN BENEFIT Charities benefiting children

The village, town, borough, parish or other geographical area the trust is prepared to fund

WHERE FUNDING CAN BE GIVEN UK

The types of grant or loan the trust is prepared to give, eg one-off, recurring, interest-free loan

TYPE OF GRANT One-off, capital, running costs

The smallest, largest and typical size of grant normally given

RANGE OF GRANTS £250–£5,000

The top ten grants given by the trust in the last financial year

SAMPLE GRANTS £5,000 to a school; £1,000 to a university; £800 to a school library; £600 to a school; £500 to a community school; £500 to a grammar school; £500 for classroom equipment; £400 towards the building of a science block; £400 to a university appeal; £250 for a wheelchair ramp

The trust's most recent financial figures including the total amount of grants given

FINANCES *Year* 1997 *Income* £55,000 *Grants* £50,000

Names of the Trustees

TRUSTEES Peter Brown, BA (Chairman), Mrs Mary Brown, Alistair Johnson, Miss Natalie Jones

Titles of publications the trust has produced which are of interest to grant seekers

PUBLICATIONS Annual Report and Accounts, *The Fictitious Trust – the first twenty years*

Any other information which might be useful to grant seekers

NOTES Owing to the large number of applications, some considerable time may elapse before a response is received

Any information which is useful to those preparing their grant application

HOW TO APPLY In writing to the address below. A sae should be included if an acknowledgement is required

The name and address of the person to whom applications should be sent

WHO TO APPLY TO Peter Brown, Chairman, The Fictitious Trust, 1 The Street, Any Town, AT13 4LY
Tel 0171-000 0000 *Fax* 0171-000 0000
E-mail person@abc.efghijklmn.org
Website http://www.efghijklmn.co.uk

Charity Commission number / *Year established*

CC NO 1234567 **ESTABLISHED** 1977

Telephone numbers

This directory was compiled prior to the introduction of the new UK telephone numbering system. As of 1 June 1999 the following new national codes have been introduced:

Cardiff 01222 XXXXXX becomes 029 20XX XXXX

Coventry 01203 XXXXXX becomes 024 76XX XXXX

London 0171 XXX XXXX becomes 020 7XXX XXXX

London 0181 XXX XXXX becomes 020 8XXX XXXX

Portsmouth 01705 XXXXXX becomes 023 92XX XXXX

Southampton 01703 XXXXXX becomes 023 80XX XXXX

Northern Ireland the new area code is 028, followed by new eight digit local numbers.

However, it should be noted that the old numbers will still work alongside the new codes untill 22 April 2000.

How to use the directory
key steps

This directory is designed to enable fundraisers to draw up a hit list of trusts which might support their cause in eight easy steps.

STEP 1
Define the project, programme or work for which you are seeking funding.

▼

STEP 2
Geographical area: find the area most local to your requirements. Note down the names of the trusts listed here.

▼

STEP 3
Field of interest: identify the categories that match your project. Note down the names of the trusts listed here.

▼

STEP 4
Grant type: identify the grant type that you are looking for. Note down the names of the trusts listed here.

▼

STEP 5
Compare the three lists of trusts to produce a list of trusts whose funding policies most closely match the characteristics of the project for which you are seeking funding.

▼

STEP 6
If your list of trusts is too short you could include trusts that have a general interest in funding in your area.

STEP 7
If your list of trusts is too long you could limit yourself to trusts that regard your area of work as a 'Funding priority', and leave out those that 'Will consider' applications.

▼

STEP 8
Look up the entries for the trusts identified, studying their details carefully and paying particular attention to 'What Is Funded' and 'What Is Not Funded'.

If you need additional information, please read the relevant note overleaf.

STEP 1 — **The following checklist will help you assemble the information you need:**

- What is the geographical location of the people who will benefit from any funding received?
- What facilities or services will the funding provide?
- What type of grant are you looking for?

EXAMPLE — *Funding is being sought for an animal welfare project in the north east of England*

- The geographical location is:
  UK → England → **North East**
- The project you are seeking funding for is: **animal welfare**
- The type of grant being sought is: **Project**

STEP 2 — **Look up the area where your project is based in the list of geographical area headings on pages 2–3.**

Turn to the relevant pages in the list of trusts by geographical area and note down the names of the trusts which have stated that they will consider funding projects in your area.

EXAMPLE — *Look up the area most local to your requirements (North East) in the list of geographical area headings. Then turn to the relevant page in the list of trusts by geographical area and look up the names of the trusts listed under North East. Note down the names so that they can be compared with the lists produced through the field of interest and grant type indexes.*

It is also worth looking at trusts listed under 'England' or 'UK', as a trust listed under a more general heading may be just as willing to fund activity in a specific region as another which states that it has a specific interest in that region.

STEP 3 — **Using the categorisation of fields of interest on page 18, identify all the categories that match the project, programme or work for which you are seeking funding.**

Turn to the relevant pages in the list of trusts by field of interest and look up the heading identified. Look first at the trusts that appear under the heading 'Funding priority', then look under the heading 'Will consider'.

Note down the names of the trusts appearing under these headings so that you can compare them with the names identified through the geographical area and grant type indexes.

EXAMPLE *With an animal welfare project, you will probably look first under the main heading 'Rural conservation and animal welfare'. Under this heading you will find the sub-heading 'Animal facilities and services' and under this you will find the heading 'Animal welfare'. Note down the page numbers beside 'Animal facilities and services' and 'Animal welfare'. Trusts that have expressed an interest in funding animal welfare may represent your best prospects, but trusts with a more general interest in funding animal facilities and services might be worth approaching – particularly if they like to fund projects in your area.*

STEP 4 **Look up the type of grant that you are seeking in the list of grant types on page 32.**

Turn to the relevant pages in the list of trusts by grant type and note down the names of the trusts that will consider giving the type of grant that you are seeking, so that you can compare them with the names identified through the geographical area and field of interest indexes.

EXAMPLE *Look up the type of grant you are seeking (project) in the list of grant types. Then turn to the relevant page of the list of trusts by grant type and look at the names of the trusts listed under 'Project'. Note down the names of all these trusts.*

STEP 5 **Compare the lists of trust names produced via steps 2, 3 and 4, and make a list of all the trusts which appear on more than one list. This will produce a list of trusts whose funding policies most closely match the characteristics of the project for which you are seeking funding.**

In order to achieve a ranking, you could assign a certain number of points to each element of the criteria you have devised and then 'score' each trust on the basis of the number of 'matches'.

STEP 6 **If the list turns out to be too short it can easily be adjusted.**

EXAMPLE *You find that you have ended up with a list of five trusts. Going back to step 3, you could include the trusts which come under 'Animal facilities and services', or, going back to step 2, you could include trusts which will consider funding projects in England.*

xiii

STEP 7 **If your list turns out to be too long it can easily be adjusted.**

EXAMPLE *You find that you have ended up with a list of 150 trusts. Going back to step 3, you could limit yourself to trusts that regard your particular area of activity as a 'Funding priority' and leave out those that 'Will consider' applications. You could also discard the names of trusts that have a general interest in funding animal facilities and services and confine your list to trusts that are interested in funding animal facilities.*

STEP 8 **Look up the entries for the trusts identified and study their details carefully, paying particular attention to 'What Is Funded' and 'What Is Not Funded'.**

If you feel that there is a good match between the characteristics of the project for which you require support and the funding policies of the trust identified, you could submit an application.

About CAF

CAF, Charities Aid Foundation, is a registered charity with a unique mission – to increase the substance of charity in the UK and overseas. It provides services that are both charitable and financial which help donors make the most of their giving and charities make the most of their resources.

Many of CAF's publications reflect the organisation's purpose: *Dimensions of the Voluntary Sector* offers the definitive financial overview of the UK voluntary sector, while the *Directory of Grant Making Trusts* provides the most comprehensive source of funding information available.

As an integral part of its activities, CAF works to raise standards of management in voluntary organisations. This includes the making of grants by its own Grants Council, sponsorship of the Charity Annual Report and Accounts Awards, seminars, training courses and the Charities Annual Conference, the largest regular gathering of key people from within the voluntary sector. In addition, Charitynet (www.charitynet.org) is now established as the leading Internet site on voluntary action.

For decades, CAF has led the way in developing tax-effective services to donors, and these are now used by more than 250,000 individuals and 2,000 of the UK's leading companies, between them giving £150 million each year to charity. Many are also using CAF's CharityCard, the world's first debit card designed exclusively for charitable giving. CAF's unique range of investment and administration services for charities includes the CafCash High Interest Cheque Account, two common investment funds for longer-term investment and a full appeals and subscription management service.

CAF's activities are not limited to the UK, however. Increasingly, CAF is looking to apply the same principles and develop similar services internationally, in its drive to increase the substance of charity across the world. CAF has offices and sister organisations in the United States, Bulgaria, South Africa, Russia, India and Brussels.

For more information about CAF, please visit www.charitynet.org/caf

Other publications from CAF

The Directory of Grant Making Trusts 1999–2000
16th Edition
ISBN 1-85934-078-4
£89.95 FOR THREE VOLUMES
Published January 1999

Grant making trusts represent a major source of support for charitable activity in the UK – in 1997 alone they contributed over £1.9 billion.

Grant making trusts support a wide variety of causes and their criteria for allocating funds are often very specific. *The Directory of Grant Making Trusts (DGMT)* keeps fundraisers in touch with changes in trusts' funding priorities. Its extensive indexing allows great precision in the targeting of trusts – thus reducing the flow of irrelevant applications and saving time and money at both ends.

The information published in the *DGMT* is the result of extensive research and close liaison with the trust community; it provides one of the most comprehensive pictures of UK trusts currently published. As well as listing over 3,500 trusts – of which 1,500 are new to this edition – this directory now features top 10 sample grants for hundreds of trusts and a new index by grant type. With the addition of the new third volume providing detailed commentaries on 250 of the major trusts, the *DGMT* now truly represents a complete, one-stop information shop for trust fundraisers.

And it works! Feedback from the fundraising community has been overwhelmingly positive. As essential tool for every trust fundraiser, in most cases it more than pays for itself – it does so many, many times over.

Grantseeker
The interactive CD-ROM for fundraisers
£58.69 (INCL VAT) FOR EACH SIX-MONTHLY RELEASE

Drawing on CAF's years of experience as a publisher of *The Directory of Grant Making Trusts*, *Grantseeker* is the tailor-made solution to the information needs of trust fundraisers in the electronic age. Published for the first time as a subscription service, users will receive a completely new updated edition every six months.

Fully interactive, *Grantseeker*'s specially designed search engine will quickly scan the entire *DGMT* database on the basis of a user's own selection criteria and generate a 'hit list' of trusts whose funding preferences match their project or cause. There are two additional search functions: the ability to search on trustees' names and a key word search by town or city which allows users a more closely defined geographical search. Users' bookmarks and notes automatically carry over to each new release.

Taking full advantage of the extra options available via an electronic search tool, *Grantseeker* offers a more sophisticated matching service than can be provided by traditional methods, enabling fundraisers to save weeks of effort and frustration. A simple hypertext link can provide them with a complete *DGMT* entry on a potential funder within moments of loading the CD. The days of ultimate dependence on a paper-based directory are over.

Designed for use by fundraisers with little or no experience of electronic directories, as well as the more technically minded, *Grantseeker* provides step-by-step instructions on every stage of the search process, backed by comprehensive help files. Even the most confirmed Luddite should not be intimidated!

Grantseeker runs under Windows 3.1 or above.

The Directory of Smaller Grant Making Trusts
1st Edition
ISBN 1–85934–062–8
£26.95
Published February 1998

For many years *The Directory of Grant Making Trusts*, known colloquially as the 'fundraiser's bible', has thrown a spotlight on the funding policies and preferences of the majority of the UK's leading trusts and foundations. Of necessity, however, space constraints have meant that many of the smaller trusts have not been listed. *The Directory of Smaller Grant Making Trusts*, which is to be published every two years, has been developed to remedy this situation and ensure that grant seekers have access to the information they need on these important sources of funding.

The Directory of Smaller Grant Making Trusts contains details of over 1,000 smaller trusts with an income of less than £13,000 per annum. Many of them have not previously been included in directory listings. The individual entries demonstrate that a large number of the trusts have a particular preference for funding activities in selected local, community-based arenas, which will make the directory of particular interest to fundraisers with a regional focus.

FOCUS SERIES

Designed to make the search for funds easier still, many directories from the *Focus Series* collect together, in individual volumes, details of trusts which have expressed an intention to support charitable activity in a particular field or in a particular geographical area.

In addition to comprehensive details of the funding policies of the trusts listed, information is also provided on recent grants they have made.

These directories will give grant seekers working in the relevant fields a head-start in identifying sympathetic trusts and presenting well-tailored funding applications.

Environment, Animal Welfare and Heritage
ISBN 1-85934-016-4
£19.95

Social Care
ISBN 1-85934-051-2
£16.95

International
ISBN 1-85934-052-0
£19.95

Schools, Colleges and Educational Establishments
ISBN 1-85934-053-9
£19.95

Children and Youth 2nd Edition
ISBN 1-85934-072-5
£19.95

Older People
ISBN 1-85934-102-0
£19.95
Published April 1999

Religion 2nd Edition
ISBN 1-85934-080-6
£19.95
Published April 1999

Cambridgeshire, Norfolk and the East Midlands
ISBN 1-85934-087-3
£19.95
Published April 1999

Manchester, Liverpool and the North West
ISBN 1-85934-099-7
£19.95
Published April 1999

Yorkshire, Humberside and the North East
ISBN 1-85934-086-5
£19.95
Published April 1999

HOW TO SERIES

The *How To Series* has been developed for use by anyone working with smaller voluntary organisations. Whatever your background, this series is designed to provide practical one-stop guides on a variety of core activities to give both volunteers and inexperienced salaried staff essential information and guidance on good practice.

Each title provides a clear picture of the subject matter in a jargon-free format for non-specialists. The books include information on relevant legislation, contact details of useful organisations, examples of practical worksheets – all the necessary tools to help develop your understanding, step by step, of the topic being discussed.

Applying to a Grant Making Trust
Anne Villemur
ISBN 1-85934-033-4
£7.95

Effective Media Relations
Ian Gilchrist
ISBN 1-85934-063-6
£7.95

Payroll Giving
Willemina Bell
ISBN 1-85934-061-X
£7.95

Public Speaking and Presentations
Ian Gilchrist
ISBN 1-85934-064-4
£7.95

Running a Local Fundraising Campaign
Janet Hilderley
ISBN 1-85934-040-7
£9.95

Running a Public Collection
Jennie Whiting
ISBN 1-85934-060-1
£7.95

The Treasurer's Handbook
Ian Caulfeild Grant
ISBN 1-85934-018-0
£7.95

Promotional Materials
Karen Gilchrist
ISBN 1-85934-084-9
£9.95

Fundraising for Education
Karen Gilchrist
ISBN 1-85934-083-0
£9.95
Published April 1999

Fundraising using a Database
Peter Flory
ISBN 1-85934-082-2
£11.95
Published June 1999

To order any of the above publications, please ring Biblios Publishers' Distribution Services Ltd on 01403 710851 or you can order online using our website: http://www.ngobooks.org

Trusts by geographical area

Geographical area headings

Worldwide
Full area 4

■ Europe
Full region 5

■ Asia
Full region 5

■ Africa
Full region 5

■ Australasia
Full region 5

■ America
Full region 5

■ Antarctica
Full region 5

■ Eire
Full area 5

United Kingdom
Full area 5

England
Full area 7

■ North East
Full region 7
Darlington 7
Durham 7
Gateshead 7
Hartlepool 7
Middlesbrough 7
Newcastle upon Tyne 7
Northumberland 7
North Tyneside 7
Redcar & Cleveland 7
South Tyneside 7
Stockton on Tees 7
Sunderland 7

■ North West
Full region 8
Blackburn with Darwen 8
Blackpool 8
Bolton 8
Bury 8
Cheshire 8
Cumbria 8
Halton 8
Knowsley 8
Lancashire 8
Liverpool City 8
Manchester City 8
Oldham 8
Rochdale 8
St Helens 8
Salford 8
Sefton 8
Stockport 8
Tameside 8
Trafford 9
Warrington 9
Wigan 9
Wirral 9

■ East Midlands
Full region 9
Derby City 9
Derbyshire 9
Leicester City 9
Leicestershire 9
Lincolnshire 9
Northamptonshire 9
Nottingham City 9
Nottinghamshire 9
Rutland 9

■ West Midlands
Full region 9
Birmingham City 9
Coventry City 9
Shropshire 9
Staffordshire 9
Warwickshire 9
Worcestershire 9

■ Eastern
Full region 9
Bedfordshire 9
Cambridgeshire 10
Essex 10
Hertfordshire 10
Luton 10
Norfolk 10
Peterborough 10
Suffolk 10

Geographical area headings

■ Yorks & Humberside

Full region *10*
Barnsley *10*
Bradford City *10*
Calderdale *10*
Doncaster *10*
East Riding of Yorkshire *10*
Kingston upon Hull *10*
Kirklees *10*
Leeds *11*
North Lincolnshire *11*
North East Lincolnshire *11*
North Yorkshire *11*
Rotherham *11*
Sheffield City *11*
Wakefield *11*
York *11*

■ South East

Full region *11*
Bracknell Forest *11*
Brighton & Hove *11*
Buckinghamshire *11*
East Sussex *11*
Hampshire *11*
Isle of Wight *12*
Kent *12*
The Medway Towns *12*
Oxfordshire *12*
Portsmouth *12*
Reading *12*
Slough *12*
Southampton *12*
Surrey *12*
West Berkshire *12*
West Sussex *12*
Windsor & Maidenhead *12*
Wokingham *12*

■ London

Full region *12*
Barnet *12*
Camden *12*
Greenwich *12*
Hackney *12*
Hammersmith & Fulham *12*
Harrow *12*
Islington *12*
Kensington & Chelsea *12*
Kingston upon Thames *12*
Lewisham *12*
Newham *12*
Richmond upon Thames *13*
Southwark *13*
Tower Hamlets *13*
Wandsworth *13*

■ South West & Channel Islands

Full region *13*
Bath & North East Somerset *13*
Bristol *13*
Channel Islands (Jersey & Guernsey) *13*
Cornwall *13*
Devon *13*
Dorset *13*
Gloucestershire *13*
North Somerset *13*
Plymouth *13*
Somerset *13*
South Gloucestershire *13*
Wiltshire *13*

Northern Ireland

Full area *14*

Scotland

Full area *14*
Aberdeen *14*
Aberdeenshire *14*
Angus *14*
Argyll & Bute *14*
Dumfries & Galloway *14*
East Lothian *14*
East Renfrewshire *14*
Edinburgh *14*
Fife *14*
Glasgow *14*
Highland *14*
Midlothian *14*
North Ayrshire *14*
North Lanarkshire *14*
Perth & Kinross *14*
Renfrewshire *14*
Shetland *14*
South Ayrshire *14*
Stirling *15*
West Ayrshire *15*
West Lothian *15*

Wales

Full area *15*

■ North Wales

Full region *15*
Denbighshire *15*
Gwynedd *15*
Wrexham *15*

■ South Wales

Full region *15*
Blaenau Gwent *15*
Caerphilly *15*
Cardiff *15*
Glamorgan, Vale of *15*
Merthyr Tydfil *15*
Rhondda Cynon Taff *15*

Page references refer to the list of trusts by geographical area that begins on page 4

Trusts by geographical area

Worldwide

Full area

Alchemy Foundation, The 49
Anne's Charities Trust, The Princess 50
Astor Foundation, The 51
BP Conservation Programme 53
Body Charitable Trust, Bernard Richard 57
Body Shop Foundation, The 58
Born Free Foundation, The 58
Bromley Trust, The 62
Cadbury Charitable Trust, William Adlington 66
Carron Charitable Trust, The 70
Chestnut Trust, The 73
Clark Charitable Trust, J A 74
Cobb Charity 76
Coote Animal Charity Fund, The Marjorie 78
Earle Charitable Trust, Audrey 86
Ecological Foundation, The 86
Ericson Trust 87
Eves Charitable Trust, Douglas Heath 88
Foreman 1980 Charitable Trust, The Russell and Mary 92
Franklin Deceased's New Second Charity, Sydney E 93
Guido's Charitable Trust, Mrs Margaret 100
HCD Memorial Fund 100
Haddon Charitable Trust, William 100
Hall Trust, The Christine 102
Haramead Trust, The 102
Hayward Foundation, The 104
Headley Trust, The 106
Hogg Charitable Trust, The J G 109
Hunt Charitable Trust, The Michael and Shirley 110
Kleinwort Charitable Trust, The Ernest 114
Kweller Charitable Trust, The Harry 116
Laurence 1976 Charitable Settlement, The Mrs F B 117
Livesley 1992 Charitable Trust, Mrs C M 120
McMorran Charitable Foundation, The Helen Isabella 123
Malachi (Family) Charitable Trust 123
March's Trust Company Ltd, The Earl of 124
Methodist Relief and Development Fund, The 127

Norman Trust, The 136
Oakdale Trust, The 137
Onaway Trust, The 138
Peacock Charitable Trust, The 141
Peartree Trust, The 142
Personal Assurance Charitable Trust 142
Persula Foundation, The 142
Philanthropic Trust, The 144
Radley Charitable Trust 148
Rausing Trust, The Ruben and Elizabeth 151
Reuter Foundation, The 153
Reynall Charitable Trust, Joan K 154
Rickard Animals' Charity, Miss Maria Susan 154
Rotary Club of Arbury Charity Trust Fund 156
Rotary Club of Eastleigh Trust Fund 156
Rotary Club of Thornbury Trust Fund, The 157
Rufford Foundation 159
Salisbury Pool Charity, The 161
Schuster Charitable Trust, The 161
Schweitzer's Hospital Fund, Dr 162
Shah Trust, The Dr N K 163
Shark Trust, The 163
Shepherd Conservation Foundation, The David 163
Simon Memorial Fund, The Andre 165
Smith (UK) Horticultural Trust, Stanley 167
Sunley Charitable Foundation, The Bernard 172
Sykes Trust, The Charles 175
Sylvanus Charitable Trust, The 176
Symons Charitable Trust, The Stella 176
Thackray General Charitable Trust, The C P 177
Torrs Charitable Trust, The 178
Walker 597 Trust, The 184
Walker Charitable Trust, The Ruth 184
Whitbread First Charitable Trust, H 188
Wolfe Charitable Settlement C, Ruth 192
Wyre Animal Welfare 194

Trusts by geographical area

United Kingdom

■ Europe

Full region

Briggs Animal Welfare Trust, The 61
Burton 1960 Charitable Trust, Audrey and Stanley 63
Chelsea Square 1994 Trust, The 73
Criffel Charitable Trust 80
Douglas Charitable Trust, R M 84
Grocers' Charity 99
Harebell Centenary Fund, The 102
Marchig Animal Welfare Trust 124
Mitsubishi Corporation Fund for Europe and Africa 128
Paget Trust, The 140
Rotary Club of Hadleigh Charitable Trust Fund 157
Sainsbury Animal Welfare Trust, Jean 160
Staples Trust 168
Wyford Charitable Trust, The 194

■ Asia

Full region

Cleopatra Trust 75
Criffel Charitable Trust 80
Dorus Trust 84
Douglas Charitable Trust, R M 84
Epigoni Trust 87
Great Britain Sasakawa Foundation, The 97
INTACH (UK) Trust 111
Marchig Animal Welfare Trust 124
Paget Trust, The 140
Pilkington Charitable Trust, The Cecil 144
Rotary Club of Hadleigh Charitable Trust Fund 157
Rowan Charitable Trust, The 158
Staples Trust 168
Tho Memorial Foundation, Loke Wan 177
Tisbury Telegraph Trust, The 178

■ Africa

Full region

Briggs Animal Welfare Trust, The 61
Burton 1960 Charitable Trust, Audrey and Stanley 63
Chelsea Square 1994 Trust, The 73
Cleopatra Trust 75

Criffel Charitable Trust 80
Dorus Trust 84
Douglas Charitable Trust, R M 84
Epigoni Trust 87
Marchig Animal Welfare Trust 124
Mitsubishi Corporation Fund for Europe and Africa 128
Paget Trust, The 140
Pilkington Charitable Trust, The Cecil 144
Rotary Club of Hadleigh Charitable Trust Fund 157
Rowan Charitable Trust, The 158
Sainsbury Animal Welfare Trust, Jean 160
Sedgwick Trust, The 162
Staples Trust 168
Tisbury Telegraph Trust, The 178

■ Australasia

Full region

Baker Trust, The C Alma 53

■ America

Full region

Cleopatra Trust 75
Cohen Foundation, The John S 76
Dorus Trust 84
Epigoni Trust 87
Moores Foundation, The Peter 130
Rowan Charitable Trust, The 158
Staples Trust 168
Tisbury Telegraph Trust, The 178

■ Antarctica

Full region

Paget Trust, The 140
Tisbury Telegraph Trust, The 178

■ Eire

Full area

Douglas Charitable Trust, R M 84
Gillman's Trust, Horace 95
Inland Waterways Association, The 112
Wills 1965 Charitable Trust, The H D H 190

■ United Kingdom

Full area

Alchemy Foundation, The 49
Anne's Charities Trust, The Princess 50
Astor Foundation, The 51
BP Conservation Programme 53
Baker Trust, The C Alma 53
Barnby's Foundation, Lord 55
Benham Charitable Settlement 56
Body Charitable Trust, Bernard Richard 57
Body Shop Foundation, The 58
Born Free Foundation, The 58
Briggs Animal Welfare Trust, The 61
Britten-Pears Foundation, The 62
Bromley Trust, The 62
CHK Charities Limited 65
Calypso Browning Trust 69
Canine Supporters Charity, The 69
Carron Charitable Trust, The 70
Carter Charitable Trust, The Leslie Mary 70
Charities Aid Foundation 71
Chestnut Trust, The 73
Cinderford Charitable Trust, The 74
Clarke's Charitable Trust, The Late Miss Doris Evelyn 74
Clutterbuck Charitable Trust, Robert 75
Coates Charitable Trust 1969, Lance 75
Cobb Charity 76
Cohen Foundation, The John S 76
Coote Animal Charity Fund, The Marjorie 78
Corden Trust, Cyril 79
Countryside Business Group Charitable Trust 79
Criffel Charitable Trust 80
EBM Charitable Trust 85
Earle Charitable Trust, Audrey 86
Ecological Foundation, The 86
Englefield Charitable Trust, The 86
Ericson Trust 87
Eves Charitable Trust, Douglas Heath 88
Evetts & Robert Luff Animal Welfare Trust, Beryl 88
Fairbairn Charitable Trust, The Esmée 89
Foreman 1980 Charitable Trust, The Russell and Mary 92

5

United Kingdom

Trusts by geographical area

Franklin Deceased's New Second Charity, Sydney E 93
Frognal Trust 93
Gibson Charitable Trust, The Simon 94
Gillman's Trust, Horace 95
Great Britain Sasakawa Foundation, The 97
Green Memorial Fund, The Barry 99
Grocers' Charity 99
Guido's Charitable Trust, Mrs Margaret 100
HCD Memorial Fund 100
Haddon Charitable Trust, William 100
Haramead Trust, The 102
Harebell Centenary Fund, The 102
Harryhausen's 1969 Trust, Mrs D L 103
Hawthorne Charitable Trust, The 104
Hayward Foundation, The 104
Headley Trust, The 106
Heritage Lottery Fund 107
Higgs Charitable Trust, The 107
Hogg Charitable Trust, The J G 109
Hogg Charity Trust, E S 109
Homelands Charitable Trust 109
Hornby's Charitable Settlement, Mrs E G 110
Hughes Charitable Trust, The Geoffrey C 110
Hunt Charitable Trust, The Michael and Shirley 110
IFAW Charitable Trust 111
Idlewild Trust, The 111
Inland Waterways Association, The 112
Kennel Club Charitable Trust, The 113
Kirkham Foundation, The Graham 113
Kleinwort Charitable Trust, The Ernest 114
Kweller Charitable Trust, The Harry 116
Laing Charitable Trust, The David 117
Landale Charitable Trust, The 117
Laurence 1976 Charitable Settlement, The Mrs F B 117
Leach Charitable Trust, The Eric and Dorothy 118
Leach Fourteenth Trust, The 118
Leche Trust, The 118
Lewis Foundation, The John Spedan 119

Linder Foundation, The Enid 119
Livesley 1992 Charitable Trust, Mrs C M 120
Loraine Trust 120
Loyd Charitable Trust, The C L 121
Lyndhurst Settlement 121
McCorquodale Charitable Trust, The 122
McMorran Charitable Foundation, The Helen Isabella 123
Malachi (Family) Charitable Trust 123
Marchig Animal Welfare Trust 124
March's Trust Company Ltd, The Earl of 124
Marsh and McLennan (Charities Fund) Ltd, J and H 124
Martin Charitable Trust, Michael D 125
Medical Equestrian Association 125
Mitsubishi Corporation Fund for Europe and Africa 128
Monument Trust, The 129
Moores Foundation, The Peter 130
Murphy Foundation, Edith 131
Nabarro Charitable Trust, The Kitty and Daniel 132
National Animal Sanctuaries Support League 132
National Lottery Charities Board 132
New Horizons Trust, The 135
Norman Trust, The 136
Oakdale Trust, The 137
Onaway Trust, The 138
Owen Family Trust, The 138
PF Charitable Trust 139
Peacock Charitable Trust, The 141
Peartree Trust, The 142
Personal Assurance Charitable Trust 142
Persula Foundation, The 142
Pet Plan Charitable Trust 143
Pewterers' Charity Trust 143
Philanthropic Trust, The 144
Pilkington Charitable Trust, The Cecil 144
Pittecroft Trust, The 145
Pye's No 1 Charitable Settlement, Mr and Mrs J A 146
RAC Foundation for Motoring and the Environment Ltd, The 148
Radley Charitable Trust 148
Rank Foundation, The 149
Rausing Trust, The Ruben and Elizabeth 151
Reekie Trust, R A & V B 153

Reuter Foundation, The 153
Reynall Charitable Trust, Joan K 154
Rickard Animals' Charity, Miss Maria Susan 154
Rivington Heritage Trust 154
Rotaract Club, Bristol North West 156
Rotary Club of Arbury Charity Trust Fund 156
Rotary Club of Thornbury Trust Fund, The 157
Rowan Charitable Trust, The 158
Rufford Foundation 159
Sainsbury Animal Welfare Trust, Jean 160
St John's Wood Trust, The 161
Salisbury Pool Charity, The 161
Sarnia Charitable Trust 161
Schuster Charitable Trust, The 161
Schweitzer's Hospital Fund, Dr 162
Shah Trust, The Dr N K 163
Shark Trust, The 163
Shepherd Conservation Foundation, The David 163
Simon Memorial Fund, The Andre 165
Smith Charitable Trust for Nature, The Peter 166
Smith Foundation, The Leslie 166
Smith Foundation, The Martin 166
Smith (UK) Horticultural Trust, Stanley 167
South Square Trust 167
Stanhope-Palmer Charity 168
Staples Trust 168
Stephenson (Deceased), Will Trust of Edgar John Henry 170
Stevens Foundation, The June 170
Sunley Charitable Foundation, The Bernard 172
Swann-Morton Foundation, The 175
Symons Charitable Trust, The Stella 176
Tay Charitable Trust, The 177
Tho Memorial Foundation, Loke Wan 177
Thoresby Charitable Trust 178
Tisbury Telegraph Trust, The 178
Torrs Charitable Trust, The 178
Van Norden's Charitable Foundation, Mrs Maud 180
Vodafone Group Charitable Trust, The 181

Trusts by geographical area **North East**

WWF UK (World Wide Fund for Nature) *182*
Wales's Charitable Foundation, The Prince of *183*
Walker 597 Trust, The *184*
Walker Charitable Trust, The Anthony *184*
Walker Charitable Trust, The Ruth *184*
Waterhouse Charitable Trust, Mrs *185*
Weatherby Charity, The *186*
Weston Foundation, Garfield *187*
Whitbread First Charitable Trust, H *188*
Whitley Animal Protection Trust *189*
Wild Flower Society, The *190*
Wills 1965 Charitable Trust, The H D H *190*
Wilson Trust for Animal Welfare, The Kit *191*
Wolfe Charitable Settlement C, Ruth *192*
Woodward Charitable Trust, The *192*
Worshipful Company of Gardeners of London Charity, The *193*
Wyre Animal Welfare *194*
Zaiger Trust, The Elizabeth and Prince *196*

England

Full area
Astor Foundation, The *51*
Belsize Charitable Trust No1 *56*
Chiron Trust, The *74*
Cobb Charity *76*
Countryside Trust, The *79*
de Freitas Charitable Trust, The Helen and Geoffrey *82*
Dixon Charitable Trust, C H *83*
Fox Memorial Trust *92*
Green Memorial Fund, The Barry *99*
Harebell Centenary Fund, The *102*
Hogg Charitable Trust, The J G *109*
Homfray Trust, The *109*
Leche Trust, The *118*
Linder Foundation, The Enid *119*
Portrack Charitable Trust, The *145*
Sainsbury Animal Welfare Trust, Jean *160*
Symons Charitable Trust, The Stella *176*
Tho Memorial Foundation, Loke Wan *177*
Van Norden's Charitable Foundation, Mrs Maud *180*

■ North East
Full region
Barbour Trust, The *54*
Burton 1960 Charitable Trust, Audrey and Stanley *63*
Chase Charity, The *73*
Chiron Trust, The *74*
Hogg Charitable Trust, The J G *109*
Jacobson Charitable Trust (No 2), The Ruth & Lionel *112*
Sykes Trust, The Charles *175*
Vaux Group Foundation, The *180*
Yorkshire Agricultural Society *195*

Darlington
Burton 1960 Charitable Trust, Audrey and Stanley *63*
Hadrian Trust, The *101*
Yorkshire Agricultural Society *195*

Durham
Hadrian Trust, The *101*
Knott Trust, Sir James *115*
Shears Charitable Trust, The *163*

Gateshead
Burton 1960 Charitable Trust, Audrey and Stanley *63*
Hadrian Trust, The *101*
Haswell Memorial Trust, The John *103*
Knott Trust, Sir James *115*
Shears Charitable Trust, The *163*

Hartlepool
Hadrian Trust, The *101*
Knott Trust, Sir James *115*

Middlesbrough
Yorkshire Agricultural Society *195*

Newcastle upon Tyne
Hadrian Trust, The *101*
Knott Trust, Sir James *115*
Mann Trustees Limited, R W *123*
Shears Charitable Trust, The *163*

Northumberland
Bell Trust, The Henry *55*
Hadrian Trust, The *101*
Knott Trust, Sir James *115*
Shears Charitable Trust, The *163*

North Tyneside
Hadrian Trust, The *101*
Knott Trust, Sir James *115*
Mann Trustees Limited, R W *123*
Shears Charitable Trust, The *163*

Redcar & Cleveland
Hillards Charitable Trust, Gay & Peter Hartley's *108*
Yorkshire Agricultural Society *195*

South Tyneside
Hadrian Trust, The *101*
Knott Trust, Sir James *115*
Shears Charitable Trust, The *163*

Stockton on Tees
Hadrian Trust, The *101*
Knott Trust, Sir James *115*
Yorkshire Agricultural Society *195*

Sunderland
Hadrian Trust, The *101*
Knott Trust, Sir James *115*
Shears Charitable Trust, The *163*

North West

Trusts by geographical area

■ North West

Full region
Chase Charity, The 73
Chiron Trust, The 74
Harvey's Discretionary Settlement, William Geoffrey 103
Hogg Charitable Trust, The J G 109
Oldham Foundation 137
Royal Botanical & Horticultural Society of Manchester and the Northern Counties, The 159
Vaux Group Foundation, The 180

Blackburn with Darwen
Mersey Basin Trust – Stream Care Project 126
Mersey Basin Trust – Waterside Revival Grants 127
Scott Charitable Trust, The Frieda 162

Blackpool
Scott Charitable Trust, The Frieda 162

Bolton
Community Trust for Greater Manchester, The 78
Hillards Charitable Trust, Gay & Peter Hartley's 108
Mersey Basin Trust – Stream Care Project 126
Mersey Basin Trust – Waterside Revival Grants 127

Bury
Community Trust for Greater Manchester, The 78
Hillards Charitable Trust, Gay & Peter Hartley's 108
Mersey Basin Trust – Stream Care Project 126
Mersey Basin Trust – Waterside Revival Grants 127

Cheshire
Brotherton Trust, The Charles 63
Clutterbuck Charitable Trust, Robert 75
Lord Mayor of Chester Charitable Trust 121
Mersey Basin Trust – ICI Green Action Grants 126
Mersey Basin Trust – Stream Care Project 126
Mersey Basin Trust – Waterside Revival Grants 127

Cumbria
Eskdale (Cumbria) Trust, The 88
Rawdon-Smith Trust, The 152
Scott Charitable Trust, The Frieda 162

Halton
Mersey Basin Trust – ICI Green Action Grants 126
Mersey Basin Trust – Stream Care Project 126
Mersey Basin Trust – Waterside Revival Grants 127

Knowsley
Hemby Trust, The 107
Johnson Foundation, The 112
Mersey Basin Trust – Stream Care Project 126
Mersey Basin Trust – Waterside Revival Grants 127
Rowan Charitable Trust, The 158

Lancashire
Hillards Charitable Trust, Gay & Peter Hartley's 108
Mersey Basin Trust – Stream Care Project 126
Mersey Basin Trust – Waterside Revival Grants 127
Scott Charitable Trust, The Frieda 162
Waterhouse Charitable Trust, Mrs 185
Wyre Animal Welfare 194

Liverpool City
Brotherton Trust, The Charles 63
Burton 1960 Charitable Trust, Audrey and Stanley 63
Hemby Trust, The 107
Johnson Foundation, The 112
Mersey Basin Trust – Stream Care Project 126
Mersey Basin Trust – Waterside Revival Grants 127
Rowan Charitable Trust, The 158

Manchester City
Burton 1960 Charitable Trust, Audrey and Stanley 63
Community Trust for Greater Manchester, The 78
Mersey Basin Trust – Stream Care Project 126
Mersey Basin Trust – Waterside Revival Grants 127

Oldham
Community Trust for Greater Manchester, The 78
Hillards Charitable Trust, Gay & Peter Hartley's 108
Mersey Basin Trust – Stream Care Project 126
Mersey Basin Trust – Waterside Revival Grants 127

Rochdale
Community Trust for Greater Manchester, The 78
Mersey Basin Trust – Stream Care Project 126
Mersey Basin Trust – Waterside Revival Grants 127

St Helens
Hemby Trust, The 107
Johnson Foundation, The 112
Mersey Basin Trust – Stream Care Project 126
Mersey Basin Trust – Waterside Revival Grants 127
Rowan Charitable Trust, The 158

Salford
Community Trust for Greater Manchester, The 78
Mersey Basin Trust – Stream Care Project 126
Mersey Basin Trust – Waterside Revival Grants 127

Sefton
Hemby Trust, The 107
Johnson Foundation, The 112
Mersey Basin Trust – Stream Care Project 126
Mersey Basin Trust – Waterside Revival Grants 127
Rowan Charitable Trust, The 158
Talbot Bridge Will Trust, The Elsie 177

Stockport
Community Trust for Greater Manchester, The 78
Mersey Basin Trust – Stream Care Project 126
Mersey Basin Trust – Waterside Revival Grants 127

Tameside
Community Trust for Greater Manchester, The 78
Mersey Basin Trust – Stream Care Project 126
Mersey Basin Trust – Waterside Revival Grants 127

Trusts by geographical area

Eastern

Trafford
Community Trust for Greater Manchester, The 78
Mersey Basin Trust – Stream Care Project 126
Mersey Basin Trust – Waterside Revival Grants 127

Warrington
Mersey Basin Trust – Stream Care Project 126
Mersey Basin Trust – Waterside Revival Grants 127
Warrington Animal Welfare 184

Wigan
Mersey Basin Trust – Stream Care Project 126
Mersey Basin Trust – Waterside Revival Grants 127
Wigan Town Relief in Need Charity 189

Wirral
Brotherton Trust, The Charles 63
Hemby Trust, The 107
Johnson Foundation, The 112
Mersey Basin Trust – Stream Care Project 126
Mersey Basin Trust – Waterside Revival Grants 127
Rotary Club of Wallasey, The Charitable Fund of the 157
Rowan Charitable Trust, The 158

■ East Midlands
Full region
Chase Charity, The 73
Hogg Charitable Trust, The J G 109
Owen Family Trust, The 138
Paget Trust, The 140

Derby City
Derbyshire Community Foundation 83
Hillards Charitable Trust, Gay & Peter Hartley's 108

Derbyshire
Bingham Trust, The 57
Derbyshire Community Foundation 83
Moore Charitable Trust, The Horace 130

Leicester City
Hillards Charitable Trust, Gay & Peter Hartley's 108
Melton Mowbray Building Society Charitable Foundation 125

Leicestershire
Cadbury Charitable Trust, William Adlington 66
Melton Mowbray Building Society Charitable Foundation 125
Paget Trust, The 140

Lincolnshire
Bergne-Coupland Charity 57
British Sugar Foundation 61
Hodgkinson Charitable Trust, The Peter and Gwyneth 108
Melton Mowbray Building Society Charitable Foundation 125
Nickerson Charitable Foundation, The Joseph 135
Skells, Bequest of Harry 166
Wright Deceased Trust, John William 193

Northamptonshire
Benham Charitable Settlement 56
Fitzwilliam Charitable Trust, The Earl 92
Hillards Charitable Trust, Gay & Peter Hartley's 108
Wicksteed Village Trust, The 189

Nottingham City
Cadbury Charitable Trust, William Adlington 66
Hillards Charitable Trust, Gay & Peter Hartley's 108
Melton Mowbray Building Society Charitable Foundation 125

Nottinghamshire
British Sugar Foundation 61
Dunn Charitable Trust, The Harry 84
Melton Mowbray Building Society Charitable Foundation 125
Moore Charitable Trust, The Horace 130
Thoresby Charitable Trust 178

Rutland
Melton Mowbray Building Society Charitable Foundation 125
Moore Charitable Trust, The Horace 130

■ West Midlands
Full region
Cadbury Charitable Trust, William Adlington 66
Chase Charity, The 73
Douglas Charitable Trust, R M 84
Elkes Charity Fund, The Wilfred & Elsie 86
Gerefa Charitable Trust 94
Hogg Charitable Trust, The J G 109
Oakley Charitable Trust, The 137
Owen Family Trust, The 138
Woodlands Trust 192

Birmingham City
Barrow Trust, Dr 55
Brotherton Trust, The Charles 63
Cadbury Charitable Trust, Richard 66
Sutton Coldfield Municipal Charities, The 173

Coventry City
Cadbury Charitable Trust, Richard 66

Shropshire
British Sugar Foundation 61
Westcroft Trust 186

Staffordshire
Douglas Charitable Trust, R M 84
Elkes Charity Fund, The Wilfred & Elsie 86

Warwickshire
Elkes Charity Fund, The Wilfred & Elsie 86
Town Lands, The 179

Worcestershire
British Sugar Foundation 61
Cadbury Charitable Trust, Richard 66

■ Eastern
Full region
Chase Charity, The 73
Chiron Trust, The 74
Hogg Charitable Trust, The J G 109

Bedfordshire
Whitbread First Charitable Trust, H 188

Yorks & Humberside

Cambridgeshire
BAA 21st Century Communities Trust, The 52
Fitzwilliam Charitable Trust, The Earl 92
Hall Charity, Robert 101
Radley Charitable Trust 148
Whitbread First Charitable Trust, H 188

Essex
BAA 21st Century Communities Trust, The 52
Whitbread First Charitable Trust, H 188

Hertfordshire
Ashby Will Trust, A J H 51
BAA 21st Century Communities Trust, The 52
Clutterbuck Charitable Trust, Robert 75
Salisbury Pool Charity, The 161
Whitbread First Charitable Trust, H 188

Luton
Whitbread First Charitable Trust, H 188

Norfolk
Adnams Charity, The 49
British Sugar Foundation 61
Carter Charitable Trust, The Leslie Mary 70
Fitzmaurice Charitable Trust, The 91
Macfarlane Walker Trust 123
Raptor Trust, The 151
Sheringham and District Preservation Society 164
Wensum Residents Association 186
Whitbread First Charitable Trust, H 188
Whitlingham Charitable Trust, The 189

Peterborough
British Sugar Foundation 61
Fitzwilliam Charitable Trust, The Earl 92
Whitbread First Charitable Trust, H 188

Suffolk
Adnams Charity, The 49
British Sugar Foundation 61
Burton Charitable Trust, The Geoffrey 64
Carter Charitable Trust, The Leslie Mary 70
Colyer-Fergusson Charitable Trust, Sir James 77

Gibson Charitable Trust, The Simon 94
Raptor Trust, The 151
Rotary Club of Hadleigh Charitable Trust Fund 157
Whitbread First Charitable Trust, H 188

■ Yorks & Humberside

Full region
Burton 1960 Charitable Trust, Audrey and Stanley 63
Chase Charity, The 73
Hall Trust, The Christine 102
Hogg Charitable Trust, The J G 109
Moore Charitable Trust, The Horace 130
Sykes Trust, The Charles 175

Barnsley
Fitzwilliam Charitable Trust, The Earl 92
Hillards Charitable Trust, Gay & Peter Hartley's 108
Kirkham Foundation, The Graham 113
Spooner Charitable Trust, W W 168
Thackray General Charitable Trust, The C P 177
Vaux Group Foundation, The 180
Yorkshire Agricultural Society 195

Bradford City
Hillards Charitable Trust, Gay & Peter Hartley's 108
Homfray Trust, The 109
Ramsden Charitable Trust, The Edward 148
Shears Charitable Trust, The 163
Spooner Charitable Trust, W W 168
Thackray General Charitable Trust, The C P 177
Vaux Group Foundation, The 180
Yorkshire Agricultural Society 195

Calderdale
Hillards Charitable Trust, Gay & Peter Hartley's 108
Homfray Trust, The 109
Ramsden Charitable Trust, The Edward 148
Shears Charitable Trust, The 163
Spooner Charitable Trust, W W 168

Thackray General Charitable Trust, The C P 177
Vaux Group Foundation, The 180
Yorkshire Agricultural Society 195

Doncaster
Fitzwilliam Charitable Trust, The Earl 92
Hillards Charitable Trust, Gay & Peter Hartley's 108
Kirkham Foundation, The Graham 113
Spooner Charitable Trust, W W 168
Thackray General Charitable Trust, The C P 177
Vaux Group Foundation, The 180
Yorkshire Agricultural Society 195

East Riding of Yorkshire
Hillards Charitable Trust, Gay & Peter Hartley's 108
Reckitt Charity, Sir James 152
Rollit Trust, The Vera Kaye 155
Spooner Charitable Trust, W W 168
Thackray General Charitable Trust, The C P 177
Vaux Group Foundation, The 180
Yorkshire Agricultural Society 195

Kingston upon Hull
Middleton Fund, The 128
Reckitt Charity, Sir James 152
Rollit Trust, The Vera Kaye 155
Yorkshire Agricultural Society 195

Kirklees
Hillards Charitable Trust, Gay & Peter Hartley's 108
Homfray Trust, The 109
Ramsden Charitable Trust, The Edward 148
Shears Charitable Trust, The 163
Spooner Charitable Trust, W W 168
Thackray General Charitable Trust, The C P 177
Vaux Group Foundation, The 180
Yorkshire Agricultural Society 195

Trusts by geographical area

South East

Leeds
Armitage Charitable Trust, G C 50
Brotherton Trust, The Charles 63
Hillards Charitable Trust, Gay & Peter Hartley's 108
Homfray Trust, The 109
Ramsden Charitable Trust, The Edward 148
Shears Charitable Trust, The 163
Spooner Charitable Trust, W W 168
Thackray General Charitable Trust, The C P 177
Vaux Group Foundation, The 180
Wade & Others, The Charity of Thomas 183
Yorkshire Agricultural Society 195

North Lincolnshire
Hillards Charitable Trust, Gay & Peter Hartley's 108
Hodgkinson Charitable Trust, The Peter and Gwyneth 108
Middleton Fund, The 128

North East Lincolnshire
Hillards Charitable Trust, Gay & Peter Hartley's 108
Hodgkinson Charitable Trust, The Peter and Gwyneth 108
Middleton Fund, The 128

North Yorkshire
Armitage Charitable Trust, G C 50
Fitzwilliam Charitable Trust, The Earl 92
Hillards Charitable Trust, Gay & Peter Hartley's 108
Middleton Fund, The 128
Ramsden Charitable Trust, The Edward 148
Spooner Charitable Trust, W W 168
Thackray General Charitable Trust, The C P 177
Vaux Group Foundation, The 180
Yorkshire Agricultural Society 195

Rotherham
Dearne Valley Community Forum 82
Fitzwilliam Charitable Trust, The Earl 92
Hillards Charitable Trust, Gay & Peter Hartley's 108
Kirkham Foundation, The Graham 113

Pryor Charity, The Ronald & Kathleen 146
Spooner Charitable Trust, W W 168
Thackray General Charitable Trust, The C P 177
Twil Group Charitable Trust, The 180
Vaux Group Foundation, The 180
Yorkshire Agricultural Society 195

Sheffield City
Fitzwilliam Charitable Trust, The Earl 92
Graves Charitable Trust, J G 96
Hillards Charitable Trust, Gay & Peter Hartley's 108
Kirkham Foundation, The Graham 113
Pryor Charity, The Ronald & Kathleen 146
Spooner Charitable Trust, W W 168
Thackray General Charitable Trust, The C P 177
Twil Group Charitable Trust, The 180
Vaux Group Foundation, The 180
Winstone Foundation, Hyman 191
Yorkshire Agricultural Society 195

Wakefield
Armitage Charitable Trust, G C 50
Brotherton Trust, The Charles 63
Hillards Charitable Trust, Gay & Peter Hartley's 108
Homfray Trust, The 109
Ramsden Charitable Trust, The Edward 148
Shears Charitable Trust, The 163
Spooner Charitable Trust, W W 168
Thackray General Charitable Trust, The C P 177
Vaux Group Foundation, The 180
Yorkshire Agricultural Society 195

York
Armitage Charitable Trust, G C 50
British Sugar Foundation 61
Brotherton Trust, The Charles 63
Hillards Charitable Trust, Gay & Peter Hartley's 108

Spooner Charitable Trust, W W 168
Thackray General Charitable Trust, The C P 177
Vaux Group Foundation, The 180
Yorkshire Agricultural Society 195

■ South East

Full region
Bentall Charitable Trust, The Gerald 56
Chase Charity, The 73
Chelsea Square 1994 Trust, The 73
EBM Charitable Trust 85
Hannay Charitable Trust, The Lennox 102
Hogg Charitable Trust, The J G 109
Moore Charitable Trust, The Horace 130
Wyford Charitable Trust, The 194

Bracknell Forest
Loyd Charitable Trust, The C L 121

Brighton & Hove
Nikeno Trust, The 136
Rausing Charitable Foundation, Marit and Hans 151

Buckinghamshire
Balney Charitable Trust, The 54
Schuster Charitable Trust, The 161

East Sussex
BAA 21st Century Communities Trust, The 52
HCD Memorial Fund 100
Kleinwort Charitable Trust, The Ernest 114
Lawson Charitable Trust, Raymond and Blanche 117
March's Trust Company Ltd, The Earl of 124
Nikeno Trust, The 136
Rausing Charitable Foundation, Marit and Hans 151
Roberts Charitable Trust, The E E 154
Robinson Trust No 3, The J C 155

Hampshire
BAA 21st Century Communities Trust, The 52
Belmont Trust, The 56

11

South East

RSPCA – Winchester and Romsey Branch *148*
Rotary Club of Eastleigh Trust Fund *156*
Stephenson (Deceased), Will Trust of Edgar John Henry *170*

Isle of Wight
BAA 21st Century Communities Trust, The *52*
Belmont Trust, The *56*
Brading Town Trust, The *59*
Isle of Wight Gardens Trust *112*
Shears Charitable Trust, The *163*

Kent
Blakey Charitable Trust, The Celia and Conrad *57*
Colyer-Fergusson Charitable Trust, Sir James *77*
D'Avigdor Goldsmid Charitable Trust, The Sarah *82*
Lawson Charitable Trust, Raymond and Blanche *117*
Rausing Charitable Foundation, Marit and Hans *151*
Roberts Charitable Trust, The E E *154*
Rochester Bridge Trust, The *155*
Rotary Club Samaritan Fund Trust, Folkestone *157*

The Medway Towns
Rochester Bridge Trust, The *155*

Oxfordshire
Ammco Trust, The *50*
Ashendene Trust, The *51*
Cooper Charitable Trust, The *78*
DLM Charitable Trust, The *82*
Lions Charity Trust Fund, Carterton *120*
Loyd Charitable Trust, The C L *121*
Pye's No 1 Charitable Settlement, Mr and Mrs J A *146*
Schuster Charitable Trust, The *161*
Wills 1965 Charitable Trust, The H D H *190*

Portsmouth
Belmont Trust, The *56*

Reading
Loyd Charitable Trust, The C L *121*

Slough
BAA 21st Century Communities Trust, The *52*
Loyd Charitable Trust, The C L *121*

Southampton
BAA 21st Century Communities Trust, The *52*

Surrey
BAA 21st Century Communities Trust, The *52*
Challice Trust, The *70*
Evelyn Charitable Settlement, The *88*
Loseley & Guildway Charitable Trust, The *121*
Rotary Club of Ashtead Trust Fund *156*

West Berkshire
Ashendene Trust, The *51*
Loyd Charitable Trust, The C L *121*

West Sussex
BAA 21st Century Communities Trust, The *52*
Belmont Trust, The *56*
HCD Memorial Fund *100*
Kleinwort Charitable Trust, The Ernest *114*
Longley Trust *120*
March's Trust Company Ltd, The Earl of *124*
Nikeno Trust, The *136*
Rausing Charitable Foundation, Marit and Hans *151*
Rotary Club of Ashtead Trust Fund *156*

Windsor & Maidenhead
BAA 21st Century Communities Trust, The *52*
Loyd Charitable Trust, The C L *121*

Wokingham
Loyd Charitable Trust, The C L *121*

■ London

Full region
Ashendene Trust, The *51*
BAA 21st Century Communities Trust, The *52*
Bentall Charitable Trust, The Gerald *56*
Bridge House Estates Trust Fund, The *59*
Chiron Trust, The *74*
Hannay Charitable Trust, The Lennox *102*
Hogg Charitable Trust, The J G *109*
Leach Fourteenth Trust, The *118*
Pye's No 1 Charitable Settlement, Mr and Mrs J A *146*
Tisbury Telegraph Trust, The *178*
Whitbread First Charitable Trust, H *188*

Barnet
Nabarro Charitable Trust, The Kitty and Daniel *132*

Camden
Macfarlane Walker Trust *123*

Greenwich
Macfarlane Walker Trust *123*

Hackney
Evans Memorial Trust, The Eric *88*

Hammersmith & Fulham
Chelsea Square 1994 Trust, The *73*

Harrow
Chelsea Square 1994 Trust, The *73*

Islington
Evans Memorial Trust, The Eric *88*

Kensington & Chelsea
Cadogan Charity, The *68*
Chelsea Square 1994 Trust, The *73*
Macfarlane Walker Trust *123*
Moore Charitable Trust, The Horace *130*

Kingston upon Thames
Chelsea Square 1994 Trust, The *73*
Moore Charitable Trust, The Horace *130*

Lewisham
Evans Memorial Trust, The Eric *88*

Newham
Evans Memorial Trust, The Eric *88*

South West & Channel Islands

Richmond upon Thames
Chelsea Square 1994 Trust, The *73*
Moore Charitable Trust, The Horace *130*

Southwark
Chelsea Square 1994 Trust, The *73*
Evans Memorial Trust, The Eric *88*

Tower Hamlets
Evans Memorial Trust, The Eric *88*

Wandsworth
Chelsea Square 1994 Trust, The *73*

■ South West & Channel Islands

Full region
Arnold Foundation, The *50*
Boyd Charitable Trust, The Viscountess *58*
Chase Charity, The *73*
Chelsea Square 1994 Trust, The *73*
Clark Charitable Trust, J A *74*
Garnett Charitable Trust, The *94*
Hannay Charitable Trust, The Lennox *102*
Hogg Charitable Trust, The J G *109*
Leach Fourteenth Trust, The *118*
Oakley Charitable Trust, The *137*
Oldham Foundation *137*

Bath & North East Somerset
Batten and Co Charitable Trust *55*
Greater Bristol Foundation *98*
Norman Family Charitable Trust, The *136*
Verdon-Smith Family Charitable Settlement, The *181*
Zaiger Trust, The Elizabeth and Prince *196*

Bristol
Crook Foundation, The Harry *80*
Greater Bristol Foundation *98*
Pye's No 1 Charitable Settlement, Mr and Mrs J A *146*

Robinson Trust No 3, The J C *155*
Verdon-Smith Family Charitable Settlement, The *181*

Channel Islands (Jersey & Guernsey)
Oakley Charitable Trust, The *137*
Sarnia Charitable Trust *161*
Wills 1965 Charitable Trust, The H D H *190*

Cornwall
Norman Family Charitable Trust, The *136*

Devon
Batten and Co Charitable Trust *55*
Mayor of Torbay's Appeal Fund, The *125*
Norman Family Charitable Trust, The *136*
Pelly Charitable Trust, The J B *142*
Pike Woodlands Trust, Claude & Margaret *144*
Yeo Trust, The Ash *195*

Dorset
Salisbury Pool Charity, The *161*
Shears Charitable Trust, The *163*
Stephenson (Deceased), Will Trust of Edgar John Henry *170*

Gloucestershire
CHK Charities Limited *65*
Gloucestershire Environmental Trust Company *96*
Macfarlane Walker Trust *123*
Moore Charitable Trust, The Horace *130*
Robinson Trust No 3, The J C *155*
Schuster Charitable Trust, The *161*
Stevens Foundation, The June *170*
Summerfield Charitable Trust, The *170*
Verdon-Smith Family Charitable Settlement, The *181*

North Somerset
Batten and Co Charitable Trust *55*
Greater Bristol Foundation *98*
Verdon-Smith Family Charitable Settlement, The *181*

Plymouth
Pelly Charitable Trust, The J B *142*

Somerset
Batten and Co Charitable Trust *55*
Glastonbury Conservation Society, The *95*
Norman Family Charitable Trust, The *136*
Verdon-Smith Family Charitable Settlement, The *181*
Zaiger Trust, The Elizabeth and Prince *196*

South Gloucestershire
Greater Bristol Foundation *98*
Pye's No 1 Charitable Settlement, Mr and Mrs J A *146*
Verdon-Smith Family Charitable Settlement, The *181*

Wiltshire
Moore Charitable Trust, The Horace *130*
Reekie Trust, R A & V B *153*
Verdon-Smith Family Charitable Settlement, The *181*
Wiltshire Gardens Trust *191*

Northern Ireland

Northern Ireland

Full area
Cadbury Charitable Trust, William Adlington 66
Garnett Charitable Trust, The 94
Green Memorial Fund, The Barry 99
Hogg Charitable Trust, The J G 109
Pye's No 1 Charitable Settlement, Mr and Mrs J A 146

Scotland

Full area
Cargill Charitable Trust, The W A 69
Chase Charity, The 73
Fox Memorial Trust 92
Gillman's Trust, Horace 95
Green Memorial Fund, The Barry 99
Harryhausen's 1969 Trust, Mrs D L 103
Hogg Charitable Trust, The J G 109
McCorquodale Charitable Trust, The 122
Macdonald Charitable Trust, The R S 122
Miller Foundation, The 128
Portrack Charitable Trust, The 145
Symons Charitable Trust, The Stella 176
Tay Charitable Trust, The 177
Wilson Trust, J and J R 190

Aberdeen
BAA 21st Century Communities Trust, The 52

Aberdeenshire
BAA 21st Century Communities Trust, The 52

Angus
Hill Memorial Trust, L E 108

Argyll & Bute
Schuster Charitable Trust, The 161
Stenhouse Foundation, The Hugh 170
Walton Foundation, The Isidore and David 184
Wilson Trust, J and J R 190

Dumfries & Galloway
Stenhouse Foundation, The Hugh 170
Walton Foundation, The Isidore and David 184
Wilson Trust, J and J R 190

East Lothian
BAA 21st Century Communities Trust, The 52
Mickel Fund 128

East Renfrewshire
Mickel Fund 128

Edinburgh
BAA 21st Century Communities Trust, The 52
Mickel Fund 128

Fife
Carnegie Dunfermline Trust 69

Glasgow
BAA 21st Century Communities Trust, The 52
Mickel Fund 128
Stenhouse Foundation, The Hugh 170
Trades House of Glasgow – Commonweal Fund, The 179
Walton Foundation, The Isidore and David 184
Wilson Trust, J and J R 190

Highland
Cromarty Trust, The 80
Gerefa Charitable Trust 94

Midlothian
Mickel Fund 128

North Ayrshire
Mickel Fund 128
Stenhouse Foundation, The Hugh 170
Walton Foundation, The Isidore and David 184
Wilson Trust, J and J R 190

North Lanarkshire
Mickel Fund 128

Perth & Kinross
Cadogan Charity, The 68

Renfrewshire
BAA 21st Century Communities Trust, The 52
Mickel Fund 128

Shetland
Shetland Islands Council Charitable Trust, The 164

South Ayrshire
Mickel Fund 128
Stenhouse Foundation, The Hugh 170
Walton Foundation, The Isidore and David 184
Wilson Trust, J and J R 190

Stirling
Walton Foundation, The Isidore and David *184*

West Ayrshire
Mickel Fund *128*

West Lothian
Mickel Fund *128*

Wales

Full area
Chase Charity, The *73*
Dinam Charity *83*
Green Memorial Fund, The Barry *99*
Hogg Charitable Trust, The J G *109*
Oakdale Trust, The *137*
Prince's Trust - BRO, The *145*
Symons Charitable Trust, The Stella *176*

■ North Wales

Full region
Hogg Charitable Trust, The J G *109*

Denbighshire
Fitzwilliam Charitable Trust, The Earl *92*

Gwynedd
Owen Family Trust, The *138*

Wrexham
Owen Family Trust, The *138*

■ South Wales

Full region
Gibson Charitable Trust, The Simon *94*
Hogg Charitable Trust, The J G *109*

Blaenau Gwent
Cwmbran Trust, The *81*

Caerphilly
South East Wales Community Foundation *167*

Cardiff
South East Wales Community Foundation *167*

Glamorgan, Vale of
South East Wales Community Foundation *167*

Merthyr Tydfil
South East Wales Community Foundation *167*

Rhondda Cynon Taff
South East Wales Community Foundation *167*

Trusts by field of interest

Categorisation of fields of interest

Rural conservation & animal welfare

■ Rural conservation 27
Endangered species 22
Environmental issues 23
Fauna 24
Flora 24
Lakes 25
Landscapes 25
Nature reserves 26
Waterways 28
Woodlands 29

■ Animal facilities & services 19
Animal homes 20
Animal welfare 20
Bird sanctuaries 21
Cats – catteries & other facilities for cats 22
Dogs – kennels & other facilities for dogs 22
Horses – stables & other facilities for horses 25
Wildlife parks 28
Wildlife sanctuaries 28
Zoos 29

■ Environmental & animal sciences 23
Agriculture 19
Agroforestry 19
Animal breeding 19
Arbiculture 21
Botany 22
Ecology 22
Entomology 23
Forestry 25
Horticulture 25
Natural history 26
Organic food production 26
Ornithology & zoology 26

Trusts by field of interest

■ Agriculture

Funding priority
Baker Trust, The C Alma 53
Great Britain Sasakawa Foundation, The 97
Reynall Charitable Trust, Joan K 154
Sedgwick Trust, The 162
Worshipful Company of Gardeners of London Charity, The 193
Yorkshire Agricultural Society 195

Will consider
Douglas Charitable Trust, R M 84
Fairbairn Charitable Trust, The Esmée 89
Fitzwilliam Charitable Trust, The Earl 92
Gibson Charitable Trust, The Simon 94
Gloucestershire Environmental Trust Company 96
Hayward Foundation, The 104
Knott Trust, Sir James 115
Landale Charitable Trust, The 117
Mitsubishi Corporation Fund for Europe and Africa 128
Moore Charitable Trust, The Horace 130
Nickerson Charitable Foundation, The Joseph 135
Paget Trust, The 140
Pilkington Charitable Trust, The Cecil 144
Roberts Charitable Trust, The E E 154
Rowan Charitable Trust, The 158
Schuster Charitable Trust, The 161
Simon Memorial Fund, The Andre 165
Summerfield Charitable Trust, The 170
Sunley Charitable Foundation, The Bernard 172
Thoresby Charitable Trust 178
Verdon-Smith Family Charitable Settlement, The 181
Weston Foundation, Garfield 187

■ Agroforestry

Funding priority
Methodist Relief and Development Fund, The 127

■ Animal breeding

Will consider
Adnams Charity, The 49
Baker Trust, The C Alma 53
Douglas Charitable Trust, R M 84
Gibson Charitable Trust, The Simon 94
Hawthorne Charitable Trust, The 104
Hayward Foundation, The 104
Schuster Charitable Trust, The 161
South Square Trust 167
Stevens Foundation, The June 170
Sunley Charitable Foundation, The Bernard 172
Yorkshire Agricultural Society 195

■ Animal facilities & services

Funding priority
Born Free Foundation, The 58
Cargill Charitable Trust, The W A 69
Clarke's Charitable Trust, The Late Miss Doris Evelyn 74
Clutterbuck Charitable Trust, Robert 75
Coote Animal Charity Fund, The Marjorie 78
Dixon Charitable Trust, C H 83
Earle Charitable Trust, Audrey 86
Hogg Charity Trust, E S 109
Hunt Charitable Trust, The Michael and Shirley 110
Kweller Charitable Trust, The Harry 116
Leach Charitable Trust, The Eric and Dorothy 118
Murphy Foundation, Edith 131
RSPCA – Winchester and Romsey Branch 148
Rickard Animals' Charity, Miss Maria Susan 154
Rochester Bridge Trust, The 155
Stevens Foundation, The June 170
Weatherby Charity, The 186
Yeo Trust, The Ash 195
Zaiger Trust, The Elizabeth and Prince 196

Will consider
Astor Foundation, The 51
Batten and Co Charitable Trust 55
Bergne-Coupland Charity 57
Bingham Trust, The 57

Animal facilities & services

Body Charitable Trust, Bernard Richard 57
CHK Charities Limited 65
Cadbury Charitable Trust, Richard 66
Carter Charitable Trust, The Leslie Mary 70
Charities Aid Foundation 71
Cohen Foundation, The John S 76
Colyer-Fergusson Charitable Trust, Sir James 77
Community Trust for Greater Manchester, The 78
Corden Trust, Cyril 79
Crook Foundation, The Harry 80
Cwmbran Trust, The 81
DLM Charitable Trust, The 82
EBM Charitable Trust 85
Elkes Charity Fund, The Wilfred & Elsie 86
Englefield Charitable Trust, The 86
Evetts & Robert Luff Animal Welfare Trust, Beryl 88
Foreman 1980 Charitable Trust, The Russell and Mary 92
Fox Memorial Trust 92
Gloucestershire Environmental Trust Company 96
Green Memorial Fund, The Barry 99
Haramead Trust, The 102
Harebell Centenary Fund, The 102
Haswell Memorial Trust, The John 103
Higgs Charitable Trust, The 107
Hodgkinson Charitable Trust, The Peter and Gwyneth 108
Hogg Charitable Trust, The J G 109
IFAW Charitable Trust 111
Lawson Charitable Trust, Raymond and Blanche 117
Livesley 1992 Charitable Trust, Mrs C M 120
Lord Mayor of Chester Charitable Trust 121
Loyd Charitable Trust, The C L 121
McCorquodale Charitable Trust, The 122
Macdonald Charitable Trust, The R S 122
Marsh and McLennan (Charities Fund) Ltd, J and H 124
Mayor of Torbay's Appeal Fund, The 125
Miller Foundation, The 128
Mitsubishi Corporation Fund for Europe and Africa 128
National Animal Sanctuaries Support League 132

Oakdale Trust, The 137
Oldham Foundation 137
Onaway Trust, The 138
PF Charitable Trust 139
Personal Assurance Charitable Trust 142
Persula Foundation, The 142
Pewterers' Charity Trust 143
Rank Foundation, The 149
Rotaract Club, Bristol North West 156
Rotary Club of Arbury Charity Trust Fund 156
Rotary Club of Eastleigh Trust Fund 156
Rotary Club of Thornbury Trust Fund, The 157
Rotary Club of Wallasey, The Charitable Fund of the 157
Salisbury Pool Charity, The 161
Shark Trust, The 163
Shears Charitable Trust, The 163
Shepherd Conservation Foundation, The David 163
Smith Charitable Trust for Nature, The Peter 166
South East Wales Community Foundation 167
Sutton Coldfield Municipal Charities, The 173
Swann-Morton Foundation, The 175
Sylvanus Charitable Trust, The 176
Symons Charitable Trust, The Stella 176
Talbot Bridge Will Trust, The Elsie 177
Town Lands, The 179
Trades House of Glasgow – Commonweal Fund, The 179
Van Norden's Charitable Foundation, Mrs Maud 180
Vaux Group Foundation, The 180
Waterhouse Charitable Trust, Mrs 185
Wensum Residents Association 186
Whitley Animal Protection Trust 189
Wilson Trust, J and J R 190
Wyre Animal Welfare 194

■ Animal homes
Funding priority
Calypso Browning Trust 69
Evetts & Robert Luff Animal Welfare Trust, Beryl 88
Pet Plan Charitable Trust 143

Sainsbury Animal Welfare Trust, Jean 160
Scott Charitable Trust, The Frieda 162
Wyre Animal Welfare 194

Will consider
Challice Trust, The 70
Chelsea Square 1994 Trust, The 73
Douglas Charitable Trust, R M 84
Gerefa Charitable Trust 94
Gibson Charitable Trust, The Simon 94
Green Memorial Fund, The Barry 99
Haddon Charitable Trust, William 100
Harryhausen's 1969 Trust, Mrs D L 103
Harvey's Discretionary Settlement, William Geoffrey 103
Hillards Charitable Trust, Gay & Peter Hartley's 108
Knott Trust, Sir James 115
Marchig Animal Welfare Trust 124
March's Trust Company Ltd, The Earl of 124
Moore Charitable Trust, The Horace 130
Oakley Charitable Trust, The 137
Paget Trust, The 140
Raptor Trust, The 151
Rollit Trust, The Vera Kaye 155
Schuster Charitable Trust, The 161
Sunley Charitable Foundation, The Bernard 172
Whitbread First Charitable Trust, H 188
Wigan Town Relief in Need Charity 189
Wilson Trust, J and J R 190

■ Animal welfare
Funding priority
Body Charitable Trust, Bernard Richard 57
Briggs Animal Welfare Trust, The 61
CHK Charities Limited 65
Calypso Browning Trust 69
Corden Trust, Cyril 79
EBM Charitable Trust 85
Hannay Charitable Trust, The Lennox 102
Haramead Trust, The 102
Hawthorne Charitable Trust, The 104

Trusts by field of interest

Bird sanctuaries

Hornby's Charitable Settlement, Mrs E G *110*
IFAW Charitable Trust *111*
Linder Foundation, The Enid *119*
Lions Charity Trust Fund, Carterton *120*
Livesley 1992 Charitable Trust, Mrs C M *120*
Lord Mayor of Chester Charitable Trust *121*
Loseley & Guildway Charitable Trust, The *121*
Loyd Charitable Trust, The C L *121*
Macdonald Charitable Trust, The R S *122*
Marchig Animal Welfare Trust *124*
Mayor of Torbay's Appeal Fund, The *125*
Miller Foundation, The *128*
National Animal Sanctuaries Support League *132*
Norman Family Charitable Trust, The *136*
Onaway Trust, The *138*
Paget Trust, The *140*
Persula Foundation, The *142*
Pet Plan Charitable Trust *143*
Philanthropic Trust, The *144*
RSPCA – Winchester and Romsey Branch *148*
Ramsden Charitable Trust, The Edward *148*
Raptor Trust, The *151*
Reynall Charitable Trust, Joan K *154*
Rickard Animals' Charity, Miss Maria Susan *154*
Rotary Club of Wallasey, The Charitable Fund of the *157*
Rufford Foundation *159*
Sainsbury Animal Welfare Trust, Jean *160*
Scott Charitable Trust, The Frieda *162*
Shah Trust, The Dr N K *163*
Sylvanus Charitable Trust, The *176*
Tho Memorial Foundation, Loke Wan *177*
Van Norden's Charitable Foundation, Mrs Maud *180*
Verdon-Smith Family Charitable Settlement, The *181*
Walker 597 Trust, The *184*
Walton Foundation, The Isidore and David *184*
Weatherby Charity, The *186*
Whitley Animal Protection Trust *189*
Wicksteed Village Trust, The *189*
Wilson Trust for Animal Welfare, The Kit *191*

Wyford Charitable Trust, The *194*
Yeo Trust, The Ash *195*

Will consider
Adnams Charity, The *49*
Bentall Charitable Trust, The Gerald *56*
Boyd Charitable Trust, The Viscountess *58*
Cadogan Charity, The *68*
Carnegie Dunfermline Trust *69*
Challice Trust, The *70*
Chelsea Square 1994 Trust, The *73*
Chiron Trust, The *74*
Dinam Charity *83*
Douglas Charitable Trust, R M *84*
Franklin Deceased's New Second Charity, Sydney E *93*
Gerefa Charitable Trust *94*
Gibson Charitable Trust, The Simon *94*
Green Memorial Fund, The Barry *99*
Haddon Charitable Trust, William *100*
Hadrian Trust, The *101*
Harryhausen's 1969 Trust, Mrs D L *103*
Harvey's Discretionary Settlement, William Geoffrey *103*
Hillards Charitable Trust, Gay & Peter Hartley's *108*
Homelands Charitable Trust *109*
Homfray Trust, The *109*
Kirkham Foundation, The Graham *113*
Knott Trust, Sir James *115*
Laing Charitable Trust, The David *117*
Lawson Charitable Trust, Raymond and Blanche *117*
McMorran Charitable Foundation, The Helen Isabella *123*
March's Trust Company Ltd, The Earl of *124*
Melton Mowbray Building Society Charitable Foundation *125*
Oakley Charitable Trust, The *137*
Rollit Trust, The Vera Kaye *155*
Rotary Club of Hadleigh Charitable Trust Fund *157*
Schuster Charitable Trust, The *161*
Schweitzer's Hospital Fund, Dr *162*
South Square Trust *167*

Sunley Charitable Foundation, The Bernard *172*
Sykes Trust, The Charles *175*
Tisbury Telegraph Trust, The *178*
Vodafone Group Charitable Trust, The *181*
Whitbread First Charitable Trust, H *188*
Wigan Town Relief in Need Charity *189*
Wilson Trust, J and J R *190*

■ Arbiculture
Funding priority
Pelly Charitable Trust, The J B *142*

■ Bird sanctuaries
Funding priority
Calypso Browning Trust *69*
Evetts & Robert Luff Animal Welfare Trust, Beryl *88*
Gillman's Trust, Horace *95*
Peacock Charitable Trust, The *141*
Pelly Charitable Trust, The J B *142*
Sainsbury Animal Welfare Trust, Jean *160*
Scott Charitable Trust, The Frieda *162*
Stenhouse Foundation, The Hugh *170*
Tho Memorial Foundation, Loke Wan *177*
Wright Deceased Trust, John William *193*

Will consider
Adnams Charity, The *49*
Boyd Charitable Trust, The Viscountess *58*
Bromley Trust, The *62*
Burton 1960 Charitable Trust, Audrey and Stanley *63*
Cadbury Charitable Trust, William Adlington *66*
Chelsea Square 1994 Trust, The *73*
Cooper Charitable Trust, The *78*
Criffel Charitable Trust *80*
Dunn Charitable Trust, The Harry *84*
Gerefa Charitable Trust *94*
Gibson Charitable Trust, The Simon *94*
Green Memorial Fund, The Barry *99*
Grocers' Charity *99*
Haddon Charitable Trust, William *100*

21

Botany

Harvey's Discretionary Settlement, William Geoffrey *103*
Hillards Charitable Trust, Gay & Peter Hartley's *108*
Kirkham Foundation, The Graham *113*
Knott Trust, Sir James *115*
Lyndhurst Settlement *121*
Macfarlane Walker Trust *123*
McMorran Charitable Foundation, The Helen Isabella *123*
Marchig Animal Welfare Trust *124*
Oakley Charitable Trust, The *137*
Raptor Trust, The *151*
Rotary Club of Hadleigh Charitable Trust Fund *157*
Schuster Charitable Trust, The *161*
South Square Trust *167*
Sykes Trust, The Charles *175*
Weston Foundation, Garfield *187*
Whitbread First Charitable Trust, H *188*
Wilson Trust, J and J R *190*
Winstone Foundation, Hyman *191*

■ Botany

Funding priority
Smith (UK) Horticultural Trust, Stanley *167*
Wild Flower Society, The *190*

Will consider
Garnett Charitable Trust, The *94*
Johnson Foundation, The *112*
Norman Trust, The *136*
Sunley Charitable Foundation, The Bernard *172*

■ Cats – catteries & other facilities for cats

Funding priority
Briggs Animal Welfare Trust, The *61*
Calypso Browning Trust *69*
Evetts & Robert Luff Animal Welfare Trust, Beryl *88*
Lions Charity Trust Fund, Carterton *120*
Pet Plan Charitable Trust *143*
Sainsbury Animal Welfare Trust, Jean *160*
Scott Charitable Trust, The Frieda *162*

Will consider
Chelsea Square 1994 Trust, The *73*
Green Memorial Fund, The Barry *99*
Hillards Charitable Trust, Gay & Peter Hartley's *108*
Kirkham Foundation, The Graham *113*
Marchig Animal Welfare Trust *124*
Oakley Charitable Trust, The *137*
Rollit Trust, The Vera Kaye *155*

■ Dogs – kennels & other facilities for dogs

Funding priority
Briggs Animal Welfare Trust, The *61*
Calypso Browning Trust *69*
Canine Supporters Charity, The *69*
Evelyn Charitable Settlement, The *88*
Evetts & Robert Luff Animal Welfare Trust, Beryl *88*
Kennel Club Charitable Trust, The *113*
Lions Charity Trust Fund, Carterton *120*
Pet Plan Charitable Trust *143*
Sainsbury Animal Welfare Trust, Jean *160*
Scott Charitable Trust, The Frieda *162*
Wyford Charitable Trust, The *194*

Will consider
Cadogan Charity, The *68*
Chelsea Square 1994 Trust, The *73*
Douglas Charitable Trust, R M *84*
Gibson Charitable Trust, The Simon *94*
Green Memorial Fund, The Barry *99*
Harryhausen's 1969 Trust, Mrs D L *103*
Harvey's Discretionary Settlement, William Geoffrey *103*
Hillards Charitable Trust, Gay & Peter Hartley's *108*
Kirkham Foundation, The Graham *113*
Marchig Animal Welfare Trust *124*
Moore Charitable Trust, The Horace *130*
Oakley Charitable Trust, The *137*
Paget Trust, The *140*
Rollit Trust, The Vera Kaye *155*
Schuster Charitable Trust, The *161*
South Square Trust *167*
Warrington Animal Welfare *184*

■ Ecology

Funding priority
Pelly Charitable Trust, The J B *142*
Shah Trust, The Dr N K *163*
Thackray General Charitable Trust, The C P *177*

Will consider
Dunn Charitable Trust, The Harry *84*
Foreman 1980 Charitable Trust, The Russell and Mary *92*
Garnett Charitable Trust, The *94*
Hayward Foundation, The *104*
Johnson Foundation, The *112*
Mersey Basin Trust – ICI Green Action Grants *126*
Norman Trust, The *136*
Radley Charitable Trust *148*
Smith Foundation, The Martin *166*
Summerfield Charitable Trust, The *170*
Sunley Charitable Foundation, The Bernard *172*

■ Endangered species

Funding priority
BP Conservation Programme *53*
Born Free Foundation, The *58*
Briggs Animal Welfare Trust, The *61*
Cooper Charitable Trust, The *78*
Criffel Charitable Trust *80*
Franklin Deceased's New Second Charity, Sydney E *93*
Haddon Charitable Trust, William *100*
Hill Memorial Trust, L E *108*
Hodgkinson Charitable Trust, The Peter and Gwyneth *108*
Pelly Charitable Trust, The J B *142*
Philanthropic Trust, The *144*
Raptor Trust, The *151*
Rufford Foundation *159*
Schuster Charitable Trust, The *161*
Shark Trust, The *163*

Trusts by field of interest — **Environmental issues**

Shepherd Conservation Foundation, The David 163
Shetland Islands Council Charitable Trust, The 164
Van Norden's Charitable Foundation, Mrs Maud 180
WWF UK (World Wide Fund for Nature) 182

Will consider
Cadogan Charity, The 68
Chelsea Square 1994 Trust, The 73
Cinderford Charitable Trust, The 74
D'Avigdor Goldsmid Charitable Trust, The Sarah 82
Dearne Valley Community Forum 82
Fairbairn Charitable Trust, The Esmée 89
Gerefa Charitable Trust 94
Hall Charity, Robert 101
Harvey's Discretionary Settlement, William Geoffrey 103
IFAW Charitable Trust 111
Leach Charitable Trust, The Eric and Dorothy 118
Mersey Basin Trust – Stream Care Project 126
Mersey Basin Trust – Waterside Revival Grants 127
Moores Foundation, The Peter 130
Nabarro Charitable Trust, The Kitty and Daniel 132
National Lottery Charities Board 132
Pike Woodlands Trust, Claude & Margaret 144
Rotary Club of Arbury Charity Trust Fund 156
Stevens Foundation, The June 170
Sunley Charitable Foundation, The Bernard 172
Tisbury Telegraph Trust, The 178
Wild Flower Society, The 190

■ Entomology
Funding priority
Lewis Foundation, The John Spedan 119

■ Environmental & animal sciences
Funding priority
Dixon Charitable Trust, C H 83
Hodgkinson Charitable Trust, The Peter and Gwyneth 108
Hogg Charity Trust, E S 109

Rochester Bridge Trust, The 155
Yeo Trust, The Ash 195

Will consider
Astor Foundation, The 51
Batten and Co Charitable Trust 55
Bergne-Coupland Charity 57
Bingham Trust, The 57
Cadbury Charitable Trust, Richard 66
Charities Aid Foundation 71
Cohen Foundation, The John S 76
Colyer-Fergusson Charitable Trust, Sir James 77
Community Trust for Greater Manchester, The 78
Cwmbran Trust, The 81
DLM Charitable Trust, The 82
Englefield Charitable Trust, The 86
Evetts & Robert Luff Animal Welfare Trust, Beryl 88
Fox Memorial Trust 92
Gloucestershire Environmental Trust Company 96
Haswell Memorial Trust, The John 103
Hogg Charitable Trust, The J G 109
Lewis Foundation, The John Spedan 119
Longley Trust 120
Loraine Trust 120
McCorquodale Charitable Trust, The 122
Marsh and McLennan (Charities Fund) Ltd, J and H 124
Moores Foundation, The Peter 130
Oakdale Trust, The 137
Oldham Foundation 137
Personal Assurance Charitable Trust 142
Pewterers' Charity Trust 143
Rank Foundation, The 149
Rotaract Club, Bristol North West 156
Rotary Club of Eastleigh Trust Fund 156
Rotary Club of Thornbury Trust Fund, The 157
St John's Wood Trust, The 161
Salisbury Pool Charity, The 161
Shears Charitable Trust, The 163
Smith Charitable Trust for Nature, The Peter 166
South East Wales Community Foundation 167
Sutton Coldfield Municipal Charities, The 173

Swann-Morton Foundation, The 175
Symons Charitable Trust, The Stella 176
Talbot Bridge Will Trust, The Elsie 177
Town Lands, The 179
Trades House of Glasgow – Commonweal Fund, The 179
Waterhouse Charitable Trust, Mrs 185
Whitbread First Charitable Trust, H 188

■ Environmental issues
Funding priority
Ammco Trust, The 50
Ashby Will Trust, A J H 51
BAA 21st Century Communities Trust, The 52
Body Shop Foundation, The 58
Bridge House Estates Trust Fund, The 59
Britten-Pears Foundation, The 62
Burton Charitable Trust, The Geoffrey 64
Clark Charitable Trust, J A 74
Countryside Trust, The 79
Ecological Foundation, The 86
Fairbairn Charitable Trust, The Esmée 89
Garnett Charitable Trust, The 94
Gloucestershire Environmental Trust Company 96
Great Britain Sasakawa Foundation, The 97
Greater Bristol Foundation 98
Haddon Charitable Trust, William 100
Hill Memorial Trust, L E 108
Hodgkinson Charitable Trust, The Peter and Gwyneth 108
Johnson Foundation, The 112
Macfarlane Walker Trust 123
Martin Charitable Trust, Michael D 125
Mersey Basin Trust – Waterside Revival Grants 127
Nikeno Trust, The 136
Norman Trust, The 136
Pelly Charitable Trust, The J B 142
Philanthropic Trust, The 144
Pike Woodlands Trust, Claude & Margaret 144
Pittecroft Trust, The 145
Pryor Charity, The Ronald & Kathleen 146
Rausing Trust, The Ruben and Elizabeth 151

23

Fauna

Trusts by field of interest

Reuter Foundation, The 153
Rufford Foundation 159
Shetland Islands Council Charitable Trust, The 164
South East Wales Community Foundation 167
Thackray General Charitable Trust, The C P 177
Tisbury Telegraph Trust, The 178
Van Norden's Charitable Foundation, Mrs Maud 180
WWF UK (World Wide Fund for Nature) 182
Wales's Charitable Foundation, The Prince of 183
Walker Charitable Trust, The Anthony 184
Yeo Trust, The Ash 195
Yorkshire Agricultural Society 195

Will consider
Alchemy Foundation, The 49
BP Conservation Programme 53
Belmont Trust, The 56
British Sugar Foundation 61
Carnegie Dunfermline Trust 69
Cleopatra Trust 75
D'Avigdor Goldsmid Charitable Trust, The Sarah 82
Dearne Valley Community Forum 82
Derbyshire Community Foundation 83
Dinam Charity 83
Dorus Trust 84
Epigoni Trust 87
Ericson Trust 87
Fitzwilliam Charitable Trust, The Earl 92
Franklin Deceased's New Second Charity, Sydney E 93
Frognal Trust 93
Gerefa Charitable Trust 94
Graves Charitable Trust, J G 96
HCD Memorial Fund 100
Hadrian Trust, The 101
Hall Charity, Robert 101
Hillards Charitable Trust, Gay & Peter Hartley's 108
IFAW Charitable Trust 111
Lawson Charitable Trust, Raymond and Blanche 117
Leach Charitable Trust, The Eric and Dorothy 118
Marchig Animal Welfare Trust 124
Melton Mowbray Building Society Charitable Foundation 125
Moores Foundation, The Peter 130

Nabarro Charitable Trust, The Kitty and Daniel 132
National Lottery Charities Board 132
Prince's Trust - BRO, The 145
RAC Foundation for Motoring and the Environment Ltd, The 148
Raptor Trust, The 151
Roberts Charitable Trust, The E E 154
Rotary Club of Arbury Charity Trust Fund 156
Rotary Club Samaritan Fund Trust, Folkestone 157
Sheringham and District Preservation Society 164
Simon Memorial Fund, The Andre 165
Smith Foundation, The Martin 166
Summerfield Charitable Trust, The 170
Sunley Charitable Foundation, The Bernard 172
Thoresby Charitable Trust 178
Twil Group Charitable Trust, The 180
Winstone Foundation, Hyman 191

■ Fauna

Funding priority
Burton Charitable Trust, The Geoffrey 64
Carron Charitable Trust, The 70
Clark Charitable Trust, J A 74
Eskdale (Cumbria) Trust, The 88
Gloucestershire Environmental Trust Company 96
Great Britain Sasakawa Foundation, The 97
Haddon Charitable Trust, William 100
Mitsubishi Corporation Fund for Europe and Africa 128
Pike Woodlands Trust, Claude & Margaret 144
Raptor Trust, The 151
Rufford Foundation 159
Shetland Islands Council Charitable Trust, The 164
Van Norden's Charitable Foundation, Mrs Maud 180

Will consider
BP Conservation Programme 53
Brading Town Trust, The 59
Chelsea Square 1994 Trust, The 73
Countryside Trust, The 79

D'Avigdor Goldsmid Charitable Trust, The Sarah 82
Fairbairn Charitable Trust, The Esmée 89
Frognal Trust 93
Gerefa Charitable Trust 94
Grocers' Charity 99
Harvey's Discretionary Settlement, William Geoffrey 103
Mersey Basin Trust – Stream Care Project 126
Mersey Basin Trust – Waterside Revival Grants 127
Nikeno Trust, The 136
Pelly Charitable Trust, The J B 142
Philanthropic Trust, The 144
Rausing Charitable Foundation, Marit and Hans 151
Reckitt Charity, Sir James 152
Shepherd Conservation Foundation, The David 163
Sunley Charitable Foundation, The Bernard 172
Tisbury Telegraph Trust, The 178
Winstone Foundation, Hyman 191
Yorkshire Agricultural Society 195

■ Flora

Funding priority
Burton Charitable Trust, The Geoffrey 64
Carron Charitable Trust, The 70
Clark Charitable Trust, J A 74
Countryside Trust, The 79
Eskdale (Cumbria) Trust, The 88
Gloucestershire Environmental Trust Company 96
Great Britain Sasakawa Foundation, The 97
Haddon Charitable Trust, William 100
Mitsubishi Corporation Fund for Europe and Africa 128
Pelly Charitable Trust, The J B 142
Pike Woodlands Trust, Claude & Margaret 144
Rufford Foundation 159
Shetland Islands Council Charitable Trust, The 164
Wild Flower Society, The 190

Will consider
Ashendene Trust, The 51
BP Conservation Programme 53
Brading Town Trust, The 59

Trusts by field of interest **Landscapes**

D'Avigdor Goldsmid Charitable Trust, The Sarah *82*
Fairbairn Charitable Trust, The Esmée *89*
Frognal Trust *93*
Gerefa Charitable Trust *94*
Grocers' Charity *99*
Isle of Wight Gardens Trust *112*
Mersey Basin Trust – Stream Care Project *126*
Mersey Basin Trust – Waterside Revival Grants *127*
Nikeno Trust, The *136*
Peartree Trust, The *142*
Prince's Trust - BRO, The *145*
Rausing Charitable Foundation, Marit and Hans *151*
Reckitt Charity, Sir James *152*
Shepherd Conservation Foundation, The David *163*
Sunley Charitable Foundation, The Bernard *172*
Tisbury Telegraph Trust, The *178*
Yorkshire Agricultural Society *195*

■ **Forestry**

Funding priority

Pilkington Charitable Trust, The Cecil *144*

■ **Horses – stables & other facilities for horses**

Funding priority

Briggs Animal Welfare Trust, The *61*
Calypso Browning Trust *69*
Evetts & Robert Luff Animal Welfare Trust, Beryl *88*
Medical Equestrian Association *125*
Pet Plan Charitable Trust *143*
Sainsbury Animal Welfare Trust, Jean *160*

Will consider

Barnby's Foundation, Lord *55*
Burton 1960 Charitable Trust, Audrey and Stanley *63*
Cadbury Charitable Trust, William Adlington *66*
Gibson Charitable Trust, The Simon *94*
Green Memorial Fund, The Barry *99*
Harryhausen's 1969 Trust, Mrs D L *103*

Harvey's Discretionary Settlement, William Geoffrey *103*
Hillards Charitable Trust, Gay & Peter Hartley's *108*
Kirkham Foundation, The Graham *113*
Marchig Animal Welfare Trust *124*
Moore Charitable Trust, The Horace *130*
Rollit Trust, The Vera Kaye *155*
Sunley Charitable Foundation, The Bernard *172*

■ **Horticulture**

Funding priority

Lewis Foundation, The John Spedan *119*
Loraine Trust *120*
Pelly Charitable Trust, The J B *142*
Royal Botanical & Horticultural Society of Manchester and the Northern Counties, The *159*
St John's Wood Trust, The *161*
Smith (UK) Horticultural Trust, Stanley *167*

Will consider

Armitage Charitable Trust, G C *50*
Garnett Charitable Trust, The *94*
Hayward Foundation, The *104*
Idlewild Trust, The *111*
Johnson Foundation, The *112*
Sunley Charitable Foundation, The Bernard *172*
Woodlands Trust *192*

■ **Lakes**

Funding priority

Carron Charitable Trust, The *70*
Gloucestershire Environmental Trust Company *96*
Pelly Charitable Trust, The J B *142*
Scott Charitable Trust, The Frieda *162*

Will consider

BP Conservation Programme *53*
Belmont Trust, The *56*
Countryside Trust, The *79*
Fairbairn Charitable Trust, The Esmée *89*
Frognal Trust *93*
Grocers' Charity *99*

Haddon Charitable Trust, William *100*
Isle of Wight Gardens Trust *112*
Melton Mowbray Building Society Charitable Foundation *125*
Mersey Basin Trust – Stream Care Project *126*
Mersey Basin Trust – Waterside Revival Grants *127*
Moore Charitable Trust, The Horace *130*
Prince's Trust - BRO, The *145*
Rawdon-Smith Trust, The *152*
Reckitt Charity, Sir James *152*
Tisbury Telegraph Trust, The *178*
Wade & Others, The Charity of Thomas *183*
Wolfe Charitable Settlement C, Ruth *192*

■ **Landscapes**

Funding priority

Carron Charitable Trust, The *70*
Countryside Trust, The *79*
Gloucestershire Environmental Trust Company *96*
Pelly Charitable Trust, The J B *142*
Radley Charitable Trust *148*
Scott Charitable Trust, The Frieda *162*
Whitlingham Charitable Trust, The *189*
Wiltshire Gardens Trust *191*

Will consider

Belmont Trust, The *56*
Brading Town Trust, The *59*
Britten-Pears Foundation, The *62*
Brotherton Trust, The Charles *63*
Fairbairn Charitable Trust, The Esmée *89*
Fitzwilliam Charitable Trust, The Earl *92*
Frognal Trust *93*
Graves Charitable Trust, J G *96*
Grocers' Charity *99*
Haddon Charitable Trust, William *100*
Hadrian Trust, The *101*
Hillards Charitable Trust, Gay & Peter Hartley's *108*
Isle of Wight Gardens Trust *112*
Leche Trust, The *118*

25

Natural history

Melton Mowbray Building Society Charitable Foundation 125
Mersey Basin Trust – Stream Care Project 126
Mersey Basin Trust – Waterside Revival Grants 127
Moore Charitable Trust, The Horace 130
Pike Woodlands Trust, Claude & Margaret 144
Prince's Trust - BRO, The 145
Reckitt Charity, Sir James 152
Rotary Club of Hadleigh Charitable Trust Fund 157
Sheringham and District Preservation Society 164
Skells, Bequest of Harry 166
Summerfield Charitable Trust, The 170
Tisbury Telegraph Trust, The 178
Wade & Others, The Charity of Thomas 183
Wolfe Charitable Settlement C, Ruth 192
Yorkshire Agricultural Society 195

■ Natural history
Will consider
Clutterbuck Charitable Trust, Robert 75
Hayward Foundation, The 104
Mersey Basin Trust – ICI Green Action Grants 126
Sunley Charitable Foundation, The Bernard 172

■ Nature reserves
Funding priority
Bell Trust, The Henry 55
Belsize Charitable Trust No1 56
Briggs Animal Welfare Trust, The 61
Burton Charitable Trust, The Geoffrey 64
Carron Charitable Trust, The 70
Carter Charitable Trust, The Leslie Mary 70
Countryside Trust, The 79
Gloucestershire Environmental Trust Company 96
Haddon Charitable Trust, William 100
Hannay Charitable Trust, The Lennox 102
Nikeno Trust, The 136
Pelly Charitable Trust, The J B 142
Pryor Charity, The Ronald & Kathleen 146
Radley Charitable Trust 148
Rausing Charitable Foundation, Marit and Hans 151
Reynall Charitable Trust, Joan K 154
Scott Charitable Trust, The Frieda 162
Shetland Islands Council Charitable Trust, The 164
Stenhouse Foundation, The Hugh 170
Van Norden's Charitable Foundation, Mrs Maud 180

Will consider
BP Conservation Programme 53
Belmont Trust, The 56
Bentall Charitable Trust, The Gerald 56
Brading Town Trust, The 59
British Sugar Foundation 61
Britten-Pears Foundation, The 62
Brotherton Trust, The Charles 63
Chase Charity, The 73
Chelsea Square 1994 Trust, The 73
Chiron Trust, The 74
D'Avigdor Goldsmid Charitable Trust, The Sarah 82
Fairbairn Charitable Trust, The Esmée 89
Fitzmaurice Charitable Trust, The 91
Frognal Trust 93
Grocers' Charity 99
Hadrian Trust, The 101
Harvey's Discretionary Settlement, William Geoffrey 103
Hillards Charitable Trust, Gay & Peter Hartley's 108
Jacobson Charitable Trust (No 2), The Ruth & Lionel 112
Mann Trustees Limited, R W 123
Melton Mowbray Building Society Charitable Foundation 125
Mersey Basin Trust – Stream Care Project 126
Mersey Basin Trust – Waterside Revival Grants 127
Moore Charitable Trust, The Horace 130
Prince's Trust - BRO, The 145
Raptor Trust, The 151
Reckitt Charity, Sir James 152
Rotary Club of Hadleigh Charitable Trust Fund 157
Sheringham and District Preservation Society 164
Skells, Bequest of Harry 166
Smith Foundation, The Leslie 166
Summerfield Charitable Trust, The 170
Sunley Charitable Foundation, The Bernard 172
Thoresby Charitable Trust 178
Twil Group Charitable Trust, The 180
Wild Flower Society, The 190
Winstone Foundation, Hyman 191
Wolfe Charitable Settlement C, Ruth 192

■ Organic food production
Funding priority
Coates Charitable Trust 1969, Lance 75
Pelly Charitable Trust, The J B 142

Will consider
Chiron Trust, The 74
Ecological Foundation, The 86
Loraine Trust 120
Paget Trust, The 140
Radley Charitable Trust 148
Summerfield Charitable Trust, The 170

■ Ornithology & zoology
Funding priority
BP Conservation Programme 53
Lewis Foundation, The John Spedan 119
Pelly Charitable Trust, The J B 142
Pryor Charity, The Ronald & Kathleen 146
Tho Memorial Foundation, Loke Wan 177

Will consider
Adnams Charity, The 49
Cadbury Charitable Trust, William Adlington 66
D'Avigdor Goldsmid Charitable Trust, The Sarah 82
Douglas Charitable Trust, R M 84
Gloucestershire Environmental Trust Company 96
Leach Fourteenth Trust, The 118
Raptor Trust, The 151
Stevens Foundation, The June 170

Trusts by field of interest **Rural conservation**

Tisbury Telegraph Trust, The *178*
Weston Foundation, Garfield *187*

■ Rural conservation

Funding priority

Chestnut Trust, The *73*
Cobb Charity *76*
Countryside Business Group Charitable Trust *79*
de Freitas Charitable Trust, The Helen and Geoffrey *82*
Dixon Charitable Trust, C H *83*
Glastonbury Conservation Society, The *95*
Heritage Lottery Fund *107*
Hogg Charity Trust, E S *109*
Kleinwort Charitable Trust, The Ernest *114*
Longley Trust *120*
Mersey Basin Trust – ICI Green Action Grants *126*
Middleton Fund, The *128*
Pilkington Charitable Trust, The Cecil *144*
Rochester Bridge Trust, The *155*
Sarnia Charitable Trust *161*
Spooner Charitable Trust, W W *168*
Tho Memorial Foundation, Loke Wan *177*
Whitbread First Charitable Trust, H *188*
Worshipful Company of Gardeners of London Charity, The *193*
Wright Deceased Trust, John William *193*
Yeo Trust, The Ash *195*

Will consider

Adnams Charity, The *49*
Ammco Trust, The *50*
Anne's Charities Trust, The Princess *50*
Arnold Foundation, The *50*
Ashby Will Trust, A J H *51*
Astor Foundation, The *51*
BAA 21st Century Communities Trust, The *52*
Balney Charitable Trust, The *54*
Barbour Trust, The *54*
Barnby's Foundation, Lord *55*
Barrow Trust, Dr *55*
Batten and Co Charitable Trust *55*
Belsize Charitable Trust No1 *56*
Benham Charitable Settlement *56*
Bergne-Coupland Charity *57*

Bingham Trust, The *57*
Boyd Charitable Trust, The Viscountess *58*
Bromley Trust, The *62*
Burton 1960 Charitable Trust, Audrey and Stanley *63*
CHK Charities Limited *65*
Cadbury Charitable Trust, Richard *66*
Cadbury Charitable Trust, William Adlington *66*
Carter Charitable Trust, The Leslie Mary *70*
Challice Trust, The *70*
Charities Aid Foundation *71*
Cohen Foundation, The John S *76*
Colyer-Fergusson Charitable Trust, Sir James *77*
Community Trust for Greater Manchester, The *78*
Cooper Charitable Trust, The *78*
Criffel Charitable Trust *80*
Cromarty Trust, The *80*
Crook Foundation, The Harry *80*
Cwmbran Trust, The *81*
DLM Charitable Trust, The *82*
Dunn Charitable Trust, The Harry *84*
Ecological Foundation, The *86*
Elkes Charity Fund, The Wilfred & Elsie *86*
Englefield Charitable Trust, The *86*
Eves Charitable Trust, Douglas Heath *88*
Fitzwilliam Charitable Trust, The Earl *92*
Fox Memorial Trust *92*
Gibson Charitable Trust, The Simon *94*
Gloucestershire Environmental Trust Company *96*
Guido's Charitable Trust, Mrs Margaret *100*
Hall Trust, The Christine *102*
Harebell Centenary Fund, The *102*
Haswell Memorial Trust, The John *103*
Hayward Foundation, The *104*
Headley Trust, The *106*
Hemby Trust, The *107*
Higgs Charitable Trust, The *107*
Hodgkinson Charitable Trust, The Peter and Gwyneth *108*
Hogg Charitable Trust, The J G *109*
Hughes Charitable Trust, The Geoffrey C *110*
INTACH (UK) Trust *111*
Knott Trust, Sir James *115*

Laing Charitable Trust, The David *117*
Landale Charitable Trust, The *117*
Laurence 1976 Charitable Settlement, The Mrs F B *117*
Lawson Charitable Trust, Raymond and Blanche *117*
Leach Fourteenth Trust, The *118*
Lord Mayor of Chester Charitable Trust *121*
Lyndhurst Settlement *121*
McCorquodale Charitable Trust, The *122*
Macfarlane Walker Trust *123*
McMorran Charitable Foundation, The Helen Isabella *123*
Malachi (Family) Charitable Trust *123*
Marsh and McLennan (Charities Fund) Ltd, J and H *124*
Martin Charitable Trust, Michael D *125*
Mitsubishi Corporation Fund for Europe and Africa *128*
Monument Trust, The *129*
Nabarro Charitable Trust, The Kitty and Daniel *132*
New Horizons Trust, The *135*
Nickerson Charitable Foundation, The Joseph *135*
Oakdale Trust, The *137*
Oakley Charitable Trust, The *137*
Oldham Foundation *137*
Onaway Trust, The *138*
Owen Family Trust, The *138*
PF Charitable Trust *139*
Paget Trust, The *140*
Peacock Charitable Trust, The *141*
Personal Assurance Charitable Trust *142*
Pewterers' Charity Trust *143*
Pittecroft Trust, The *145*
Portrack Charitable Trust, The *145*
Pye's No 1 Charitable Settlement, Mr and Mrs J A *146*
Radley Charitable Trust *148*
Rank Foundation, The *149*
Reekie Trust, R A & V B *153*
Reuter Foundation, The *153*
Rivington Heritage Trust *154*
Robinson Trust No 3, The J C *155*
Rotaract Club, Bristol North West *156*
Rotary Club of Ashtead Trust Fund *156*

27

Waterways

Trusts by field of interest

Rotary Club of Eastleigh Trust Fund 156
Rotary Club of Thornbury Trust Fund, The 157
Rowan Charitable Trust, The 158
Salisbury Pool Charity, The 161
Schuster Charitable Trust, The 161
Shears Charitable Trust, The 163
Smith Charitable Trust for Nature, The Peter 166
South East Wales Community Foundation 167
South Square Trust 167
Stanhope-Palmer Charity 168
Staples Trust 168
Sutton Coldfield Municipal Charities, The 173
Swann-Morton Foundation, The 175
Sykes Trust, The Charles 175
Symons Charitable Trust, The Stella 176
Talbot Bridge Will Trust, The Elsie 177
Tay Charitable Trust, The 177
Thackray General Charitable Trust, The C P 177
Torrs Charitable Trust, The 178
Town Lands, The 179
Trades House of Glasgow – Commonweal Fund, The 179
Vaux Group Foundation, The 180
Vodafone Group Charitable Trust, The 181
Wales's Charitable Foundation, The Prince of 183
Walker Charitable Trust, The Anthony 184
Walker Charitable Trust, The Ruth 184
Waterhouse Charitable Trust, Mrs 185
Weston Foundation, Garfield 187
Whitlingham Charitable Trust, The 189
Wills 1965 Charitable Trust, The H D H 190
Woodward Charitable Trust, The 192

■ Waterways

Funding priority

Burton Charitable Trust, The Geoffrey 64
Countryside Trust, The 79
Evans Memorial Trust, The Eric 88
Gloucestershire Environmental Trust Company 96
Mersey Basin Trust – Stream Care Project 126
Mersey Basin Trust – Waterside Revival Grants 127
Pelly Charitable Trust, The J B 142
Rausing Trust, The Ruben and Elizabeth 151
Verdon-Smith Family Charitable Settlement, The 181

Will consider

Alchemy Foundation, The 49
Belmont Trust, The 56
Blakey Charitable Trust, The Celia and Conrad 57
Britten-Pears Foundation, The 62
Brotherton Trust, The Charles 63
Fairbairn Charitable Trust, The Esmée 89
Fitzmaurice Charitable Trust, The 91
Fitzwilliam Charitable Trust, The Earl 92
Frognal Trust 93
Grocers' Charity 99
Haddon Charitable Trust, William 100
Hadrian Trust, The 101
Hillards Charitable Trust, Gay & Peter Hartley's 108
Idlewild Trust, The 111
Inland Waterways Association, The 112
Melton Mowbray Building Society Charitable Foundation 125
Moore Charitable Trust, The Horace 130
Prince's Trust - BRO, The 145
Reckitt Charity, Sir James 152
Summerfield Charitable Trust, The 170
Sunley Charitable Foundation, The Bernard 172
Thoresby Charitable Trust 178
Tisbury Telegraph Trust, The 178
Van Norden's Charitable Foundation, Mrs Maud 180

■ Wildlife parks

Funding priority

Carron Charitable Trust, The 70
Carter Charitable Trust, The Leslie Mary 70
Hodgkinson Charitable Trust, The Peter and Gwyneth 108
Sarnia Charitable Trust 161
Shetland Islands Council Charitable Trust, The 164

Will consider

Anne's Charities Trust, The Princess 50
Ashby Will Trust, A J H 51
Barrow Trust, Dr 55
Benham Charitable Settlement 56
Britten-Pears Foundation, The 62
Brotherton Trust, The Charles 63
Cadbury Charitable Trust, William Adlington 66
Cinderford Charitable Trust, The 74
Cromarty Trust, The 80
Gloucestershire Environmental Trust Company 96
Haddon Charitable Trust, William 100
Knott Trust, Sir James 115
Laurence 1976 Charitable Settlement, The Mrs F B 117
Macfarlane Walker Trust 123
Marchig Animal Welfare Trust 124
Paget Trust, The 140
Roberts Charitable Trust, The E E 154
Rufford Foundation 159
Schuster Charitable Trust, The 161
Stephenson (Deceased), Will Trust of Edgar John Henry 170
Tisbury Telegraph Trust, The 178
Weston Foundation, Garfield 187
Wills 1965 Charitable Trust, The H D H 190

■ Wildlife sanctuaries

Funding priority

Briggs Animal Welfare Trust, The 61
Britten-Pears Foundation, The 62
Carron Charitable Trust, The 70
Carter Charitable Trust, The Leslie Mary 70
Evetts & Robert Luff Animal Welfare Trust, Beryl 88
Hodgkinson Charitable Trust, The Peter and Gwyneth 108

Pelly Charitable Trust, The J B *142*
Sainsbury Animal Welfare Trust, Jean *160*
Sarnia Charitable Trust *161*
Shetland Islands Council Charitable Trust, The *164*
Sylvanus Charitable Trust, The *176*
Tho Memorial Foundation, Loke Wan *177*
Wright Deceased Trust, John William *193*

Will consider
Anne's Charities Trust, The Princess *50*
Arnold Foundation, The *50*
Ashby Will Trust, A J H *51*
Barrow Trust, Dr *55*
Benham Charitable Settlement *56*
Boyd Charitable Trust, The Viscountess *58*
Bromley Trust, The *62*
Burton 1960 Charitable Trust, Audrey and Stanley *63*
Cadbury Charitable Trust, William Adlington *66*
Carnegie Dunfermline Trust *69*
Chelsea Square 1994 Trust, The *73*
Cinderford Charitable Trust, The *74*
Cooper Charitable Trust, The *78*
Criffel Charitable Trust *80*
Cromarty Trust, The *80*
Ecological Foundation, The *86*
Gibson Charitable Trust, The Simon *94*
Gloucestershire Environmental Trust Company *96*
Haddon Charitable Trust, William *100*
Laurence 1976 Charitable Settlement, The Mrs F B *117*
Leach Fourteenth Trust, The *118*
Longley Trust *120*
Lyndhurst Settlement *121*
Macfarlane Walker Trust *123*
Marchig Animal Welfare Trust *124*
Melton Mowbray Building Society Charitable Foundation *125*
Paget Trust, The *140*
Philanthropic Trust, The *144*
Portrack Charitable Trust, The *145*
Raptor Trust, The *151*
Roberts Charitable Trust, The E E *154*

Rotary Club of Hadleigh Charitable Trust Fund *157*
Rufford Foundation *159*
Schuster Charitable Trust, The *161*
South Square Trust *167*
Stephenson (Deceased), Will Trust of Edgar John Henry *170*
Tisbury Telegraph Trust, The *178*
Weston Foundation, Garfield *187*
Whitbread First Charitable Trust, H *188*
Wills 1965 Charitable Trust, The H D H *190*
Winstone Foundation, Hyman *191*

....

■ **Woodlands**
Funding priority
Burton Charitable Trust, The Geoffrey *64*
Carron Charitable Trust, The *70*
Countryside Trust, The *79*
Gloucestershire Environmental Trust Company *96*
Haddon Charitable Trust, William *100*
Nikeno Trust, The *136*
Pelly Charitable Trust, The J B *142*
Pike Woodlands Trust, Claude & Margaret *144*
Radley Charitable Trust *148*
Rausing Charitable Foundation, Marit and Hans *151*
Reynall Charitable Trust, Joan K *154*
Scott Charitable Trust, The Frieda *162*
Stenhouse Foundation, The Hugh *170*
Verdon-Smith Family Charitable Settlement, The *181*
Wiltshire Gardens Trust *191*
Woodlands Trust *192*
Yorkshire Agricultural Society *195*

Will consider
Armitage Charitable Trust, G C *50*
BP Conservation Programme *53*
Belmont Trust, The *56*
Brading Town Trust, The *59*
British Sugar Foundation *61*
Britten-Pears Foundation, The *62*
Brotherton Trust, The Charles *63*

Chelsea Square 1994 Trust, The *73*
Chiron Trust, The *74*
Douglas Charitable Trust, R M *84*
Ericson Trust *87*
Fairbairn Charitable Trust, The Esmée *89*
Fitzwilliam Charitable Trust, The Earl *92*
Frognal Trust *93*
Graves Charitable Trust, J G *96*
Greater Bristol Foundation *98*
Grocers' Charity *99*
HCD Memorial Fund *100*
Hadrian Trust, The *101*
Hillards Charitable Trust, Gay & Peter Hartley's *108*
Idlewild Trust, The *111*
Mann Trustees Limited, R W *123*
Melton Mowbray Building Society Charitable Foundation *125*
Mersey Basin Trust – Stream Care Project *126*
Mersey Basin Trust – Waterside Revival Grants *127*
Moore Charitable Trust, The Horace *130*
Prince's Trust - BRO, The *145*
Raptor Trust, The *151*
Rawdon-Smith Trust, The *152*
Reckitt Charity, Sir James *152*
Rotary Club of Hadleigh Charitable Trust Fund *157*
Rufford Foundation *159*
Skells, Bequest of Harry *166*
Summerfield Charitable Trust, The *170*
Sunley Charitable Foundation, The Bernard *172*
Thoresby Charitable Trust *178*
Tisbury Telegraph Trust, The *178*
Wade & Others, The Charity of Thomas *183*
Westcroft Trust *186*
Winstone Foundation, Hyman *191*
Wolfe Charitable Settlement C, Ruth *192*

....

■ **Zoos**
Funding priority
Mickel Fund *128*
Pryor Charity, The Ronald & Kathleen *146*

Zoos

Will consider
Cadbury Charitable Trust, William Adlington *66*
Gloucestershire Environmental Trust Company *96*
Haddon Charitable Trust, William *100*
Paget Trust, The *140*
Stanhope-Palmer Charity *168*
Tisbury Telegraph Trust, The *178*
Weston Foundation, Garfield *187*

Trusts by grant type

List of grant types

Grant Type	Period of Funding
■ Buildings 33	■ One year or less 43
■ Capital other than buildings (computers, vehicles, etc) 34	■ Up to two years 44
■ Core costs (costs of running the organisation as a whole) 35	■ Up to three years 45
■ Endowment 36	■ More than three years 45
■ Feasibility study 36	
■ Interest free loans 36	
■ One-off (no future funding needs) 36	
■ Project only 38	
■ Research 40	
■ Recurring costs 41	
■ Running costs (eg post, telephone, rent, etc) 41	
■ Salaries 42	
■ Start-up costs 43	

Trusts by grant type

■ Buildings

Funding priority

Bridge House Estates Trust Fund, The *59*
Chase Charity, The *73*
Dixon Charitable Trust, C H *83*
Gloucestershire Environmental Trust Company *96*
Leche Trust, The *118*
Personal Assurance Charitable Trust *142*
Pet Plan Charitable Trust *143*
Rochester Bridge Trust, The *155*
Scott Charitable Trust, The Frieda *162*
Skells, Bequest of Harry *166*
Sykes Trust, The Charles *175*
Verdon-Smith Family Charitable Settlement, The *181*
Wright Deceased Trust, John William *193*

Will consider

Adnams Charity, The *49*
Astor Foundation, The *51*
BAA 21st Century Communities Trust, The *52*
Barnby's Foundation, Lord *55*
Batten and Co Charitable Trust *55*
Bingham Trust, The *57*
Body Shop Foundation, The *58*
Brading Town Trust, The *59*
Bromley Trust, The *62*
Brotherton Trust, The Charles *63*
Burton Charitable Trust, The Geoffrey *64*
Cadbury Charitable Trust, Richard *66*
Cadbury Charitable Trust, William Adlington *66*
Carnegie Dunfermline Trust *69*
Carter Charitable Trust, The Leslie Mary *70*
Chelsea Square 1994 Trust, The *73*
Chiron Trust, The *74*
Cinderford Charitable Trust, The *74*
Colyer-Fergusson Charitable Trust, Sir James *77*
Criffel Charitable Trust *80*
Crook Foundation, The Harry *80*
Cwmbran Trust, The *81*
Douglas Charitable Trust, R M *84*
Englefield Charitable Trust, The *86*
Fairbairn Charitable Trust, The Esmée *89*
Fitzwilliam Charitable Trust, The Earl *92*
Frognal Trust *93*
Gibson Charitable Trust, The Simon *94*
Graves Charitable Trust, J G *96*
Greater Bristol Foundation *98*
Green Memorial Fund, The Barry *99*
Grocers' Charity *99*
HCD Memorial Fund *100*
Haddon Charitable Trust, William *100*
Hadrian Trust, The *101*
Hall Charity, Robert *101*
Harryhausen's 1969 Trust, Mrs D L *103*
Harvey's Discretionary Settlement, William Geoffrey *103*
Hayward Foundation, The *104*
Hemby Trust, The *107*
Heritage Lottery Fund *107*
Hill Memorial Trust, L E *108*
Hillards Charitable Trust, Gay & Peter Hartley's *108*
Hogg Charitable Trust, The J G *109*
Hunt Charitable Trust, The Michael and Shirley *110*
Idlewild Trust, The *111*
Jacobson Charitable Trust (No 2), The Ruth & Lionel *112*
Knott Trust, Sir James *115*
Landale Charitable Trust, The *117*
Lawson Charitable Trust, Raymond and Blanche *117*
Leach Fourteenth Trust, The *118*
Lyndhurst Settlement *121*
McCorquodale Charitable Trust, The *122*
Mann Trustees Limited, R W *123*
Marsh and McLennan (Charities Fund) Ltd, J and H *124*
Melton Mowbray Building Society Charitable Foundation *125*
Mickel Fund *128*
Monument Trust, The *129*
Moores Foundation, The Peter *130*
National Lottery Charities Board *132*
New Horizons Trust, The *135*
Nikeno Trust, The *136*
Oakdale Trust, The *137*
Oakley Charitable Trust, The *137*
Owen Family Trust, The *138*
PF Charitable Trust *139*
Persula Foundation, The *142*
Portrack Charitable Trust, The *145*
Prince's Trust - BRO, The *145*
Radley Charitable Trust *148*

Capital

Rank Foundation, The *149*
Rawdon-Smith Trust, The *152*
Robinson Trust No 3, The J C *155*
Rollit Trust, The Vera Kaye *155*
Rotaract Club, Bristol North West *156*
Rotary Club of Arbury Charity Trust Fund *156*
Rotary Club of Ashtead Trust Fund *156*
Sainsbury Animal Welfare Trust, Jean *160*
Schuster Charitable Trust, The *161*
Sheringham and District Preservation Society *164*
Smith (UK) Horticultural Trust, Stanley *167*
South Square Trust *167*
Sunley Charitable Foundation, The Bernard *172*
Sutton Coldfield Municipal Charities, The *173*
Talbot Bridge Will Trust, The Elsie *177*
Tay Charitable Trust, The *177*
Thoresby Charitable Trust *178*
Trades House of Glasgow – Commonweal Fund, The *179*
Vodafone Group Charitable Trust, The *181*
Weston Foundation, Garfield *187*
Woodward Charitable Trust, The *192*
Yorkshire Agricultural Society *195*

■ Capital other than buildings (computers, vehicles, etc)

Funding priority

Bridge House Estates Trust Fund, The *59*
Carnegie Dunfermline Trust *69*
Chase Charity, The *73*
Cobb Charity *76*
Franklin Deceased's New Second Charity, Sydney E *93*
Haswell Memorial Trust, The John *103*
Personal Assurance Charitable Trust *142*
Pet Plan Charitable Trust *143*
Rochester Bridge Trust, The *155*
Scott Charitable Trust, The Frieda *162*
Wade & Others, The Charity of Thomas *183*
Wright Deceased Trust, John William *193*
Yorkshire Agricultural Society *195*

Will consider

Adnams Charity, The *49*
Alchemy Foundation, The *49*
Ashendene Trust, The *51*
Astor Foundation, The *51*
BAA 21st Century Communities Trust, The *52*
Barbour Trust, The *54*
Barnby's Foundation, Lord *55*
Batten and Co Charitable Trust *55*
Bingham Trust, The *57*
Body Shop Foundation, The *58*
Boyd Charitable Trust, The Viscountess *58*
Bromley Trust, The *62*
Brotherton Trust, The Charles *63*
Burton Charitable Trust, The Geoffrey *64*
Cadbury Charitable Trust, Richard *66*
Cadbury Charitable Trust, William Adlington *66*
Carter Charitable Trust, The Leslie Mary *70*
Challice Trust, The *70*
Cinderford Charitable Trust, The *74*
Clutterbuck Charitable Trust, Robert *75*
Colyer-Fergusson Charitable Trust, Sir James *77*
Corden Trust, Cyril *79*
Criffel Charitable Trust *80*
Crook Foundation, The Harry *80*
Cwmbran Trust, The *81*
Derbyshire Community Foundation *83*
Douglas Charitable Trust, R M *84*
Elkes Charity Fund, The Wilfred & Elsie *86*
Englefield Charitable Trust, The *86*
Fairbairn Charitable Trust, The Esmée *89*
Fitzwilliam Charitable Trust, The Earl *92*
Frognal Trust *93*
Gibson Charitable Trust, The Simon *94*
Graves Charitable Trust, J G *96*
Green Memorial Fund, The Barry *99*
Grocers' Charity *99*
Hadrian Trust, The *101*
Hall Charity, Robert *101*
Harebell Centenary Fund, The *102*
Harryhausen's 1969 Trust, Mrs D L *103*
Harvey's Discretionary Settlement, William Geoffrey *103*
Hayward Foundation, The *104*
Headley Trust, The *106*
Hemby Trust, The *107*
Heritage Lottery Fund *107*
Hillards Charitable Trust, Gay & Peter Hartley's *108*
Hodgkinson Charitable Trust, The Peter and Gwyneth *108*
Hogg Charitable Trust, The J G *109*
Idlewild Trust, The *111*
Knott Trust, Sir James *115*
Landale Charitable Trust, The *117*
Lawson Charitable Trust, Raymond and Blanche *117*
Leach Charitable Trust, The Eric and Dorothy *118*
Leach Fourteenth Trust, The *118*
Linder Foundation, The Enid *119*
Lord Mayor of Chester Charitable Trust *121*
Mann Trustees Limited, R W *123*
Marsh and McLennan (Charities Fund) Ltd, J and H *124*
Melton Mowbray Building Society Charitable Foundation *125*
Methodist Relief and Development Fund, The *127*
Mickel Fund *128*
Monument Trust, The *129*
Moores Foundation, The Peter *130*
National Lottery Charities Board *132*
Oakdale Trust, The *137*
Owen Family Trust, The *138*
Paget Trust, The *140*
Peacock Charitable Trust, The *141*
Persula Foundation, The *142*
Portrack Charitable Trust, The *145*
Prince's Trust - BRO, The *145*
Pye's No 1 Charitable Settlement, Mr and Mrs J A *146*
Radley Charitable Trust *148*
Rank Foundation, The *149*
Rawdon-Smith Trust, The *152*
Roberts Charitable Trust, The E E *154*
Robinson Trust No 3, The J C *155*
Rollit Trust, The Vera Kaye *155*

Trusts by grant type **Core costs**

Rotaract Club, Bristol North West 156
Rotary Club of Arbury Charity Trust Fund 156
Rotary Club of Ashtead Trust Fund 156
Rotary Club of Hadleigh Charitable Trust Fund 157
Sainsbury Animal Welfare Trust, Jean 160
Schuster Charitable Trust, The 161
Sheringham and District Preservation Society 164
Shetland Islands Council Charitable Trust, The 164
Smith Foundation, The Leslie 166
Smith Foundation, The Martin 166
Smith (UK) Horticultural Trust, Stanley 167
South East Wales Community Foundation 167
South Square Trust 167
Sunley Charitable Foundation, The Bernard 172
Sutton Coldfield Municipal Charities, The 173
Sykes Trust, The Charles 175
Symons Charitable Trust, The Stella 176
Talbot Bridge Will Trust, The Elsie 177
Thackray General Charitable Trust, The C P 177
Tisbury Telegraph Trust, The 178
Torrs Charitable Trust, The 178
Trades House of Glasgow – Commonweal Fund, The 179
Verdon-Smith Family Charitable Settlement, The 181
Vodafone Group Charitable Trust, The 181
Wales's Charitable Foundation, The Prince of 183
Waterhouse Charitable Trust, Mrs 185
Westcroft Trust 186
Weston Foundation, Garfield 187
Whitbread First Charitable Trust, H 188
Woodward Charitable Trust, The 192

■ **Core costs (costs of running the organisation as a whole)**

Funding priority
Bell Trust, The Henry 55
Calypso Browning Trust 69
Cobb Charity 76
HCD Memorial Fund 100
Hannay Charitable Trust, The Lennox 102
Hogg Charity Trust, E S 109
Personal Assurance Charitable Trust 142
Schuster Charitable Trust, The 161
South Square Trust 167
Tisbury Telegraph Trust, The 178
Wyford Charitable Trust, The 194
Yorkshire Agricultural Society 195

Will consider
Ammco Trust, The 50
Ashendene Trust, The 51
Astor Foundation, The 51
Barbour Trust, The 54
Barnby's Foundation, Lord 55
Batten and Co Charitable Trust 55
Boyd Charitable Trust, The Viscountess 58
Bridge House Estates Trust Fund, The 59
Bromley Trust, The 62
Brotherton Trust, The Charles 63
Burton Charitable Trust, The Geoffrey 64
CHK Charities Limited 65
Cadbury Charitable Trust, William Adlington 66
Carter Charitable Trust, The Leslie Mary 70
Challice Trust, The 70
Chase Charity, The 73
Chiron Trust, The 74
Cinderford Charitable Trust, The 74
Colyer-Fergusson Charitable Trust, Sir James 77
Criffel Charitable Trust 80
Crook Foundation, The Harry 80
Cwmbran Trust, The 81
D'Avigdor Goldsmid Charitable Trust, The Sarah 82
Dearne Valley Community Forum 82
Derbyshire Community Foundation 83
Dunn Charitable Trust, The Harry 84

Elkes Charity Fund, The Wilfred & Elsie 86
Englefield Charitable Trust, The 86
Ericson Trust 87
Fairbairn Charitable Trust, The Esmée 89
Fitzwilliam Charitable Trust, The Earl 92
Franklin Deceased's New Second Charity, Sydney E 93
Gibson Charitable Trust, The Simon 94
Green Memorial Fund, The Barry 99
Grocers' Charity 99
Haddon Charitable Trust, William 100
Hadrian Trust, The 101
Hall Trust, The Christine 102
Harryhausen's 1969 Trust, Mrs D L 103
Harvey's Discretionary Settlement, William Geoffrey 103
Hillards Charitable Trust, Gay & Peter Hartley's 108
Hodgkinson Charitable Trust, The Peter and Gwyneth 108
Hogg Charitable Trust, The J G 109
Homfray Trust, The 109
Johnson Foundation, The 112
Knott Trust, Sir James 115
Landale Charitable Trust, The 117
Laurence 1976 Charitable Settlement, The Mrs F B 117
Lawson Charitable Trust, Raymond and Blanche 117
Leach Charitable Trust, The Eric and Dorothy 118
Leach Fourteenth Trust, The 118
Livesley 1992 Charitable Trust, Mrs C M 120
Lyndhurst Settlement 121
McCorquodale Charitable Trust, The 122
Mann Trustees Limited, R W 123
March's Trust Company Ltd, The Earl of 124
Marsh and McLennan (Charities Fund) Ltd, J and H 124
Melton Mowbray Building Society Charitable Foundation 125
Methodist Relief and Development Fund, The 127
New Horizons Trust, The 135
Oakdale Trust, The 137

35

Endowment

Trusts by grant type

Oakley Charitable Trust, The *137*
PF Charitable Trust *139*
Paget Trust, The *140*
Persula Foundation, The *142*
Pye's No 1 Charitable Settlement, Mr and Mrs J A *146*
Radley Charitable Trust *148*
Rank Foundation, The *149*
Rawdon-Smith Trust, The *152*
Rollit Trust, The Vera Kaye *155*
Rotaract Club, Bristol North West *156*
Rotary Club of Arbury Charity Trust Fund *156*
Rotary Club of Ashtead Trust Fund *156*
Sainsbury Animal Welfare Trust, Jean *160*
Smith Foundation, The Martin *166*
Smith (UK) Horticultural Trust, Stanley *167*
Stanhope-Palmer Charity *168*
Stenhouse Foundation, The Hugh *170*
Sykes Trust, The Charles *175*
Symons Charitable Trust, The Stella *176*
Torrs Charitable Trust, The *178*
Trades House of Glasgow – Commonweal Fund, The *179*
WWF UK (World Wide Fund for Nature) *182*
Wade & Others, The Charity of Thomas *183*
Wales's Charitable Foundation, The Prince of *183*
Weston Foundation, Garfield *187*
Wigan Town Relief in Need Charity *189*
Woodlands Trust *192*
Woodward Charitable Trust, The *192*

■ Endowment

Will consider

Boyd Charitable Trust, The Viscountess *58*
Cinderford Charitable Trust, The *74*
D'Avigdor Goldsmid Charitable Trust, The Sarah *82*
Elkes Charity Fund, The Wilfred & Elsie *86*
Englefield Charitable Trust, The *86*
Fairbairn Charitable Trust, The Esmée *89*

Fitzwilliam Charitable Trust, The Earl *92*
Hadrian Trust, The *101*
Hayward Foundation, The *104*
Hunt Charitable Trust, The Michael and Shirley *110*
Idlewild Trust, The *111*
Persula Foundation, The *142*
Rollit Trust, The Vera Kaye *155*
Westcroft Trust *186*
Weston Foundation, Garfield *187*

■ Feasibility study

Funding priority

Carnegie Dunfermline Trust *69*
Charities Aid Foundation *71*
Gloucestershire Environmental Trust Company *96*
Wiltshire Gardens Trust *191*

Will consider

Boyd Charitable Trust, The Viscountess *58*
Bridge House Estates Trust Fund, The *59*
Chase Charity, The *73*
Cinderford Charitable Trust, The *74*
Cohen Foundation, The John S *76*
Corden Trust, Cyril *79*
Crook Foundation, The Harry *80*
DLM Charitable Trust, The *82*
de Freitas Charitable Trust, The Helen and Geoffrey *82*
Dearne Valley Community Forum *82*
Derbyshire Community Foundation *83*
Ecological Foundation, The *86*
Elkes Charity Fund, The Wilfred & Elsie *86*
Englefield Charitable Trust, The *86*
Fairbairn Charitable Trust, The Esmée *89*
Great Britain Sasakawa Foundation, The *97*
Greater Bristol Foundation *98*
Hayward Foundation, The *104*
Idlewild Trust, The *111*
Inland Waterways Association, The *112*
Lewis Foundation, The John Spedan *119*
Lyndhurst Settlement *121*
Macfarlane Walker Trust *123*
Mann Trustees Limited, R W *123*
March's Trust Company Ltd, The Earl of *124*

Melton Mowbray Building Society Charitable Foundation *125*
Mersey Basin Trust – Waterside Revival Grants *127*
Methodist Relief and Development Fund, The *127*
Persula Foundation, The *142*
Prince's Trust - BRO, The *145*
Rollit Trust, The Vera Kaye *155*
Smith (UK) Horticultural Trust, Stanley *167*
Sykes Trust, The Charles *175*
Symons Charitable Trust, The Stella *176*
Trades House of Glasgow – Commonweal Fund, The *179*
WWF UK (World Wide Fund for Nature) *182*
Yorkshire Agricultural Society *195*

■ Interest free loans

Funding priority

Carnegie Dunfermline Trust *69*

Will consider

Cinderford Charitable Trust, The *74*
Crook Foundation, The Harry *80*
Cwmbran Trust, The *81*
Englefield Charitable Trust, The *86*
Fairbairn Charitable Trust, The Esmée *89*
Inland Waterways Association, The *112*
Laing Charitable Trust, The David *117*
Mann Trustees Limited, R W *123*
March's Trust Company Ltd, The Earl of *124*
Norman Family Charitable Trust, The *136*
Pye's No 1 Charitable Settlement, Mr and Mrs J A *146*
Smith (UK) Horticultural Trust, Stanley *167*
WWF UK (World Wide Fund for Nature) *182*

■ One-off (no future funding needs)

Funding priority

Adnams Charity, The *49*
Arnold Foundation, The *50*
Baker Trust, The C Alma *53*

Trusts by grant type **One-off**

Balney Charitable Trust, The 54
Bell Trust, The Henry 55
Bridge House Estates Trust Fund, The 59
Britten-Pears Foundation, The 62
Carnegie Dunfermline Trust 69
Charities Aid Foundation 71
Clark Charitable Trust, J A 74
Cobb Charity 76
Community Trust for Greater Manchester, The 78
de Freitas Charitable Trust, The Helen and Geoffrey 82
Dixon Charitable Trust, C H 83
Evans Memorial Trust, The Eric 88
Eves Charitable Trust, Douglas Heath 88
Franklin Deceased's New Second Charity, Sydney E 93
Gloucestershire Environmental Trust Company 96
Haddon Charitable Trust, William 100
Haswell Memorial Trust, The John 103
Hemby Trust, The 107
Hillards Charitable Trust, Gay & Peter Hartley's 108
Homfray Trust, The 109
Inland Waterways Association, The 112
Kirkham Foundation, The Graham 113
Knott Trust, Sir James 115
Laing Charitable Trust, The David 117
McMorran Charitable Foundation, The Helen Isabella 123
Melton Mowbray Building Society Charitable Foundation 125
Paget Trust, The 140
Pelly Charitable Trust, The J B 142
Pittecroft Trust, The 145
Pryor Charity, The Ronald & Kathleen 146
Reynall Charitable Trust, Joan K 154
Rotary Club of Hadleigh Charitable Trust Fund 157
Rotary Club of Wallasey, The Charitable Fund of the 157
Schuster Charitable Trust, The 161
Scott Charitable Trust, The Frieda 162
Sykes Trust, The Charles 175
Talbot Bridge Will Trust, The Elsie 177

Tisbury Telegraph Trust, The 178
Trades House of Glasgow – Commonweal Fund, The 179
Van Norden's Charitable Foundation, Mrs Maud 180
Wade & Others, The Charity of Thomas 183
Wales's Charitable Foundation, The Prince of 183
Warrington Animal Welfare 184
Whitbread First Charitable Trust, H 188
Wild Flower Society, The 190
Worshipful Company of Gardeners of London Charity, The 193
Wright Deceased Trust, John William 193
Yeo Trust, The Ash 195
Yorkshire Agricultural Society 195

Will consider

Alchemy Foundation, The 49
Ashby Will Trust, A J H 51
Astor Foundation, The 51
BAA 21st Century Communities Trust, The 52
Barbour Trust, The 54
Barnby's Foundation, Lord 55
Batten and Co Charitable Trust 55
Belsize Charitable Trust No1 56
Benham Charitable Settlement 56
Bentall Charitable Trust, The Gerald 56
Bergne-Coupland Charity 57
Bingham Trust, The 57
Body Shop Foundation, The 58
Boyd Charitable Trust, The Viscountess 58
Brading Town Trust, The 59
Bromley Trust, The 62
Brotherton Trust, The Charles 63
Burton 1960 Charitable Trust, Audrey and Stanley 63
Cadbury Charitable Trust, Richard 66
Cadbury Charitable Trust, William Adlington 66
Cadogan Charity, The 68
Carter Charitable Trust, The Leslie Mary 70
Chase Charity, The 73
Chelsea Square 1994 Trust, The 73
Cinderford Charitable Trust, The 74
Colyer-Fergusson Charitable Trust, Sir James 77
Cooper Charitable Trust, The 78

Corden Trust, Cyril 79
Countryside Trust, The 79
Criffel Charitable Trust 80
Crook Foundation, The Harry 80
Cwmbran Trust, The 81
DLM Charitable Trust, The 82
Dearne Valley Community Forum 82
Derbyshire Community Foundation 83
Douglas Charitable Trust, R M 84
Dunn Charitable Trust, The Harry 84
EBM Charitable Trust 85
Earle Charitable Trust, Audrey 86
Elkes Charity Fund, The Wilfred & Elsie 86
Englefield Charitable Trust, The 86
Ericson Trust 87
Fairbairn Charitable Trust, The Esmée 89
Fitzmaurice Charitable Trust, The 91
Fitzwilliam Charitable Trust, The Earl 92
Foreman 1980 Charitable Trust, The Russell and Mary 92
Gerefa Charitable Trust 94
Gibson Charitable Trust, The Simon 94
Graves Charitable Trust, J G 96
Great Britain Sasakawa Foundation, The 97
Green Memorial Fund, The Barry 99
Grocers' Charity 99
HCD Memorial Fund 100
Hadrian Trust, The 101
Hall Trust, The Christine 102
Harebell Centenary Fund, The 102
Harryhausen's 1969 Trust, Mrs D L 103
Hayward Foundation, The 104
Headley Trust, The 106
Higgs Charitable Trust, The 107
Hodgkinson Charitable Trust, The Peter and Gwyneth 108
Hogg Charitable Trust, The J G 109
Hunt Charitable Trust, The Michael and Shirley 110
INTACH (UK) Trust 111
Idlewild Trust, The 111
Jacobson Charitable Trust (No 2), The Ruth & Lionel 112
Johnson Foundation, The 112
Kennel Club Charitable Trust, The 113

37

One-off

Kleinwort Charitable Trust, The Ernest 114
Landale Charitable Trust, The 117
Laurence 1976 Charitable Settlement, The Mrs F B 117
Lawson Charitable Trust, Raymond and Blanche 117
Leach Charitable Trust, The Eric and Dorothy 118
Leach Fourteenth Trust, The 118
Lewis Foundation, The John Spedan 119
Linder Foundation, The Enid 119
Lions Charity Trust Fund, Carterton 120
Longley Trust 120
Lord Mayor of Chester Charitable Trust 121
Loyd Charitable Trust, The C L 121
Lyndhurst Settlement 121
Macdonald Charitable Trust, The R S 122
Macfarlane Walker Trust 123
Malachi (Family) Charitable Trust 123
Mann Trustees Limited, R W 123
March's Trust Company Ltd, The Earl of 124
Marsh and McLennan (Charities Fund) Ltd, J and H 124
Mersey Basin Trust – Waterside Revival Grants 127
Methodist Relief and Development Fund, The 127
Mickel Fund 128
Monument Trust, The 129
Moores Foundation, The Peter 130
Nabarro Charitable Trust, The Kitty and Daniel 132
National Lottery Charities Board 132
New Horizons Trust, The 135
Norman Family Charitable Trust, The 136
Oldham Foundation 137
PF Charitable Trust 139
Peartree Trust, The 142
Persula Foundation, The 142
Pet Plan Charitable Trust 143
Pewterers' Charity Trust 143
Portrack Charitable Trust, The 145
Prince's Trust - BRO, The 145
Pye's No 1 Charitable Settlement, Mr and Mrs J A 146
Radley Charitable Trust 148
Rank Foundation, The 149

Raptor Trust, The 151
Rawdon-Smith Trust, The 152
Reekie Trust, R A & V B 153
Reuter Foundation, The 153
Robinson Trust No 3, The J C 155
Rochester Bridge Trust, The 155
Rollit Trust, The Vera Kaye 155
Rotaract Club, Bristol North West 156
Rotary Club of Arbury Charity Trust Fund 156
Rotary Club of Ashtead Trust Fund 156
Rotary Club of Eastleigh Trust Fund 156
Rotary Club Samaritan Fund Trust, Folkestone 157
Rotary Club of Thornbury Trust Fund, The 157
Rowan Charitable Trust, The 158
Rufford Foundation 159
Sainsbury Animal Welfare Trust, Jean 160
Salisbury Pool Charity, The 161
Shark Trust, The 163
Shears Charitable Trust, The 163
Shetland Islands Council Charitable Trust, The 164
Skells, Bequest of Harry 166
Smith Foundation, The Leslie 166
Smith Foundation, The Martin 166
Smith (UK) Horticultural Trust, Stanley 167
South East Wales Community Foundation 167
Spooner Charitable Trust, W W 168
Stanhope-Palmer Charity 168
Staples Trust 168
Stenhouse Foundation, The Hugh 170
Summerfield Charitable Trust, The 170
Sunley Charitable Foundation, The Bernard 172
Sutton Coldfield Municipal Charities, The 173
Sylvanus Charitable Trust, The 176
Symons Charitable Trust, The Stella 176
Tay Charitable Trust, The 177
Thoresby Charitable Trust 178
Torrs Charitable Trust, The 178
Vodafone Group Charitable Trust, The 181
WWF UK (World Wide Fund for Nature) 182

Westcroft Trust 186
Weston Foundation, Garfield 187
Wigan Town Relief in Need Charity 189
Winstone Foundation, Hyman 191
Wolfe Charitable Settlement C, Ruth 192
Woodlands Trust 192
Woodward Charitable Trust, The 192
Wyre Animal Welfare 194
Zaiger Trust, The Elizabeth and Prince 196

■ **Project only**

Funding priority
BP Conservation Programme 53
Bell Trust, The Henry 55
Bridge House Estates Trust Fund, The 59
Britten-Pears Foundation, The 62
Carnegie Dunfermline Trust 69
Carron Charitable Trust, The 70
Cleopatra Trust 75
Cobb Charity 76
Countryside Trust, The 79
de Freitas Charitable Trust, The Helen and Geoffrey 82
Dorus Trust 84
Epigoni Trust 87
Franklin Deceased's New Second Charity, Sydney E 93
Gloucestershire Environmental Trust Company 96
Greater Bristol Foundation 98
Hall Trust, The Christine 102
Heritage Lottery Fund 107
Hillards Charitable Trust, Gay & Peter Hartley's 108
Inland Waterways Association, The 112
Linder Foundation, The Enid 119
Mersey Basin Trust – ICI Green Action Grants 126
Mersey Basin Trust – Stream Care Project 126
Mersey Basin Trust – Waterside Revival Grants 127
Nikeno Trust, The 136
Pelly Charitable Trust, The J B 142
Personal Assurance Charitable Trust 142
Pet Plan Charitable Trust 143
Philanthropic Trust, The 144
Rausing Charitable Foundation, Marit and Hans 151

Trusts by grant type **Project only**

Reynall Charitable Trust, Joan K 154
Schuster Charitable Trust, The 161
Scott Charitable Trust, The Frieda 162
Shepherd Conservation Foundation, The David 163
South Square Trust 167
Tho Memorial Foundation, Loke Wan 177
Wiltshire Gardens Trust 191
Worshipful Company of Gardeners of London Charity, The 193
Wright Deceased Trust, John William 193
Yorkshire Agricultural Society 195

Will consider
Adnams Charity, The 49
Ashendene Trust, The 51
Astor Foundation, The 51
BAA 21st Century Communities Trust, The 52
Barbour Trust, The 54
Barnby's Foundation, Lord 55
Batten and Co Charitable Trust 55
Belsize Charitable Trust No1 56
Bingham Trust, The 57
Body Shop Foundation, The 58
Brading Town Trust, The 59
British Sugar Foundation 61
Bromley Trust, The 62
Brotherton Trust, The Charles 63
Burton 1960 Charitable Trust, Audrey and Stanley 63
Burton Charitable Trust, The Geoffrey 64
Cadbury Charitable Trust, William Adlington 66
Carter Charitable Trust, The Leslie Mary 70
Chase Charity, The 73
Chelsea Square 1994 Trust, The 73
Chestnut Trust, The 73
Cinderford Charitable Trust, The 74
Cohen Foundation, The John S 76
Colyer-Fergusson Charitable Trust, Sir James 77
Corden Trust, Cyril 79
Criffel Charitable Trust 80
Crook Foundation, The Harry 80
D'Avigdor Goldsmid Charitable Trust, The Sarah 82
Dearne Valley Community Forum 82
Ecological Foundation, The 86

Elkes Charity Fund, The Wilfred & Elsie 86
Englefield Charitable Trust, The 86
Ericson Trust 87
Fairbairn Charitable Trust, The Esmée 89
Fitzwilliam Charitable Trust, The Earl 92
Gerefa Charitable Trust 94
Gibson Charitable Trust, The Simon 94
Graves Charitable Trust, J G 96
Great Britain Sasakawa Foundation, The 97
Green Memorial Fund, The Barry 99
Grocers' Charity 99
Haddon Charitable Trust, William 100
Hadrian Trust, The 101
Headley Trust, The 106
Hodgkinson Charitable Trust, The Peter and Gwyneth 108
Hogg Charitable Trust, The J G 109
Idlewild Trust, The 111
Isle of Wight Gardens Trust 112
Jacobson Charitable Trust (No 2), The Ruth & Lionel 112
Johnson Foundation, The 112
Kleinwort Charitable Trust, The Ernest 114
Knott Trust, Sir James 115
Laing Charitable Trust, The David 117
Landale Charitable Trust, The 117
Laurence 1976 Charitable Settlement, The Mrs F B 117
Lawson Charitable Trust, Raymond and Blanche 117
Leach Charitable Trust, The Eric and Dorothy 118
Leach Fourteenth Trust, The 118
Lewis Foundation, The John Spedan 119
Lyndhurst Settlement 121
McCorquodale Charitable Trust, The 122
Macdonald Charitable Trust, The R S 122
Macfarlane Walker Trust 123
Mann Trustees Limited, R W 123
March's Trust Company Ltd, The Earl of 124
Marsh and McLennan (Charities Fund) Ltd, J and H 124
Melton Mowbray Building Society Charitable Foundation 125

Methodist Relief and Development Fund, The 127
Mickel Fund 128
Monument Trust, The 129
Nabarro Charitable Trust, The Kitty and Daniel 132
National Lottery Charities Board 132
New Horizons Trust, The 135
Norman Family Charitable Trust, The 136
Oakdale Trust, The 137
PF Charitable Trust 139
Paget Trust, The 140
Peacock Charitable Trust, The 141
Persula Foundation, The 142
Pilkington Charitable Trust, The Cecil 144
Prince's Trust - BRO, The 145
Pye's No 1 Charitable Settlement, Mr and Mrs J A 146
Radley Charitable Trust 148
Raptor Trust, The 151
Rausing Trust, The Ruben and Elizabeth 151
Reckitt Charity, Sir James 152
Reuter Foundation, The 153
Robinson Trust No 3, The J C 155
Rollit Trust, The Vera Kaye 155
Rotaract Club, Bristol North West 156
Rotary Club of Arbury Charity Trust Fund 156
Rotary Club of Ashtead Trust Fund 156
Rotary Club of Eastleigh Trust Fund 156
Rufford Foundation 159
Sainsbury Animal Welfare Trust, Jean 160
Sedgwick Trust, The 162
Shah Trust, The Dr N K 163
Shark Trust, The 163
Sheringham and District Preservation Society 164
Shetland Islands Council Charitable Trust, The 164
Smith Foundation, The Martin 166
Smith (UK) Horticultural Trust, Stanley 167
Summerfield Charitable Trust, The 170
Sunley Charitable Foundation, The Bernard 172
Sutton Coldfield Municipal Charities, The 173
Sykes Trust, The Charles 175
Symons Charitable Trust, The Stella 176
Thackray General Charitable Trust, The C P 177

Research

Thoresby Charitable Trust 178
Trades House of Glasgow – Commonweal Fund, The 179
Vodafone Group Charitable Trust, The 181
WWF UK (World Wide Fund for Nature) 182
Wensum Residents Association 186
Weston Foundation, Garfield 187
Whitbread First Charitable Trust, H 188
Winstone Foundation, Hyman 191
Wolfe Charitable Settlement C, Ruth 192
Woodlands Trust 192
Woodward Charitable Trust, The 192

■ Research

Funding priority

BP Conservation Programme 53
Carron Charitable Trust, The 70
Cobb Charity 76
Gloucestershire Environmental Trust Company 96
Linder Foundation, The Enid 119
Nikeno Trust, The 136
Pelly Charitable Trust, The J B 142
Personal Assurance Charitable Trust 142
Pet Plan Charitable Trust 143
Pryor Charity, The Ronald & Kathleen 146
RAC Foundation for Motoring and the Environment Ltd, The 148
Rausing Charitable Foundation, Marit and Hans 151
South Square Trust 167
Sykes Trust, The Charles 175
Tho Memorial Foundation, Loke Wan 177
Tisbury Telegraph Trust, The 178
Van Norden's Charitable Foundation, Mrs Maud 180
Whitbread First Charitable Trust, H 188
Yorkshire Agricultural Society 195

Will consider

Adnams Charity, The 49
Astor Foundation, The 51
Barbour Trust, The 54
Barnby's Foundation, Lord 55

Batten and Co Charitable Trust 55
Body Shop Foundation, The 58
Britten-Pears Foundation, The 62
Bromley Trust, The 62
Brotherton Trust, The Charles 63
Burton Charitable Trust, The Geoffrey 64
Cadbury Charitable Trust, William Adlington 66
Carter Charitable Trust, The Leslie Mary 70
Chelsea Square 1994 Trust, The 73
Cinderford Charitable Trust, The 74
Cohen Foundation, The John S 76
Colyer-Fergusson Charitable Trust, Sir James 77
Criffel Charitable Trust 80
DLM Charitable Trust, The 82
D'Avigdor Goldsmid Charitable Trust, The Sarah 82
Dearne Valley Community Forum 82
Derbyshire Community Foundation 83
Douglas Charitable Trust, R M 84
Ecological Foundation, The 86
Elkes Charity Fund, The Wilfred & Elsie 86
Englefield Charitable Trust, The 86
Ericson Trust 87
Fairbairn Charitable Trust, The Esmée 89
Fitzwilliam Charitable Trust, The Earl 92
Frognal Trust 93
Gibson Charitable Trust, The Simon 94
Great Britain Sasakawa Foundation, The 97
Haddon Charitable Trust, William 100
Harebell Centenary Fund, The 102
Hayward Foundation, The 104
Higgs Charitable Trust, The 107
Hill Memorial Trust, L E 108
Hillards Charitable Trust, Gay & Peter Hartley's 108
Hogg Charitable Trust, The J G 109
INTACH (UK) Trust 111
Idlewild Trust, The 111
Inland Waterways Association, The 112
Jacobson Charitable Trust (No 2), The Ruth & Lionel 112
Johnson Foundation, The 112

Landale Charitable Trust, The 117
Lawson Charitable Trust, Raymond and Blanche 117
Leach Charitable Trust, The Eric and Dorothy 118
Leach Fourteenth Trust, The 118
Lewis Foundation, The John Spedan 119
Lyndhurst Settlement 121
McCorquodale Charitable Trust, The 122
Macdonald Charitable Trust, The R S 122
Macfarlane Walker Trust 123
Marsh and McLennan (Charities Fund) Ltd, J and H 124
Melton Mowbray Building Society Charitable Foundation 125
Methodist Relief and Development Fund, The 127
Mickel Fund 128
National Lottery Charities Board 132
Norman Family Charitable Trust, The 136
Oakdale Trust, The 137
PF Charitable Trust 139
Paget Trust, The 140
Persula Foundation, The 142
Portrack Charitable Trust, The 145
Prince's Trust - BRO, The 145
Pye's No 1 Charitable Settlement, Mr and Mrs J A 146
Radley Charitable Trust 148
Rank Foundation, The 149
Rausing Trust, The Ruben and Elizabeth 151
Reuter Foundation, The 153
Roberts Charitable Trust, The E E 154
Rollit Trust, The Vera Kaye 155
St John's Wood Trust, The 161
Schuster Charitable Trust, The 161
Shark Trust, The 163
Smith Foundation, The Leslie 166
Smith Foundation, The Martin 166
Smith (UK) Horticultural Trust, Stanley 167
Stanhope-Palmer Charity 168
Sunley Charitable Foundation, The Bernard 172
Symons Charitable Trust, The Stella 176
Talbot Bridge Will Trust, The Elsie 177
Thoresby Charitable Trust 178

Trusts by grant type **Running costs**

Trades House of Glasgow –
   Commonweal Fund, The
   179
Vodafone Group Charitable
   Trust, The *181*
Westcroft Trust *186*
Weston Foundation, Garfield
   187
Woodlands Trust *192*
Woodward Charitable Trust, The
   192

■ **Recurring costs**

Funding priority
Bell Trust, The Henry *55*
Bridge House Estates Trust
   Fund, The *59*
Calypso Browning Trust *69*
Carron Charitable Trust, The
   70
Cobb Charity *76*
Nikeno Trust, The *136*
Personal Assurance Charitable
   Trust *142*

Will consider
Ashby Will Trust, A J H *51*
BAA 21st Century Communities
   Trust, The *52*
Barbour Trust, The *54*
Benham Charitable Settlement
   56
Bentall Charitable Trust, The
   Gerald *56*
Bergne-Coupland Charity *57*
Bromley Trust, The *62*
Brotherton Trust, The Charles
   63
Burton Charitable Trust, The
   Geoffrey *64*
CHK Charities Limited *65*
Carter Charitable Trust, The
   Leslie Mary *70*
Chestnut Trust, The *73*
Cinderford Charitable Trust, The
   74
Clarke's Charitable Trust, The
   Late Miss Doris Evelyn *74*
Colyer-Fergusson Charitable
   Trust, Sir James *77*
Criffel Charitable Trust *80*
Crook Foundation, The Harry
   80
DLM Charitable Trust, The *82*
Dearne Valley Community
   Forum *82*
Douglas Charitable Trust, R M
   84
EBM Charitable Trust *85*
Earle Charitable Trust, Audrey
   86
Elkes Charity Fund, The Wilfred
   & Elsie *86*
Englefield Charitable Trust, The
   86

Eskdale (Cumbria) Trust, The
   88
Fairbairn Charitable Trust, The
   Esmée *89*
Gibson Charitable Trust, The
   Simon *94*
Glastonbury Conservation
   Society, The *95*
Graves Charitable Trust, J G
   96
Green Memorial Fund, The Barry
   99
Grocers' Charity *99*
Haddon Charitable Trust,
   William *100*
Hall Charity, Robert *101*
Hall Trust, The Christine *102*
Harebell Centenary Fund, The
   102
Harryhausen's 1969 Trust, Mrs
   D L *103*
Harvey's Discretionary
   Settlement, William Geoffrey
   103
Hillards Charitable Trust, Gay &
   Peter Hartley's *108*
Hodgkinson Charitable Trust,
   The Peter and Gwyneth *108*
Hogg Charitable Trust, The J G
   109
INTACH (UK) Trust *111*
Johnson Foundation, The *112*
Kennel Club Charitable Trust,
   The *113*
Knott Trust, Sir James *115*
Laing Charitable Trust, The
   David *117*
Landale Charitable Trust, The
   117
Lawson Charitable Trust,
   Raymond and Blanche *117*
Leach Charitable Trust, The Eric
   and Dorothy *118*
Leach Fourteenth Trust, The
   118
Loraine Trust *120*
Loyd Charitable Trust, The C L
   121
Lyndhurst Settlement *121*
Macdonald Charitable Trust,
   The R S *122*
Melton Mowbray Building
   Society Charitable
   Foundation *125*
Methodist Relief and
   Development Fund, The
   127
Mickel Fund *128*
Moores Foundation, The Peter
   130
Owen Family Trust, The *138*
PF Charitable Trust *139*
Paget Trust, The *140*
Peacock Charitable Trust, The
   141
Peartree Trust, The *142*

Persula Foundation, The *142*
Pet Plan Charitable Trust *143*
Portrack Charitable Trust, The
   145
Pye's No 1 Charitable
   Settlement, Mr and Mrs J A
   146
Radley Charitable Trust *148*
Rank Foundation, The *149*
Reckitt Charity, Sir James *152*
Reekie Trust, R A & V B *153*
Reuter Foundation, The *153*
Robinson Trust No 3, The J C
   155
Rollit Trust, The Vera Kaye *155*
Rotary Club Samaritan Fund
   Trust, Folkestone *157*
Rowan Charitable Trust, The
   158
Sainsbury Animal Welfare Trust,
   Jean *160*
Salisbury Pool Charity, The
   161
Schweitzer's Hospital Fund, Dr
   162
Sedgwick Trust, The *162*
Shark Trust, The *163*
Shetland Islands Council
   Charitable Trust, The *164*
Smith Foundation, The Leslie
   166
Spooner Charitable Trust, W W
   168
Staples Trust *168*
Stenhouse Foundation, The
   Hugh *170*
Sykes Trust, The Charles *175*
Sylvanus Charitable Trust, The
   176
Symons Charitable Trust, The
   Stella *176*
Wade & Others, The Charity of
   Thomas *183*
Wensum Residents Association
   186
Westcroft Trust *186*
Whitbread First Charitable
   Trust, H *188*
Wigan Town Relief in Need
   Charity *189*
Woodlands Trust *192*
Woodward Charitable Trust, The
   192
Zaiger Trust, The Elizabeth and
   Prince *196*

■ **Running costs (eg post, telephone, rent, etc)**

Funding priority
Bell Trust, The Henry *55*
Bridge House Estates Trust
   Fund, The *59*
Calypso Browning Trust *69*

41

Running costs *Trusts by grant type*

Cobb Charity 76
Haswell Memorial Trust, The John 103
Scott Charitable Trust, The Frieda 162

Will consider
Adnams Charity, The 49
Barbour Trust, The 54
Batten and Co Charitable Trust 55
Bingham Trust, The 57
Bromley Trust, The 62
Brotherton Trust, The Charles 63
Cadbury Charitable Trust, William Adlington 66
Carter Charitable Trust, The Leslie Mary 70
Chiron Trust, The 74
Cinderford Charitable Trust, The 74
Colyer-Fergusson Charitable Trust, Sir James 77
Criffel Charitable Trust 80
Cwmbran Trust, The 81
DLM Charitable Trust, The 82
Dearne Valley Community Forum 82
Derbyshire Community Foundation 83
Elkes Charity Fund, The Wilfred & Elsie 86
Englefield Charitable Trust, The 86
Ericson Trust 87
Fairbairn Charitable Trust, The Esmée 89
Gibson Charitable Trust, The Simon 94
Graves Charitable Trust, J G 96
Greater Bristol Foundation 98
Green Memorial Fund, The Barry 99
Grocers' Charity 99
Hadrian Trust, The 101
Hall Trust, The Christine 102
Harryhausen's 1969 Trust, Mrs D L 103
Harvey's Discretionary Settlement, William Geoffrey 103
Heritage Lottery Fund 107
Hillards Charitable Trust, Gay & Peter Hartley's 108
Hodgkinson Charitable Trust, The Peter and Gwyneth 108
Hogg Charitable Trust, The J G 109
Knott Trust, Sir James 115
Lawson Charitable Trust, Raymond and Blanche 117
Leach Fourteenth Trust, The 118
Linder Foundation, The Enid 119

Lyndhurst Settlement 121
Macfarlane Walker Trust 123
March's Trust Company Ltd, The Earl of 124
Marsh and McLennan (Charities Fund) Ltd, J and H 124
Melton Mowbray Building Society Charitable Foundation 125
Methodist Relief and Development Fund, The 127
Moores Foundation, The Peter 130
National Lottery Charities Board 132
New Horizons Trust, The 135
Oakdale Trust, The 137
PF Charitable Trust 139
Paget Trust, The 140
Personal Assurance Charitable Trust 142
Persula Foundation, The 142
Pye's No 1 Charitable Settlement, Mr and Mrs J A 146
Radley Charitable Trust 148
Reckitt Charity, Sir James 152
Robinson Trust No 3, The J C 155
Rollit Trust, The Vera Kaye 155
Rotaract Club, Bristol North West 156
Rotary Club of Ashtead Trust Fund 156
Sainsbury Animal Welfare Trust, Jean 160
Shetland Islands Council Charitable Trust, The 164
Sykes Trust, The Charles 175
Symons Charitable Trust, The Stella 176
Trades House of Glasgow – Commonweal Fund, The 179
WWF UK (World Wide Fund for Nature) 182
Wade & Others, The Charity of Thomas 183
Westcroft Trust 186
Weston Foundation, Garfield 187
Woodlands Trust 192
Wyre Animal Welfare 194

■ **Salaries**

Funding priority
Bridge House Estates Trust Fund, The 59
Carron Charitable Trust, The 70
Cobb Charity 76
Nikeno Trust, The 136

Will consider
Alchemy Foundation, The 49
Barbour Trust, The 54
Batten and Co Charitable Trust 55
Bingham Trust, The 57
Bromley Trust, The 62
Brotherton Trust, The Charles 63
Chase Charity, The 73
Cinderford Charitable Trust, The 74
Colyer-Fergusson Charitable Trust, Sir James 77
Dearne Valley Community Forum 82
Derbyshire Community Foundation 83
Elkes Charity Fund, The Wilfred & Elsie 86
Englefield Charitable Trust, The 86
Fairbairn Charitable Trust, The Esmée 89
Gibson Charitable Trust, The Simon 94
Grocers' Charity 99
HCD Memorial Fund 100
Hadrian Trust, The 101
Harryhausen's 1969 Trust, Mrs D L 103
Heritage Lottery Fund 107
Hillards Charitable Trust, Gay & Peter Hartley's 108
Hogg Charitable Trust, The J G 109
Knott Trust, Sir James 115
Leach Fourteenth Trust, The 118
Lyndhurst Settlement 121
March's Trust Company Ltd, The Earl of 124
Marsh and McLennan (Charities Fund) Ltd, J and H 124
Methodist Relief and Development Fund, The 127
National Lottery Charities Board 132
Oakdale Trust, The 137
Paget Trust, The 140
Personal Assurance Charitable Trust 142
Persula Foundation, The 142
Pet Plan Charitable Trust 143
Rank Foundation, The 149
Robinson Trust No 3, The J C 155
Rollit Trust, The Vera Kaye 155
Rotary Club of Ashtead Trust Fund 156
Symons Charitable Trust, The Stella 176
Trades House of Glasgow – Commonweal Fund, The 179

Trusts by grant type

WWF UK (World Wide Fund for Nature) *182*
Woodlands Trust *192*
Woodward Charitable Trust, The *192*

■ **Start-up costs**

Funding priority
Carnegie Dunfermline Trust *69*
Cobb Charity *76*
Countryside Trust, The *79*
Gloucestershire Environmental Trust Company *96*
Greater Bristol Foundation *98*
Haswell Memorial Trust, The John *103*
Hillards Charitable Trust, Gay & Peter Hartley's *108*
Knott Trust, Sir James *115*
Pelly Charitable Trust, The J B *142*
Scott Charitable Trust, The Frieda *162*
Wiltshire Gardens Trust *191*
Yorkshire Agricultural Society *195*

Will consider
Adnams Charity, The *49*
Astor Foundation, The *51*
BAA 21st Century Communities Trust, The *52*
Balney Charitable Trust, The *54*
Barbour Trust, The *54*
Batten and Co Charitable Trust *55*
Bingham Trust, The *57*
Bromley Trust, The *62*
CHK Charities Limited *65*
Cadbury Charitable Trust, William Adlington *66*
Chase Charity, The *73*
Chiron Trust, The *74*
Cinderford Charitable Trust, The *74*
Clark Charitable Trust, J A *74*
Colyer-Fergusson Charitable Trust, Sir James *77*
Cwmbran Trust, The *81*
DLM Charitable Trust, The *82*
de Freitas Charitable Trust, The Helen and Geoffrey *82*
Dearne Valley Community Forum *82*
Derbyshire Community Foundation *83*
Elkes Charity Fund, The Wilfred & Elsie *86*
Englefield Charitable Trust, The *86*
Ericson Trust *87*
Fairbairn Charitable Trust, The Esmée *89*

Fitzwilliam Charitable Trust, The Earl *92*
Gibson Charitable Trust, The Simon *94*
Graves Charitable Trust, J G *96*
Great Britain Sasakawa Foundation, The *97*
Green Memorial Fund, The Barry *99*
HCD Memorial Fund *100*
Hadrian Trust, The *101*
Hall Charity, Robert *101*
Harryhausen's 1969 Trust, Mrs D L *103*
Hayward Foundation, The *104*
Hemby Trust, The *107*
Heritage Lottery Fund *107*
Hogg Charitable Trust, The J G *109*
Hunt Charitable Trust, The Michael and Shirley *110*
Idlewild Trust, The *111*
Laing Charitable Trust, The David *117*
Laurence 1976 Charitable Settlement, The Mrs F B *117*
Lawson Charitable Trust, Raymond and Blanche *117*
Lyndhurst Settlement *121*
Macfarlane Walker Trust *123*
March's Trust Company Ltd, The Earl of *124*
Melton Mowbray Building Society Charitable Foundation *125*
National Lottery Charities Board *132*
New Horizons Trust, The *135*
Norman Family Charitable Trust, The *136*
Onaway Trust, The *138*
Paget Trust, The *140*
Personal Assurance Charitable Trust *142*
Persula Foundation, The *142*
Prince's Trust - BRO, The *145*
Pye's No 1 Charitable Settlement, Mr and Mrs J A *146*
Radley Charitable Trust *148*
Reuter Foundation, The *153*
Robinson Trust No 3, The J C *155*
Rollit Trust, The Vera Kaye *155*
Rotaract Club, Bristol North West *156*
Rotary Club of Arbury Charity Trust Fund *156*
Rotary Club of Ashtead Trust Fund *156*
Rotary Club Samaritan Fund Trust, Folkestone *157*
Rotary Club of Thornbury Trust Fund, The *157*

One year or less

Smith (UK) Horticultural Trust, Stanley *167*
South East Wales Community Foundation *167*
Summerfield Charitable Trust, The *170*
Sykes Trust, The Charles *175*
Symons Charitable Trust, The Stella *176*
Tay Charitable Trust, The *177*
Thoresby Charitable Trust *178*
Trades House of Glasgow – Commonweal Fund, The *179*
WWF UK (World Wide Fund for Nature) *182*
Wade & Others, The Charity of Thomas *183*
Westcroft Trust *186*
Weston Foundation, Garfield *187*
Woodlands Trust *192*

■ **One year or less**

Funding priority
Adnams Charity, The *49*
Astor Foundation, The *51*
BP Conservation Programme *53*
Balney Charitable Trust, The *54*
Britten-Pears Foundation, The *62*
Burton 1960 Charitable Trust, Audrey and Stanley *63*
Burton Charitable Trust, The Geoffrey *64*
Carnegie Dunfermline Trust *69*
Charities Aid Foundation *71*
Cleopatra Trust *75*
Countryside Trust, The *79*
de Freitas Charitable Trust, The Helen and Geoffrey *82*
Dixon Charitable Trust, C H *83*
Dorus Trust *84*
Englefield Charitable Trust, The *86*
Epigoni Trust *87*
Ericson Trust *87*
Fitzwilliam Charitable Trust, The Earl *92*
Greater Bristol Foundation *98*
Grocers' Charity *99*
Hadrian Trust, The *101*
Hall Trust, The Christine *102*
Hannay Charitable Trust, The Lennox *102*
Harvey's Discretionary Settlement, William Geoffrey *103*
Haswell Memorial Trust, The John *103*
Hemby Trust, The *107*

43

One year or less

Trusts by grant type

Hillards Charitable Trust, Gay & Peter Hartley's 108
Hogg Charity Trust, E S 109
Hunt Charitable Trust, The Michael and Shirley 110
Inland Waterways Association, The 112
Knott Trust, Sir James 115
Leach Charitable Trust, The Eric and Dorothy 118
Leach Fourteenth Trust, The 118
Linder Foundation, The Enid 119
Longley Trust 120
Lyndhurst Settlement 121
Mersey Basin Trust – ICI Green Action Grants 126
Mersey Basin Trust – Stream Care Project 126
Mersey Basin Trust – Waterside Revival Grants 127
Paget Trust, The 140
Personal Assurance Charitable Trust 142
Pet Plan Charitable Trust 143
Philanthropic Trust, The 144
Raptor Trust, The 151
Rawdon-Smith Trust, The 152
Robinson Trust No 3, The J C 155
Rochester Bridge Trust, The 155
Rotary Club of Hadleigh Charitable Trust Fund 157
Rufford Foundation 159
Schuster Charitable Trust, The 161
Sutton Coldfield Municipal Charities, The 173
Sykes Trust, The Charles 175
Talbot Bridge Will Trust, The Elsie 177
Tho Memorial Foundation, Loke Wan 177
Thoresby Charitable Trust 178
Tisbury Telegraph Trust, The 178
Torrs Charitable Trust, The 178
Trades House of Glasgow – Commonweal Fund, The 179
Van Norden's Charitable Foundation, Mrs Maud 180
Verdon-Smith Family Charitable Settlement, The 181
Warrington Animal Welfare 184
Wiltshire Gardens Trust 191
Worshipful Company of Gardeners of London Charity, The 193
Wright Deceased Trust, John William 193

Wyford Charitable Trust, The 194
Yeo Trust, The Ash 195

Will consider
Ammco Trust, The 50
Barbour Trust, The 54
Batten and Co Charitable Trust 55
Bentall Charitable Trust, The Gerald 56
Brading Town Trust, The 59
Cadbury Charitable Trust, Richard 66
Cadbury Charitable Trust, William Adlington 66
Carron Charitable Trust, The 70
Chelsea Square 1994 Trust, The 73
Cohen Foundation, The John S 76
Corden Trust, Cyril 79
Crook Foundation, The Harry 80
Cwmbran Trust, The 81
Derbyshire Community Foundation 83
Dunn Charitable Trust, The Harry 84
Elkes Charity Fund, The Wilfred & Elsie 86
Fairbairn Charitable Trust, The Esmée 89
Frognal Trust 93
Gerefa Charitable Trust 94
Green Memorial Fund, The Barry 99
Harebell Centenary Fund, The 102
Harryhausen's 1969 Trust, Mrs D L 103
Hill Memorial Trust, L E 108
Hogg Charitable Trust, The J G 109
Isle of Wight Gardens Trust 112
Jacobson Charitable Trust (No 2), The Ruth & Lionel 112
Laurence 1976 Charitable Settlement, The Mrs F B 117
Lions Charity Trust Fund, Carterton 120
Malachi (Family) Charitable Trust 123
Mann Trustees Limited, R W 123
Marsh and McLennan (Charities Fund) Ltd, J and H 124
Melton Mowbray Building Society Charitable Foundation 125
National Lottery Charities Board 132
Norman Family Charitable Trust, The 136

Oakley Charitable Trust, The 137
Pewterers' Charity Trust 143
Radley Charitable Trust 148
Reynall Charitable Trust, Joan K 154
Rollit Trust, The Vera Kaye 155
Rotaract Club, Bristol North West 156
Rotary Club of Arbury Charity Trust Fund 156
Rotary Club of Ashtead Trust Fund 156
Sainsbury Animal Welfare Trust, Jean 160
Salisbury Pool Charity, The 161
Smith Foundation, The Leslie 166
South Square Trust 167
Symons Charitable Trust, The Stella 176
Weston Foundation, Garfield 187
Wolfe Charitable Settlement C, Ruth 192

■ Up to two years

Funding priority
Burton 1960 Charitable Trust, Audrey and Stanley 63
Franklin Deceased's New Second Charity, Sydney E 93
Gloucestershire Environmental Trust Company 96
Pet Plan Charitable Trust 143
Skells, Bequest of Harry 166

Will consider
Astor Foundation, The 51
Barnby's Foundation, Lord 55
Cadogan Charity, The 68
Carron Charitable Trust, The 70
Colyer-Fergusson Charitable Trust, Sir James 77
Ecological Foundation, The 86
Englefield Charitable Trust, The 86
Ericson Trust 87
Fairbairn Charitable Trust, The Esmée 89
Fitzwilliam Charitable Trust, The Earl 92
Frognal Trust 93
Green Memorial Fund, The Barry 99
Hadrian Trust, The 101
Harryhausen's 1969 Trust, Mrs D L 103
Hogg Charitable Trust, The J G 109
Hunt Charitable Trust, The Michael and Shirley 110

Trusts by grant type

Inland Waterways Association, The *112*
Johnson Foundation, The *112*
Knott Trust, Sir James *115*
Melton Mowbray Building Society Charitable Foundation *125*
National Lottery Charities Board *132*
New Horizons Trust, The *135*
Oakdale Trust, The *137*
Paget Trust, The *140*
Personal Assurance Charitable Trust *142*
Philanthropic Trust, The *144*
Raptor Trust, The *151*
Robinson Trust No 3, The J C *155*
Rollit Trust, The Vera Kaye *155*
Rotary Club of Arbury Charity Trust Fund *156*
Rotary Club Samaritan Fund Trust, Folkestone *157*
Sainsbury Animal Welfare Trust, Jean *160*
Schuster Charitable Trust, The *161*
Sutton Coldfield Municipal Charities, The *173*
Tisbury Telegraph Trust, The *178*
Torrs Charitable Trust, The *178*
Whitbread First Charitable Trust, H *188*

■ **Up to three years**

Funding priority

Bridge House Estates Trust Fund, The *59*
Cobb Charity *76*
Pelly Charitable Trust, The J B *142*
Pet Plan Charitable Trust *143*
Sainsbury Animal Welfare Trust, Jean *160*
Scott Charitable Trust, The Frieda *162*
Yorkshire Agricultural Society *195*

Will consider

Armitage Charitable Trust, G C *50*
Arnold Foundation, The *50*
Ashendene Trust, The *51*
Astor Foundation, The *51*
BAA 21st Century Communities Trust, The *52*
Bingham Trust, The *57*
Body Shop Foundation, The *58*
Boyd Charitable Trust, The Viscountess *58*
Britten-Pears Foundation, The *62*

Brotherton Trust, The Charles *63*
Burton 1960 Charitable Trust, Audrey and Stanley *63*
Carnegie Dunfermline Trust *69*
Carron Charitable Trust, The *70*
Charities Aid Foundation *71*
Chase Charity, The *73*
Chiron Trust, The *74*
Cinderford Charitable Trust, The *74*
Clark Charitable Trust, J A *74*
DLM Charitable Trust, The *82*
Dearne Valley Community Forum *82*
Englefield Charitable Trust, The *86*
Fairbairn Charitable Trust, The Esmée *89*
Franklin Deceased's New Second Charity, Sydney E *93*
Gibson Charitable Trust, The Simon *94*
Graves Charitable Trust, J G *96*
Great Britain Sasakawa Foundation, The *97*
Green Memorial Fund, The Barry *99*
HCD Memorial Fund *100*
Hadrian Trust, The *101*
Hall Charity, Robert *101*
Harryhausen's 1969 Trust, Mrs D L *103*
Hayward Foundation, The *104*
Headley Trust, The *106*
Hogg Charitable Trust, The J G *109*
Idlewild Trust, The *111*
Inland Waterways Association, The *112*
Knott Trust, Sir James *115*
Lewis Foundation, The John Spedan *119*
Macdonald Charitable Trust, The R S *122*
Macfarlane Walker Trust *123*
March's Trust Company Ltd, The Earl of *124*
Methodist Relief and Development Fund, The *127*
Monument Trust, The *129*
National Lottery Charities Board *132*
Nikeno Trust, The *136*
PF Charitable Trust *139*
Paget Trust, The *140*
Personal Assurance Charitable Trust *142*
Philanthropic Trust, The *144*
Portrack Charitable Trust, The *145*
Prince's Trust - BRO, The *145*

More than three years

Pye's No 1 Charitable Settlement, Mr and Mrs J A *146*
Rausing Charitable Foundation, Marit and Hans *151*
Rollit Trust, The Vera Kaye *155*
Schuster Charitable Trust, The *161*
Skells, Bequest of Harry *166*
Stanhope-Palmer Charity *168*
Staples Trust *168*
Sunley Charitable Foundation, The Bernard *172*
Sutton Coldfield Municipal Charities, The *173*
Vodafone Group Charitable Trust, The *181*
Wade & Others, The Charity of Thomas *183*
Westcroft Trust *186*
Woodlands Trust *192*
Woodward Charitable Trust, The *192*

■ **More than three years**

Funding priority

Bell Trust, The Henry *55*
Pryor Charity, The Ronald & Kathleen *146*

Will consider

Armitage Charitable Trust, G C *50*
Arnold Foundation, The *50*
Astor Foundation, The *51*
Bentall Charitable Trust, The Gerald *56*
Boyd Charitable Trust, The Viscountess *58*
Bromley Trust, The *62*
CHK Charities Limited *65*
Carron Charitable Trust, The *70*
Cinderford Charitable Trust, The *74*
Cobb Charity *76*
Criffel Charitable Trust *80*
Douglas Charitable Trust, R M *84*
Englefield Charitable Trust, The *86*
Fairbairn Charitable Trust, The Esmée *89*
Green Memorial Fund, The Barry *99*
Harryhausen's 1969 Trust, Mrs D L *103*
Higgs Charitable Trust, The *107*
Hogg Charitable Trust, The J G *109*
Landale Charitable Trust, The *117*

45

More than three years

Lawson Charitable Trust, Raymond and Blanche *117*
Leach Fourteenth Trust, The *118*
Macfarlane Walker Trust *123*
Mickel Fund *128*
Owen Family Trust, The *138*
Paget Trust, The *140*
Pye's No 1 Charitable Settlement, Mr and Mrs J A *146*
Roberts Charitable Trust, The E E *154*
Rollit Trust, The Vera Kaye *155*
Schuster Charitable Trust, The *161*
Smith (UK) Horticultural Trust, Stanley *167*
Stenhouse Foundation, The Hugh *170*
Westcroft Trust *186*

Alphabetical register of grant making trusts

A

■ The Adnams Charity

WHAT IS FUNDED Rural conservation; animal welfare; bird sanctuaries; animal breeding; and ornithology and zoology

WHAT IS NOT FUNDED No grants to individuals, students or national charities

WHO CAN BENEFIT Small local projects and innovative projects

WHERE FUNDING CAN BE GIVEN Within a 25-mile radius of Southwold (strictly)

TYPE OF GRANT One-off, buildings, capital, project, research, running costs and start-up costs will be considered. Funding may be given for up to one year

RANGE OF GRANTS £250–£1,500

SAMPLE GRANTS £8,000 to RSPB for the creation of a dipping pond

FINANCES
- Year 1996
- Grants £31,000
- Income £31,000

TRUSTEES B Segrave-Daly, S P D Loftus, J P A Adnams, R J Nicholson, M Horn, A Rous

PUBLICATIONS Annual Report

HOW TO APPLY Trustees meet quarterly. Applications for specific grants in writing to the address below

WHO TO APPLY TO Mrs E M Utting, Trust Administrator, The Adnams Charity, Sole Bay Brewery, Southwold, Suffolk IP18 6JW
Tel 01502 727200
Fax 01502 727201

CC NO 1000203   **ESTABLISHED** 1990

■ The Alchemy Foundation (154)

WHAT IS FUNDED Third world water projects

WHO CAN BENEFIT Community projects, voluntary sector and registered charities working in the areas outlined above

WHERE FUNDING CAN BE GIVEN UK and overseas

TYPE OF GRANT Capital, revenue, one-off, salaries

FINANCES
- Year 1997
- Grants £1,205,386
- Income £1,560,396

TRUSTEES A Armitage, A Murison, Esther Rantzen, The Rev Donald Reeves, Dr M Smith, A Stilgoe, H Stilgoe, J Stilgoe, Dr J Stilgoe, R Stilgoe, R Stilgoe

PUBLICATIONS Annual Report and Accounts

HOW TO APPLY Applications should not be too formal or bureaucratic

WHO TO APPLY TO Richard Stilgoe, The Alchemy Foundation, Trevereux Manor, Limpsfield Chart, Oxted, Surrey RH8 0TL

CC NO 292500   **ESTABLISHED** 1985

Commentary

The Alchemy Foundation was established for humanitarian reasons by Richard Stilgoe as the Starlight Foundation in 1985, and the name was changed to The Alchemy Foundation in 1987. The Alchemy Foundation is linked with the Orpheus Trust (see Volume 2), with which it collaborates to achieve its objectives. Both charities have identical Boards of Trustees

The Foundation was established with the following aims: (a) To promote the welfare of people suffering from mental or physical illness or disability; particularly children and babies. (b) To assist people suffering from the effects of famine. (c) To support charities benefiting the elderly, dying, medical research, children. (d) The Orpheus Trust. The Foundation prefers to fund projects in the following order of preference: third world water projects; disability; social welfare; individual enterprise; salary support for a small number of voluntary sector individuals; medical research and aid; respite for carers; penal reform and work with prisoners and their families; and holidays for disadvantaged children. The funding policies of the Foundation are set through discussions with the Trustees and change as and when necessary. The Foundation will support charities both in the UK and overseas

The Foundation offers a large number of small grants across a wide field. The Trustees have no particular grant type preferences and offer capital and recurring grants, although the latter means limited funds are available for new projects. For larger appeals, the Foundation offers grants that are one-off or payable over a number of years. It does not give loans.

The Foundation requests that applications should avoid excessive formal or bureaucratic qualities. As the Trustees receive more than 100 applications each week, they are unable to respond to all of them. However, the Trustees are most likely to show interest where there is assurance of personnel commitment and clear advantages to the applicant's beneficiaries. Once the grants have been distributed, recipients may receive a visit from an assessor, although this is only done on occasion

SAMPLE GRANTS
The top ten grants made in 1997 were:
£100,000 to Water Aid
£50,000 to Save The Children
£30,000 to Oxfam
£20,000 to Osteopathic Centre For Children
£18,000 to Bridgets
£10,000 to Trust for the Rehabilitation of the Paralysed in Bangladesh
£8,000 to Camphill Communities of Ireland
£8,000 to Imperial College – St Marys
£7,000 to Crossroads
£7,000 to Toynbee Hall

■The Ammco Trust

WHAT IS FUNDED Environmental resources and conservation

WHAT IS NOT FUNDED No grants to individuals or students

WHO CAN BENEFIT Small local projects; national, new organisations; and established organisations working in the areas outlined above

WHERE FUNDING CAN BE GIVEN Oxfordshire and adjoining counties

TYPE OF GRANT One-off and recurrent for core costs. Funding is available for up to one year

RANGE OF GRANTS £50–£5,000

FINANCES
- Year 1997–98
- Income £128,327
- Grants £80,829

TRUSTEES Mrs E M R Lewis, Mrs R S E Vickers, N P Cobbold

PUBLICATIONS Annual Report

HOW TO APPLY In writing at any time. No application forms. An sae is appreciated

WHO TO APPLY TO Mrs E M R Lewis, The Ammco Trust, Glebe Farm, Hinton Waldrist, Faringdon, Oxfordshire SN7 8RX
Tel 01865 820269
Fax 01865 821188

CC NO 327962   **ESTABLISHED** 1988

■The Princess Anne's Charities Trust

WHAT IS FUNDED Wildlife

WHAT IS NOT FUNDED No grants are made to individuals

WHO CAN BENEFIT Registered charities only

WHERE FUNDING CAN BE GIVEN UK and overseas

FINANCES
- Year 1996
- Income £241,335
- Grants £110,607

TRUSTEES Lt Col Sir Peter Gibbs, KCVO, Captain T J H Laurence, MVO, RN, The Hon Mark Bridges

HOW TO APPLY In writing to the address below

WHO TO APPLY TO Lt Col Sir Peter Gibbs, KCVO, The Princess Anne's Charities Trust, Buckingham Palace, London SW1A 1AA

CC NO 277814   **ESTABLISHED** 1979

■G C Armitage Charitable Trust

WHAT IS FUNDED Charities working in the fields of: woodlands and horticulture

WHAT IS NOT FUNDED Individual applications will not be considered, expenses kept to absolute minimum, do not favour other than local/known charities

WHO CAN BENEFIT Organisations working in the areas outlined above

WHERE FUNDING CAN BE GIVEN Leeds, North Yorkshire, Wakefield and York

TYPE OF GRANT Funding for up to and over three years will be considered

RANGE OF GRANTS £100–£2,500; average approximately £800

FINANCES
- Year 1998
- Income £32,500
- Grants £32,700

TRUSTEES Mrs V M Armitage, Mrs C J Greig

HOW TO APPLY In writing to the address below

WHO TO APPLY TO Mrs V M Armitage, G C Armitage Charitable Trust, Aldborough House, Aldborough, Boroughbridge YO51 9EY

CC NO 326418   **ESTABLISHED** 1985

■The Arnold Foundation

WHAT IS FUNDED Only to support local (South West England) charities in which the Trustees have a personal knowledge and interest. Particularly charities working in the fields of: rural conservation and wildlife sanctuaries

WHAT IS NOT FUNDED Registered charities only. Applications from individuals, including students, are ineligible. No grants made in response to appeals from large national organisations, nor from any organisation working outside South West England

WHO CAN BENEFIT Small charities in South West England personally known to the Trustees

WHERE FUNDING CAN BE GIVEN South West England

TYPE OF GRANT One-off grants funded for up to, or more than, three years will be considered

RANGE OF GRANTS £250–£1,000

FINANCES
- Year 1997
- Grants £19,300
- Income £15,657

TRUSTEES J L S Arnold (Chairman), Mrs M S Grantham, A J Meek, FRIBA, D F Smith, FCA

NOTES Funds of this Trust are fully committed

HOW TO APPLY This Trust states that it does not respond to unsolicited applications

WHO TO APPLY TO The Secretary, The Arnold Foundation, 37 Nightingale Rise, Portishead, Bristol BS20 8LN
Tel 01275 842414

CC NO 277430   **ESTABLISHED** 1979

■ A J H Ashby Will Trust

WHAT IS FUNDED Environmental resources; wildlife and conservation

WHAT IS NOT FUNDED No grants to individuals or students

WHO CAN BENEFIT Small local projects working in the areas outlined above

WHERE FUNDING CAN BE GIVEN Lea Valley, Hertfordshire only

TYPE OF GRANT One-off and recurrent range of grants

FINANCES
- Year 1995
- Grants £72,000
- Income £62,725

TRUSTEES Midland Bank Trust Co Ltd

HOW TO APPLY To the address below in writing

WHO TO APPLY TO C M Woodrow, Trust Manager, A J H Ashby Will Trust, Midland Trusts, Cumberland House, 15–17 Cumberland Place, Southampton SO15 2UY
Tel 01703 531364

CC NO 803291   **ESTABLISHED** 1990

■ The Ashendene Trust

WHAT IS FUNDED Charities working in the field of the conservation of flora

WHAT IS NOT FUNDED No large organisations, education or health

WHO CAN BENEFIT Registered charities working in the areas outlined above

WHERE FUNDING CAN BE GIVEN London, Oxfordshire and Berkshire

TYPE OF GRANT Capital, core costs and project. Funding available for up to three years

RANGE OF GRANTS £500–£25,000 (4 years). Average grant £2,500

FINANCES
- Year 1997–98
- Grants £36,000
- Income £36,000

TRUSTEES Sir Simon Hornby, Sir Edward Cazalet, A D Loehnis

NOTES This a small Trust that gives to organisations where the grant will really make an impact

HOW TO APPLY In writing to the address below. There is no application form and guidelines are not issued

WHO TO APPLY TO Sir Simon Hornby, Trustee, The Ashendene Trust, The Ham, Wantage, Oxfordshire OX12 0JA

CC NO 270749   **ESTABLISHED** 1975

■ The Astor Foundation

WHAT IS FUNDED New and imaginative charities in their early days, including those working in the fields of rural conservation; animal facilities and services; and environmental and animal sciences

WHAT IS NOT FUNDED Positively no grants to individuals. Normally not capital building works. No grants made to post-graduates or those requiring funding for travel, etc

WHO CAN BENEFIT Mainly headquarters organisations. Innovatory projects rather than long established or well endowed ones (with some exceptions)

WHERE FUNDING CAN BE GIVEN UK and overseas

TYPE OF GRANT Grants are usually one-off though buildings, capital, core costs, project, research and start-up costs will be considered. Salaries are rarely given. Funding may be for up to and over three years

RANGE OF GRANTS Smallest £250, average grant £1,500

SAMPLE GRANTS £2,000 to Environmental Investigations Agency
£1,000 to WSPA (World Society Protection of Animals)

FINANCES
- Year 1997
- Grants £77,750
- Income £151,000

TRUSTEES Sir William Slack, KCVO, Lord Astor of Hever, J R Astor, R H Astor, Dr H Swanton, C Money-Coutts

HOW TO APPLY Applications are eventually acknowledged. Annual Accounts whilst not necessary are useful. Initial telephone calls are not welcome

WHO TO APPLY TO The Secretary, The Astor Foundation, 5 Northview, Hungerford, Berkshire RG17 0DA

CC NO 225708   **ESTABLISHED** 1963

B

■ The BAA 21st Century Communities Trust

WHAT IS FUNDED The Trust will consider funding conservation including environmental issues

WHAT IS NOT FUNDED No grants for religious or political groups

WHO CAN BENEFIT Organisations in local communities around BAA airports working in the areas outlined above

WHERE FUNDING CAN BE GIVEN Local communities around BAA airports, situated in: East and West Sussex: Hampshire; Isle of Wight; Slough; Southampton; Surrey; Windsor and Maidenhead; London; Cambridgeshire; Essex; Hertfordshire; Aberdeen; Aberdeenshire; East Lothian; Edinburgh; Glasgow; and Renfrewshire

TYPE OF GRANT One-off, recurring, buildings, capital, project and start-up costs. Funding is available for up to three years

RANGE OF GRANTS £100–£50,000, typical grant £5,000–£10,000

FINANCES
- Year 1997–98   • Income £565,000

TRUSTEES D Wilson, R Everitt, A Barrell, C Hoare, V Gooding

PUBLICATIONS *BAA Environment and Community Report 1998–99*

HOW TO APPLY In writing the the Community Relations Manager at the local BAA airport

WHO TO APPLY TO Please apply to the appropriate address below

REGIONAL OFFICES
BAA Heathrow: Community Relations Manager, The BAA 21st Century Communities Trust, BAA Heathrow, Heathrow Point, 234 Bath Road, Harlington, Middlesex UB3 5AP
BAA Gatwick: Community Relations Manager, The BAA 21st Century Communities Trust, BAA Gatwick, Gatwick, West Sussex RH6 0HP
BAA Glasgow: Public Relations Manager, The BAA 21st Century Communities Trust, BAA Glasgow, Paisley, Renfrewshire PA3 2ST
BAA Edinburgh: Community Liason Executive, The BAA 21st Century Communities Trust, BAA Edinburgh, Edinburgh EH12 9DN
BAA Aberdeen: Passenger Services Manager, The BAA 21st Century Communities Trust, BAA Aberdeen, Dyce, Aberdeenshire AB2 0DU
BAA Stansted: Community Relations Manager, The BAA 21st Century Communities Trust, BAA Stansted, Stansted, Essex CM24 1QN

BAA Southampton: Public Affairs Manager, The BAA 21st Century Communities Trust, BAA Southampton, Southampton, Hampshire SO18 2NL

CC NO 1058617   ESTABLISHED 1996

■ BP Conservation Programme

WHAT IS FUNDED Conservation research on globally threatened species (including all types of flora and fauna), and habitats

WHAT IS NOT FUNDED 50 per cent of any funds granted must be used for the involvement of national counterparts. No longer consider applications from individuals applying for funding to join an expedition, ie only consider the whole expedition team

WHO CAN BENEFIT Teams should be a majority of university students (under- or postgraduates)

WHERE FUNDING CAN BE GIVEN Expeditions to and from anywhere in the world

TYPE OF GRANT Four main grants of £5,000 are awarded, one each, to projects with the themes of globally threatened species; oceanic islands and marine habitats; tropical forests; wetlands, grasslands, savannahs and deserts. Eight runners-up are each awarded £3,000. To encourage on-going conservation work a single award of £10,000 is given to the best follow-up proposal from a previous winning project

RANGE OF GRANTS £3,000–£10,000

SAMPLE GRANTS £10,000 to Action Simper, Indonesia for a conservation research and education project being carried out by a group of British and Indonesians
£7,500 to Project Eakehei for a project in Podocarpus National Park, Ecuador by a group of Ecuadorians and Australians
£5,000 to Colombia/Venezuela Sea Turtle Project for bi-national sea turtle project
£5,000 to Diadema for a study of New Caledonia's threatened bird and reptile species by a group of British and New Caledonians
£5,000 to Jaran Hawk Eagle Project for a group of Indonesians to study the Jaran Hawk Eagle
£5,000 to Project Kasigau for a group of Kenyans and British studying threatened birds in Kenya
£3,000 to Ascension 1998 for British team studying threatened endemic plants on Ascensia
£3,000 to Birds of Bolivian Yungas for studying threatened birds of Yungas Habitat, Bolivia by a British and Bolivian Team
£3,000 to Tainjing Wetlands for a Chinese Team studying the conservation of birds in Tainjing Wetlands of China
£3,000 to Adji Lake for a Russian and Ukrainian team studying the conservation of birds in and around Adji Lake, Dagestan

FINANCES
- Year 1996
- Income £3,202,229
- Grants £2,902,316

NOTES BP Conservation Programme is organised by Birdlife International, Fauna and Flora International, and BP Amoco plc

HOW TO APPLY Awards are granted annually. Applications should be received by 16 November. Contact the Programme Manager at Birdlife International for guidelines for applicants and application forms

WHO TO APPLY TO Programme Manager, BP Conservation Programme, Birdlife International, Wellbrook Court, Girton Road, Cambridge CB3 0NA
Web Site http://www.bp.com/conservation

CC NO 1042125   ESTABLISHED 1994

■ The C Alma Baker Trust

WHAT IS FUNDED Agriculture and education with an agricultural connection particularly in New Zealand and UK. (a) Agricultural research particularly New Zealand. (b) Massey University, New Zealand – Wye College, UK. Undergraduate Scheme. (c) UK YFC Scheme for young farmers to experience New Zealand farming on the Trust's property in New Zealand. (d) Annual Travel Fellowship New Zealand-UK, UK-New Zealand. (e) Maori Language Education Scholarship, Wailato University, New Zealand

WHO CAN BENEFIT Individuals or scientific research institutions

WHERE FUNDING CAN BE GIVEN UK and overseas, particularly New Zealand

TYPE OF GRANT Range of grants, though normally one-off annual grants

RANGE OF GRANTS For education £200–£10,000, typical grant £1,600

SAMPLE GRANTS £5,792 to an individual at Massey University, New Zealand for work on parasitology in the sheep abnomasum
£4,644 to an individual at Lincoln University, New Zealand for doctoral scholarship in inorganic nitrogen in woolscour sludge
£4,633 to an individual at Massey University, New Zealand for work into efficient venison production with minimal imputs
£4,633 to an individual at Lincoln University, New Zealand for doctoral scholarship re Asochyta disease in broad beans and peas
£3,861 to an individual at Massey University, New Zealand for evaluation of once bred heifer beef production
£3,352 to an individual at Reading University, UK for travel fellowship to New Zealand

Institute of Agricultural Science
£2,836 to an individual from Chipping Sodbury, UK for YFC Scheme to Limestone Down, New Zealand
£2,706 to an individual from Brecon, Powys, UK for YFC Scheme to Limestone Downs, New Zealand
£2,689 to an individual from Murchison, New Zealand for Wool Diploma Study Tour to UK textile Industry
£2,507 to an individual at Wye College, UK for Undergraduate Exchange to Massey University, New Zealand

FINANCES
- Year 1996–97
- Income £456,416
- Grants £64,487

TRUSTEES C R Boyes, R Moore, S F B Taylor. New Zealand Committee: C T Horton, Prof A Frampton, D J Frith, K I Lowe, Prof B MacDonald, Mrs M Millard

PUBLICATIONS Limestone Downs Annual Report in New Zealand

NOTES The Trust's main asset is Limestone Downs, a sheep and beef property in the North Island, New Zealand utilised for new ideas and development in agriculture to be explored and debated in a working farm environment

HOW TO APPLY In writing for annual grant review at the end of November each year. The Trust only has a limited number of grants available. For New Zealand applicants apply to: Professor B Macdonald, Secretary to New Zealand Committee, The C Alma Baker Trust, Massey University, Bag 11-222, Palmerston North, New Zealand. Fax: 00 64 63 505686

WHO TO APPLY TO Mrs Scott, Secretary to the Trustees, The C Alma Baker Trust, Warrens Boyes & Archer, 20 Hartford Road, Huntingdon, Cambridgeshire PE18 6QE
Fax 01480 459012
E-mail wba.law@btinternet.com

CC NO 283015   **ESTABLISHED** 1981

■ The Balney Charitable Trust

WHAT IS FUNDED Rural conservation. The Trustees lean towards local appeals

WHAT IS NOT FUNDED Local community projects outside North Buckinghamshire will not be funded

WHO CAN BENEFIT Registered charities and institutions

WHERE FUNDING CAN BE GIVEN North Buckinghamshire

TYPE OF GRANT One-off and start-up costs. Funding is given for one year or less

RANGE OF GRANTS £200–£5,000

SAMPLE GRANTS £2,000 to Kew Millennium Seed Bank Appeal towards the formation of rare seed bank

FINANCES
- Year 1997
- Income £50,569
- Grants £38,255

TRUSTEES J G B Chester, R Ruck-Keene

HOW TO APPLY Written applications only. Sae if acknowledgement is required

WHO TO APPLY TO G C Beazley, The Balney Charitable Trust, The Chicheley Estate, Bartlemas Office, Pavenham, Bedford MK43 7PF
Tel 01234 823661
Fax 01234 825058

CC NO 288575   **ESTABLISHED** 1983

■ The Barbour Trust

WHAT IS FUNDED The preservation of countryside of environmental interest. Applications from organisations based in the North East of England are looked at favourably, particularly those based in Tyne and Wear and County Durham. Northumberland and Cleveland are considered. However, it should be noted that very few donations are made in this field

WHAT IS NOT FUNDED Grants are made to registered charities only and not to individuals

WHO CAN BENEFIT The Trust likes to support local activities. The Trust also supports local branches of national charities

WHERE FUNDING CAN BE GIVEN North East England (Tyne & Wear, Northumberland, Co Durham & Cleveland)

TYPE OF GRANT Capital, core costs, one-off, project, research, running costs, recurring costs, salaries and start-up costs. Funding for up to one year will be considered

FINANCES
- Year 1996
- Income £367,158

TRUSTEES Mrs M Barbour, CBE, DL (Chairman), H J Tavroges, A A E Clenton, Helen M Barbour, BA

PUBLICATIONS A statement of the accounts of the Trust is published annually

HOW TO APPLY The Trust meets every two months to consider applications

WHO TO APPLY TO Mrs A Harvey, The Barbour Trust, PO Box 21, Guisborough, Cleveland TS14 8YH

CC NO 328081   **ESTABLISHED** 1988

■ Lord Barnby's Foundation

WHAT IS FUNDED The preservation of the countryside, and the welfare of horses

WHAT IS NOT FUNDED No grants to individuals; grants to registered charities only

WHO CAN BENEFIT Registered charities working in the areas outlined above

WHERE FUNDING CAN BE GIVEN UK

TYPE OF GRANT One-off, buildings, capital, core costs, project, research. Funding is up to two years

RANGE OF GRANTS Grants range from £500 to £50,000; but are generally £1,000 to £2,000

SAMPLE GRANTS £10,000 to Countryside Foundation

FINANCES
- Year 1998
- Income £181,164
- Grants £289,450

TRUSTEES Rt Hon Lord Newall, Sir John L Lowther, Sir Michael Farquhar, Bt, The Hon G Lopes, The Rt Hon Countess Peel

NOTES Annual review of permanent lists of donations and additions or deletions at Trustees' discretion. Appeals are considered three times a year in March, July and October. Once only donations to special appeals or capital projects

HOW TO APPLY Applications should be made in writing, accompanied by a set of the latest Accounts. Applicants do not need to send sae

WHO TO APPLY TO Lord Barnby's Foundation, Messrs Payne Hicks Beach, 10 New Square, Lincoln's Inn, London WC2A 3QG
Tel 0171-465 4300
Fax 0171-465 4400

CC NO 251016   **ESTABLISHED** 1966

■ Dr Barrow Trust

WHAT IS FUNDED Wildlife and the countryside

WHO CAN BENEFIT Individuals and organisations working in the areas outlined above

WHERE FUNDING CAN BE GIVEN Birmingham

FINANCES
- Year 1996
- Income £9,862

TRUSTEES B J M Delray, R L Cole

HOW TO APPLY To the address below in writing

WHO TO APPLY TO The Clerk, c/o NatWest Bank Plc, Dr Barrow Trust, PO Box 198, 4th Floor, Cornwall Court, Cornwall Street, Birmingham B3 2DT

CC NO 261160   **ESTABLISHED** 1970

■ Batten and Co Charitable Trust

WHAT IS FUNDED Rural conservation; animal facilities and services; and animal sciences

WHAT IS NOT FUNDED No grants for expeditions abroad

WHERE FUNDING CAN BE GIVEN Somerset and North and West Devon

TYPE OF GRANT Buildings, capital, core costs, one-off, project, research, running costs, salaries and start-up costs. Funding may be given for one year or less

SAMPLE GRANTS £250 to Dorset Wildlife Trust for general funds

FINANCES
- Year 1997
- Income £2,975
- Grants £4,452

TRUSTEES S R Allen, R M Edwards, D G March, R J Vaughan

HOW TO APPLY In writing to the address below

WHO TO APPLY TO R J Gibbons, Clerk, Batten and Co Charitable Trust, Church House, Church Street, Yeovil, Somerset BA20 1HB

CC NO 293500   **ESTABLISHED** 1985

■ The Henry Bell Trust

WHAT IS FUNDED Nature reserves and other charitable purposes

WHAT IS NOT FUNDED No grants to individuals

WHERE FUNDING CAN BE GIVEN Hexham, Hexham Low Quarter and Hexhamshire

TYPE OF GRANT Core costs, one-off, project, recurring and running costs. Funding is available for over three years

FINANCES
- Year 1996–97
- Income £16,407
- Grants £14,350

TRUSTEES A Brogdon, J M Clark, Canon M Nelson, M Howard, I Brogdon

HOW TO APPLY To the address under Who To Apply To in writing

WHO TO APPLY TO J M Clark, Trustee, The Henry Bell Trust, c/o Clark Scott-Harden, Market Place, Haltwhistle, Northumberland NE49 0BP
Tel 01434 320363

CC NO 702166   **ESTABLISHED** 1989

Belmont

■ The Belmont Trust

WHAT IS FUNDED Small donations for environmental purposes

WHAT IS NOT FUNDED Applications from individuals and for religious purposes are excluded

WHO CAN BENEFIT Organisations working in the areas outlined above

WHERE FUNDING CAN BE GIVEN Hampshire and adjacent counties preferred

TYPE OF GRANT No loans

RANGE OF GRANTS Largest £750, typical grants £50–£150

FINANCES
- Year 1997–98
- Income £21,000
- Grants £12,000

TRUSTEES Mrs L Steel, Miss H E F Corbett, BSc

HOW TO APPLY In writing with full supporting details. Trustees regret that they cannot acknowledge unsuccessful applications. Please note that a large proportion of donations are made in March/April of each year via the Charities Aid Foundation

WHO TO APPLY TO The Belmont Trust, PO Box 89, Havant, Hampshire PO9 3YU

CC NO 265946 **ESTABLISHED** 1973

■ Belsize Charitable Trust No1

WHAT IS FUNDED Nature conversation, including nature reserves

WHAT IS NOT FUNDED No grants made to individuals

WHO CAN BENEFIT Organisations working in the areas outlined above

WHERE FUNDING CAN BE GIVEN England

TYPE OF GRANT One-off and project

RANGE OF GRANTS Typical grant £5,000

FINANCES
- Year 1997
- Income £27,231
- Grants £11,000

TRUSTEES Lloyds Bank A/C 42392/CR

HOW TO APPLY All letters considered half yearly at the end of February and August. No acknowledgements issued

WHO TO APPLY TO Lloyds Private Banking Ltd, Belsize Charitable Trust No1, UK Trust Centre, The Clock House, 22–26 Ock Street, Abingdon, Oxfordshire OX14 5SW

CC NO 262535 **ESTABLISHED** 1958

■ Benham Charitable Settlement

WHAT IS FUNDED Established by the late Cedric and Hilda Benham, the Trust's policy is to make a large number of relatively small grants to groups working in many charitable fields – including charities working in the fields of wildlife and the environment. The emphasis is very much on activities within Northamptonshire

WHAT IS NOT FUNDED Registered charities only. No individuals

WHO CAN BENEFIT Organisations working in the areas outlined above. Most good causes considered, including national appeals, or branches of the same in Northamptonshire

WHERE FUNDING CAN BE GIVEN UK, but with special interest in Northamptonshire

TYPE OF GRANT One-off and recurring grants will be considered

RANGE OF GRANTS £50–£25,000; typically £300

FINANCES
- Year 1997–98
- Income £147,171
- Grants £138,000

TRUSTEES Mrs M M Tittle, Mrs R A Nickols, E N Langley

NOTES Only successful applications are acknowledged

HOW TO APPLY Must be in writing to the address under Who To Apply To. No telephone calls. No application forms or guidelines. Applications considered any time, but only once each year

WHO TO APPLY TO Mrs M M Tittle, Benham Charitable Settlement, Hurstbourne, Portnall Drive, Virginia Water, Surrey GU25 4NR

CC NO 239371 **ESTABLISHED** 1964

■ The Gerald Bentall Charitable Trust

WHAT IS FUNDED Nature reserves and animal welfare

WHAT IS NOT FUNDED Grants are not made to individuals, students or expeditions

WHO CAN BENEFIT Organisations working in the areas outlined above

WHERE FUNDING CAN BE GIVEN London and South East England

TYPE OF GRANT Recurring and one-off

FINANCES
- Year 1997
- Income £8,317

TRUSTEES Anthony J D Anstee, Jacqueline de Courcy Digby-Smith, Susan E Digby-Smith

HOW TO APPLY All applications are acknowledged. The Trustees usually require a copy of applicants Annual Accounts

WHO TO APPLY TO A J D Anstee, The Gerald Bentall Charitable Trust, Bentall's Plc, Anstee House, Wood Street, Kingston Upon Thames, KT1 1TS
Tel 0181-546 2002
Fax 0181-546 3880

CC NO 271993   **ESTABLISHED** 1976

■ Bergne-Coupland Charity

WHAT IS FUNDED Rural conservation; animal facilities and services; and environmental and animal sciences

WHO CAN BENEFIT Individuals and institutions working in the areas outlined above

WHERE FUNDING CAN BE GIVEN Lincolnshire

TYPE OF GRANT One-off and recurring

FINANCES
- Year 1995–96
- Income £8,016
- Grants £7,428

TRUSTEES Mrs A Coltman (Chairman), C Coltman, Miss S Coltman, Miss J Coltman

HOW TO APPLY To the address below

WHO TO APPLY TO J J Ware, Bergne-Coupland Charity, 3 Middlegate, Newark, Nottinghamshire NG24 1AQ
Tel 01636 71881

CC NO 1023682   **ESTABLISHED** 1993

■ The Bingham Trust

WHAT IS FUNDED Identifiable community needs in the areas of: rural conservation; animal facilities and services; and environmental and animal sciences

WHAT IS NOT FUNDED Generally, limited to the town of Buxton and district

WHO CAN BENEFIT Primarily charitable organisations working in the areas outlined above. Occasionally individuals

WHERE FUNDING CAN BE GIVEN Buxton, Derbyshire

TYPE OF GRANT One-off, capital, buildings, project, running costs, salaries and start-up costs. Funding available is for up to three years

RANGE OF GRANTS £50–£15,000

FINANCES
- Year 1997
- Income £63,729
- Grants £62,960

TRUSTEES J I Fraser, R A Horne, Mrs J H Lawton, Rev P J Meek, Dr R G B Willis

HOW TO APPLY Apply in writing, on not more than two sides of A4 paper, stating total cost of the project and sources of other funding. Apply before the end of June, September, December and February each year

WHO TO APPLY TO The Bingham Trust, Bennett Brooke-Taylor & Wright, 4 The Quadrant, Buxton, Derbyshire SK17 6AW

CC NO 287636   **ESTABLISHED** 1977

■ The Celia and Conrad Blakey Charitable Trust

WHAT IS FUNDED Among the areas of interest to the Trust is the sea

WHAT IS NOT FUNDED No grants to individuals. No grants to national appeals. Grants rarely made to bodies outside Kent

WHO CAN BENEFIT Registered charities only

WHERE FUNDING CAN BE GIVEN South East Kent

RANGE OF GRANTS £250–£5,000

FINANCES
- Year 1997
- Income £24,165
- Grants £19,500

TRUSTEES Mrs C Blakey, C C Blakey, Miss J S Portrait

WHO TO APPLY TO Miss J S Portrait, The Celia and Conrad Blakey Charitable Trust, Messrs Portrait, 1 Chancery Lane, Clifford's Inn, London WC2A 1LF

CC NO 263482   **ESTABLISHED** 1971

■ Bernard Richard Body Charitable Trust

WHAT IS FUNDED For the protection and benefit of animals, particularly for our own animal sanctuary in Berkshire. Some other charities on a regular basis

WHAT IS NOT FUNDED No grants for scholarships or expeditions

WHO CAN BENEFIT Organisations benefiting animals

WHERE FUNDING CAN BE GIVEN UK and overseas

TYPE OF GRANT Regular grants given to certain charities. Only restricted funds available for further grants

RANGE OF GRANTS Some annual grants of £1,000 or less; one-off grants of £500 or less

SAMPLE GRANTS £500 to Brooke Hospital for Animals

£200 to Society for the Protection of Animals Abroad
£200 to Wood Green Animal Shelter
£150 to International League for the Protection of Horses
£150 to Animal Health Trust

FINANCES
- Year 1997–98
- Income £17,476
- Grants £4,950

TRUSTEES B R Body, Mrs A Burfoot, J Coleman

HOW TO APPLY To the address under Who To Apply To in writing

WHO TO APPLY TO Lady Body, Bernard Richard Body Charitable Trust, Jewells Farm, Stanford Dingley, Reading, Berkshire RG7 6LX

CC NO 800320   **ESTABLISHED** 1988

■The Body Shop Foundation

WHAT IS FUNDED Innovative, grassroots projects in the field of environmental protection

WHAT IS NOT FUNDED No grants to individuals, sport or the arts, capital investment, low likelihood of sustainability, emergency aid, dependent relationships

WHO CAN BENEFIT Registered charities as outlined above

WHERE FUNDING CAN BE GIVEN UK and overseas

TYPE OF GRANT Buildings, capital, one-off, project and research. Funding of up to three years will be considered

RANGE OF GRANTS Up to £10,000

SAMPLE GRANTS £39,000 to Global Witness for research costs into the deforestation of Cambodia
£25,000 to World Society for the Protection of Animals to help reintroduce spectacled bears into the wild
£21,200 to Environmental Investigation Agency to investigate the trade of endangered species in Northern India

FINANCES
- Year 1997
- Income £1,118,146
- Grants £701,980

TRUSTEES Mrs A Roddick, G Roddick, M Barrett, R Cockerill, R Godfrey, J Floodgate, A Kinney-Eiltinger, S Scott

HOW TO APPLY This Trust states that it does not respond to unsolicited applications

WHO TO APPLY TO The Body Shop Foundation Watersmead, Littlehampton, West Sussex BN17 6LS

CC NO 802757   **ESTABLISHED** 1988

■The Born Free Foundation

WHAT IS FUNDED Preservation and conservation of animal species in their natural habitats, on an international basis. The Foundation undertakes all relevant educational and research activities and publishes the useful results of such research. Prevention of all types of cruelty and abuse of animals and wildlife, particularly in zoos and other places where animals are kept in captivity

WHO CAN BENEFIT Organisations working in the areas outlined above

WHERE FUNDING CAN BE GIVEN UK and overseas

FINANCES
- Year 1996
- Income £615,097

HOW TO APPLY In writing to the address below

WHO TO APPLY TO Miss Alison Hood, Trustee, The Born Free Foundation, 3 Grove House, Foundry Lane, Horsham, West Sussex RH13 5PL

CC NO 296024   **ESTABLISHED** 1987

■The Viscountess Boyd Charitable Trust

WHAT IS FUNDED General charitable purposes in Devon and Cornwall including rural conservation; animal welfare; bird sanctuaries; and wildlife sanctuaries

WHO CAN BENEFIT Organisations working in the areas outlined above

WHERE FUNDING CAN BE GIVEN South West England

TYPE OF GRANT Capital, core costs, endowment, feasibility studies and one-off funding. Grants can be given for up to and over three years

FINANCES
- Year 1997–98
- Income £19,736
- Grants £34,000

TRUSTEES The Iveagh Trustees Limited, Viscountess Boyd, Viscount Boyd

NOTES The Trustees are particularly interested in organisations from the Devon and Cornwall areas. Only applications enclosing an sae are ensured of a reply

HOW TO APPLY First of the month, no application form is used

WHO TO APPLY TO Miss Yvonne White, The Viscountess Boyd Charitable Trust, The Iveagh Trustees Limited, Iveagh House, 41 Harrington Gardens, London SW7 4JU

CC NO 284270   **ESTABLISHED** 1982

■ The Brading Town Trust

WHAT IS FUNDED General charitable objectives benefiting: fauna; flora; landscapes; nature reserves; and woodlands

WHAT IS NOT FUNDED No grants to individuals

WHO CAN BENEFIT Organisations within the area Where Funding Can Be Given

WHERE FUNDING CAN BE GIVEN Brading, Isle of Wight

TYPE OF GRANT Buildings, one-off grants and project. Funding is available for up to one year

SAMPLE GRANTS £20 to Horticultural Society for the cost of show and hire of hall

FINANCES
- Year 1995
- Income £14,257
- Grants £15,900

TRUSTEES Betty Howell (Chairman), Margaret Wetherick, Peter Wright, Paul Eccles, Roger Woodcock

HOW TO APPLY To the address under Who To Apply To in writing

WHO TO APPLY TO J Lee, Clerk, The Brading Town Trust, 42 High Street, Brading, Isle of Wight PO36 0DJ
Tel 01983 407560

CC NO 202053   **ESTABLISHED** 1898

■ The Bridge House Estates Trust Fund (16)

WHAT IS FUNDED Environmental conservation

WHAT IS NOT FUNDED The Trust cannot fund: political parties; political lobbying; non charitable activities; statutory bodies. The Trust does not fund: individuals; schools, universities or other educational establishments; other grant making bodies to make grants on its behalf; medical or academic research; churches or other religious bodies for the construction maintenance and repair of religious buildings and for other religious purposes; hospitals. Grants will not usually be given to organisations seeking funding to replace cuts by statutory authorities; organisations seeking to replace cuts by statutory authorities; organisations seeking funding to top up on under-priced contracts

WHERE FUNDING CAN BE GIVEN Greater London (33 boroughs)

TYPE OF GRANT Capital and revenue grants. Recurring revenue grants up to three years. Applicants should note that revenue grants are usually project grants not core revenue/running costs. Funding may be given for up to three years

FINANCES
- Year 1998
- Income £36,606,000
- Grants £9,991,000

TRUSTEES The Mayor and Commonality & Citizens of the City of London

NOTES The Trust's income is also applied for maintaining the bridges for which the Trust is responsible. The Trust's income and assets relate to the entire Bridge House Estates, of which, the Charitable Trust Fund is part

HOW TO APPLY Application forms are available from the address below. The Trust's staff are willing to advise potential applicants over the telephone. There are no application deadlines. The Trustees meet 10 times per annum

WHO TO APPLY TO Chief Grants Officer, The Bridge House Estates Trust Fund, Corporation of London, PO Box 270, Guildhall, London EC2P 2EJ
Tel 0171-332 3710
Fax 0171-332 3720

CC NO 1035628   **ESTABLISHED** 1995

Commentary

In 1176 when Peter de Colechurch, a priest and head of the Brethren of London Bridge, began to build the first stone bridge in the City he set in motion the creation of the Bridge House Estates Trust Fund. The Trust was run from a house on the south side of London Bridge called Bridge House, hence the name. Today the Trust has under its care not only London Bridge, but Tower Bridge, Southwark Bridge and Blackfriars Bridge – the gateways to the City. In 1995 the objectives of the Trust were extended to enable it to provide vital support for Greater London, including the provision of transport and access to Greater London for elderly or disabled people, and other charitable purposes for the general benefit of the inhabitants of Greater London.

The Trust supports a number of different programmes within their quite broad outlook. The first of these aims to improve opportunities and services for older people and disabled people, and encourages their active involvement in the management by supporting initiatives which give them: (a) access to transport, especially community transport schemes. Projects where vehicles are shared or their use is maximised in another way are favoured as well as schemes improving transport services through better co-ordination; (b) access to buildings. Projects improving access to buildings in the voluntary and community sectors and access to the built environment in general are supported, also schemes increasing access awareness, information and design; and (c) access to opportunities. Initiatives from organisations providing training, employment, arts, sports and leisure facilities are supported, as are schemes providing information, advocacy and community support; training for independent living; specialist aids, equipment or communication facilities including signing; disability equality training; increased social participation and integration.

A second scheme supports projects which will sustain, protect and improve London's environment and help to create a better environmental future for London and maintaining the Capital's biodiversity or variety of life. The Trust seeks to achieve this by supporting organisations who are: (a) developing environmental education work; (b) seeking to protect and improve the natural environment; (c) helping maintain London's biodiversity; (d) helping raise awareness and knowledge of environmental issues within the wider community; and (e) working to ensure that resources are used in the least harmful and most efficient way. Within the programme of environmental conservation the Trust is also interested in supporting smaller organisations and organisations that do not have the environment as their main area of focus.

The third major scheme has three themes. The first concentrates upon preventative work with children and young people (aged 5–16) and includes work with families, individuals and groups, particularly: work preventing homelessness or drug and alcohol misuse; advice, counselling and information services; life skills and personal development projects; and work breaking cycles of violence, abuse, crime and mental illness. A second theme promotes the active involvement of young people (aged 11–18), encouraging work: enabling young people to realise their potential; encouraging young people to take responsibility; involving young people in their communities, including inter-generational work; and developing personal and emotional skills, especially in the areas of parenting, life skills and relationships. The third theme is aimed at young people in crisis, and supports: projects tackling drug and alcohol problems and homelessness; groups supporting young parents, young carers or those with mental health problems; and projects offering fresh opportunities to those who are living in poverty or deprivation.

A fourth scheme supports a wide range of services aimed at improving the lives of older people and assisting them to stay within the community. Priorities within this area are aiding organisations which are working to: (a) represent and empower older people without a strong or clear voice; (b) enable older people to make informed choices; (c) address the needs of older people with dementia and their carers; (d) support older people affected by depression and other mental health problems; and (e) enable older people in residential or nursing home care to maintain their involvement in the wider community.

The last scheme aims to strengthen the voluntary sector and assist voluntary organisations in their long-term development and financial planning. The Trust aims to do this through the provision of technical assistance including information, advice, training and consultancy to help voluntary organisations to develop. The Trust welcomes schemes put forward by groups which are working to: (a) improve the delivery of services by second tier organisations to other voluntary organisations, especially smaller voluntary organisations; (b) assist voluntary organisations with their organisational development; (c) provide specialist training and information to non-specialist organisations; (d) develop councils for voluntary services in boroughs which lack co-ordinating bodies; and (e) support organisations which promote volunteering. In exceptional cases the Trust may fund outside of these priority areas, but in practice rarely does so.

Of the programmes, the most important, and the one that will continue to receive the greatest amount of funding, is that of transport and access for older and disabled people, closely followed by the Trust's youth programme, then the older people, technical support to voluntary organisations, and environmental conservation programmes. The categories are the result of a long policy review and consultation process in June 1996, and have been set in areas where there is a demonstrable long-term need. This being the case, it is unlikely that any truly major policy changes will occur in the near future, although the Trust is committed to on-going consultation and responsiveness to need.

Funding is only given for benefit within Greater London, reflecting the Trust's long-standing connection with the Capital. No funding is given which will in any way directly relieve any statutory body of funding which they have a duty to provide, nor will any funding be given to organisations seeking to replace the shortfall left by a cut in statutory funding.

The Trustees are open to 'match' or 'partnership' funding, they are interested in working collaboratively with other funders where more can be achieved through pooling resources. In terms of their own funding of projects and organisations, the Trustees give a large proportion of their grants in the form of project running costs (for up to a maximum of three years), and capital or revenue grants. Other forms of grant are considered, though, including pump-priming and salaries.

There is a comprehensive form for applicants which can be obtained from the Trust, and applications should be limited to the form and supporting information. This includes a photocopy of the completed application form and: two copies of the most recent audited accounts; two copies of the projected income and expenditure for the current year; a copy of the latest Annual Report; and a copy of the organisation's constitution. The applicant's information is entered into the Trust's database and then checked to see that it is complete. If anything is missing, it will be returned to be amended. A further check is made to ensure that it meets the criteria of the Trust. If it does not a recommendation will be written for it to be rejected. Those that are recommended for further consideration will then receive a visit from a Trust Officer who will assess the proposed project. The report of the Officer together with the original application is presented to the Trustees at one of their ten annual meetings.

The Trust has a grant monitoring process in place and assess all of their grants, although the Trust expects the applicant to set up their own monitoring processes as well

SAMPLE GRANTS

The top ten grants given in 1997 were:
£815,000 to Peabody Trust towards a social and community centre in a ground-breaking scheme offering housing, social and community services
£428,000 over two years to London Wildlife Trust to increase community participation in the conservation of London's natural heritage
£400,000 to Centrepoint towards work aiming to prevent homelessness amongst young people and towards a young runaways' refuge
£400,000 to the London Playing Fields Society to develop changing facilities for young women and to improve disabled access
£300,000 to Interchange Trust towards the purchase of land for a children and young people's arts centre and facilities for young disabled people
£299,773 over two years to Hackney Community Transport towards the development of a co-ordinating centre for special needs transport provision
£277,552 to London Connection over three years towards extending the opening of the day centre for young homeless people to seven days a week
£220,000 to Jewish Care towards a special day centre for people suffering from Alzheimer's disease
£191,232 to SHARE Community for the renovation of SHARE's training facilities, including disabled toilets, for disabled people
£180,000 to the Foundation for Young Musicians over three years towards a salary and running costs at the Centre for Young Musicians
Please note that the majority of grants were considerably smaller

■ The Briggs Animal Welfare Trust

WHAT IS FUNDED Animals in distress caused by man including: endangered species; nature reserves; animal welfare; cats, catteries and other facilities for cats; dogs, kennels and other facilities for dogs; and horses, stables and other facilities for horses; and wildlife sanctuaries

WHAT IS NOT FUNDED No grants for expeditions or scholarships

WHO CAN BENEFIT Organisations working in the fields outlined above benefiting animals in distress

WHERE FUNDING CAN BE GIVEN UK, Europe and Africa

SAMPLE GRANTS £1,000 to RSPCA
£1,000 to Brooke Hospital for Animals, Cairo
£1,000 to Born Free Foundation
£1,000 to Cranmer Cat Sanctuary
£1,000 to North Clwyd Animal Rescue
£1,000 to Sebakwe Black Rhino
£1,000 to Thoroughbred Rehabilitation Centre
£1,000 to Bleakholt Sanctuary
£1,000 to CEWA Hammond Trust
£1,000 to Woodside Animal Welfare

FINANCES
- Year 1997
- Income £31,818
- Grants £31,000

TRUSTEES A J Hartnett, L M Hartnett

HOW TO APPLY In writing to the address below, enclosing an sae

WHO TO APPLY TO Mrs A J Hartnett, The Briggs Animal Welfare Trust, Belmoredean. Maplehurst Road, West Grinstead, West Sussex RH13 6RN

CC NO 276459   **ESTABLISHED** 1978

■ British Sugar Foundation (formerly Bristar Foundation)

WHAT IS FUNDED General charitable purposes including environmental issues, nature reserves and woodlands

WHAT IS NOT FUNDED Generally not large national organisations. Applications from individuals, including students are not eligible. No overseas aid. No grants to animal charities

WHO CAN BENEFIT Volunteer organisations only

WHERE FUNDING CAN BE GIVEN Communities local to British Sugar sites only. Areas include Lincolnshire, Nottinghamshire, Shropshire, Worcestershire, Norfolk, Peterborough, Suffolk and York

TYPE OF GRANT Usually one-off for specific project

Britten-Pears

Alphabetical register of grant making trusts

FINANCES
- Year 1997
- Income £94,000
- Grants £94,000

PUBLICATIONS Policy and Guidelines

NOTES Projects inspired by company employees and benefiting the communities in which company employees and their families live, will receive special attention

HOW TO APPLY At any time in writing to the address below

WHO TO APPLY TO The Secretary, British Sugar Foundation, Oundle Road, Peterborough, Cambridgeshire PE2 9QU
Tel 01733 422902
Fax 01733 422487
E-mail amacdoug@britishsugar.co.uk

CC NO 290966   **ESTABLISHED** 1984

■ The Britten-Pears Foundation (438)

WHAT IS FUNDED Environmental issues; landscapes; nature reserves; waterways; wildlife parks and wildlife sanctuaries

WHAT IS NOT FUNDED Grants are not given for: general charitable purposes; festivals other than Aldeburgh; individual scholarships, bursaries and course grants other than those for Britten-Pears School; the purchase or restoration of equipment; or capital projects

WHO CAN BENEFIT Environmental organisations

WHERE FUNDING CAN BE GIVEN UK

TYPE OF GRANT One-off, project and research. Funding may be given for one year or less, or more than three years

RANGE OF GRANTS £100–£2,500

FINANCES
- Year 1996
- Income £1,182,041
- Grants £292,141

TRUSTEES Michael Berkley, Sir Robert Carnwath, Peter Carter, Hugh Cobbe, David Drew, Mark Fisher, MP, Dr Colin Matthews, Dr Donald Mitchell, Noel Periton, Prof Rhian Samuel, Marion Thorpe (Chair), Sir John Tooley

HOW TO APPLY To the General Director in writing. Telephone for guidelines if required

WHO TO APPLY TO General Director, The Britten-Pears Foundation, Unit 4G Leroy House, 436 Essex Road, London N1 3QP
Tel 0171-359 5552
Fax 0717-288 0252
E-mail britten@verger.demon.co.uk

CC NO 295595   **ESTABLISHED** 1986

Commentary

The Britten-Pears Foundation was established on 11 November 1986 to: (a) promote the musical works and writing of Benjamin Britten and Peter Pears, and the principals of musical education and performance developed by them; and (b) generally to encourage and promote the knowledge, teaching and practice of music and the arts. The Foundation is also the owner of the Britten-Pears Library at Aldeburgh, Suffolk.

The principal activities of the Foundation are: (i) the furtherance of music by living composers; (ii) the promotion of live performance, commissions and recordings; and (iii) musical educational projects. Funding is also given to environmental issues; gay and lesbian rights; support to voluntary and community organisations; and the advancement of peace. It is not known if there is a scale of preference within the funding policies of the Foundation.

The Foundation's objects do not permit the funding of statutory bodies or the replacement of statutory funding. The Foundation does take part in co-funding with other organisations,

One-off, project and research grants are made; however, the Foundation does not make loans.

Applications should be by letter containing both project and budgetary information. Decisions are made by the Foundation's Grants Panel (comprising four of the Trustees) on a case by case basis

SAMPLE GRANTS

The top ten grants made by the Trust in 1996 are not known as no grants list was issued with the Annual Accounts for that year

■ The Bromley Trust

WHAT IS FUNDED Preservation of the world environment; preservation of rainforests; and national and international conservation issues

WHAT IS NOT FUNDED Non-registered charities and individuals. No grants for expeditions or scholarships

WHO CAN BENEFIT National schemes and organisations, and international organisations

WHERE FUNDING CAN BE GIVEN UK and overseas

TYPE OF GRANT Mainly recurrent: one-off grants are occasionally made, but these are rare. It is our declared policy to give larger amounts to fewer charities rather than to spread our income over a large number of small grants. Buildings, capital, core costs, project, research, recurring costs, running costs, salaries and start-up costs will be considered. Funding can be given for any length of time

RANGE OF GRANTS £250–£10,000

SAMPLE GRANTS Greenpeace Environmental Trust
Worldwide Land Conservation Trust
Birdlife International
Fauna and Flora International
British Butterfly Conservation Society
Wildfowl and Wetlands Trust
Wildlife Conservation Research Unit
Countryside Restoration Trust
Jersey Wildlife Preservation Trust

FINANCES
- Year 1997–98
- Income £168,624
- Grants £163,050

TRUSTEES Keith Bromley, Anna Home OBE, Alan P Humphries, Lady Ann Wood, Lady Anne Prance, Peter Winfield

NOTES The Trustees meet twice a year, usually in April and October. Urgent appeals may be dealt with at any time

HOW TO APPLY To the address under Who To Apply To in writing. Single general information sheet sent on request

WHO TO APPLY TO Keith Bromley, The Bromley Trust, Ashley Manor, King's Somborne, Stockbridge, Hampshire SO20 6RQ
Tel 01794 388241
Fax 01794 388264

CC NO 801875   **ESTABLISHED** 1989

■ The Charles Brotherton Trust

WHAT IS FUNDED Charities working in the fields of: landscapes; nature reserves; waterways; woodlands; and wildlife parks

WHAT IS NOT FUNDED No grants to individuals – only to registered charities and recognised bodies

WHO CAN BENEFIT Organisations only

WHERE FUNDING CAN BE GIVEN Birmingham, Liverpool, Wirral, Wakefield, York, Leeds, Borough of Bebington (Cheshire)

TYPE OF GRANT Buildings, capital, core costs, one-off, project, research, recurring costs, running costs and salaries will be considered. Funding may be given for up to three years

RANGE OF GRANTS £100–£350

FINANCES
- Year 1996
- Income £88,000
- Grants £80,000

TRUSTEES D R Brotherton (Custodian), C M Brotherton-Ratcliffe, J S Riches, Management: D R Brotherton, Mrs A Henson, Mrs P L M H Seeley, C M Brotherton-Ratcliffe

HOW TO APPLY Applicants Annual Accounts are required. Applications not acknowledged. Distribution made annually in June for successful applications received by 31 January

WHO TO APPLY TO C Brotherton-Ratcliffe, Secretary, The Charles Brotherton Trust, PO Box 374, Harrogate, North Yorkshire HG1 4YW

CC NO 227067   **ESTABLISHED** 1940

■ Audrey and Stanley Burton 1960 Charitable Trust (376)

WHAT IS FUNDED Grants are given for specific charitable purposes including: rural conservation; bird sanctuaries; horses, stables and other facilities for horses; and wildlife sanctuaries. Preference is given to charities in Yorkshire

WHAT IS NOT FUNDED No grants are made to individuals. New charities must provide detailed information and accounts

WHO CAN BENEFIT Registered charities working in the areas outlined above

WHERE FUNDING CAN BE GIVEN North East England, particularly Darlington and Durham; Liverpool; Manchester; Yorkshire and Humberside. Also Europe and Africa

TYPE OF GRANT Preferably one-off donations and project grants. Funding may be given for up to three years

FINANCES
- Year 1997
- Income £389,018
- Grants £379,395

TRUSTEES Amanda C Burton, Audrey R Burton, Deborah M Hazan, Phillip E Morris, David J Solomon

HOW TO APPLY In writing to the Trust Managers. Unsuccessful applications are not necessarily acknowledged

WHO TO APPLY TO Audrey and Stanley Burton 1960 Charitable Trust, Trustee Management Ltd, 27 East Parade, Leeds LS1 5SX
Tel 0113-297 8782

CC NO 1028430   **ESTABLISHED** 1960

Commentary

The Audrey and Stanley Burton 1960 Charitable Trust was created under a Trust Deed in 1960 by the late Stanley H Burton.

The funding policies of the Trust were originally set out in the Trust Deed of 1960. It was created to support general charitable purposes in the UK and overseas. The Trustees currently prefer to make grants for specific charitable purposes, and particularly to organisations involved in health, the arts, education, conservation and social needs. There are no stated scales of preference within these areas of interest.

Burton

The Trustees have total discretion concerning where grants should be made. Grants are made to organisations throughout the UK, but particular favour is given to those in the Yorkshire area.

It is not known whether the Trust will make grants to statutory bodies or replace statutory funding. Neither is the Trust's attitude to co-funding known, or whether it will make loans or support infrastructure costs. The Trust prefers to make one-off grants. It will not make grants to individuals.

Applications should be in writing to the Trust Managers. Unsuccessful applications are not necessarily acknowledged

SAMPLE GRANTS
The top ten grants made in 1997 were:
£82,600 to Oxfam
£77,986 to the Mental Health Foundation
60530 to Actionaid
£52,300 to JPAIME
£20,000 to DFS Extension Charitable Trust
£13,000 to the Jerusalem Foundation
£12,000 to United World College of Atlanta
£10,000 to Children in Crisis
£10,000 to University of York
£10,000 to Leeds Grand Theatre and Opera House

Tel 01394 285537
Fax 01394 670073

CC NO 290854   **ESTABLISHED** 1984

■ The Geoffrey Burton Charitable Trust

WHAT IS FUNDED General charitable purposes including environmental issues; fauna; flora; nature reserves; waterways and woodlands

WHAT IS NOT FUNDED No grants to individuals

WHO CAN BENEFIT Organisations in the UK

WHERE FUNDING CAN BE GIVEN Suffolk

TYPE OF GRANT Buildings, capital, core costs, project, research and recurring costs. Funding is given for one year or less

RANGE OF GRANTS 45 grants in year, largest to Blond McIndoe

SAMPLE GRANTS £2,500 to Suffolk Wildlife Trust for butterfly project
£2,000 to RSPB for excavation and renovation work at Berney Marshes
£1,000 to Suffolk Wildlife Trust for heathlands appeal

FINANCES
- Year 1997–98
- Income £52,815
- Grants £32,681

TRUSTEES E de B Nash, E E Maule

HOW TO APPLY To the address under Who To Apply To in writing

WHO TO APPLY TO E E Maule, The Geoffrey Burton Charitable Trust, 1 Gainsborough Road, Felixstowe, Suffolk IP11 7HT

■ CHK Charities Limited (151)

WHAT IS FUNDED There are no restrictions upon the type of project funded. Funding may be given for animal welfare and conservation and preservation

WHAT IS NOT FUNDED No grants are made to individuals

WHO CAN BENEFIT Registered charities working in the areas outlined above

WHERE FUNDING CAN BE GIVEN UK, especially Gloucestershire

TYPE OF GRANT Start-up capital costs and ongoing expenses (three to five years)

RANGE OF GRANTS £2,000–£5,000

FINANCES
- Year 1998
- Income £1,786,177
- Grants £1,239,532

TRUSTEES D A E R Peake (Chairman), D A Acland, Mrs S E Acland, Mrs K S Assheton, Mrs C S Heber Percy, Mrs L H Morris, Mrs S Peake, Mrs J A S Prest

HOW TO APPLY To the Administrator in writing, enclosing a copy of the most recent Annual Accounts

WHO TO APPLY TO The Administrator, CHK Charities Limited, PO Box 191, 10 Fenchurch Street, London EC3M 3LB
Tel 0171-956 6246

CC NO 1050900   **ESTABLISHED** 1995

Commentary

CHK Charities Limited, formerly the Sir Cyril Kleinwort Charitable Trust, was originally formed in 1963. When Kleinwort Benson was taken over in 1995 by the Dresdner Bank Group a new trust was formed using £11 million from Sir Cyril Kleinwort Charitable Trust and an injection of new capital. The organisation is still a family trust, with the Trustees coming from branches of the original settlor's family.

The Charities fund a very wide range of causes, and particularly encourage applications from organisations working in these eighteen different areas: animal welfare and disease; artistic causes; blindness/deafness; care of the elderly; conservation/preservation; countryside matters; crime prevention; disabled/handicapped treatment and care; drug abuse prevention and treatment; education; employment and job creation; general medical research; general welfare and social problems; homeless/housing; hospices; hospital/nursing home building and equipment; population control; and youth care. The above areas are all given an equal priority for receiving funding, with the Charities being totally reactive to applications they receive. With the relative newness of CHK Charities, they have not yet undergone a full review of their own grant making; however, one is scheduled for 1999. It is anticipated that there may be some shifts in emphasis as a result, although the overall policies of the organisation are unlikely to change.

Charities from Gloucestershire are given priority as the family come from the county, but applications from anywhere else in the UK will be considered, as well as national charities. The CHK Charities are unable to consider applications from individuals or very localised charities, for example church appeals, unless they are in Gloucestershire.

The Trustees will not support the replacement of statutory funding, although on rare occasions they may consider making grants for costs not covered by statutory funding, for example for medical equipment or research. The Charities tend not to match fund with other charitable trusts, as there is a feeling that the organisation is large enough to stand alone. On the other hand, there is a positive attitude towards match funding with European funds, and organisations that apply to the Charities with either Lottery or European funding will be looked upon favourably – partly because any such organisations will have been investigated fully.

Grants are generally given in the range £2,000 to £5,000, and are given for capital costs and for start-up funding (generally over three to five years). The Trustees are particularly keen on start-up funding, as they find it gratifying to help a charity or project get off of the ground. Revenue funding is a much lower priority. Loans may be given for shortfall funding for charities, but these loans are only likely to happen when there is an existing relationship.

Applications should be made in a letter to the Administrator enclosing a set of accounts. There is no application form. All applications are acknowledged when they are first received, but only those which are successful will be contacted again, generally after two to three months.

When an application is received, and approximately 20 are received daily, they are split up into the eighteen different categories by the Administrator and the Chairman of the Trustees. Those applications that are unsuitable will be responded to immediately. The Trustees examine the rest and pass their decisions back to the Administrator, who will tell the applicant that they have been successful.

The monitoring and evaluation of grants depends upon whether the grant is one-off or a series of payments. For one-off payments the Trustees do not generally expect a detailed report, though they do require receipts for equipment and services that the grant pays for. For grants over a number of years, reports are required annually, and have to be provided for funding to continue. Visits are not generally made to projects either before or after a grant has been made

SAMPLE GRANTS
The top ten grants given in 1997 were:
£100,000 to DGAA Homelife
£91,032 to the Durrell Institute of Conservation & Ecology
£82,500 to the Royal Shakespeare Theatre, Stratford upon Avon
£50,000 to Brace – Alzheimer's research
£51,500 to the British Museum
£50,000 to Education 2000 Trust
£50,000 to Home-Start
£35,000 to Life Education Centre
£25,000 to Goldsmiths College
£20,000 to Margaret Pyke Memorial Trust

■ Richard Cadbury Charitable Trust

WHAT IS FUNDED This Trust is willing to support: rural conservation; animal facilities and services; and environmental and animal sciences

WHAT IS NOT FUNDED Registered charities only. No student grants or support of individuals

WHO CAN BENEFIT Organisations working in the areas outlined above

WHERE FUNDING CAN BE GIVEN Mainly local to Birmingham, Worcester and Coventry

TYPE OF GRANT One-off for capital and buildings (preferred). Funding is available for one year or less

RANGE OF GRANTS £200–£1,000

FINANCES
- Year 1997
- Income £43,534
- Grants £42,000

TRUSTEES R B Cadbury, Mrs M M Eardley, D G Slora, Miss J A Slora

NOTES Restricted from small unregistered groups

HOW TO APPLY By letter including costings and current set of accounts if appropriate. Trustee meetings held February, June and October

WHO TO APPLY TO Mrs M M Eardley, Administrator, Richard Cadbury Charitable Trust, 6 Middleborough Road, Coventry, West Midlands CV1 4DE

CC NO 224348   **ESTABLISHED** 1948

■ William Adlington Cadbury Charitable Trust (292)

WHAT IS FUNDED In the West Midlands: the environment and conservation work. In the UK: UK environmental education programmes. Fund may be given for rural conservation; bird sanctuaries; horses, stables and other facilities for horses; wildlife sanctuaries; wildlife parks; zoos; and ornithology and zoology

WHAT IS NOT FUNDED The Trust does not fund: individuals (whether for research, expeditions or educational purposes, etc); local projects or groups outside the West Midlands; or projects concerned with travel or adventure.

WHO CAN BENEFIT Organisations serving Birmingham and the West Midlands, organisations whose work has a national significance, organisations outside the West Midlands where the Trust has well-established links, organisations in Ireland, and UK based charities working overseas

WHERE FUNDING CAN BE GIVEN Birmingham and the West Midlands, Ireland, overseas

TYPE OF GRANT Specific grant applications are favoured. Grants are generally one-off or for projects of one year or less. The Trust will consider building grants, capital, core and running costs, start-up costs and research. Grants are not usually awarded on an annual basis, except to a small number of charities for revenue costs. Grants are only made to or through registered charities and range from £100 to £5,000. Larger grants are seldom awarded. Major appeals are considered by Trustees at meetings in May and November. Small grants of up to £500 are made on a continuing basis under the Trust's Small Grants Programme

FINANCES
- Year 1998
- Income £571,394
- Grants £535,978

TRUSTEES Brandon Cadbury, Rupert A Cadbury, Mrs Katherine van Hagen Cadbury, John C Penny, Mrs C M Salmon, Mrs Sarah Stafford, Mrs Hannah H Taylor, W James B Taylor, Adrian D M Thomas

PUBLICATIONS Policy Statement and Guidelines for Applicants

NOTES Telephone calls should only be made in the mornings

HOW TO APPLY There is no formal application form. Applicants should write to the Secretary giving the charity's registration number, a brief description of the charity's activities, and details of the specific project for which a grant is being sought. Applicants should also include a budget of the proposed work together with a copy of the charity's most recent Accounts.

Trustees will also wish to know what funds have already been raised for the project and how the shortfall is going to be met. Applications are not acknowledged unless accompanied by a stamped, addressed envelope. The Trust encourages applications from ethnic minority groups and women-led initiatives. The Trust receives more applications than it is able to support. Even if an appeal falls within the Trust's policy, they may not be able to help, particularly if the project is outside the West Midlands

WHO TO APPLY TO Mrs Christine M Stober, Secretary to the Trustees, William Adlington Cadbury Charitable Trust, 2 College Walk, Selly Oak, Birmingham B29 6LQ
Tel 0121-472 1464

CC NO 213629   **ESTABLISHED** 1923

Commentary

The William Adlington Cadbury Charitable Trust was established on 21 December 1923 by William Adlington Cadbury, for general charitable purposes. The Founder lived in the Birmingham area and this is now reflected in the preference given by the Trustees to appeals from the West Midlands area. It is a family Trust in which all the Trustees are family members. The Trust sometimes works with the Barrow Cadbury Trust, advising each other about potential applicants.

The Trust will support charities working in various different fields. In Birmingham and the West Midlands it will support: churches of The Religious Society of Friends (Quakers) and other churches; medical causes, including hospitals and nursing homes, and health care projects; social welfare – community groups, children and young people, the elderly, people with disabilities, the homeless, housing initiatives, and counselling and mediation agencies; education and training – schools and universities, adult literacy schemes and employment training; the environment and conservation work; preservation – museums and art galleries; the arts – music, drama and visual arts; and penal affairs – work with offenders and ex-offenders and police projects. In the UK the Trust will support: The Religious Society of Friends (Quakers); UK medical research; education projects which have a national significance; UK environmental education programmes; the preservation of listed buildings and monuments; penal affairs, such as penal reform and work with offenders and ex-offenders; and Ireland for cross community health and social welfare projects. Internationally the Trust will support: UK charities working overseas on long-term development projects.

The Trustees have absolute discretion to distribute the Trust's income to charitable institutions and the funding policies are set at their discretion. The policies were originally set in the Trust Deed in 1923, but in 1993–94 the policies were greatly narrowed down, from simply general charitable purposes, to the situation in force today. This was done to try to reduce the vast number of applications that were being received each year, because far more were being received than could possibly be dealt with, and the Trustees felt that by narrowing the range of causes supported by the Trust, they could better target their grant making.

Within the priorities outlined above, preference is given to charities within the West Midlands, followed then by charities working outside the West Midlands and finally by UK based charities working abroad. Even if an application falls within the funding policies, if it is outside the West Midlands area it is much less likely to be supported.

The Trust supports statutory bodies in the sense that it has made several grants to schools, the police and to the Royal Orthopaedic Hospital in Birmingham, but it will not replace statutory funding. It may, however, consider meeting a shortfall in funding. The Trust is prepared to consider co-funding, for example with the National Lottery, but it is up to the applicant to obtain the balance of the funds needed from the 'co-funder'. The Trust prefers to make grants for specific projects, for example for new equipment, but they will occasionally give revenue grants. They will also support infrastructure costs. The range of grants given by the Trust normally fall between £100 and £5,000. Interest free loans are given to some applicants, and in 1997 loans were made to a total of £20,000.

There is no formal application form, so applicants should write to the Secretary giving the charity's registration number, a brief description of the charity's activities, and details of the specific project for which a grant is being sought. Applicants should also include a budget of the proposed work together with a copy of the charity's most recent accounts. Trustees will also wish to know what funds have already been raised for the project and how the shortfall is going to be met. Applications are not acknowledged unless accompanied by a stamped, addressed envelope. The Trust encourages applications from ethnic minority groups and women-led initiatives. The Trust receives more applications than it is able to support, so even if an appeal falls within the Trust's policy, they may not be able to help, particularly if the project is outside the West Midlands.

The Trustees meet twice a year to consider applications, and if an application is successful at this point it will then receive an application form. Applications are assessed firstly to see if it falls within the Trust's funding preferences, and secondly, by whether or not the project is of interest to the Trustees at that point in time. In

Cadogan

1997–98, 1,020 applications were received. One Trustee can authorise grants of up to £500 under the Trust's small grants programme, but larger grants must be considered at the Trustees meetings. Grant applicants or recipients are rarely ever visited

SAMPLE GRANTS

The top ten grants awarded in 1997–98 were:
£30,000 to Medical Foundation for Victims of Torture
£30,000 to Vaccine Research Trust
£20,000 to Save the Children
£10,000 to Birmingham Settlement
£10,000 to British Red Cross
£10,000 to City of Belfast YMCA
£10,000 to the Karuna Trust for work in India
£10,000 to the National Gallery of Ireland
£10,000 to Oxfam for work in Uganda and South Africa
£10,000 to Quaker Peace and Service
£10,000 to Ulster Guide Association

■The Cadogan Charity (296)

WHAT IS FUNDED The Charity will consider funding: endangered species; animal welfare; and dogs, kennels and other facilities for dogs

WHAT IS NOT FUNDED No grants are made to individuals

WHO CAN BENEFIT Charities and organisations working in the areas outlined above

WHERE FUNDING CAN BE GIVEN London, with a preference for the Borough of Kensington & Chelsea, and Perth and the surrounding area in Scotland

TYPE OF GRANT Support is usually given over one to two years, although some one-off grants may be made

FINANCES
- Year 1997
- Income £695,887
- Grants £524,800

TRUSTEES The Rt Hon The Eighth Earl Cadogan, DL, Countess Cadogan, The Dowager Countess Cadogan, Viscount Chelsea

HOW TO APPLY Applications in writing, including some background on the specifics of the appeal as well as a set of recent accounts if available

WHO TO APPLY TO Mrs B J Wizard, Secretary to the Earl Cadogan, The Cadogan Charity, 18 Cadogan Gardens, London SW3 2RP

CC NO 247773   **ESTABLISHED** 1966

Commentary

The Trust was originally known as Earl Cadogan's Charity and was formed by the Seventh Earl Cadogan under a Deed of Trust dated 31 March 1966 to represent the families interest in charity.

In 1996 the Trustees of Viscount Chelsea's Charity resolved to transfer their whole trust fund to the Trustees of Earl Cadogan's Charity, and to combine the Trusts into one, whereupon the name was changed to The Cadogan Charity.

Although the Trustees have a free rein in terms of what the Charity is able to support, in practice the giving is concentrated upon medical charities, and predominantly medical research charities. However, the Charity will not rule out giving in other areas and in 1997 they supported social welfare charities, children's charities, education bodies, community organisations, arts organisations and animal welfare charities. The Charity's priority area of medical support is a long established one and is unlikely to change in the near future. Any minor changes in policy are set at the Trustee meetings, when they may be influenced by the funding requests that are under discussion. Grants are made in Perth and the surrounding area in Scotland, and in the Borough of Kensington & Chelsea in London, where the Cadogan family has strong historical connections. Preference is given to those charities with whom a direct family member is involved.

The Charity will not become involved where there is a government responsibility to fund a project or an organisation. However, support can be given for appeals of the kind not covered by statutory responsibility, for example hospital appeals for a specific piece of equipment. The Charity does not become involved in any form of pre-arranged partnership funding, although they are more than happy to be one of many co-funders of a project or organisation. Applications arising as a result of a lottery grant are considered using the same criteria as any other application. The Charity has a nucleus of grant recipients which they fund on a regular basis, but one-off grants may also be made if there is a particular appeal that requires a single grant. No loans are made. When grants are given the Trustees prefer to see the money reaching those areas that are involved in the direct tackling of the problem, and for this reason they tend not to give grants for the infrastructure costs of an organisation.

Applications should be made to the Earl Cadogan's secretary, and should contain some background on the specific appeal, and a copy of the most recent Annual Report and Accounts. Applications are filtered initially before being discussed by the Trustees, and with so many applications received they may be rejected if they are poorly presented or do not contain adequate information. The Trustees do not meet at regular intervals throughout the year, but three Trustee meetings a year take place when applications may be discussed.

After a grant has been given, the Charity does not have a formal assessment process, although where there is already a relationship between the

Trust and the grant recipient (as is often the case) there is likely to be some form of contact. Also, the Trustees often have contact with the Trustees of other charities, and so they are able to keep track of some of their grant making that way

SAMPLE GRANTS
The top ten grants made in 1997 were:
£60,000 to Royal Veterinary College
£50,000 to St Wilfrids
£45,000 to Dockland Settlements
£25,000 to NSPCC
£20,000 to Covent Garden Royal Opera House Appeal
£15,000 to Christ Church Primary School
£15,000 to Imperial Cancer Research Fund
£15,000 to Leukaemia Research Fund
£15,000 to WNCCC Cancer Aware
£12,000 to St Mary's Church, Birnam

■ Calypso Browning Trust

WHAT IS FUNDED Animal welfare including: animal homes; bird sanctuaries; cats, catteries and other facilities for cats; dogs, kennels and other facilities for dogs; and horses, stables and other facilities for horses. Regular grants made to some chosen charities but do include occasional new charities in line with trust funding policies

WHAT IS NOT FUNDED No grants to individuals

WHO CAN BENEFIT Organisations benefiting animals

WHERE FUNDING CAN BE GIVEN UK

TYPE OF GRANT Core costs, recurring costs and running costs

RANGE OF GRANTS £500–£4,664

SAMPLE GRANTS £1,000 to People's Dispensary for Sick Animals
£1,000 to RSPCA
£500 to the Donkey Sanctuary

FINANCES
- Year 1998
- Income £37,335
- Grants £37,039

TRUSTEES A B S Weir, Mrs J M Kapp

HOW TO APPLY By letter to the address under Who To Apply To

WHO TO APPLY TO Calypso Browning Trust, Tweedie & Prideaux, Solicitors, 5 Lincoln's Inn Fields, London WC2A 3BT

CC NO 281986   **ESTABLISHED** 1979

■ The Canine Supporters Charity

WHAT IS FUNDED Academic and practical study, and opportunities to bring people together to discuss dogs

WHO CAN BENEFIT Registered charities and organisations associated with dogs

WHERE FUNDING CAN BE GIVEN UK

FINANCES
- Year 1996–97
- Income £20,528
- Grants £18,500

TRUSTEES The Committee: Mrs H Morse, Mrs K le Mare, K Forrest, M Harvey, Mrs B Harvey, M Mcmillan, G Payne, Mrs L Skeritt, Mrs L Burtenshaw, P Burtenshaw, Mrs S Clark, Ms A Messenger

WHO TO APPLY TO K M Forrest, The Canine Supporters Charity, Wey Farm, Guildford Road, Ottershaw, Surrey KT16 0QW

CC NO 289046   **ESTABLISHED** 1984

■ The W A Cargill Charitable Trust

WHAT IS FUNDED Animals and wildlife

WHO CAN BENEFIT Organisations working in the areas outlined above

WHERE FUNDING CAN BE GIVEN Scotland

FINANCES
- Year 1996
- Income £90,000
- Grants £80,000

TRUSTEES A C Fyfe, W G Peacock, N A Fyfe, Mirren E Graham

HOW TO APPLY Applications should be made in writing to the address below

WHO TO APPLY TO Alexander C Fyfe, The W A Cargill Charitable Trust, 190 St Vincent Street, Glasgow G2 5SP

SC NO SCO 12076   **ESTABLISHED** 1954

■ Carnegie Dunfermline Trust

WHAT IS FUNDED Social, educational, cultural and recreational purposes in Dunfermline and its immediate environs including: environmental issues; animal welfare; and wildlife sanctuaries

WHAT IS NOT FUNDED Operates only within Dunfermline and its immediate environs. Grants rarely given to individuals

WHO CAN BENEFIT Local clubs and societies, and special projects

WHERE FUNDING CAN BE GIVEN Dunfermline and its immediate environs only

TYPE OF GRANT Grants/loans are given for projects, equipment, and feasibility studies generally on a one-off basis

RANGE OF GRANTS £100–£75,000. Typical grant £500–£1,000

Carron

Alphabetical register of grant making trusts

SAMPLE GRANTS £5,057 to School Children's Spring Flower Show for bulbs and associated materials

FINANCES
- Year 1998
- Income £383,000
- Grants £320,000

TRUSTEES Appointed in terms of Royal Charter

PUBLICATIONS Several, all related to Dumfermline area

HOW TO APPLY To the address under Who To Apply To. Initial telephone calls are welcome. Application forms and guidelines available. There are no deadlines for applications. Sae is not required. Applications considered monthly

WHO TO APPLY TO The Secretary, Carnegie Dunfermline Trust, Abbey Park House, Dunfermline, Fife KY12 7PB
Tel 01383 723638
Fax 01383 721862

SC NO SCO 00729   **ESTABLISHED** 1903

■ The Carron Charitable Trust

WHAT IS FUNDED Applications from charities linked to wildlife and the countryside including: fauna and flora, lakes, landscapes, nature reserves; woodlands; wildlife parks and wildlife sanctuaries

WHAT IS NOT FUNDED No grants to individuals

WHO CAN BENEFIT Organisations working in the areas outlined above

WHERE FUNDING CAN BE GIVEN UK and overseas

TYPE OF GRANT Project, research, recurring costs and salaries

FINANCES
- Year 1998
- Income £43,541
- Grants £24,182

TRUSTEES P G Fowler, Mrs J Wells, W M Allen, D L Morgan, FCA

HOW TO APPLY **Almost all of the Charity's funds are committed for the foreseeable future and the Trustees therefore do not invite applications from the general public**

WHO TO APPLY TO Mrs C S Cox, The Carron Charitable Trust, Messrs Rothman Pantall & Co, 10 Romsey Road, Eastleigh, Hampshire SO50 9AL
Tel 01703 614555

CC NO 289164   **ESTABLISHED** 1984

■ The Leslie Mary Carter Charitable Trust

WHAT IS FUNDED The Trustees prefer well thought-out applications for larger gifts, than many applicants for smaller grants. The preferred areas for grant giving are nature conservation and wildlife. Other applications will be considered but acknowledgements may not always be sent

WHAT IS NOT FUNDED Applications for grants from individuals will not be entertained

WHO CAN BENEFIT Organisations working in the areas outlined above

WHERE FUNDING CAN BE GIVEN UK with preference for East Anglia

TYPE OF GRANT Buildings, capital, core costs, one-off, project, research, running costs and recurring costs will be considered

RANGE OF GRANTS £500–£5,000, typical grant £4,000

FINANCES
- Year 1997
- Income £66,640
- Grants £59,500

TRUSTEES Miss L M Carter, S R M Wilson

HOW TO APPLY Telephone calls are not welcome. There is no application form, guidelines, deadlines for applications or a requirement for a sae, unless the applicant wishes to have material returned

WHO TO APPLY TO S R M Wilson, The Leslie Mary Carter Charitable Trust, Messrs Birketts, 24–26 Museum Street, Ipswich, Suffolk IP1 1HZ

CC NO 284782   **ESTABLISHED** 1982

■ The Challice Trust

WHAT IS FUNDED This Trust will consider: rural conservation; animal homes and animal welfare. Help for local needs has priority

WHAT IS NOT FUNDED Only local students helped

WHO CAN BENEFIT Local organisations and individuals working in the areas outlined above

WHERE FUNDING CAN BE GIVEN Surrey

TYPE OF GRANT Small capital and maintenance

FINANCES
- Year 1998
- Income £13,282
- Grants £11,362

TRUSTEES P W Smith, Mrs B Munro Thomson, R W Edmondson, B E Farley

HOW TO APPLY By brief letter to the address below. There are no deadline dates

WHO TO APPLY TO P W Smith, The Challice Trust, 29 Poltimore Road, Guildford, Surrey GU2 5PR

CC NO 222360   **ESTABLISHED** 1962

■ Charities Aid Foundation (277)

WHAT IS FUNDED Grants are made to assist a charitable organisation: (a) improve its effectiveness in meeting its objectives; (b) improve its use of financial resources, facilities, members, staff or volunteers; (c) improve its strength or sustainability; (d) research or move into new types of activity; (e) in exceptional or unforeseen circumstances, to meet an emergency financial setback or to provide a single injection of funds to maintain the viability of the charitable organisation; (f) training needed to fulfil the above objectives; (g) staff funding in fulfilling the above (not regular/core costs). The CAF Grants Council are particularly interested in funding applications with a wide and lasting benefit and work which will improve the capacity, strength and sustainability of a charitable organisation. Any registered charity which fulfils the above objectives may apply for funding, including those working in the fields of rural conservation; animal facilities and services; and animal sciences

WHAT IS NOT FUNDED Grants will not be given for: (a) capital items, buildings, vehicles, maintenance costs; (b) core, routine or continuation costs of running or expanding the charitable organisation and associated general appeals; (c) start-up costs of a new charitable organisation; (d) academic or scientific research projects; (e) retrospective, debt, deficit or loan funding; (f) funding that should properly be the responsibility of statutory agencies; (g) support or services to individuals or other beneficiaries; (h) schools, universities and NHS trusts

WHO CAN BENEFIT Any registered (or Inland revenue approved) organisation benefiting any beneficiary group anywhere in the UK. Small and medium charitable organisations, with a maximum total income of £1 million. Preference is given to those with limited freely available funds or insufficient reserves to meet the need themselves

WHERE FUNDING CAN BE GIVEN National and UK charities working overseas

TYPE OF GRANT One-off grants and feasibility studies. Normally non-recurring and not in excess of £10,000

RANGE OF GRANTS Smallest £300, largest £10,000; average grant £4,000

FINANCES
- Year 1997–98
- Grants £576,300
- Income £636,800

TRUSTEES The Grants Council: Rev Dr Gordon Barritt, OBE, MA, John Bateman, Babu Bhattacherjee, David Carrington (Chairman), Yogesh Chauhan, Ms Gillian Crosby, Anthony Hewson, OBE, Miss Jane Lewis, ACIS, Mrs Dorothy McGahan, Prof Peter Quilliam, OBE, Ms Ceridwen Roberts, Prof Naomi Sargant, Ms Miranda Spitteler, Peter Woodward

HOW TO APPLY Meetings of the Grants Council in 1999 will take place in February, May, September and November, and applications should be submitted by the beginning of the preceding month in order to be considered at each meeting. The schedule for 2000 will be similar. An application pack including guidelines, an application form and notes for applicants is available

WHO TO APPLY TO Mrs Judith McQuillan, Grants Administrator, Charities Aid Foundation, Kings Hill, West Malling, Kent ME19 4TA
Tel 01732 520031
Fax 01732 520001
E-mail swilson@caf.charitynet.org
Web Site http://www.charitynet.org

CC NO 268369   **ESTABLISHED** 1974

Commentary

The Charities Aid Foundation began in 1924 when the National Council for Social Service (now called the National Council for Voluntary Organisations) set up a Charities Department, registered as a friendly society, named as the National Council of Social Service Benevolent Fund. Its aim was to help charities to recover tax on money donated to them by Deed of Covenant. This service developed and increased over the next 50 years and additional services were implemented, including the creation of a deposit account that enabled donors to make charitable gifts throughout their lifetime. In 1959 the Fund became known as the Charities Aid Fund and in 1967 was registered as a charity. In 1974 the Fund became a wholly independent charity and was renamed as the Charities Aid Foundation. With the Duke of Edinburgh as its Patron it was at this point that CAF began its own grant making, setting up a Grants Council for this purpose.

The Grants Council receives its income from three main sources: it receives an amount from CAF itself; it manages and distributes special funds into which CAF donors can contribute, giving them the opportunity to support particular fields of charitable activity, and the Grants Council distributes funds on behalf of trust and company clients. The Council distributes these monies within its criteria, while ensuring that funds from the last two sources benefit charities working in the fields covered by the special funds, eg environment or arts, or as specified by the clients.

The Grants Council's aim is to enable charities to achieve their purposes more effectively, ie to help charities to help themselves. It does this in several ways. Funding is offered to enable a charity to improve its management and effectiveness, for example: to improve its effectiveness in meeting its objectives; to improve its use of financial resources, facilities, members, staff or volunteers; and to improve its stability or effectiveness, or to move into new areas of need. Emergency grants may be given to meet an exceptional, unforeseen financial setback, or where a single injection of funds is required to restore the viability of the charity.

In 1998 grants were awarded in nine main areas. Most grants concerned fundraising: 17 per cent of grants were towards the cost of staff fundraisers – 22 per cent of grants were towards the cost of fundraising consultants; and 1 per cent towards fundraising material; a total of 40 per cent. The Grants Council do not have a specific policy to give preference to fundraising related appeals, it is simply that such appeals have tended to receive the most support in the past. Consultancy work received the next largest proportion of funding, with 25 per cent of grants made towards the cost of organisation review/ business planning consultants, and 10 per cent of grants made towards other consultancy costs. Project funding received 9 per cent of grants and grants to organisations suffering financial setback received 5 per cent. Grants for staff training amounted to 7 per cent and provision of training received 1 per cent. Only 3 per cent of grants were made for other (unspecified) purposes.

The funding policies of the Council were set soon after the Fund became a charity in 1974. An advisory council was established to set out the criteria under which grants would be made and these have not changed much since, but they are subject to regular review. (It should be noted that the Grants Council held a review meeting in September 1998, revised guidelines were produced in early 1999). Grants are awarded to charitable organisations throughout the UK and to UK-based charitable organisations working overseas. The Grants Council will not fund statutory bodies and will not normally replace statutory funding. However, under certain circumstances the Council may, under its emergency criteria, make a bridging grant to a charity whose statutory funding has suddenly been withdrawn or delayed. Co-funding has not occurred in the past and National Lottery bids are not assisted. Grants are normally non-recurring and range in size from under £1,000 up to £10,000. Loans are not made and infrastructure costs are not supported.

Appeals to the Grants Council should be made on an application form. An application pack is available on request which includes guidelines, an application form and notes for applicants. The Grants Council meets four times a year: in 1999 they will meet in February, May, September and November. Applications must be submitted by the beginning of the preceding month in order to be considered at the next meeting. Applications are assessed by the administrative office to ensure that they meet the Council's criteria and that sufficient information is included. Suitable applications are then sent to a member of the Council who will look at each in more detail and then lead the discussion in the Grants Council meeting. The Grants Council make recommendations to the Trustees who approve the grants to be made. There is a Trustee presence on the Grants Council. Applicants are not visited as part of the assessment procedure, but grant recipients are visited very occasionally

SAMPLE GRANTS

The top ten grants made in 1998 were:
£10,000 to Fairtrade Foundation as the third and final grant to fund research to identify producers for new Fairtrade Mark products; establish Fairtrade criteria for the products; and establish the means by which the products can be brought into the market
£8,812 to Association for Rehabilitation of Communication and Oral Skills (ARCOS) to assist in its future development by covering the fees of two consultants, one to set up appropriate management and administration systems and one to prepare a fundraising strategy
£8,708 to Living Paintings Trust to cover the fees of consultants in the prospecting and enlisting phase of a major gifts fundraising campaign
£8,648 to South East London Community Foundation to cover the fees of consultants to study and enhance the capacity of the Foundation in providing fund-holding and grant making services to regeneration and other partnerships within its area of interest
£8,150 to PHAB Scotland towards the fees of consultants to carry out a feasibility study on a possible joint structure or merger with another organisation
£7,500 to Radio Lollipop to cover fees of consultants to put together a rescue package
£7,000 to Nigel Clare Network Trust to cover the fees of a consultant to train a volunteer fundraiser and to assist in the development of a fundraising strategy
£7,000 to Poweraid to cover the fees of consultants to carry out a needs assessment, prepare a business plan and funding strategy and assist in its implementation
£7,000 to Workers Educational Association Scotland towards the salary of a development officer to consult, review and make recommendations on rationalising the structure and support required by local units and the ongoing development of the voluntary movement
£6,944 to After Adoption Wales to cover the first year's salary of a worker responsible for

implementing fundraising strategy and financial management

■ The Chase Charity

WHAT IS FUNDED Landscapes and nature reserves. The Trustees do not contribute to large general appeals, nor to annual running costs. They work over a wide field but projects in rural areas of particular interest, together with strengthening vulnerable groups. They try to make an impact with each grant. Starter finance, unforeseen capital or other expenditure, even help over a bad patch are considered. Small charities and projects are preferred

WHAT IS NOT FUNDED No grants are made for projects abroad or in Greater London; individuals; travel; expeditions; sport; endowment funds; hospices; the advancement of religion; animal welfare; medical research; formal education; festivals; individual youth clubs and uniformed youth groups; holidays; projects in receipt of Millennium Lottery Board funding; urban homeless; and other grant making bodies

WHO CAN BENEFIT Mostly small organisations, often in rural areas

WHERE FUNDING CAN BE GIVEN Great Britain, except London

TYPE OF GRANT Buildings, capital, core costs, feasibility studies, one-off, project, salaries and start-up costs. Funding is available for up to three years

RANGE OF GRANTS £1,000–£10,000

FINANCES
- Year 1997–98
- Income £313,873
- Grants £201,190

TRUSTEES The Council of Management: A Ramsay Hack (Chairman), Gordon Halcrow, Richard Mills, Elizabeth Moore, Ninian Perry, Alexander Robertson, Ann Stannard

PUBLICATIONS Annual Report; *How to Apply for a Grant*

HOW TO APPLY At any time. The Trustees meet quarterly, but there is a waiting list so projects are not often considered within three months of applying

WHO TO APPLY TO Ailsa Hornsby, The Chase Charity, 2 The Court, High Street, Harwell, Didcot, Oxfordshire OX11 0EY
Tel 01235 820044

CC NO 207108   **ESTABLISHED** 1962

■ The Chelsea Square 1994 Trust

WHAT IS FUNDED Endangered species; fauna; nature reserves; and woodland. Also animal homes and animal welfare; bird sanctuaries; cats, catteries and other facilities for cats; dogs, kennels and other facilities for dogs; and wildlife sanctuaries

WHAT IS NOT FUNDED No grants for expeditions or scholarships

WHERE FUNDING CAN BE GIVEN Southern England (including the London Boroughs of Hammersmith and Fulham, Harrow, Kensington and Chelsea, Kingston upon Thames, Richmond upon Thames, Southwark and Wandsworth); and to a limited extent Europe and Africa

TYPE OF GRANT Buildings, one-off, project and research. Funding may be given for one year or less

FINANCES
- Year 1997
- Income £49,287
- Grants £59,610

HOW TO APPLY By letter with Annual Report and Accounts. Please include an sae

WHO TO APPLY TO J B Talbot, MC, The Chelsea Square 1994 Trust, The Middle House, Chapel Road, Rowledge, Farnham, Surrey GU10 4AN

CC NO 1040479   **ESTABLISHED** 1994

■ The Chestnut Trust

WHAT IS FUNDED The conservation of wildlife and the environment

WHO CAN BENEFIT Charitable organisations working in the areas outlined above

WHERE FUNDING CAN BE GIVEN UK and overseas

TYPE OF GRANT Project and recurring costs

FINANCES
- Year 1997
- Income £3,601
- Grants £4,001

TRUSTEES A R Jenkinson, G M Jenkinson

HOW TO APPLY In writing to the address below

WHO TO APPLY TO A R Jenkinson, The Chestnut Trust, Padley Knoll, Nether Padley, Grindleford, Hope Valley, S32 2HE

CC NO 326360   **ESTABLISHED** 1983

■ The Chiron Trust

WHAT IS FUNDED Support is given in the fields of nature reserves, woodlands, animal welfare, and organic food production

WHAT IS NOT FUNDED No funding for expeditions or travel bursaries

WHO CAN BENEFIT Registered charities working in the areas outlined above

WHERE FUNDING CAN BE GIVEN England, particularly North East, North West and Eastern regions and London

TYPE OF GRANT Buildings, core costs, running costs and start-up costs will be considered. Funding is available for up to three years

RANGE OF GRANTS £250–£1,000

FINANCES
- Year 1997
- Income £113,747
- Grants £144,323

TRUSTEES D M Tinson, C J Du B Tinson, I R Marks

HOW TO APPLY In writing, no application forms

WHO TO APPLY TO Mrs D M Tinson, The Chiron Trust, 30 Fitzwalter Road, Colchester, Essex CO3 3SY

CC NO 287062   **ESTABLISHED** 1983

■ The Cinderford Charitable Trust

WHAT IS FUNDED Wildlife. The bulk of the income is given to charities which have been supported over many years

WHAT IS NOT FUNDED No grants to individuals

WHO CAN BENEFIT Organisations only

WHERE FUNDING CAN BE GIVEN UK

TYPE OF GRANT Buildings, capital, core costs, endowments, feasibility studies, interest free loans, one-off, project, research, recurring costs, running costs, salaries and start-up costs. Funding for up to and over three years is available

SAMPLE GRANTS £7,883 to World Wildlife Fund

FINANCES
- Year 1997
- Income £162,357
- Grants £192,750

TRUSTEES R J Clark, R McLeod

WHO TO APPLY TO R J Clark, The Cinderford Charitable Trust, 2 Bloomsbury Street, London WC1B 3ST

CC NO 286525   **ESTABLISHED** 1983

■ J A Clark Charitable Trust

WHAT IS FUNDED Preservation of the earth including conservation of fauna and flora, and environmental issues

WHAT IS NOT FUNDED No support for independent schools (except special needs), conservation of buildings or for individuals

WHO CAN BENEFIT Organisations working in the areas outlined above

WHERE FUNDING CAN BE GIVEN The south west of England and overseas

TYPE OF GRANT One-off for up to three years, including start-up costs

RANGE OF GRANTS £500–£10,000

FINANCES
- Year 1997
- Income £171,125
- Grants £141,637

TRUSTEES Lancelot Pease Clark, John Cyprus Clark, Thomas Aldenham Clark, Caroline Pym, Aidan J R Pelly

HOW TO APPLY Written application with project details plus most recent Accounts. Receipt of applications will not be acknowledged. All applications are, however, considered and a small number are contacted with a request for a formal application. Trustees grant allocation meeting October/November

WHO TO APPLY TO The Secretary, J A Clark Charitable Trust, PO Box 1704, Glastonbury, Somerset BA16 0YB

CC NO 1010520   **ESTABLISHED** 1992

■ The Late Miss Doris Evelyn Clarke's Charitable Trust

WHAT IS FUNDED Donations primarily made to animal charities chosen from a list provided by the settlor

WHO CAN BENEFIT Established organisations as outlined above

WHERE FUNDING CAN BE GIVEN UK

TYPE OF GRANT Recurrent

RANGE OF GRANTS £205–£4,285

SAMPLE GRANTS £4,285 to Royal Society for the Prevention of Cruelty to Animals
£1,920 to the Cats' Protection League
£1,920 to the Donkey Sanctuary
£1,920 to Blue Cross Animals' Hospital
£445 to the Guide Dogs for the Blind Association
£445 to National Canine Defence League
£445 to People's Dispensary for Sick Animals
£205 to Battersea Dogs' Home
£205 to League Against Cruel Sports

£205 to Horses and Ponies Protection Association

FINANCES
- Year 1996
- Income £13,555
- Grants £13,659

TRUSTEES The Royal Bank of Scotland plc

PUBLICATIONS Annual Accounts

HOW TO APPLY In writing at any time to the address below

WHO TO APPLY TO The Late Miss Doris Evelyn Clarke's Charitable Trust, The Royal Bank of Scotland plc, Private Trust and Taxation, PO Box 356, 45 Moseley Street, Manchester M60 2BE

CC NO 281282   **ESTABLISHED** 1979

■ Cleopatra Trust

WHAT IS FUNDED Funding may be considered for environmental issues

WHAT IS NOT FUNDED No grants to individuals, or for expeditions, research or scholarships

WHO CAN BENEFIT Registered charities working in the areas outlined above

WHERE FUNDING CAN BE GIVEN Projects carried out by UK charities in Asia, Africa and America are sometimes considered

TYPE OF GRANT Project funding for one year or less

RANGE OF GRANTS £500–£10,000

SAMPLE GRANTS £5,000 to Soil Association for the cost of Responsible Forestry Programme

FINANCES
- Year 1996
- Income £154,000
- Grants £93,000

TRUSTEES Dr C Peacock, C Peacock, Mrs B Bond

HOW TO APPLY In writing only to the address under Who To Apply To. Applications are normally considered in July and December. A copy of latest Annual Report and Accounts must accompany any application

WHO TO APPLY TO Mrs Barbara Davis, Senior Information Officer, Cleopatra Trust, c/o CAF, Kings Hill, West Malling, Kent ME19 4TA
Tel 01732 520081
Fax 01732 520001
E-mail bdavis@caf.charitynet.org

CC NO 1004551   **ESTABLISHED** 1990

■ Robert Clutterbuck Charitable Trust

WHAT IS FUNDED The welfare, protection and preservation of animal life, and natural history

WHAT IS NOT FUNDED Applications for payments to individuals are not considered

WHO CAN BENEFIT The Trustees only consider applications from registered charities and they give preference to those falling within the categories mentioned above

WHERE FUNDING CAN BE GIVEN Mainly UK. Special consideration will be given to charities associated with the counties of Cheshire and Hertfordshire

TYPE OF GRANT Payments normally from income, generally for the purchase of specific items

RANGE OF GRANTS £130–£20,000; typical £2,000–£3,000

FINANCES
- Year 1997–98
- Income £49,897
- Grants £44,985

TRUSTEES Major R G Clutterbuck, C N Lindsell, A C Humphries, OBE

HOW TO APPLY To B C Berryman who will acknowledge them. Applications are only considered by Trustees at their meetings. They meet three times a year

WHO TO APPLY TO B C Berryman, Robert Clutterbuck Charitable Trust, Ashleigh Cottage, 207 Staines Road, Laleham, Staines, Middlesex TW18 2RS
Tel 01784 451651

CC NO 1010559   **ESTABLISHED** 1992

■ Lance Coates Charitable Trust 1969

WHAT IS FUNDED Promotion of biological and ecological approach to food production with the object of: (a) maintaining soil fertility for future generations; (b) improving health; (c) safeguarding scarce resources; and (d) minimising pollution

WHAT IS NOT FUNDED No grants to individuals

WHO CAN BENEFIT Organisations working in the areas outlined above. Local activities often preferred

WHERE FUNDING CAN BE GIVEN UK

RANGE OF GRANTS £100–£5,000

SAMPLE GRANTS £5,000 to Country Trust
£500 to Farm Africa

FINANCES
- Year 1996
- Income £29,017
- Grants £11,750

TRUSTEES H L T Coates, E P Serjeant, Mrs S M Coates

HOW TO APPLY In writing to the address below

WHO TO APPLY TO D Nye, Trustee, Lance Coates Charitable Trust 1969, Hillier Hopkins, 77–79 Marlows, Hemel Hempstead, Hertfordshire HP1 1LW

CC NO 261521   **ESTABLISHED** 1969

■ Cobb Charity

WHAT IS FUNDED The encouragement of co-operative values and support of a more sustainable environment with eco-friendly technologies

WHAT IS NOT FUNDED Registered charities only, no individuals. No medical organisations, no student expeditions, no building restorations

WHO CAN BENEFIT Ecological causes in the UK, related educational and co-operative projects

WHERE FUNDING CAN BE GIVEN UK and overseas, but only smaller charities need apply

TYPE OF GRANT Capital, core costs, one-off, project, research, running costs, recurring costs, salaries and start-up costs

SAMPLE GRANTS £750 to Friends of the Earth Trust for research into GM food
£750 to Good Gardeners Association for research into health/food production
£750 to Arid Lands Initiative for transformation of urban wasteland
£750 to Earth Live Fund for Artists for the Environment

FINANCES
- Year 1998
- Income £34,000
- Grants £28,000

TRUSTEES E Allitt, F Appelbe, C Cochran, M Wells

HOW TO APPLY Preferably in September or February. No phone calls. As yet no guidelines or application forms are available

WHO TO APPLY TO Eleanor Allitt, Cobb Charity, 108 Leamington Road, Kenilworth, Warwickshire CV8 2AA

CC NO 248030   **ESTABLISHED** 1964

■ The John S Cohen Foundation (375)

WHAT IS FUNDED Rural conservation; animal facilities and services; and animal sciences

WHAT IS NOT FUNDED No grants to individuals

WHERE FUNDING CAN BE GIVEN UK and America

TYPE OF GRANT Feasibility studies, project and research. Funding may be given for one year or less

FINANCES
- Year 1998
- Income £738,716
- Grants £382,448

TRUSTEES Dr David Cohen (Chairman), Richard Cohen, Elizabeth Cohen, Imogen Cohen, Jolyon Cowan

HOW TO APPLY Applications should be by letter to the Administrator on no more than two sides of A4 and should include a full budget and accounts

WHO TO APPLY TO Duncan Haldane, Administrator, The John S Cohen Foundation, 85 Albany Street, London NW1 4BT
Tel 0171-486 1117
Fax 0171-486 1118

CC NO 241598   **ESTABLISHED** 1965

Commentary

The John S Cohen Foundation was established in 1965 with assets donated by John S Cohen, his wife and his children. John Cohen died in 1974 and was succeeded as Chairman by his son, Dr David Cohen, a practising GP. His fellow Trustees are his brother Richard Cohen, his sister, Elizabeth Cohen, and his daughter Imogen Cohen and his nephew, Jolyon Cowan. The Foundation's original areas of support concentrated on Jewish causes, social welfare and relief of need; particularly in North London.

However, from these beginnings the Foundation's interests have widened considerably, to the extent that present pre-occupations are primarily with the arts and music. The Foundation is particularly interested in supporting new work and is prepared to back experimental or innovative proposals, for instance in the form of musical commissions, new writing and exhibitions. It is also particularly active in supporting Jewish charities; often of a cultural or social nature and relating to Jewish education, although support for education is not exclusive to Jewish charities. There is a definite interest in widening access to education as a whole. There is also an interest in the preservation of the built environment and conservation of the natural environment, as well as social developments mainly in the areas of prison reform, population control and the family. The Trustees prefer to support schemes which have some national importance and are particularly interested in innovative, imaginative but realistic ideas which may not have a particularly wide appeal. These areas are now unlikely to change radically, as they have developed over a number of years to their present form. The Foundation will consider projects throughout the UK, although there is a concentration upon London and the South East.

The Foundation is happy to consider co-funding. Much of this co-funding tends to be shortfall funding for both statutory bodies and charities. There is a preference for project funding, which may be over a period of years, subject to receipt of an annual review and reports. There is a stipulation that there will be no donations to large capital appeals, including capital requirements generated by the National Lottery, nor to individuals. Blanket or circular appeals will not be successful, and applications should come only from registered charities.

Applications should be by letter to the Administrator, on no more than two sides of A4 paper, outlining the aims and objectives of the organisation and the specific project for which funding is required. Applications should also include a full budget for the proposal, identifying: administration, management and core costs; details of how the project is to be funded, including other sources of funding – both those from statutory and charitable bodies; structure and staffing of the organisation; a copy of the latest Annual Report and audited Accounts. The Foundation does not normally acknowledge applications unless there is an intention to take them further, due to the extremely large number of applications received. The Chairman of the Trustees views all new applications under consideration. The Trustees normally only meet twice a year, in the Spring and the Autumn

SAMPLE GRANTS
The top ten grants made in 1998 were:
50000 to British Museum
£35,000 to the Royal Free Hospital School of Medicine
£25,000 to the Welsh National Opera
£20,000 to the National Gallery
£15,000 to Tricycle Theatre
£12,000 to Marie Stopes International
£11,000 to Lincoln College, Oxford
10800 to South Bank Centre
£10,000 to Jewish Care
£10,000 to Down House

■ Sir James Colyer-Fergusson Charitable Trust (254)

WHAT IS FUNDED Small charities in Kent and Suffolk working in the areas of rural conservation; animal facilities and services; and environmental and animal sciences

WHAT IS NOT FUNDED No individual applicants are supported

WHO CAN BENEFIT Organisations in Kent and Suffolk

WHERE FUNDING CAN BE GIVEN Kent and Suffolk

TYPE OF GRANT One-off, recurring, capital, core, running and start-up costs will all be considered, as will salaries, buildings, project and research costs. Funding may be given for up to two years

RANGE OF GRANTS £500–£10,000 and some larger one-off grants

FINANCES
- Year 1997
- Income £650,405
- Grants £632,213

TRUSTEES Hon Simon Buxton, Sir Charles M Farrer, Hon Jonathan St Q R Monckton, John A Porter

PUBLICATIONS Accounts

HOW TO APPLY An application form is available. Applications should include details of the project, its budget, and funds already raised. Applications are considered quarterly in March, June, September and December

WHO TO APPLY TO S H J Macdonald, Sir James Colyer-Fergusson Charitable Trust, c/o Messrs Farrer & Co, 66 Lincoln's Inn Fields, London WC2A 3LH
Tel 0171-242 2022
Fax 0171-831 6301

CC NO 258958   **ESTABLISHED** 1969

Commentary

The Sir James Colyer-Fergusson Charitable Trust was established in 1969 by Sir James Colyer-Fergusson to support small charities and churches in Kent and Suffolk.

The Trustees' policy is to consider appeals for charitable causes in Kent and Suffolk only and their preference is to support smaller charities. The Trustees currently regard churches as their priority for funding; of 104 donations made during 1997, 56 were to churches. The funding policies are set by the Trustees and may change at their discretion. If there is surplus income available the Trustees will consider donations for other purposes.

The Trust does not fund statutory bodies or replace statutory funding, but it participates informally in co-funding with other charities. Grants can be one-off or recurring and are generally awarded for repairs to church buildings. Infrastructure costs are also considered, but loans are not made.

Applications should be made in writing; an application form will be issued where appropriate. Requests for funding are considered on a quarterly basis, usually in March, June, September and December. A report may be requested by the Trustees upon the completion of a project

SAMPLE GRANTS
The top ten grants made in 1997 were:
£110,000 to University of Kent Musical Endowment Fund
£52,300 to University of Kent for theatre

Community

refurbishment
£20,000 to Bapchild PCC
£15,000 to St Margaret's Lee PCC
£15,000 to The Broomhill Trust
£10,000 to Kent Trust for Nature Conservation
£10,000 to Minster Abbey Restoration Appeal
£10,000 to Canterbury Youth Project
£10,000 to St Peter's PCC
£10,000 to New Medway Steam Packet Company Limited

■ The Community Trust for Greater Manchester

WHAT IS FUNDED Rural conservation; animal facilities and services; and environmental and animal sciences

WHAT IS NOT FUNDED No grants to individuals, or for political organisations

WHO CAN BENEFIT Small local projects, new and established organisations, and innovative projects

WHERE FUNDING CAN BE GIVEN Greater Manchester

TYPE OF GRANT One-off grants

RANGE OF GRANTS Up to £1,000

FINANCES
- Year 1996–97
- Income £195,352
- Grants £121,644

TRUSTEES His Grace The Duke of Westminster, OBE, TD, DL, Alan Rudden, R Gordon Humphreys, A J Farnworth, John Sandford, C Smith, M Eileen Polding, Lorraine Worsley, Jack Buckley, W T Risby, C Chan, A A Downie

PUBLICATIONS Annual Report. Guidelines. Information Packs

HOW TO APPLY In writing. Application form available

WHO TO APPLY TO R J Carter, The Community Trust for Greater Manchester, PO Box 63, Beswick House, Beswick Row, Manchester M4 4JY

CC NO 1017504   **ESTABLISHED** 1993

■ The Cooper Charitable Trust

WHAT IS FUNDED Preference to charities with little State funding in the areas of: rural conservation; bird and wildlife sanctuaries, wildlife parks and endangered species

WHAT IS NOT FUNDED Seldom to individuals

WHO CAN BENEFIT Well organised local causes and institutions working in the areas outlined above

WHERE FUNDING CAN BE GIVEN Preference to Oxford and the surrounding area

TYPE OF GRANT Single donations

RANGE OF GRANTS £100–£10,000, typical grant £500

FINANCES
- Year 1997
- Income £18,380
- Grants £32,600

TRUSTEES G R Cooper, A R Cooper

HOW TO APPLY To the address under Who To Apply To in writing. Accounts or financial statements required

WHO TO APPLY TO G R Cooper, The Cooper Charitable Trust, Shepherd's Close, Hinksey Hill, Oxford OX1 5BQ

CC NO 249879   **ESTABLISHED** 1966

■ The Marjorie Coote Animal Charity Fund

WHAT IS FUNDED The care and protection of horses, dogs and other animals and birds. It is the policy of the Trustees to concentrate on research into animal health problems and on the protection of species, whilst continuing to apply a small proportion of the income to general animal welfare, including sanctuaries

WHAT IS NOT FUNDED No grants to individuals

WHO CAN BENEFIT Registered charities for the benefit of animals

WHERE FUNDING CAN BE GIVEN UK and overseas

RANGE OF GRANTS £500–£25,000

SAMPLE GRANTS £26,000 to Animal Health Trust for equine research
£25,000 to Langford Trust for Animal Welfare for stables for Bristol University Equine Hospital
£10,000 to PDSA for capital equipment
£6,000 to Friends of Conservation for rhino monitoring in Kenya
£5,500 to British Horse Society for equine welfare
£5,000 to FRAME for general purposes
£5,000 to Guide Dogs for the Blind for general purposes
£5,000 to World Wildlife Fund for Nature for protection of the tiger
£3,500 to Devon Wildlife Trust for general welfare
£3,500 to Whiteley Wildlife Conservation Trust for animal care at Paignton Zoo

FINANCES
- Year 1998
- Income £129,744
- Grants £116,250

TRUSTEES Sir Hugh Neill, Mrs J P Holah, N H N Coote

Alphabetical register of grant making trusts **Countryside**

NOTES The list of beneficiaries is very small and changes little from year to year

HOW TO APPLY Applications should be in writing and must be received during September

WHO TO APPLY TO Sir Hugh Neill, Barn Cottage, Lindrick Common, Worksop, Nottingham S81 8BA

CC NO 208493   **ESTABLISHED** 1954

■ Cyril Corden Trust

WHAT IS FUNDED A self contained project designed to improve the work of a charity which aims to encourage animal welfare. Particularly charities working in the fields of facilities and services

WHAT IS NOT FUNDED Applications for general funds are not normally considered. No grants to individuals

WHO CAN BENEFIT Any suitable charity

WHERE FUNDING CAN BE GIVEN UK

TYPE OF GRANT Award to one project not exceeding £10,000. Capital, feasibility studies, one-off and project funding for one year or less will be considered

RANGE OF GRANTS Up to £10,000

FINANCES
- Year 1997
- Income £23,630
- Grants £18,672

TRUSTEES H Bland, P Corden, Ms D Craddock, N T Gale, J Kipling

NOTES Charities must be prepared to wait for a decision

HOW TO APPLY At any time with current statement of accounts

WHO TO APPLY TO Cyril Corden Trust, c/o Ravensdale, Sally Deards Lane, Rabley Heath, Welwyn, Hertfordshire AL6 9UE

CC NO 297595   **ESTABLISHED** 1987

■ Countryside Business Group Charitable Trust

WHAT IS FUNDED The protection, maintenance or preservation of the countryside, to educate the public and promote any object that will benefit the countryside

WHO CAN BENEFIT Organisations working in the areas outlined above

WHERE FUNDING CAN BE GIVEN UK

FINANCES
- Year 1997
- Income £47,710

TRUSTEES Lt Col J Charteris, C Goodson-Wickes, The Earl of Stockton

HOW TO APPLY In writing to the address below

WHO TO APPLY TO Dr Charles Goodson-Wickes, Chairman, Countryside Business Group Charitable Trust, Fraser House, Albermarle Street, London W1X 3FA

CC NO 1060040   **ESTABLISHED** 1996

■ The Countryside Trust

WHAT IS FUNDED At present the Trustees only offer grants for fundraising campaigns where the money raised benefits practical conservation projects of local rather than national significance including: environmental issues; flora, fauna; lakes and landscapes; nature reserves; waterways; and woodlands

WHAT IS NOT FUNDED Applications from individuals are ineligible. Trustees wish to assist small scale, local initiatives and have set an upper limit of £5,000 for each grant

WHO CAN BENEFIT Community or voluntary bodies concerned with the care of the local countryside of England

WHERE FUNDING CAN BE GIVEN England

TYPE OF GRANT One-off payment towards a specific fundraising project. Also start-up costs. Core funding and/or salary costs are unlikely to be considered

RANGE OF GRANTS Up to £5,000

SAMPLE GRANTS £3,000 to Yorkshire Wildlife Trust - 50 Year Appeal
£1,212 to Devon Wildlife Trust for a fete and fayre
£1,172 to Yorkshire Dales Millennium Trust - Corporate Appeal
£1,000 to BTCV, Skelton for a video
£1,000 to Northumberland Wildlife Trust for a Wildlife Art Auction
£1,000 to Nottingham Wildlife Trust for a Countryside Festival
£1,000 to Silvanus for display materials
£976 to Dandelion Trust for a woodland scheme
£597 to Suffolk Wildlife Trust for a corporate pack
£555 to Lancashire Wildlife Trust for Green Krypton Factor Challenge

FINANCES
- Year 1996–97
- Income £47,723
- Grants £14,979

TRUSTEES E Cameron, R Wakeford, J L Evans

HOW TO APPLY Trustees meet twice yearly, in February and August, to consider applications. Applications can be sent in at any time but must be received by the end of December and

---

Does the trust you have chosen match your needs? Haphazard applications waste postage and time

Criffel

Alphabetical register of grant making trusts

the end of June respectively for consideration at those meetings

WHO TO APPLY TO Mrs Sarah Stone, Secretary, The Countryside Trust, John Dower House, Crescent Place, Cheltenham, Gloucestershire GL50 3RA
Tel 01242 521381
Fax 01242 584270

CC NO 803496   **ESTABLISHED** 1990

■ Criffel Charitable Trust

WHAT IS FUNDED Conservation; bird and wildlife sanctuaries; and endangered species

WHAT IS NOT FUNDED No personal applications

WHO CAN BENEFIT Organisations working in the areas outlined above

WHERE FUNDING CAN BE GIVEN UK, Europe, Asia and Africa

TYPE OF GRANT Buildings, capital, core costs, one-off, projects, research, recurring costs and running costs. Funding is available for more than three years

FINANCES
- Year 1997
- Income £58,404
- Grants £51,120

TRUSTEES Mrs J I Harvey, Mrs J C Lees, J C Lees

HOW TO APPLY This Trust states that it does not respond to unsolicited applications

WHO TO APPLY TO J C Lees and Mrs J E Lees, Criffel Charitable Trust, 4 Wentworth Road, Sutton Coldfield, West Midlands B74 2SG
Tel 0121-308 1575

CC NO 1040680   **ESTABLISHED** 1994

■ The Cromarty Trust

WHAT IS FUNDED Grants are given largely to organisations which work to preserve the wildlife of Cromarty

WHO CAN BENEFIT Organisations benefiting Cromarty

WHERE FUNDING CAN BE GIVEN Mainly the Parish of Cromarty

FINANCES
- Year 1997
- Income £22,778
- Grants £17,466

TRUSTEES J Nightingale, Michael Nightingale of Cromarty, Miss E V de B Murray

HOW TO APPLY Applications are not invited

WHO TO APPLY TO John Nightingale, The Cromarty Trust, 25 West Square, London SE11 4SP

CC NO 272843   **ESTABLISHED** 1976

■ The Harry Crook Foundation (377)

WHAT IS FUNDED Rural conservation, and animal facilities and services

WHAT IS NOT FUNDED No grants to individuals

WHO CAN BENEFIT Registered charities working in the areas outlined above

WHERE FUNDING CAN BE GIVEN Bristol and District only

TYPE OF GRANT One-off, capital, recurring. Also buildings, core costs, feasibility studies, interest free loans and project. Funding is given for one year or less

RANGE OF GRANTS £100–£250,000

FINANCES
- Year 1998
- Income £121,156
- Grants £377,693

TRUSTEES D J Bellew, T G Bickle, J D Gough (Chairman), R G West, Mrs I Wollen

NOTES Address appeals to D J Bellew c/o Solicitor to the Trustees, Miss J Pierce

HOW TO APPLY In writing to the address below

WHO TO APPLY TO D J Bellew, c/o Miss J Pierce, Solicitor, The Harry Crook Foundation, Veale Wasbrough, Solicitors, Orchard Court, Orchard Lane, Bristol BS1 5DS
Tel 0117-927 6402

CC NO 231470   **ESTABLISHED** 1963

Commentary

The Harry Crook Charitable Trust was established on 31 May 1963 by Dr Harry Crook for general charitable purposes. Harry Crook founded the Kleeneze Brush Company in the 1920s and led that company throughout his lifetime. He was also an Alderman on Bristol City Council for 25 years, and in 1955 was Lord Mayor of the City. During his lifetime, Harry Crook supported a wide number of charitable causes in the City of Bristol, and the Trustees consider their primary duty to be to maintain and support those causes which were dear to his heart.

The policy of the Trustees is to follow the express wishes of Harry Crook and support charitable causes which serve the City of Bristol, or its immediate environs, or those which are personally known to the Trustees. The Trustees have given support to a wide range of charities including those concerned with education, poverty, the disabled and the arts. However, on the whole, funding is given to registered charities working in the following areas: (a) elderly, (b) homeless, (c) education, (d) young, (e) civic, and (f) sundry small donations. There are no scales of preference between these categories; the Trustees seek to maintain a balance between them. The Trustees also aim to support one main project from time to time. The Trustees do not fund statutory bodies; nor are they willing to replace statutory funding. The Trustees attitudes to co-funding are not known. The Trust prefers to make one-off, recurring and capital grants.

Applications should be in writing. The Trustees meet in July and December to approve donations from the Foundation. There is a selection process prior to the full meetings where appeals are either rejected or put back to the main meeting. At the less formal meetings one-off small grants are sometimes made. It is not known if the Foundation has an assessment process for grant recipients

SAMPLE GRANTS
The top ten grants made in 1998 were:
£250,000 to St Peter's Hospice
£50,000 to Brunelcare
£13,136 to Bristol 5 Boys Club
£5,000 to The Salvation Army
£5,000 to Boys Brigade
£5,000 to Countryside Business Group Charitable Trust
£5,000 to Rotary Club of Chelwood Bridge (Bristol Branch of the Multiple Sclerosis Society)
£3,000 to NSPCC
£2,500 to Bristol Children's Hospital
£2,000 to St John Ambulance

■The Cwmbran Trust (formerly The Girling (Cwmbran) Trust)

WHAT IS FUNDED Rural conservation; animal facilities and services; and animal sciences

WHAT IS NOT FUNDED No grants are made outside of Cwmbran in Gwent

WHO CAN BENEFIT Neighbourhood-based community projects

WHERE FUNDING CAN BE GIVEN Cwmbran

TYPE OF GRANT Buildings, capital, core costs, interest free loans, one-off, running costs, recurring costs and start-up costs. Funding may be given for one year or less

RANGE OF GRANTS £100–£10,000

FINANCES
- Year 1998
- Income £64,854
- Grants £44,685

TRUSTEES B Cunningham, P M Harris, K L Maddox, A Rippon, B E Smith

HOW TO APPLY To the address under Who To Apply To in writing. The Trustees usually meet every two months, starting at the end of February

WHO TO APPLY TO K L Maddox, The Cwmbran Trust, Grange Road, Cwmbran, Gwent NP44 3XU
Tel 01633 834040

CC NO 505855   **ESTABLISHED** 1976

The DLM Charitable Trust

WHAT IS FUNDED To support charities operating in Oxford and the surrounding areas, including charities working in the fields of: rural conservation; animal facilities and services; and animal sciences

WHAT IS NOT FUNDED No grants to individuals

WHERE FUNDING CAN BE GIVEN Oxfordshire

TYPE OF GRANT Feasibility studies, one-off, research, recurring costs, running costs and start-up costs. Funding of up to three years will be considered

FINANCES
- Year 1996
- Income £102,480
- Grants £37,509

TRUSTEES Dr E A de la Mare, Mrs P Sawyer, J A Cloke

WHO TO APPLY TO J A Cloke, The DLM Charitable Trust, Messrs Cloke & Co, Warnford Court, Throgmorton Street, London EC2N 2AT

CC NO 328520   **ESTABLISHED** 1990

The Sarah D'Avigdor Goldsmid Charitable Trust

WHAT IS FUNDED No specific policy, but see What Is Not Funded. Endangered species, environmental issues, fauna and flora, and nature reserves. Also ornithology and zoology

WHAT IS NOT FUNDED Applications by individuals not considered. Unsuccessful applications not acknowledged. Needs of the County of Kent favoured

WHO CAN BENEFIT Registered charities only

WHERE FUNDING CAN BE GIVEN Kent

TYPE OF GRANT Core costs, endowments, project and research

RANGE OF GRANTS £25–£1,000; typical grant £50–£100

SAMPLE GRANTS £1,500 to Kent Trust for Nature Conservation
£1,000 to Game Conservancy Scottish Research Trust

FINANCES
- Year 1997
- Income £27,387
- Grants £26,646

TRUSTEES A J M Teacher, Mrs A J M Teacher, Harry Teacher

PUBLICATIONS Annual Report and Accounts

HOW TO APPLY By post only

WHO TO APPLY TO James Teacher, The Sarah D'Avigdor Goldsmid Charitable Trust, Hadlow Place Farm, Golden Green, Tonbridge, Kent TN11 0BW

CC NO 233083   **ESTABLISHED** 1963

The Helen and Geoffrey de Freitas Charitable Trust

WHAT IS FUNDED The Trustees wish to fund charities or voluntary umbrella bodies with charitable status working in the preservation of wildlife and rural England and conservation and environment

WHAT IS NOT FUNDED No medical causes or charities. No grants to individuals. Registered charities only

WHO CAN BENEFIT Mainly headquarters organisations working in the areas outlined above

WHERE FUNDING CAN BE GIVEN England

TYPE OF GRANT Feasibility studies; one-off; project and start-up costs. Funding for one year or less will be considered

RANGE OF GRANTS £1,000–£5,000

FINANCES
- Year 1998
- Income £28,250
- Grants £15,850

TRUSTEES R C Kirby, Frances de Freitas, Roger de Freitas

HOW TO APPLY In writing only to the address below. Initial telephone calls are not welcome. No application form or guidelines. Trustees meet only twice a year. No sae required

WHO TO APPLY TO , The Helen and Geoffrey de Freitas Charitable Trust, PO Box 18667, London NW3 5WB

CC NO 258597   **ESTABLISHED** 1969

Dearne Valley Community Forum

WHAT IS FUNDED Support will be given to endangered species and environmental issues

WHAT IS NOT FUNDED No support for services which are the responsibility of a statutory body, mainstream school activities, or private and religious activity

WHO CAN BENEFIT Organisations in the Dearne Valley area

WHERE FUNDING CAN BE GIVEN Dearne Valley, including the Bolton-On-Dearne, Goldthorpe and Thurnscoe areas of Barnsley and the

Conisbrough, Denaby and Mexborough areas of Doncaster and Swinton, Kilnhurst, Wath and Bramron areas of Rotherham

TYPE OF GRANT One-off, recurring, core costs, feasibility studies, projects, research, running costs, salaries and start-up costs will be considered. Funding may be for up to three years

RANGE OF GRANTS Typical grant £500–£3,000, some grants of up to £8,000

FINANCES
- Year 1998
- Income £90,000

HOW TO APPLY Telephone for an application form

WHO TO APPLY TO Ms J C Bibby, Secretary, Dearne Valley Community Forum, Manvers House, PO Box 109, Wath Upon Dearne, Rotherham, South Yorkshire S63 7YZ
Tel 01709 760207

CC NO 1064193   **ESTABLISHED** 1997

■ Derbyshire Community Foundation

WHAT IS FUNDED Community groups and voluntary organisations working to tackle disadvantage and improve quality of life, including environmental issues

WHAT IS NOT FUNDED No grants to individuals; work that replaces statutory funding; animal welfare; party politics or religious evangelism; general appeals; or national charities (unless it is a local project)

WHO CAN BENEFIT Voluntary groups and volunteers and the people they work with in Derbyshire across a wide spectrum of activity tackling disadvantage and promoting quality of life

WHERE FUNDING CAN BE GIVEN Derby City and Derbyshire. We have exceptionally made grants outside the county for one donor but it required special arrangement and is unlikely to be repeated

TYPE OF GRANT Usually one-off, though depending on the programme and donor's wishes, we may give more than one grant to the same group for different projects or items. Capital, core costs, feasibility studies, research, running costs, salaries and start-up costs. Funding for up to one year will be considered

RANGE OF GRANTS Usually up to £1,000

FINANCES
- Year 1997–98
- Income £368,269
- Grants £81,355

TRUSTEES B A Ashby (Chair), B Archbold, C J Baker, R Beck, P R Binks, A Blackwood, A Borkowski, D Forman, G R Ingram, K Martin, M McGlade, D G W Moss, E Quicke, J Rivers, C E Wilkinson

NOTES Nearly all grantmaking to date has been administration of grant programmes for other donors, who set their own criteria. By 1999 we hope to make our first grants using our own policy, with funds generated by our infant endowment fund

HOW TO APPLY Please contact our office. It is worth phoning first to check that we have a pot of money suitable for your needs. We have a standard form and we will tell you the deadline for current round. Grants are usually made in two annual rounds, with applications invited from April and October

WHO TO APPLY TO Hilary Gilbert, Director, Derbyshire Community Foundation, The Arkwright Suite, University of Derby, Kedleston Road, Derby DE22 1EB
Tel 01332 621348
Fax 01332 621348

CC NO 1039485   **ESTABLISHED** 1994

■ Dinam Charity

WHAT IS FUNDED Support for organisations dealing with environmental protection, and animal welfare

WHAT IS NOT FUNDED No grants to individuals

WHO CAN BENEFIT Charitable organisations working in the areas outlined above

WHERE FUNDING CAN BE GIVEN Wales

FINANCES
- Year 1996
- Income £178,143
- Grants £117,130

TRUSTEES Hon Mrs Mary M Noble, Hon Mrs G R Jean Cormack, Hon Edward D G Davies, J S Tyres

HOW TO APPLY In writing to the address below

WHO TO APPLY TO The Hon J H Davies, Dinam Charity, 8 Southampton Place, London WC1A 2EA

CC NO 231295   **ESTABLISHED** 1926

■ C H Dixon Charitable Trust

WHAT IS FUNDED The Trust will consider funding: rural conservation; animal facilities and services; and animal sciences

WHO CAN BENEFIT Organisations working in the fields outlined above

WHERE FUNDING CAN BE GIVEN England

TYPE OF GRANT One-off and buildings

RANGE OF GRANTS £100–£2,000

SAMPLE GRANTS £1,000 to Blue Cross for general purposes

FINANCES
- Year 1998
- Income £12,176
- Grants £10,200

TRUSTEES Miss A Dixon, R M Robinson

HOW TO APPLY In writing to the address below

WHO TO APPLY TO R M Robinson, C H Dixon Charitable Trust, Messrs Dixon Ward, 16 The Green, Richmond, Surrey TW9 1QD

CC NO 282936   **ESTABLISHED** 1981

■ Dorus Trust

WHAT IS FUNDED Funding specific projects including environmental issues

WHAT IS NOT FUNDED No grants to individuals, or for expeditions, research or scholarships

WHO CAN BENEFIT Registered charities only working in the areas outlined above

WHERE FUNDING CAN BE GIVEN Projects carried out by UK charities in Asia, Africa and America are sometimes considered

TYPE OF GRANT Project funding for up to one year will be considered

RANGE OF GRANTS £500–£10,000

SAMPLE GRANTS £15,000 to Voluntary Service Overseas for funding a forestry policy adviser
£15,000 to UK Foundation for the South Pacific for encouraging sustainable harvest of rain forests

FINANCES
- Year 1996
- Income £154,000
- Grants £98,000

TRUSTEES C Peacock, B Bond, M Bond

HOW TO APPLY In writing only to the address under Who To Apply To. Applications are normally considered in July and December. A copy of latest Annual Report and Accounts must accompany any application

WHO TO APPLY TO Mrs B Davis, Senior Information Officer, Dorus Trust, c/o CAF, Kings Hill, West Malling, Kent ME19 4TA
Tel 01732 520081
Fax 01732 520001
E-mail bdavis@caf.charitynet.org

CC NO 328724   **ESTABLISHED** 1990

■ R M Douglas Charitable Trust

WHAT IS FUNDED Registered charities at discretion of Trustees, including those working in the areas of: woodlands; animal homes; animal welfare; dogs, kennels and other facilities for dogs; agriculture; animal breeding; and ornithology and zoology

WHAT IS NOT FUNDED No grants to individuals. No grants for scholarships or participation in expeditions or adventurous activities

WHO CAN BENEFIT Registered charities working in the areas outlined above

WHERE FUNDING CAN BE GIVEN Staffordshire a priority, but the West Midlands, South Wales, Europe, Asia, Africa and Ireland are also considered

TYPE OF GRANT Mostly small grants at the discretion of Trustees including buildings, capital, core costs, one-off, research, and recurring costs. Funding is available for over three years

RANGE OF GRANTS £50–£5,000. Typically £200–£250

FINANCES
- Year 1997
- Income £55,453
- Grants £46,350

TRUSTEES J R T Douglas, OBE, F W Carder, TD, Mrs J E Lees

NOTES New applications not normally considered

HOW TO APPLY By letter. Not all acknowledged. No application form or guidelines

WHO TO APPLY TO The Administrator, R M Douglas Charitable Trust, 68 Liverpool Road, Stoke-on-Trent ST4 1BG

CC NO 248775   **ESTABLISHED** 1966

■ The Harry Dunn Charitable Trust

WHAT IS FUNDED To pursue own concerns in the locality, mainly in relation to environmental charities. Particularly charities working in the fields of: rural conservation; bird sanctuaries and ecology

WHAT IS NOT FUNDED Only to causes known to the Trustees personally and never to individual applicants

WHO CAN BENEFIT Organisations working in the areas outlined above

WHERE FUNDING CAN BE GIVEN Nottinghamshire

TYPE OF GRANT Core costs and one-off, funding for one year or less will be considered

RANGE OF GRANTS £500–£5,000

FINANCES
- Year 1998
- Income £68,075
- Grants £29,000

TRUSTEES A H Dunn, C N Dunn, A J Kennedy, N A Dunn, R M Dunn

WHO TO APPLY TO A J Kennedy, The Harry Dunn Charitable Trust, Messrs Cooper-Parry, 56 High Pavement, Nottingham NG1 1HX

CC NO 297389　　　**ESTABLISHED** 1987

■ EBM Charitable Trust (222)

WHAT IS FUNDED General charitable purposes, especially animal welfare

WHAT IS NOT FUNDED No grants to individuals. No worldwide charities

WHO CAN BENEFIT Animal welfare charities

WHERE FUNDING CAN BE GIVEN UK, particularly South-East England

TYPE OF GRANT Recurring and one-off

FINANCES
- Year 1998
- Income £5,132,918
- Grants £762,960

TRUSTEES Cyril Fitzgerald, Harry Holgate, Michael Macfayden, Richard Moore

PUBLICATIONS Annual Accounts

HOW TO APPLY This Trust states that it does not respond to unsolicited applications

WHO TO APPLY TO Keith Lawrence, EBM Charitable Trust, Moore Stephens, St Paul's House, Warwick Lane, London EC4P 4BN
Tel 0171-248 4499
Fax 0171-3347973
E-mail Keith_Lawrence@moorestephens.com

CC NO 326186　　　**ESTABLISHED** 1982

Commentary

The EBM Charitable Trust was established by E B Moller in 1982 for general charitable purposes and with a particular interest in animal welfare. The funding policy is at the Trustees' discretion and the Trust funds a range of charitable projects, many of them in the South-East of England.

The Trust has not so far funded statutory bodies, replaced statutory funding or provided match-funding. It does not make loans.

The Trust makes one-off grants and recurring grants and will cover infrastructure costs.

The Trust has stated that its funds are fully committed and that therefore unsolicited applications are not invited. The Trustees will often visit a project before awarding a grant in order to determine what help is needed. They like to support long-term projects and will visit beneficiaries and request reports which demonstrate how the grants have been used

SAMPLE GRANTS
The top ten grants made in 1998 were:
£300,000 to The Salvation Army
£200,000 to British Racing School

£33,199 to Chicken Shed Theatre Company
£30,000 to Worshipful Company of Shipwrights Charitable Fund
£30,000 to Youth Sport Trust
£28,411 to Evelina Children's Hospital Appeal
£24,000 to Cambridge University Veterinary School Trust
£22,500 to Sea Cadets Association
£20,000 to Community Links
£10,000 to Cancer Research Campaign

■ Audrey Earle Charitable Trust

WHAT IS FUNDED Mostly animal charities

WHO CAN BENEFIT Animal charities

WHERE FUNDING CAN BE GIVEN UK and overseas

TYPE OF GRANT Small one-off and recurrent range of grants

RANGE OF GRANTS Usually £1,000 or less

FINANCES
- Year 1996
- Income £16,944

TRUSTEES J F Russell Smith, John W H Carey, C R L Coubrough

HOW TO APPLY No further applications can be considered at present. Existing commitments to be continued

WHO TO APPLY TO Audrey Earle Charitable Trust, Messrs Moon Beever & Hewlett, 24 Bloomsbury Square, London WC1A 2PL
Tel 0171-637 0661

CC NO 290028   **ESTABLISHED** 1984

■ The Ecological Foundation

WHAT IS FUNDED Conservation, wildlife sanctuaries, organic food production and environmental issues

WHO CAN BENEFIT Individuals and voluntary organisations working in the areas outlined above

WHERE FUNDING CAN BE GIVEN UK and overseas

TYPE OF GRANT Feasibility studies, project and research. Funding can be given for up to two years

FINANCES
- Year 1997
- Income £54,755
- Grants £85,051

TRUSTEES The Marquis of Londonderry, John Aspinall, R Hanbury-Tension, E R Goldsmith

HOW TO APPLY To the address under Who To Apply To in writing

WHO TO APPLY TO J Faull, Director, The Ecological Foundation, Lower Bosneives, Withiel, Bodmin, Cornwall PL30 5NQ

Tel 01208 831236
Fax 01208 831083

CC NO 264947   **ESTABLISHED** 1972

■ The Wilfred & Elsie Elkes Charity Fund

WHAT IS FUNDED The Trustees have a particular interest in rural conservation and animal facilities and services

WHAT IS NOT FUNDED The Trustees normally only make donations to other charitable organisations, and only exceptionally direct to individuals

WHO CAN BENEFIT Organisations working in the areas outlined above

WHERE FUNDING CAN BE GIVEN West Midlands, particularly Staffordshire and Stoke-on-Trent

TYPE OF GRANT Recurrent grants are given in a number of cases but more normally the grant is a one-off payment. Also capital, core costs, endowments, feasibility studies, project, research, recurring and running costs, salaries and start-up costs. Funding may be given for one year or less

FINANCES
- Year 1997–98
- Income £105,070
- Grants £92,500

TRUSTEES Royal Bank of Scotland plc, F A Barnes

HOW TO APPLY Any time, but Trustees meetings are only held at approximately quarterly intervals

WHO TO APPLY TO The Trust Officer, Trustee & Taxation Office, The Wilfred & Elsie Elkes Charity Fund, Royal Bank of Scotland plc, PO Box 356, 45 Mosley Street, Manchester M60 2BE

CC NO 326573   **ESTABLISHED** 1984

■ The Englefield Charitable Trust

WHAT IS FUNDED Charitable organisations generally, with particular consideration to those in Berkshire. Particularly charities working in the fields of: rural conservation; animal facilities and services; and animal sciences

WHAT IS NOT FUNDED Applications from individuals for study or travel will not be considered

WHERE FUNDING CAN BE GIVEN UK

TYPE OF GRANT Buildings, capital, core costs, endowments, feasibility studies, interest free loans, one-off, project, research, recurring and running costs, salaries and start-up costs.

Funding may be given for up to and over three years

RANGE OF GRANTS £250–£40,000. Average grant £1,000

FINANCES
- Year 1997–98
- Income £398,000
- Grants £355,000

TRUSTEES Sir William Benyon, Lady Benyon, Richard Benyon, James Shelley, Catherine Haig

NOTES Finances: funds are being withheld in addition to the figure for Grants as follows: £41,000 for St Mary the Virgin, Reading and £20,000 for St Mary the Virgin, Burghfield

HOW TO APPLY Unsuccessful applications will not be acknowledged. Trustees meet March and October

WHO TO APPLY TO The Secretary, The Englefield Charitable Trust, Englefield Estate Office, Theale, Reading RG7 5DU
Tel 01734 302504
Fax 01734 323748

CC NO 258123   **ESTABLISHED** 1968

■Epigoni Trust

WHAT IS FUNDED Funding specific projects including environmental issues

WHAT IS NOT FUNDED No grants to individuals, or for expeditions, research or scholarships

WHO CAN BENEFIT Registered charities only working in the areas outlined above

WHERE FUNDING CAN BE GIVEN Projects carried out by UK charities in Asia, Africa and America are sometimes considered

TYPE OF GRANT Project funding for one year or less

RANGE OF GRANTS £500–£10,000

SAMPLE GRANTS £20,000 to Voluntary Service Overseas for funding a forestry worker

FINANCES
- Year 1996
- Income £155,000
- Grants £93,000

TRUSTEES C Peacock, B Bond, M Bond

HOW TO APPLY In writing only to the address under Who To Apply To. Applications are normally considered in July and December. A copy of the latest Annual Report and Accounts must accompany any application

WHO TO APPLY TO Mrs B Davis, Senior Information Officer, Epigoni Trust, c/o CAF, Kings Hill, West Malling, Kent ME19 4TA
Tel 01732 520081
Fax 01732 520001
E-mail bdavis@caf.charitynet.org

CC NO 328700   **ESTABLISHED** 1990

■Ericson Trust

WHAT IS FUNDED Environmental projects or research

WHAT IS NOT FUNDED No grants to individuals. Applications from the following areas are generally not considered unless closely connected with one of the above; children's and young people's clubs, centres, etc; schools; charities dealing with illness or disability (except psychiatric); religious institutions, except in their social project

WHO CAN BENEFIT Registered charities only

WHERE FUNDING CAN BE GIVEN UK and overseas projects by UK charities

TYPE OF GRANT Project. Requests for core funding, running costs or particular items are considered. Funding may be given for up to two years

RANGE OF GRANTS Maximum £2,000

FINANCES
- Year 1998
- Income £29,554
- Grants £60,500

TRUSTEES Mrs Valerie J Barrow, Mrs A M Claudia Cotton, Miss Rebecca C Cotton

HOW TO APPLY Applicants should send a concise descriptive document (leaflet, brochure or letter) and be prepared to send a copy of the Accounts. There is no special application form, but guidelines are available for applicants. It may be useful if small, new projects include a commendation by a respected and relevant public person. Successful applicants are asked to return an official receipt as soon as possible after receiving their cheques and to report on progress after a specified period of time. As the Trust has many commitments, very few new requests are successful in each round of grants. Unfortunately, explanatory letters cannot be sent to every unsuccessful applicant. Applications are considered in February and September, and cheques sent in March and October

WHO TO APPLY TO Mrs A M C Cotton, Ericson Trust, Flat 2, 53 Carleton Road, London N7 0ET

CC NO 219762   **ESTABLISHED** 1962

Eskdale

■ The Eskdale (Cumbria) Trust

WHAT IS FUNDED To conserve and control flora and fauna in Ravenglass and Eskdale

WHO CAN BENEFIT Organisations working in the areas outlined above

WHERE FUNDING CAN BE GIVEN Ravenglass, Eskdale and district, Cumbria

TYPE OF GRANT Recurring

FINANCES
- Year 1996
- Income £9,808

HOW TO APPLY In writing to the address below

WHO TO APPLY TO C W Musson, The Eskdale (Cumbria) Trust, 13 Maude Street, Kendal, Cumbria LA9 4QD

CC NO 505295   **ESTABLISHED** 1976

■ The Eric Evans Memorial Trust

WHAT IS FUNDED This Trust will consider funding the conservation of waterways

WHO CAN BENEFIT Individuals and organisations working in the areas outlined above

WHERE FUNDING CAN BE GIVEN Islington, East London and East Anglia

TYPE OF GRANT One-off

RANGE OF GRANTS £100–£400

FINANCES
- Year 1997
- Income £98,854

TRUSTEES D Boehm, Mrs O Evans, J M Kinder

WHO TO APPLY TO J M Kinder, Trustee, The Eric Evans Memorial Trust, 55 Thornhill Square, London N1 1BE
Tel 0171-285 3007

CC NO 1047709   **ESTABLISHED** 1995

■ The Evelyn Charitable Settlement

WHAT IS FUNDED Dogs, kennels and other facilities for dogs

WHAT IS NOT FUNDED Grants are rarely awarded to individuals

WHO CAN BENEFIT Organisations working in the areas outlined above

WHERE FUNDING CAN BE GIVEN Surrey, especially the Parishes of Wotton and Abinger (North Ward) near Dorking

FINANCES
- Year 1996–97
- Income £6,000
- Grants £5,500

TRUSTEES J P M H Evelyn, Mrs A P Evelyn, Mrs S Lyons

HOW TO APPLY To the Secretary in writing. The Trustees meet annually in the autumn

WHO TO APPLY TO P A C Trower, Secretary to the Trustees, The Evelyn Charitable Settlement, Bartram House, Station Road, Pulborough, West Sussex RH20 1AJ

CC NO 293867   **ESTABLISHED** 1986

■ Douglas Heath Eves Charitable Trust

WHAT IS FUNDED Charities which benefit the environment

WHAT IS NOT FUNDED Grants never made to individuals. Registered charities only

WHO CAN BENEFIT Organisations working in the areas outlined above

WHERE FUNDING CAN BE GIVEN UK and occasionally overseas

TYPE OF GRANT One-off single non-continuing

RANGE OF GRANTS £50–£250

FINANCES
- Year 1997
- Income £25,125
- Grants £18,812

TRUSTEES D H Eves, Mrs M Alderdice, P J Sheahan

HOW TO APPLY In writing to the address below

WHO TO APPLY TO Douglas Heath Eves, Douglas Heath Eves Charitable Trust, Cocklands, Lower Basildon, Reading, Berkshire RG8 9PD

CC NO 248003   **ESTABLISHED** 1964

■ Beryl Evetts & Robert Luff Animal Welfare Trust

WHAT IS FUNDED The protection and shelter of lost or starving birds or animals. The promotion of hospitals for animals or birds (permanent site or mobile). The funding of veterinary research

WHO CAN BENEFIT Registered charities working in the areas outlined above

WHERE FUNDING CAN BE GIVEN UK

RANGE OF GRANTS £100–£35,000

SAMPLE GRANTS £35,000 to Animal Health Trust
£26,000 to Royal Veterinary College
£1,000 to National Equine (and smaller animals) Defence League
£1,000 to People's Dispensary for Sick Animals
£500 to Pet Search

£100 to Paignton Zoo
£100 to Tusk Trust
£100 to National Federation of Badgers

FINANCES
- Year 1997
- Income £88,771
- Grants £63,800

TRUSTEES R C W Luff, CBE, Sir Robert Johnson, M Tomlinson, Mrs J Tomlinson, Lady Johnson, R P J Price, Ms G Favot, B D Nicholson

HOW TO APPLY In writing to the address below

WHO TO APPLY TO M D Lock, Beryl Evetts & Robert Luff Animal Welfare Trust, c/o Parker Cavendish, 28 Church Road, Stanmore, Middlesex HA7 4XR

CC NO 283944   **ESTABLISHED** 1981

■The Esmée Fairbairn Charitable Trust (25)

WHAT IS FUNDED Rural conservation and agriculture. The Trust's policies in these areas are outlined in further detail below, although applicants are urged to obtain a copy of the Trust's guidelines, which are updated regularly. The Trust is committed to the preservation and development of a free society and to free market principles. It seeks to encourage the pursuit of excellence and innovation

WHAT IS NOT FUNDED Voluntary and charitable organisations only. Applications on behalf of individuals and student expeditions are not supported. Nor are medical causes (especially research); individual schools; sectarian religions; animal welfare; individual parish churches; overseas travel; commercial publications; sports; general appeals; conferences or seminars; branches of national charities; large national charities which enjoy wide support; charities whose operational area is outside the UK. Retrospective grants are not made

WHO CAN BENEFIT Voluntary and charitable organisations working in the areas outlined above

WHERE FUNDING CAN BE GIVEN UK

TYPE OF GRANT Primarily core and project grants, with a limited number of capital projects. Also buildings, endowments, feasibility studies, one-off, research, recurring costs, running costs, salaries and start-up costs. Funding can be given for up to or over three years

RANGE OF GRANTS Typically £1,000–£250,000; occasionally much larger grants are made. In 1998 the average grant size was just below £15,000

FINANCES
- Year 1998
- Income £15,451,000
- Grants £14,694,000

TRUSTEES John S Fairbairn, DL (Chairman), Jeremy Hardie, CBE (Treasurer), Sir Antony Acland, GCMG, GCVO, Ashley G Down, Mrs Penelope Hughes-Hallett, Martin Lane Fox, Baroness Linklater, Lady Milford, Lord Rees-Mogg, William Sieghart

PUBLICATIONS Policy guidelines, Annual Report

NOTES Grants are paid only to registered charities

Fairbairn

HOW TO APPLY Applicants should request a copy of the Trust's policy guidelines (send an A4 sae) before submitting an application

WHO TO APPLY TO Judith Dunworth, Secretary, The Esmée Fairbairn Charitable Trust, 7 Cowley Street, London SW1P 3NB
Tel 0171-227 5400
Fax 0171-227 5401

CC NO 200051   **ESTABLISHED** 1961

Commentary

The Esmée Fairbairn Charitable Trust was established on 20 January 1961. The founder and principal settlor, Ian Fairbairn, was a leading City figure and his company, now M&G Group PLC, was the pioneer of the unit trust industry. The Trust is named after Ian Fairbairn's wife, Esmée, who had been killed by a flying bomb towards the end of the Second World War.

The Trust gives its funding in five main areas: arts and heritage; education; social welfare; the environment; and social and economic research. In the arts and heritage category the Trust aims to help extend the artistic and business development of the performing and creative arts. Priorities include: the professional development of performers and other artists who have completed their formal training and are in the early stages of their careers (although no grants are made to individuals); initiatives which improve the management, artistic or business performance of arts organisations, or their financial independence; the public presentation or performance of contemporary work; arts provision amongst groups or places less well served; audience development; and arts education work involving local communities, particularly those less well served. In the heritage field the Trust additionally supports: significant acquisitions by provincial public museums and galleries (however, this is done through another grant giving body, so direct support is limited); the preservation of buildings of historic or architectural value where these are put to public use, and the conservation of artefacts.

The Trust's education category is aimed at projects which will contribute to the development of a better educated society. Priority areas within this include: early learning, covering the years 0–7; further education of 16–19 year olds, particularly the academically less able; the professional development and further training of teachers; and adult education, especially where this combats earlier under-achievement or creates second chances. Awards are not made to individuals.

The Trust's social welfare programme aims to foster self-help and the active participation of those in need; enable less advantaged people to be independent, gain useful skills and overcome handicaps; and encourage volunteer involvement. The Trust supports practical initiatives embodying some or all of these characteristics in the fields of: permanent physical and sensory disabilities; mental health and learning disabilities; young people, especially those who are under-achieving or living in difficult circumstances; parenting and family support; carers, ie people caring for the sick, elderly or disabled people at home; homelessness; ageing, ie social aspects of elderly people living in the community; crime prevention and the rehabilitation of ex-offenders; substance abuse; and regeneration and other schemes which support and develop community resourcefulness, particularly in less advantaged areas.

The Trust's environmental grants are aimed at the promotion of sustainable development, principally through: practical projects; research where this is geared to advancing practical solutions; and education. The priority areas are as follows: the preservation of countryside and wildlife, linked to public access where appropriate; the reconciliation of the needs of the environment and the economy, for example projects which sustain the former and promote solutions to any adverse environmental effects associated with economic development; and the development of alternative technologies that help attain these priorities.

The social and economic research category aims at encouraging the application of new ideas (or the challenging of old ones), to contemporary socio-political and economic issues. Research which is designed with practical applications of these new ideas in mind is viewed particularly well, and the principal medium of the research is through independent research institutions, and Think Tanks. Of the five main funding areas, the first three are by far the most heavily concentrated upon by the Trust. Social welfare grants accounted for 41.7 per cent of the total in 1997, with arts and heritage receiving 26.2 per cent, education 17.1 per cent, and the lower priority areas of the environment receiving 10.1 per cent and social and economic research and other receiving 4.9 per cent. This differs quite significantly with the start of the year's projected guideline percentages, with social welfare originally apportioned 30 per cent, arts and heritage 25 per cent, education 27.5 per cent, the environment 10 per cent, and social and economic research 7.5 per cent. This outcome is due to the fact that social welfare is the area where budgetary pressure is always the greatest, combined with a reduction in applications for education, due to the domination of state provision in the field. In other funding areas, especially social welfare, not replacing statutory funding is becoming an increasingly difficult line to hold. There is a general review of funding policy every three years, when strategy meetings are held.

The Trust will only fund organisations and projects in the UK, although they do try and spread their funding as widely as possible. Following a first successful appointment in north west England, the Trust is appointing up to five more freelance regional advisors throughout the country in order to enhance its contact with applicants and facilitate their giving.

The Trust is more than happy to become involved in co-funding if they are unable to offer the whole sum required by an organisation. Although they do not always have the resources to actively go out and seek partnerships for projects, they are not against partnership funding in the right circumstances. The bulk of the grants made by the Trust are for core costs or for projects, often over a year or more. Capital grants are limited but when made tend to be for quite large projects.

The Trust's application procedures vary according to the size of the grant required. While there is an application form for smaller grants of up to £5,000, for larger grants a letter is required, with the appropriate supporting information. The letter should include: (i) a brief description of the organisation, its work, management and staffing structure, and current budget; (ii) a description of the purpose of the project for which funds are required, the amount sought from the Trust, who will manage the project, when the project will start and finish and the results expected; (iii) a budget for the project, details of funds already raised and other sources being approached; (iv) how your organisation intends to monitor and evaluate the project; (v) your plans for sharing information about the project and what you learn from it with others in the field; (vi) the most recent Annual Report and Audited Accounts; (vii) your organisation's charitable status, including the charity's registration number; (viii) the contact name, address and telephone number. Applicants are urged to contact the Trust prior to making an application in order to obtain up-to-date guidelines. Applications may be made at any time throughout the year, and the process of dealing with an application is liable to take anything between two to six months. Applications are assessed by the Trust's staff and external advisors. Some visits are undertaken as part of the process, especially to organisations applying for larger grants. Numbers of visits are set to increase with the appointment of the new regional advisors, as well as new members of staff at the offices of the Trust. Approximately the same amount of money is available for distribution in grants at each of the quarterly meetings of the Trustees. These meetings occur in February, May, July and November (but this is likely to change in 1999 to February, April, July and December), when all applications will be considered and decisions made upon them. Applicants are notified of the outcome of their application by letter. Once an application has been considered, the Trust does not usually accept another application from the same organisation within 12 months from the date of the decision. Where an organisation has received a grant, the Trust's evaluation process is a developing area, which, although at present concentrating on the larger grants, is continuing to expand. Most of the larger grants made require the recipient to produce progress reports, often with specific requirements such as accounts. For the majority of smaller grants, the Trust only requires that a report be made upon completion of a project

SAMPLE GRANTS

In 1998 the Trust made 1023 grants, of which 362 were over £10,000 and the rest below. A sample of larger grants made in 1998 follow:
£250,000 to King's College, University of London towards Liddell Hart Archive Development
£181,800 to Museum of Scotland towards capital funding of the Discovery Centre
£165,000 to Worcester College of Higher Education towards the Accounting Early for Life Long Learning project
£149,000 to Oxford University Psychiatry Department towards an evaluation study of a parent education programme
£105,000 to Royal Society for Nature Conservation towards a grants programme for local wildlife trusts
£100,000 to StartHere towards the development of a pilot project to establish an accessible IT-based interactive community information service
£100,000 to Aldeburgh Productions towards capital improvements to Snape Maltings Concert Hall
£60,000 to Pens Green Centre towards the Centre's early years research and development project
£50,000 to the Architecture Foundation towards core funding
£50,000 to the Pedestrians Association towards core funding costs

■The Fitzmaurice Charitable Trust

WHAT IS FUNDED Charities working in the fields of nature reserves and waterways

WHAT IS NOT FUNDED No large national charities

WHO CAN BENEFIT Individuals and small voluntary organisations working in the areas outlined above

WHERE FUNDING CAN BE GIVEN Norwich and Norfolk

TYPE OF GRANT Small one-off grants

RANGE OF GRANTS £25–£1,000, typical grant £100

Fitzwilliam

Alphabetical register of grant making trusts

FINANCES
- Year 1996
- Income £14,923
- Grants £10,755

TRUSTEES D K Fitzmaurice, K J Fitzmaurice, T P B Fitzmaurice

HOW TO APPLY In writing only to the address under Who To Apply To

WHO TO APPLY TO Mrs T M Fitzmaurice, Secretary, The Fitzmaurice Charitable Trust, Marlpit House, Wroxham Road, Coltishall, Norwich NR12 7AF

CC NO 326729 **ESTABLISHED** 1984

■ The Earl Fitzwilliam Charitable Trust

WHAT IS FUNDED Preference for charitable projects in areas with historical family connections. Chiefly in Cambridgeshire, Northamptonshire and Yorkshire. Particularly charities working in the fields of: rural conservation including: environmental issues, landscapes, waterways and woodlands. Also agriculture

WHAT IS NOT FUNDED No grants to individuals on a personal basis

WHO CAN BENEFIT Organisations working in the fields outlined above. Projects and charities connected in some way with or which will benefit rural life

WHERE FUNDING CAN BE GIVEN Priority given to Cambridgeshire, Northamptonshire and Yorkshire. Also Denbighshire

TYPE OF GRANT Buildings, capital, core costs, endowments, one-off, project, research and start-up costs. Funding may be given for up to two years

RANGE OF GRANTS £250–£5,000

SAMPLE GRANTS £10,000 to The Badminton Foundation for endowment for acquisition of woodland and land for conservation

FINANCES
- Year 1998
- Income £179,000
- Grants £122,000

TRUSTEES Sir Philip Naylor-Leyland, Bt, Lady Isabella Naylor-Leyland

HOW TO APPLY All applications in writing, no application form and no guidelines are issued

WHO TO APPLY TO J M S Thompson, Secretary to the Trustees, The Earl Fitzwilliam Charitable Trust, Estate Office, Milton Park, Peterborough PE6 7AH

CC NO 269388 **ESTABLISHED** 1975

■ The Russell and Mary Foreman 1980 Charitable Trust

WHAT IS FUNDED Ecology and animals

WHAT IS NOT FUNDED Grants to registered charities only. No grants to individuals

WHO CAN BENEFIT Registered charities working in the areas outlined above

WHERE FUNDING CAN BE GIVEN UK and overseas

TYPE OF GRANT Cash donations only. Yearly donations

FINANCES
- Year 1996
- Income £13,033
- Grants £650

TRUSTEES Royal Bank of Scotland plc

HOW TO APPLY To the address under Who To Apply To in writing at any time. No acknowledgements will be sent

WHO TO APPLY TO The Senior Trust Officer (Ref 7980), Russell and Mary Foreman 1980 Charitable Trust, Royal Bank of Scotland plc, Private Trust & Taxation, PO Box 356, 45 Mosley Street, Manchester M60 2BE

CC NO 281543 **ESTABLISHED** 1980

■ Fox Memorial Trust

WHAT IS FUNDED Support will be given to rural conservation; animal facilities and services; and environmental and animal sciences

WHO CAN BENEFIT General charities working in the areas outlined above

WHERE FUNDING CAN BE GIVEN England and Scotland

RANGE OF GRANTS £250–£3000, typical grant £500

FINANCES
- Year 1997–98
- Income £43,716
- Grants £53,032

TRUSTEES Sir Murray Fox, GBE, MA, Miss S M Crichton, Mrs F M Davies, Miss A M Fox, Miss C H Fox

HOW TO APPLY Initial telephone calls are not welcome. Sae will guarantee a response

WHO TO APPLY TO Mrs C Hardy, Fox Memorial Trust, 5 Audley Court, 32–34 Hill Street, London W1X 7FT

CC NO 262262 **ESTABLISHED** 1970

■ Sydney E Franklin Deceased's New Second Charity

WHAT IS FUNDED Donations mainly given to small charities with low overheads; focusing on endangered species, environmental issues and animal welfare

WHAT IS NOT FUNDED No grants to individuals or for scholarships. No grants to large umbrella charities

WHO CAN BENEFIT Smaller charities with low overheads dealing with endangered species

WHERE FUNDING CAN BE GIVEN UK and overseas. Priority, but not exclusively, to third world projects

TYPE OF GRANT Core costs, one-off and project. Funding may be given for up to three years

RANGE OF GRANTS £500–£5,000, typical grant £1,000–£3,000

SAMPLE GRANTS £1,000 to Diana Fossey Gorilla Fund

FINANCES
- Year 1997–98
- Income £25,800
- Grants £26,500

TRUSTEES A Franklin, Dr R C G Franklin, Ms T N Franklin

HOW TO APPLY Donations may only be requested by letter, and these are placed before the Trustees at their meeting which is normally held at the end of each year. Applications are not acknowledged

WHO TO APPLY TO Dr R C G Franklin, Sydney E Franklin Deceased's New Second Charity, c/o 39 Westleigh Avenue, London SW15 6RQ

CC NO 272047 **ESTABLISHED** 1973

■ Frognal Trust

WHAT IS FUNDED The Trustees current grant making policy is to make relatively small grants to as many qualifying charities as possible. Particularly charities working in the fields of: environmental issues; fauna and flora; lakes; landscapes; nature reserves; waterways; and woodlands. Other charitable purposes will be considered

WHAT IS NOT FUNDED No grants to charities for the benefit of animals, people living outside the UK or for the propagation of religious beliefs. The Trustees do not make grants for educational/research trips overseas

WHO CAN BENEFIT Registered charities only

WHERE FUNDING CAN BE GIVEN UK

TYPE OF GRANT Buildings, capital and research grants will be considered. Funding is available for up to two years

RANGE OF GRANTS £500–£3,800

SAMPLE GRANTS £3,000 to Woodland Trust

FINANCES
- Year 1997
- Income £69,569
- Grants £60,855

TRUSTEES Mrs P Blake-Roberts, J P van Montagu, P Fraser

WHO TO APPLY TO The Grants Administrator, Frognal Trust, Charities Aid Foundation, Kings Hill, West Malling, Kent ME19 4TA

CC NO 244444 **ESTABLISHED** 1964

Garnett

■ The Garnett Charitable Trust

WHAT IS FUNDED Environmental causes

WHAT IS NOT FUNDED No grants to individuals

WHO CAN BENEFIT Organisations working in the areas outlined above

WHERE FUNDING CAN BE GIVEN South West, Channel Islands and Northern Ireland

RANGE OF GRANTS £5–£10,000

FINANCES
- Year 1997
- Income £28,455
- Grants £26,980

TRUSTEES A J F Garnett, Mrs P Garnett, J W Sharpe

HOW TO APPLY In writing to the address below

WHO TO APPLY TO J W Sharpe, The Garnett Charitable Trust, Osborne Clarke Solicitors, 50 Queen Charlotte Street, Bristol BS1 4HE *Tel* 0117-923 0220

CC NO 327847   **ESTABLISHED** 1988

■ Gerefa Charitable Trust

WHAT IS FUNDED Endangered species; environmental issues; fauna; flora; animal homes; animal welfare; and bird sanctuaries

WHAT IS NOT FUNDED No buildings, appeals for endowment funds for charities, social welfare where it may be considered as government or local authority responsibility. No grants to individuals

WHO CAN BENEFIT Small local organisations with particular need

WHERE FUNDING CAN BE GIVEN West Midlands, especially Shropshire, Highlands in Scotland

TYPE OF GRANT One-off and project. Single donations up to £200

RANGE OF GRANTS £20–£2,500; typical £100

FINANCES
- Year 1998
- Income £8,000
- Grants £5,500

TRUSTEES Alan Grieve, MA, LLM, Karen Grieve

HOW TO APPLY To the address below in writing. Applications cannot be acknowledged

WHO TO APPLY TO Alan Grieve, Trustee, Gerefa Charitable Trust, Stoke Lodge, Clee Downton, Ludlow, Shropshire SY8 3EG

CC NO 267103   **ESTABLISHED** 1974

■ The Simon Gibson Charitable Trust (405)

WHAT IS FUNDED Charitable bodies in the UK including those working in the areas of: rural conservation; animal homes; animal welfare; bird sanctuaries; dogs, kennels and other facilities for dogs; horses, stables and other facilities for horses; wildlife sanctuaries; agriculture; and animal breeding

WHAT IS NOT FUNDED No grants are made to individuals

WHO CAN BENEFIT Registered charities and other organisations tax exempt under Charity Commission schemes

WHERE FUNDING CAN BE GIVEN UK, especially South Wales and Suffolk

TYPE OF GRANT One-off or recurring, core costs, running costs, project, research, salaries and start-up costs, buildings and capital. Funding may be given for up to three years

RANGE OF GRANTS £1,000–£50,000, normally £2,000–£5,000

FINANCES
- Year 1998
- Income £362,018
- Grants £333,100

TRUSTEES George D Gibson, Angela M Homfray, Bryan Marsh

HOW TO APPLY Applications should be in writing. No guidelines are issued. All applications are acknowledged

WHO TO APPLY TO Bryan Marsh, Trustee, The Simon Gibson Charitable Trust, Hill House, 1 Little New Street, London EC4A 3TR

CC NO 269501   **ESTABLISHED** 1975

Commentary

The Simon Gibson Charitable Trust was founded in 1975 by George Simon Gibson. Simon Gibson's father had himself set up a Trust – the G C Gibson Charitable Trust – and this Trust was established as a continuation of this tradition and with the intention of giving to any charitable cause that the Trustees determined. As well as the G C Gibson Charitable Trust, there is another family charity, Simon Gibson's sister's trust – J A M Humphreys Charitable Settlement – demonstrating the family's breadth of commitment to charity. However, these trusts are run completely separately. The Trustees of the Simon Gibson Charitable Trust include the settlor's sister and nephew.

The Trust is extremely comprehensive in its giving and does not limit the causes which it will support, although, in practice, assistance is often concentrated upon projects and organisations with which the Trust or the settlor has past connections. Areas supported in the past and therefore likely to receive consideration include: a wide range of care organisations, including those aimed at the general welfare as well as the specific care of both children and the elderly; community organisations working for the benefit of local communities, especially in Suffolk and South Wales; the arts, especially music; and organisations working with and for people with various disabilities. To a lesser extent charities interested in the welfare of animals, and those concentrating upon sailors and sailing are assisted. Many churches and schools are also assisted, although the Trust's policy on statutory funding, as outlined below, should be noted. The Trustees are anxious for their donations not to be subsumed by huge fundraising costs, and for this reason like to give small amounts to small, local organisations, where they feel that the benefits of the grant will reach the 'sharp end' as quickly as possible. The Trust does not give grants to individuals.

Although the Trust deed allows grants to be made throughout the world, in effect grants are made to organisations throughout the UK, although there is some concentration upon local charities in South Wales, where the Gibson family have strong connections, and in Suffolk, where many members of the family now live. Grants are rarely given overseas because it is felt that there are so many good and worthy causes to support within the UK.

Although the Trust is happy to help a school or a hospital provide a better service, they will not replace statutory responsibilities. What they will provide are facilities or equipment that can be seen as an added extra, that would be improving on current services and facilities, and that would not be catered for by statutory bodies in the normal course of events. Grants tend to be quite small, often around £2,000, reflecting the Trust's concentration on giving to small charities.

Applicants should choose the format that they feel best presents their organisation when making an application; there is no application form. An initial telephone call to the Trust is discouraged. When the Trust receives an application an acknowledgement card is sent out to the applicant, informing them of whether the Trust will be considering their application further or not. Due to the large number of applications, it is unusual for more than 40 per cent of these to go forward for further consideration. The Trustees meet on one day a year, in May, when they give away the entire income of the Trust in grants. Only successful applicants are informed of the outcome of their application, in order to keep the Trust's administration costs to a minimum.

The Trust itself is operated on a shoestring, without a full time administrator and with administration costs of only £2,000 to £3,000 a year. There is no mechanism in place to follow up grants; the Trustees do not have time to make visits nor do they require reports from their grantees. Often there is already a relationship between the Trust and the grant recipient, and there will be some form of contact where there has been a long-term interest

SAMPLE GRANTS
The top ten grants made in 1998 were:
£20,000 to Welsh Livery Guild Charitable Trust
£10,000 to Ely Cathedral Appeal Fund
£6,000 to New Astley Club Endowment Fund
£5,000 to Alzheimer's Research Trust
£5,000 to Exning Church
£5,000 to Framlington College
£5,000 to Princes Youth Business Trust
£5,000 to Prostate Cancer Charity
£5,000 to Save the Children Fund
£5,000 to St Edmundsbury Cathedral

■ Horace Gillman's Trust

WHAT IS FUNDED Grants are given to support the work of several bird charities, reserves and an observatory

WHO CAN BENEFIT Bird related projects

WHERE FUNDING CAN BE GIVEN UK, particularly Scotland, also Ireland

SAMPLE GRANTS £11,500 to RSPB for Loch Garten Osprey Visitors Centre
£1,500 to Scottish Seabirds Centre, North Berwick Harbour for Bass Rock Project

FINANCES
- Year 1997
- Income £20,000
- Grants £10,000

TRUSTEES J K Burleigh, F Hamilton, I Darling

HOW TO APPLY Applications should be made in writing to the address below

WHO TO APPLY TO Miss C Hope, Horace Gillman's Trust, 32 Moray Place, Edinburgh EH3 6BZ

SC NO SCO 17672   **ESTABLISHED** 1979

■ The Glastonbury Conservation Society

WHAT IS FUNDED To stimulate public interest, promote high standards of planning and preservation of features of historic importance in Glastonbury

WHO CAN BENEFIT Organisations and institutions working in the areas outlined above

Gloucestershire

Alphabetical register of grant making trusts

WHERE FUNDING CAN BE GIVEN The Borough of Glastonbury and any place within five miles of the Cross at Glastonbury

TYPE OF GRANT Recurring

FINANCES
- Year 1996
- Income £5,450

HOW TO APPLY In writing to the address below

WHO TO APPLY TO J R Brunsdon, Glastonbury Conservation Society, The Hermitage, 5 Chilkwell Street, Glastonbury, Somerset BA6 8DJ

CC NO 264036   **ESTABLISHED** 1972

■ Gloucestershire Environmental Trust Company

WHAT IS FUNDED Any project falling within the criteria for Project Approval by ENTRUST, particularly: environmental issues; flora; lakes; landscapes; nature reserves; waterways; woodlands; animal facilities and services; wildlife parks and sanctuaries; zoos; environmental and animal sciences; agriculture; and ornithology and zoology

WHAT IS NOT FUNDED Anything not approved by ENTRUST

WHO CAN BENEFIT Any bona fide body whose objects include any of the approved objects under the Landfill Tax Regulations, eg churches, community groups, wildlife trusts, village hall committees, historic buildings, waste management research establishments. There are no restrictions on the age; professional and economic group; religion and culture of the beneficiaries

WHERE FUNDING CAN BE GIVEN Projects in Gloucestershire only

TYPE OF GRANT Buildings, feasibility studies, one-off, project, research and start-up costs. Funding may be given for up to two years

RANGE OF GRANTS Maximum grants £100,000 per project, a maximum limit of £100,000 for an individual organisation per annum

SAMPLE GRANTS £54,610 to Woodchester Mansion Trust for restoration of Victorian rainwater system
£50,000 to Gloucestershire Wildlife Trust for purchase of SSSI (Salmonsbury Meadows)
£48,000 to The Natural Step for research into waste sustainibility
£41,360 to Painswick Rococo Garden for restoration of orangery
£32,000 to Gloucestershire Wildlife Trust/ Biodiversity Partnership for Biodiversity Action Plan officer for Gloucestershire (for one year)
£30,000 to Wildfowl and Wetlands Trust for creation of reedbed to take waste from Slimbridge
£30,000 to Dursley Town Hall Trust for damage limitation/revival of historic building
£29,000 to Farming and Wildlife Advisory Group for one year funding for FWAG Adviser to specialise in waste management advice to farmers/landowners
£20,000 to Gloucestershire Resource Centre for 'The Scrap Store'
£19,700 to Coltswold Water Park Society for one year funding for officer to implement Biodiversity Action Plan

FINANCES
- Year 1997–98
- Income £1,399,644
- Grants £269,850

TRUSTEES Jonathon Porritt (Chairman), David Ball, David Burton, Paul Holliday, Gordon McGlone, Jack Newell

PUBLICATIONS Leaflets: *Applying for a Grant*, *Notes on Application for Grants* and application form

NOTES The Trust receives its income through a scheme set up by Cory Environmental under the Landfill Tax Regulations. Preferential consideration is given to projects close to Hempsted, Stoke Orchard and Elmstone Hardwicke operations. Figures under Finances are for a fifteen month period to 31 March 1998

HOW TO APPLY In the first instance contact the Trust Secretary for an application form

WHO TO APPLY TO Mrs Lynne Garner, Secretary, Gloucestershire Environmental Trust Company, Moorend Cottage, Watery Lane, Upton St Leonards, Gloucestershire GL4 8DW
Tel 01452 615110
Fax 01452 613817

CC NO 1072572   **ESTABLISHED** 1997

■ J G Graves Charitable Trust

WHAT IS FUNDED Charities working in the fields of environmental issues, landscapes and woodlands. The income is mainly applied to local (Sheffield) charities for capital purposes rather than running costs

WHAT IS NOT FUNDED No grants to individuals

WHO CAN BENEFIT Charities who have similar objectives

WHERE FUNDING CAN BE GIVEN Mainly Sheffield

TYPE OF GRANT Mainly capital and one-off for start-ups. Some for running costs. Funding may given for up to three years

RANGE OF GRANTS No restrictions

FINANCES
- Year 1997
- Income £153,036
- Grants £119,561

TRUSTEES G F Young, CBE, JP, LLD, Mrs A C Womack, G W Bridge, R S Sanderson, FCA, Mrs A H Tonge, T H Reed, R T Graves, S McK Hamilton, D S W Lee, Cllr P Price, Dr D R Cullen

HOW TO APPLY In writing to reach Secretary by 31 March, 30 June, 30 September, 31 December. Guidelines available. Accounts required

WHO TO APPLY TO R H M Plews, FCA, Secretary, J G Graves Charitable Trust, Knowle House, 4 Norfolk Park Road, Sheffield S2 3QE
Tel 0114-276 7991
Fax 0114-275 3538

CC NO 207481   **ESTABLISHED** 1930

■ The Great Britain Sasakawa Foundation (283)

WHAT IS FUNDED Japan – related environmental issues, fauna, flora and agriculture

WHAT IS NOT FUNDED No funding for the purchase, construction or maintenance of land or buildings

WHO CAN BENEFIT Individuals, and voluntary and charitable organisations benefiting citizens of UK and Japan

WHERE FUNDING CAN BE GIVEN UK and overseas, but projects must be Anglo-Japanese related

TYPE OF GRANT Mainly one-off, also project and research, maximum term three years. Funding for feasibility studies and start-up costs will also be considered

RANGE OF GRANTS £500–£25,000; average grant £5,000

FINANCES
- Year 1998
- Income £774,233
- Grants £560,879

TRUSTEES Earl of St Andrews, Baroness Brigstocke, Jeremy Brown, Kazuo Chiba, Michael French, BSc (Eng), FCA (Treasurer), Akiri Iriyama, Prof Harumi Kimura, D Litt, Prof Peter Mathias, CBE, FBA, DLitt (Chairman), Baroness Park of Monmouth, CMG, OBE, Yohei Sasakawa, Prof Shoichi Watanabe

NOTES The Foundation is rarely able to consider grants for the total cost of any project and encourage applicants to seek additional support from other donors

HOW TO APPLY Applications within the UK should be addressed to the Administrator in London and those arising in Japan to the Director in Tokyo at the address below. In advance of any formal application, Foundation staff are always prepared to discuss the project with the organisation or individual concerned, and like, ideally, to meet all applicants. There are no set application forms. Applicants should apply in writing and include: a summary of the project and its aims and objectives in under 1,000 words, with details of the applicant's organisation and the principal participant(s) in the project; a budget showing details of the total cost, expected contributions from other sources and the specific amount sought as a Foundation grant; for projects designed to extend over more than one year, the period to be covered by any grant approved – grants for projects in excess of three years are not normally considered. The UK Awards Committee meets twice a year in April/May and October/November. The deadlines for applications for these meetings are 31 March and 30 September respectively. The Japan Awards committee meets at the end of March and the end of October each year. The deadlines are 28 February and 30 September respectively

WHO TO APPLY TO Peter D Hand, Administrator, The Great Britain Sasakawa Foundation, 43 North Audley Street, London W1Y 1WH
Tel 0171-355 2229
Fax 0171-355 2230
E-mail gbsf@gbsf.demon.co.uk
Web Site http//www.gbsf.demon.co.uk

REGIONAL OFFICES Tokyo Liaison Office: Mrs Setsuko Sengoku, Director - Tokyo, The Sasakawa Hall, Minato-Ku, Tokyo 108-0073, Japan
Tel (81) 03 3798 5971
Fax (81) 03 3798 5973

CC NO 290766   **ESTABLISHED** 1985

Commentary

The Great Britain Sasakawa Foundation was established in 1984. In 1987 the Chairman of the Japan Shipbuilding Industry Foundation (now the Nippon Foundation) donated 3,000,000,000 Yen (roughly equivalent to £10,000,000, at an exchange rate of 232.52 Yen to the Pound) to the Great Britain Sasakawa Foundation so that it could achieve its objectives.

The main aim of the Foundation is to advance the education of the citizens of Great Britain and Japan in certain areas of interest. These areas are: maritime science and technology; each other's institutions, people, history, language, culture, music and folklore; and the two countries' intellectual, artistic and economic life. The Foundation also supports research in these areas and will support the publishing of any useful results of such research.

The Foundation supports these areas through the following activities: (a) youth exchanges and visits between Japan and Great Britain, by artists, teachers, academics and sports teams; (b) exhibitions of fine and applied art and performance of drama, music and dance; (c) research and study in the fields of medicine,

history, industry and environment, and support of Japanese language teaching in the UK; and
(d) promoting meetings of British and Japanese Veterans of the Burma Campaign.

Funding can be given throughout the world, but must be related to Anglo-Japanese projects. The Foundation may consider funding for statutory bodies and will consider co-funding projects. Grants are generally one-off awards and loans are not considered. Infrastructure costs are not normally considered.

Applications within the UK should be addressed to the Administrator in London and those arising in Japan to the Director in Tokyo at the above addresses. In advance of any formal application, Foundation staff are always prepared to discuss the project with the organisation or individual concerned, and like, ideally, to meet all applicants.

There are no set application forms; applicants should apply in writing, including: a summary of the project and its aims and objectives in under 1,000 words, with details of the applicant organisation and principal participants in the project; a budget showing details of the total cost, expected contributions from other sources and the specific amount sought from the Foundation.

The Awards Committee meets twice a year in April/May and October/November. The deadlines for applications for these meetings are 31 March and 30 September. Immediately following each Award Committee meeting the Foundation advises all applicants in writing of the results of all applications considered

SAMPLE GRANTS

The top ten grants made in 1998 were:
£35,000 to Youth Exchange Centre (British Council) for their Japan Exchange programme to enable young people from schools and youth groups to visit Japan or the United Kingdom
£22,432 to Japan/UK Community Care for Year 2 of a three year Strategic Development Programme to assist Japanese Voluntary organisations learn from specialists in the UK voluntary sector £18,000 to Oxford Brookes University for the appointment of a Sasakawa Lecturer for a single field in Japanese Studies
£15,985 to JETRO – International Educators to Japan Programme 1998/99 sponsoring seven school teachers to visit Japan to attend 6th UK Educators to Japan Programme
£13,332 to Tanpop-No-Iye-Foundation for support with a UK-Japan Fortun on works of art created by people with disabilities
£13,332 to British Craft Open Workshop for cost of holding a craft workshop in Japan for the enhancement of rural crafts
£13,321 to Tokyo Athletic Association-Japan/UK Exchange for support of an ongoing student exchange programme with UK from 1998 to 2000

£12,660 to Tokyo LA-NPO-UK/Japan Exchange for continuation of a programme for specialists from UK to develop voluntary bcommunity sector partnerships mdth local govermnent
£11,088 to Real Life New British Art for support for an art exhibition by UK artists to be shown in Japan from April 1998 to March 1999
£10,796 to British Embassy, Tokyo for additional production of Brit Packs for 1050 UK participants on the Japanese Exchange Teachers (JET) Progranune for use in schools in Japan

■ Greater Bristol Foundation

WHAT IS FUNDED Funding may be given for environmental issues and woodlands. Funds targeted at those most disadvantaged in the community with emphasis on smaller locally-based organisations

WHAT IS NOT FUNDED No grants to individuals

WHO CAN BENEFIT Any charity working in the areas outlined above

WHERE FUNDING CAN BE GIVEN Greater Bristol (a ten mile radius of the City centre)

TYPE OF GRANT Buildings, feasibility studies, project, running costs, and start-up costs. Funding may given for one year or less.
(a) Express programme up to £1,500 at any time. (b) Catalyst programme matching designated funds to projects. (c) Impact programme £20,000 per year for three years. (d) Range of special advised funds. (e) Donor advised funds

RANGE OF GRANTS £100–£60,000; average grant £1,000

SAMPLE GRANTS £4,300 to Winterbourne Parish Council to make practical improvements to an area of land owned by the Council as part of the Forest of Avon project. The work increased access, seating and fitness trails as well as creating a still pond
£3,582 to Stoke Gifford Parish Council to plant trees and shrubs in Gypsy Patch Lane, Stoke Gifford. The Parish Council oversaw this work
£3,000 to Montpelier Conservation Group, Central Bristol to make environmental improvements to St Andrews Road Park including improving the gates, fences and play equipment
£2,000 to Lawrence Weston Community Farm to purchase a shredder to recycle all waste in the community garden run by the Farm. The organisation provides a range of environmental training and educational opportunities for local residents
£2,000 to Filton Environment Action Group to involve local schools and residents in a 3-day tree, bulb and shrub planting project
£2,000 to Easton Community Association for

environmental improvements to an area of community land close to the centre to increase its accessibility to local people

£2,000 to Bristol Recycling Consortium, Patchway, to produce and distribute a locally-written waste reduction and recycling directory in Patchway. The Patchway recycling organisation runs a number of projects including community composting and waste reduction activities

£1,000 to Southmead Development Trust to make improvements to an area of land adjacent to the Greenway Centre for the benefit of local families, turning it into an accessible picnic area

£1,000 to Avon Wildlife Trust to fund work with schools in the Bristol area helping them to make better environmental use of their grounds. The project uses volunteers and actively involves the pupils in educational as well as practical projects

£750 to Stapleton Conservation Society to restore a footpath in Stapleton Glen to increase public awareness and enjoyment of this area of the city

FINANCES
- Year 1998
- Income £450,411
- Grants £274,468

TRUSTEES Ms J Bryant-Pearson, J Burke, D Claisse, Gillian Camm, G Ferguson, Mrs M Jackson, Alfred Morris (Chairman), J Pontin, J Pool, MBE, Brig H Pye, The Rt Rev B Rogerson, Bishop of Bristol, T Stevenson, S Storvik, A Thornhill, QC, J Tidmarsh, MBE, LL, JP, Heather Wheelhouse, Ms D Wood, M Woolley

PUBLICATIONS Annual Report, regular newsheets, grant making policy and guidelines

HOW TO APPLY Application forms and guidelines on request. An initial telephone enquiry recommended and welcome. Express programme considered on a rolling basis. Enquire to Foundation for other programmes

WHO TO APPLY TO Helen Moss, Director, Greater Bristol Foundation, PO Box 383, Bristol BS99 5JG
Tel 0117-921 1311
Fax 0117-929 7965
E-mail gbf@globalnet.co.uk

CC NO 295797   **ESTABLISHED** 1987

■ The Barry Green Memorial Fund

WHAT IS FUNDED Preference for smaller charities rescuing and caring for cruelly treated animals; animal homes; animal welfare; bird sanctuaries; cats, catteries and other facilities for cats; dogs, kennels and other facilities for dogs; and horses, stables and other facilities for horses

WHAT IS NOT FUNDED No expeditions, scholarships, work outside the UK or individuals

WHO CAN BENEFIT All, but the Trustees have a preference towards smaller charities working at grass roots level

WHERE FUNDING CAN BE GIVEN UK, with preference towards Yorkshire and Lancashire

TYPE OF GRANT Buildings, capital, core costs, one-off, project, recurring costs, running costs and start-up costs. Funding available for up to and over three years

RANGE OF GRANTS £100–£15,000

FINANCES
- Year 1998
- Income £151,016
- Grants £119,500

TRUSTEES R Fitzgerald-Hart, M Fitzgerald-Hart

HOW TO APPLY Any time, in writing only to the address below

WHO TO APPLY TO Clerk to the Trustees, The Barry Green Memorial Fund, Claro Chambers, Horsefair, Boroughbridge, York YO5 9LD

CC NO 1000492   **ESTABLISHED** 1990

■ Grocers' Charity

WHAT IS FUNDED Within broad aims which are reflected in the wide pattern of grants, the Trustees currently have an interest in: fauna; flora; lakes and landscapes; nature reserves; waterways; woodlands; and bird sanctuaries

WHAT IS NOT FUNDED Organisations which are not registered charities are not funded. No support for churches, educational establishments, expeditions, hospices or research projects. Restricted to those having specific close and long standing connections with The Grocers' Company. Donations will not be made to individuals (but may be paid through registered charities)

WHO CAN BENEFIT Registered charities only

WHERE FUNDING CAN BE GIVEN UK and Europe

TYPE OF GRANT Both capital and revenue projects. Non-recurring grants of limited size. Core costs, one-off, recurring costs, running costs and salaries will be considered. Funding may be given for up to one year

FINANCES
- Year 1997–98
- Income £369,000
- Grants £328,000

TRUSTEES The Grocers' Trust Company Ltd

PUBLICATIONS Annual Report

HOW TO APPLY In writing to the address under Who To Apply To. Trustees meet four times a year in January, April, June and November. Informal telephone inquiries encouraged. Applications are not acknowledged, but are informed of outcome in due course. Copy of latest annual accounts must accompany application

WHO TO APPLY TO Miss Anne Blanchard, Charity Administrator, Grocers' Charity, Grocers' Hall, Princes Street, London EC2R 8AD
Tel 0171-606 3113
Fax 0171-600 3082

CC NO 255230   **ESTABLISHED** 1968

■ Mrs Margaret Guido's Charitable Trust

WHAT IS FUNDED The preservation of the natural environment

WHAT IS NOT FUNDED No grants to individuals

WHERE FUNDING CAN BE GIVEN UK and overseas

FINANCES
- Year 1997–98
- Income £24,000
- Grants £22,850

TRUSTEES Coutts & Co

HOW TO APPLY To the address under Who To Apply To in writing

WHO TO APPLY TO Mrs Margaret Guido's Charitable Trust, The Trustee Department, c/o Coutts & Co, 440 Strand, London WC2R 0QS

CC NO 290503   **ESTABLISHED** 1984

■ HCD Memorial Fund

WHAT IS FUNDED Environmental issues and woodlands

WHAT IS NOT FUNDED Not usually for animals or objects. No grants to individuals

WHO CAN BENEFIT Organisations working in the areas outlined above

WHERE FUNDING CAN BE GIVEN UK, particularly East and West Sussex, and overseas

TYPE OF GRANT Can be one-off or recurring, including core costs, buildings, salaries and start-up costs. Funding may be given for up to three years

RANGE OF GRANTS £1,000–£150,000, typical grant £20,000

FINANCES
- Year 1996–97
- Income £491,148
- Grants £662,689

TRUSTEES C Debenham, J Debenham, N Debenham, C Flinn, Dr C Sherman

NOTES Have a preference for seeking out own projects; do not usually respond to general appeals

HOW TO APPLY In writing to the address below, no special form

WHO TO APPLY TO J Debenham, HCD Memorial Fund, Reeds Farm, Sayers Common, Hassocks, West Sussex BN6 9JQ
Tel 01273 832173

CC NO 1044956   **ESTABLISHED** 1995

■ William Haddon Charitable Trust

WHAT IS FUNDED Rural conservation and animal welfare

WHAT IS NOT FUNDED No grants to individuals

WHO CAN BENEFIT Registered charities only

WHERE FUNDING CAN BE GIVEN UK and overseas

TYPE OF GRANT One-off grants of £1,000 or less

RANGE OF GRANTS £50–£1,000; typical grant £250

SAMPLE GRANTS £1,000 to CPRE for preservation of English countryside
£1,000 to Wildfowl and Wetlands Trust for habitat for waterbirds
£1,000 to National Trust for Scotland for conservation of landscape and buildings

£500 to Suffolk Horse Society for preservation of breed purity
£500 to International Otter Survival Fund for support for threatened species
£500 to Retired Greyhound Trust for finding homes for ex-racing dogs
£500 to Advocates for Animals for medical research without using animals

FINANCES
- Year 1995–96
- Grants £11,250
- Income £14,955

TRUSTEES M A Haddon, Mrs C J Johnson, Mrs J E Haddon, Ms C Haddon

HOW TO APPLY In writing only. There are no application forms

WHO TO APPLY TO M A Haddon, William Haddon Charitable Trust, Manor Garden, Sibbertoft, Market Harborough, Leicestershire LE16 9UA

CC NO 326540   **ESTABLISHED** 1984

■The Hadrian Trust

WHAT IS FUNDED Environmental issues; landscapes; nature reserves; waterways; woodlands and other charitable projects within the boundaries of the old counties of Northumberland and Durham (this includes Tyne and Wear)

WHAT IS NOT FUNDED General applications from large national organisations are not considered nor from smaller bodies working outside the area Where Funding Can Be Given

WHO CAN BENEFIT Organisations only

WHERE FUNDING CAN BE GIVEN Within the boundaries of the old counties of Northumberland and Durham (this includes Tyne and Wear and Cleveland north of the Tees)

TYPE OF GRANT Usually one-off for a special project or part of a project. Core funding is rarely considered. The average grant is for £1,000. Buildings, capital, endowments, project, research, recurring costs, as well as running costs, salaries and start-up costs. Funding of up to three years will be considered

RANGE OF GRANTS £250–£5,000

SAMPLE GRANTS £5,000 to Beble Foundation, Jarrow towards development of environmental museum

FINANCES
- Year 1997
- Grants £196,750
- Income £190,976

TRUSTEES P R M Harbottle, B J Gillespie, J B Parker

PUBLICATIONS Information sheet

NOTES Trustees meetings are held quarterly, usually in January, April, July and October

HOW TO APPLY By letter to the address under Who To Apply To. There is no application form but information sheet will be sent if requested. The letter of application should set out concise details of the project, the proposed funding and list any other applications being made, with results if known. Eligible applications will be acknowledged and the acknowledgement will give the date when the application will be considered. Cheques are sent out to successful applicants within two weeks of the meeting, but no further correspondence is sent to unsuccessful applicants. Applications from individuals in need are now referred to Greggs Charitable Trust to whom a block grant is now made. The address is Fernwood House, Clayton Road, Newcastle upon Tyne NE2 1TL

WHO TO APPLY TO John Parker, The Hadrian Trust, 36 Rectory Road, Gosforth, Newcastle upon Tyne NE3 1XP
Tel 0191-285 9553 (only for specific enquiries)

CC NO 272161   **ESTABLISHED** 1976

■Robert Hall Charity

WHAT IS FUNDED General at Trustees' discretion, including charities working with endangered species and environmental issues

WHAT IS NOT FUNDED No grants to individuals

WHO CAN BENEFIT Organisations working in the areas outlined above

WHERE FUNDING CAN BE GIVEN West Walton and St Augustine's area of Wisbech

TYPE OF GRANT Range of grants including buildings, capital, recurring costs and start up costs. Funding for up to three years may be available

RANGE OF GRANTS £500–£5,000

FINANCES
- Year 1997–98
- Grants £23,550
- Income £27,165

TRUSTEES Steven Whitteridge, Colin Arnold, David Ball, David Burall

HOW TO APPLY In writing to the address under Who To Apply To

WHO TO APPLY TO David Ball, Robert Hall Charity, Frasers, Solicitors, 29 Old Market, Wisbech, Cambridgeshire PE13 1ND

CC NO 1015493   **ESTABLISHED** 1992

The Christine Hall Trust

WHAT IS FUNDED General charitable purposes including rural conservation

WHAT IS NOT FUNDED No grants to individuals

WHO CAN BENEFIT Registered charities working in the areas outlined above

WHERE FUNDING CAN BE GIVEN Leeds, Yorkshire and overseas

TYPE OF GRANT One-off, running, recurring and core costs. Project funding for one year or less

RANGE OF GRANTS Up to £2,000 per grant

FINANCES
- Year 1996
- Income £6,417

TRUSTEES S L Hall, B C Stead, D C Hall

HOW TO APPLY To the address below in writing

WHO TO APPLY TO D C Hall, Trustee, The Christine Hall Trust, Mazebrook, 34 Moor Road, Far Headlingley, Leeds LS6 4BJ

CC NO 328068   **ESTABLISHED** 1988

The Lennox Hannay Charitable Trust

WHAT IS FUNDED The Trust will consider funding nature reserves and animal welfare

WHAT IS NOT FUNDED No grants to individuals or non-registered charities

WHO CAN BENEFIT Registered charities working in the areas outlined above

WHERE FUNDING CAN BE GIVEN South East and South West England, London

TYPE OF GRANT Core costs. Funding is given for one year or less

RANGE OF GRANTS £200–£47,000

SAMPLE GRANTS £23,000 to Countryside Foundation

FINANCES
- Year 1997–98
- Income £349,663
- Grants £316,950

TRUSTEES Robert Fleming Trustee Co Ltd, W L Hannay, Caroline F Wilmot-Sitwell

HOW TO APPLY In writing to the address below. No guidelines or application forms issued

WHO TO APPLY TO Robert Fleming Trustee Co Ltd, The Lennox Hannay Charitable Trust, 25 Copthall Avenue, London EC2R 7DR

CC NO 299099   **ESTABLISHED** 1988

The Haramead Trust

WHAT IS FUNDED The relief of the suffering of animals

WHO CAN BENEFIT Organisations benefiting animals

WHERE FUNDING CAN BE GIVEN UK and overseas

RANGE OF GRANTS £5,000–£35,000

FINANCES
- Year 1997
- Income £165,992
- Grants £170,000

TRUSTEES Mrs W M Linnett, M J Linnett, R H Smith, D L Tams

HOW TO APPLY In writing to the address below

WHO TO APPLY TO D L Tams, Trustee, The Haramead Trust, c/o Crane and Walton, 113–117 London Road, Leicester LE2 0RG

CC NO 1047416   **ESTABLISHED** 1995

The Harebell Centenary Fund

WHAT IS FUNDED The relief of sickness and suffering in animals; and rural conservation

WHAT IS NOT FUNDED Infrastructure. No grants to individuals. No individual scholarships or bursaries are being given at present

WHO CAN BENEFIT National and small charitable organisations working in the areas outlined above

WHERE FUNDING CAN BE GIVEN UK and Europe

TYPE OF GRANT One-off, capital, research and recurring costs. Funding may be given for one year or less

RANGE OF GRANTS £500–£2,500

SAMPLE GRANTS £2,500 to Marwell Zoological Park for general purposes
£2,500 to The Blue Cross Animals Hospital for general purposes

FINANCES
- Year 1997–98
- Income £72,000
- Grants £60,500

TRUSTEES J M Denker, M I Goodbody, F M Reed

NOTES The Trustees are unlikely to respond to unsolicited applications or to individuals

HOW TO APPLY To the address under Who To Apply To in writing

WHO TO APPLY TO Ms P J Chapman, The Harebell Centenary Fund, 20 Blackfriars Lane, London EC4V 6HD
Tel 0171-248 4282

CC NO 1003552   **ESTABLISHED** 1991

■ Mrs D L Harryhausen's 1969 Trust

WHAT IS FUNDED Grants are made to a number of specific animal welfare charities in connection with David Livingstone. At present these exhaust the income and the Trustees are not inviting applications

WHO CAN BENEFIT Animal charities

WHERE FUNDING CAN BE GIVEN UK, particularly Scotland

TYPE OF GRANT Buildings, capital, core costs, one-off, recurring costs, running costs, salaries and start-up costs. Funding may be given for up to and over three years

RANGE OF GRANTS £500–£1,500

FINANCES
- Year 1996–97
- Income £11,700
- Grants £10,374

TRUSTEES Simon Mackintosh, George Menzies, Vanessa Harryhausen

PUBLICATIONS Accounts are available from the Trust

NOTES At present the commitments are exhausting the income available

HOW TO APPLY Applications should be made in writing to the address under Who To Apply To, but at present no new applications are being invited

WHO TO APPLY TO The Correspondent, Mrs D L Harryhausen's 1969 Trust, Turcan Connell, Saltire Court, 20 Castle Terrace, Edinburgh EH1 2EF
Tel 0131-228 8111

SC NO SCO 15688

■ William Geoffrey Harvey's Discretionary Settlement

WHAT IS FUNDED To promote the well-being of and prevent cruelty to animals and birds. Also endangered species, fauna and nature reserves

WHAT IS NOT FUNDED New causes not likely to receive help. No grants to individuals

WHO CAN BENEFIT Registered charities only

WHERE FUNDING CAN BE GIVEN North West of England

TYPE OF GRANT Running costs and capital expenditure. Also core costs and recurring costs. Funding is given for one year or less

RANGE OF GRANTS £1,000–£5,000 (but may increase in 1999/2000)

SAMPLE GRANTS The following grants were given for general running costs:
£5,000 to PDSA
£5,000 to Redwings Horse Sanctuary
£4,000 to Care for the Wild
£3,500 to National Canine Defence League
£3,500 to Wildfowl and Wetlands Trust
£3,000 to The Donkey Sanctuary
£3,000 to Wildlife Hospital Trust
£1,000 to three Owl and Bird Sanctuaries/Reserves

FINANCES
- Year 1998
- Income £31,443
- Grants £28,000

TRUSTEES F R Shackleton, F A Sherring, G J Hull

NOTES Trustees make decisions after 5 April every year

HOW TO APPLY This Trust states that it does not generally respond to unsolicited applications

WHO TO APPLY TO F A Sherring, William Geoffrey Harvey's Discretionary Settlement, 1A Gibsons Road, Stockport SK4 4JX

CC NO 800473 **ESTABLISHED** 1968

■ The John Haswell Memorial Trust

WHAT IS FUNDED This fund supports the development of new work through start-up grants, grants for small pieces of equipment, and the funding of more complex initiatives. It is designed to be used by both new groups and more established voluntary organisations, including those working in the fields of rural conservation, animal facilities and services, and environmental and animal sciences

WHAT IS NOT FUNDED Grants will not be given for: (i) individuals; (ii) salary costs; (iii) any ongoing running costs of projects; (iv) partial funding for large general appeals; or (v) training course fees outside of the area where expertise will not be shared with other Gateshead groups

WHO CAN BENEFIT Organisations working in the areas outlined above

WHERE FUNDING CAN BE GIVEN Gateshead

TYPE OF GRANT Capital, one-off, running costs and start-up costs. Funding is given for one year or less. For established organisations: conference, seminar and training initiative funding

RANGE OF GRANTS £25–£400; typical approximately £200–£400

FINANCES
- Year 1998
- Income £7,525
- Grants £4,234

TRUSTEES Gateshead Voluntary Organisations Council management committee members and three additional trustees

Hawthorne

Alphabetical register of grant making trusts

NOTES Applications must be submitted on an application form and written quotes enclosed if necessary

HOW TO APPLY To the Correspondent in writing. Application form available

WHO TO APPLY TO Victoria Clark, Panel Secretary, The John Haswell Memorial Trust, John Haswell House, 8–9 Gladstone Terrace, Gateshead NE8 4DY
Tel 0191-478 4103
Fax 0191-477 1260

CC NO 510764   **ESTABLISHED** 1980

■ The Hawthorne Charitable Trust

WHAT IS FUNDED The Trustees make donations, generally on an annual basis, to a large number of charities including those concerned with research into animal health

WHAT IS NOT FUNDED It is not the Trustees' policy to make grants to individuals

WHO CAN BENEFIT Organisations working in the area outlined above

WHERE FUNDING CAN BE GIVEN UK

FINANCES
- Year 1998
- Income £151,100
- Grants £145,600

TRUSTEES Mrs A Berington, R J Clark

WHO TO APPLY TO The Hawthorne Charitable Trust, Messrs Baker Tilly, Chartered Accountants, 2 Bloomsbury Street, London WC1B 3ST

CC NO 233921   **ESTABLISHED** 1964

■ The Hayward Foundation (150)

WHAT IS FUNDED Rural conservation; agriculture; animal breeding; ecology; horticulture; and natural history are of interest to the Foundation

WHAT IS NOT FUNDED No grants to individuals, for minibuses, travel, bursaries, hospices, repairs and maintenance, general appeals, deficit or retrospective funding, loans, or state and private schools except for special schools

WHO CAN BENEFIT Mainly national or larger regional organisations, centres of excellence or innovation in their field of interest

WHERE FUNDING CAN BE GIVEN UK and overseas

TYPE OF GRANT Mainly capital costs, buildings, occasionally feasibility studies and endowments. Some revenue funding for special projects of limited duration which are not part of the recurring expenses of the organisation. Recurring commitments for research, start-up or one-off projects for up to three years

RANGE OF GRANTS £10,000–£30,000 for a single grant

FINANCES
- Year 1997
- Income £1,698,780
- Grants £1,240,969

TRUSTEES I F Donald (Chairman), Sir Jack Hayward, OBE, Sir Graham Hearne, CBE, Mrs S J Heath, Dr J C Houston, CBE, FRCP, C W Taylor, FCA, J N van Leuven

NOTES Trustees meet three times a year to consider applications. As there is often a waiting list, applicants may not receive an answer for several months

HOW TO APPLY Applications should be made in writing to the Director and include the following information: (a) A description of your present work and the priorities you are addressing. This may be in the form of an Annual Report. (b) Full set of recent audited financial accounts for the organisation. (c) A description of the project being undertaken, detailing the number of people and groups who will benefit and how. Demonstrate the need for the project and describe any increase in activities that will be achieved. (d) A timetable for the project; when it will start and be finished. (e) A full cost breakdown for the project, separating capital from revenue expenditure where applicable. (f) A list of the funds raised to date towards the target with donors identified. Specify the amount of the organisation's own resources going into the project. List bids outstanding with other funders, together with the amount requested and the date they will be considered. (g) Other information of relevance considered to be useful for consideration of the application: (i) references, recommendations or letters of support, (ii) floor plans, drawings or pictures (no larger than A4) (iii) a budget for the on-going revenue costs of the project and details of how this will be funded.
A set of guidelines for applicants is available from the Hayward Foundation's offices. The staff may be contacted by telephone to discuss projects prior to making a formal application. Once applications are received, there is an initial examination, and some are declared unsuccessful and responded to with the Foundation's regrets. After this, organisations may be contacted with a request for more information before applications are prepared for a Trustees' meeting

WHO TO APPLY TO M T Schnebli, Director, The Hayward Foundation, 45 Harrington Gardens, London SW7 4JU
Tel 0171-370 7067

CC NO 201034   **ESTABLISHED** 1961

Commentary

The Hayward Foundation was established in 1961 by Sir Charles Hayward, who had been persuaded that by setting up a grant making trust he would be able to continue his charitable giving in a much more effective manner.

The Hayward Foundation concentrates its funding programme on larger national and regional organisations and charities. In contrast, the Charles Hayward Trust concentrates on small local organisations and local branches of national organisations.

Although the Foundation has general charitable purposes, there is particular interest in a few major areas. The first of these is special needs, where the Foundation covers a wide area in the field of disability, from children and adults with learning difficulties, mental health problems, brain injuries and spinal injuries to people with facial disfigurement, addictive problems and dyslexia. The Foundation will fund a range of things including care centres, and the provision of special equipment.

The Foundation also particularly favours work in the field of youth and community with a special emphasis on youth at risk, as the Trustees regard an early investment in this area as being both meaningful and effective. There is a lot of support for community and residential facilities for young people, as well as research into prison reform and the rehabilitation of offenders, prevention of offending, as well as teaching male prisoners good parenting. There is also a focus upon projects that support people within the community, for example projects mirroring those for young male offenders, whereby young mothers are taught vital parenting skills, as well as life skills and job skills.

The Foundation takes some interest in medical research, where the Trustees try to concentrate upon rare and unpopular causes that do not have a high profile and may not receive funding from some of the larger research funders. They tend to look for projects concentrating on scientific research which could have a positive effect upon the lives of the people affected by a disease.

The Foundation is also interested in the fields of art, education, preservation and the environment. Under this category the Foundation is able to distribute funds to beneficiaries in the area of the theatre, museums and educational charities.

One of the Foundations other programmes is aimed at supporting the elderly, especially tackling dementia and care in the community; there is the possibility that good research into the field of elderly welfare may be funded.

The Foundation distributes its funds quite widely throughout the UK, although the greatest concentration is in England. This reflects the fact that the amount of applications received from Wales, Scotland and Northern Ireland are significantly less than those for England. The Foundation will not replace statutory funding, preferring to be involved with schemes which are 100 per cent charitable. They are always keen to be involved in co-funding; due to the projects they support often being for large scale capital costs – such as new buildings – it is usually necessary for other funders to be involved, though not necessarily in a planned or 'partnership' manner.

The Foundation has recently initiated a limited funding programme for overseas projects. Applications will be considered from European based voluntary or charitable organisations or from projects managed or supervised by third parties known to the Trustees. The projects considered will be developmental in terms of addressing the causes of poverty and disadvantage in a practical and sustainable manner. Projects might include housing, education, health care, water and sanitation.

There is a post-grant assessment process, for example for a capital item a grant recipient is required to provide evidence of expenditure, in the form of a receipt or an architect's certificate. For research and other more ongoing projects the Foundation requires reports of how the grant recipient is getting on, including their Accounts, either annually or at the end of the project; whichever is sooner. Representatives of the Hayward Foundation may make visits to some of their grantees. It is not unusual for the Foundation to follow up some of their previous projects to find out how they are getting on, especially where a project has been of real interest to the Trustees

SAMPLE GRANTS

The top ten grants made in 1997 were:
£100,000 to Enham Village Centre, Andover for Phase II of Phipps House refurbishment
£50,000 to Griffin Community Trust, London for construction of Lansbury Lodge
£50,000 to Imperial College of Science and Technology, London for a reader in image processing
£50,000 to Natural History Museum Development Trust towards renovation of Downe House
£50,000 to Royal Hospital for Neuro-disability, Putney for a unit for behavioural disorders and Huntington's Disease
£32,500 to Fairbridge, London for their Phase II project in Wales
£31,000 to PACE Centre, Aylesbury to equip three bathrooms at this Conductive Education Centre
£25,000 to Glebe House, Cambridgeshire for family therapy and arts development
£25,000 to Winston Churchill School, Woking for a lift in the Science Block
£23,400 to Manningford Trust, Wiltshire for Automatic Peritoneal Dialysis Machines

Headley

■ The Headley Trust (86)

WHAT IS FUNDED Rural conservation

WHAT IS NOT FUNDED No grants direct to individuals. Funding is not provided for animal welfare

WHO CAN BENEFIT Registered charities only

WHERE FUNDING CAN BE GIVEN UK and overseas

TYPE OF GRANT One-off, capital and project over three years or less

FINANCES
- Year 1997
- Income £3,227,000
- Grants £2,775,000

TRUSTEES The Rt Hon Sir Timothy Sainsbury, Lady Susan Sainsbury, T J Sainsbury, Miss J Portait, J R Benson

NOTES Please note that the Trust is not seeking further applications for rural conservation. Their limited grantmaking in this area is pro-active, not reactive

HOW TO APPLY Applications are not solicited, but if submitted are considered at any time

WHO TO APPLY TO M A Pattison, The Headley Trust, 9 Red Lion Court, London EC4A 3EF *Tel* 0171-410 0330

CC NO 266620   **ESTABLISHED** 1973

Commentary

The Headley Trust was established in 1973 and is one of the Sainsbury Family Charitable Trusts. The Trust Deed indicated that the Trust was set up 'general charitable purposes' but, since 1973, the Trustees have identified areas in which they have felt that the Trust can make a significant contribution and these are reviewed as it becomes necessary.

These areas are: (a) Arts and the environment at home – the Trustees support a wide variety of conservation projects, as well as arts projects with an educational element. They will also consider grants towards partnership funding for major National Lottery grants, particularly for museums, galleries, libraries and theatres. Grants are available for restoration work to the fabric of cathedrals and large churches of exceptional merit, but the Trustees do not respond to applications for modern amenities, organ restoration or choral scholarships. Funding for fabric repair to mediaeval parish churches in rural, sparsely populated villages is also considered through a process of review diocese by diocese. Urban churches are not eligible.
(b) Arts and the environment overseas – the Trustees support arts conservation projects of outstanding artistic or architectural importance, particularly the restoration of buildings, statuary or paintings, primarily in the countries of central and eastern Europe. Grants are channelled through reputable conservation organisations in the countries concerned. (c) Medical – the Trustees are particularly interested in research into ageing and osteoporosis. (d) Developing countries – priority is given to countries in sub-Saharan anglophone Africa, central and eastern Europe, and the former Soviet Union. Focus areas include: (i) water projects (for example those which give disadvantaged communities access to safe water, preserve ecologically or culturally important wetland areas, improve sanitary conditions, or promote better use of water); (ii) forestry projects (for example those which preserve areas of natural woodland or encourage environmentally or socially sustainable methods of forestry); (iii) education and literacy projects (for example those which improve the quality of education and literacy standards for underprivileged people through the supply of materials, construction, training support etc); (iv) health projects (particularly those which support blind or partially sighted people). (e) Health and social welfare – where the Trustees contribute to a wide range of health and social welfare projects, particularly charities supporting carers of an ill or disabled relative, and those that support elderly people of limited means. The Trustees will also consider projects which stimulate the local economy through establishing self-help activity, for example community businesses; environmental improvement projects; projects which provide support to families under pressure, for example childcare, after-school and homework clubs, supplementary schooling, family centres; and projects which stimulate the motivation of disaffected young people, for example creative and cultural activities, summer universities, peer education projects. (f) Education – where the Trustees main focus is the provision of bursary support, particularly for artistic or technical skills training. Also supported are projects which link with their health and social welfare priorities, for example early years support, pastoral care for 'at risk' students, parenting and relationship skills, school exclusion and primary/secondary transition.

The Headley Trust makes few responses to unsolicited applications because the Trustees take a proactive stance. Unsolicited applications are therefore not likely to be successful, although all applications will receive a response. Application should be made by letter at any time of the year to M A Pattison and should provide information on project objectives and costs, other likely sources of funds, the long-term funding position and background information on the organisation such as Annual Report and Accounts. Trustees request reports from those who have received funding and also arrange periodic reviews of their major programmes, but do not have an assessment process whereby all organisations are visited

SAMPLE GRANTS
The top ten grants approved in 1997 were:
£500,000 to Victoria & Albert Museum towards the British Galleries redevelopment
£250,000 to Sadler's Wells towards the redevelopment appeal
£95,000 to Contact a Family to offer mutual support networks to families of disabled children in Scotland
£90,000 to University College London Hospitals towards clinical research into Osteoporosis
£60,000 to Research into Ageing towards research into Alzheimer's disease
£52,000 to Book Aid International towards the Intra-Africa Book Support Scheme
£45,000 to Devon Child Assault Project, towards improving children's awareness of their personal safety
£45,000 to Plan International, towards a Community Water Project in Central/Eastern Ghana
£40,000 to St Alban's Cathedral trust, towards the restoration and renewal of the Presbytery Vault
£40,000 to International Trust for Croatian Monuments towards urgent restoration to St Lawrence, Trogir

■ The Hemby Trust

WHAT IS FUNDED This Trust will consider funding rural conservation

WHAT IS NOT FUNDED No grants will be made for political, religious (except churches), pressure groups, sponsorships or to individuals. No grants to animal charities

WHERE FUNDING CAN BE GIVEN The County of Merseyside and Wirral

TYPE OF GRANT Capital grants. Also buildings, one-off, and start-up costs. Funding may be given for one year or less

SAMPLE GRANTS £5,000 to Dale Farm Association

TRUSTEES R A Morris, P T Furlong, A T Morris, N A Wainwright

NOTES The Trustees meet four times a year. Applications need to be received one month prior to the meeting

HOW TO APPLY To the Secretary at the address under Who To Apply To

WHO TO APPLY TO M E Hope, Secretary, The Hemby Trust, c/o Rathbone Bros & Co Ltd, Port of Liverpool Building, Pier Head, Liverpool L3 1NW
Tel 0151-236 6666
Fax 0151-243 7001

CC NO 1073028   **ESTABLISHED** 1998

■ Heritage Lottery Fund

WHAT IS FUNDED Natural habitats and countryside

WHAT IS NOT FUNDED At present it is not expected that grants will be made for individual sites or buildings in private or commercial ownership. Grants are not normally made for objects created within the last 20 years or urban parks created within the last 30 years

WHO CAN BENEFIT Grants are normally made to public and not-for-profit organisations. As a minimum applicants should have a constitution or a set of rules and a bank or building society account

WHERE FUNDING CAN BE GIVEN UK

TYPE OF GRANT Buildings, capital, project, running costs, salaries and start-up costs

RANGE OF GRANTS Minimum project cost normally £5,000

SAMPLE GRANTS £6,650,000 for the restoration of Glasgow Green, under the Urban Parks Programme
£527,000 towards conserving the heathland of the Gower Peninsular, near Swansea

FINANCES
- Year 1998–99
- Income £300m

TRUSTEES Dr Eric Anderson (Chairman), Prof Chris Baines, Robert Boas, Sir Richard Carew Pole, W Lindsay Evans, Sir Angus Grossart, Sir Ernest Hall, Caryl Hubbard, John Keegan, Patricia Lankester, Prof Palmer Newbould, Susan Palmer, Catherine Porteous, Dame Sue Tinson, Mary Ann Seighart

HOW TO APPLY Telephone 0171-591 6041 for an application pack. Decisions for most projects are made within six months

WHO TO APPLY TO Heritage Lottery Fund, 7 Holbein Place, London SW1W 8NR
Tel 0171-591 6000
Fax 0171-591 6001
E-mail nhmf@nhmf.demon.co.uk
Web Site http://www.nhmf.org.uk

ESTABLISHED 1993

■ The Higgs Charitable Trust

WHAT IS FUNDED Rural conservation, and animal facilities and services

WHO CAN BENEFIT Organisations working in the areas outlined above

WHERE FUNDING CAN BE GIVEN UK

TYPE OF GRANT One-off and research. Funding for more than three years will be considered

FINANCES
- Year 1997
- Income £51,767
- Grants £53,881

TRUSTEES D W H Campbell, T W Higgs, Mrs L Humphris

WHO TO APPLY TO A C Nash, The Higgs Charitable Trust, Messrs Moger & Sparrow, 24 Queen Square, Bath BA1 2HY

CC NO 267036　　　**ESTABLISHED** 1982

■ L E Hill Memorial Trust

WHAT IS FUNDED Charities working in the fields of: endangered species and environmental issues

WHAT IS NOT FUNDED No grants to individuals

WHO CAN BENEFIT UK registered charities working in the areas outlined above

WHERE FUNDING CAN BE GIVEN Tayside

TYPE OF GRANT Buildings and research will be considered. Funding may be given for one year or less

RANGE OF GRANTS £200–£2,000. £5,000 in exceptional cases

FINANCES
- Year 1997
- Income £23,500
- Grants £25,000

TRUSTEES Turcan Connell (Trustees) Limited, M H J Hill, OBE, J Ivory, CA

HOW TO APPLY Applications, which should be in writing, are considered at quarterly intervals

WHO TO APPLY TO D A Connell, L E Hill Memorial Trust, Messrs Turcan Connell, Saltire Court, 20 Castle Terrace, Edinburgh EH1 2EF
Tel 0131-228 8111

SC NO SCO 03454　　　**ESTABLISHED** 1989

■ Gay & Peter Hartley's Hillards Charitable Trust

WHAT IS FUNDED The Trust will consider funding: environmental issues; landscapes; nature reserves; waterways; woodlands; animal homes; animal welfare; bird sanctuaries; cats, catteries and other facilities for cats; dogs, kennels and other facilities for dogs; and horses, stables and other facilities for horses

WHAT IS NOT FUNDED Personal applications are not usually granted unless they come through another charity. As a body, the Trustees do not give to national charities but the individual Trustees have some discretion in that respect

WHO CAN BENEFIT Local and regional organisations

WHERE FUNDING CAN BE GIVEN Areas served by Hillards stores, mainly the North of England, especially Yorkshire. Also Derby, Leicester, Northamptonshire and Nottingham

TYPE OF GRANT Buildings, capital, core costs, one-off, project, research, recurring costs, running costs, salaries and start up costs. All funding is for one year or less

RANGE OF GRANTS £50–£1,000. Two special grants of £10,000 are given each year

SAMPLE GRANTS £1,000 to Hull Animal Welfare Trust for general work

FINANCES
- Year 1997
- Income £77,463
- Grants £91,229

TRUSTEES P A H Hartley, CBE, Mrs G Hartley, MBE, S R H Hartley, ASVA, Miss S Hartley, BA, MBA, A C H Hartley, MA, MBA, MSc, Miss A Hartley

HOW TO APPLY Application forms are available from the Secretary to the Trustees upon written request and should be returned before 1 October for consideration in December. Applicants are told if they have not been successful

WHO TO APPLY TO Mrs R C Phillips, Secretary to the Trustees, Gay & Peter Hartley's Hillards Charitable Trust, 400 Shadwell Lane, Leeds LS17 8AW
Tel 0113-266 1424
Fax 0113-237 0051

CC NO 327879　　　**ESTABLISHED** 1988

■ The Peter and Gwyneth Hodgkinson Charitable Trust

WHAT IS FUNDED To protect and preserve for the benefit of the public features of the County of Lincolnshire including: rural conservation; endangered species; environmental issues; animal facilities and services; wildlife parks; wildlife sanctuaries; and environmental and animal sciences

WHAT IS NOT FUNDED Applications for grants from individuals are not normally considered

WHO CAN BENEFIT Organisations working in the areas outlined above

WHERE FUNDING CAN BE GIVEN Lincolnshire

TYPE OF GRANT Capital, core costs, one-off, project, recurring and running costs

FINANCES
- Year 1996
- Income £1,439
- Grants £2,000

TRUSTEES M P Hodgkinson (Chairman), J A Hodgkinson, P R Hodgkinson, P D Hodgkinson

NOTES Each year between £2,000 and £5,000 are given towards one of the Trust's four funding policies, on a rotational system

HOW TO APPLY To the address below in writing, describing the organisation, its funding needs, the nature of the project that the money will be used for and the people who will benefit. The letter should not be more than 1,000 words

WHO TO APPLY TO M P Hodgkinson, Chairman, The Peter and Gwyneth Hodgkinson Charitable Trust, Carlton House, High Street, Carlton-le-Moorland, Lincolnshire LN5 9HL

CC NO 700149   **ESTABLISHED** 1989

■ The J G Hogg Charitable Trust

WHAT IS FUNDED Rural conservation; animal facilities and services; and environmental and animal sciences

WHO CAN BENEFIT Organisations working in the areas outlined above

WHERE FUNDING CAN BE GIVEN UK and overseas

TYPE OF GRANT Buildings, capital, core costs, one-off, project, research, recurring and running costs, salaries and start-up costs. Funding may be given for up to and over three years

SAMPLE GRANTS £10,000 to Burstow Wildlife Sanctuary for general purposes
£5,000 to Cats Protection League for general purposes
£5,000 to National Canine Defence League for general purposes

FINANCES
- Year 1998
- Income £170,796
- Grants £222,440

TRUSTEES Joanne W Hogg, Sarah J Houldsworth

HOW TO APPLY To the address under Who To Apply To in writing

WHO TO APPLY TO C M Jones, Trustee's Accountant, The J G Hogg Charitable Trust, Chantrey Vellacott, Russell Square House, 10–12 Russell Square, London WC1A 5LF

CC NO 299042   **ESTABLISHED** 1987

■ E S Hogg Charity Trust

WHAT IS FUNDED Rural conservation; animal facilities and services; and animal sciences

WHO CAN BENEFIT Individuals and organisations working in the areas outlined above

WHERE FUNDING CAN BE GIVEN UK

TYPE OF GRANT Core costs funded for one year or less

FINANCES
- Year 1996–97
- Income £60,570
- Grants £55,000

HOW TO APPLY To the address under Who To Apply To in writing

WHO TO APPLY TO The Secretary, E S Hogg Charity Trust, Messrs Hoare Trustees, 37 Fleet Street, London EC4P 4DQ
Tel 0171-353 4522

CC NO 280138   **ESTABLISHED** 1980

■ Homelands Charitable Trust

WHAT IS FUNDED General charitable purposes in accordance with the Settlor's wishes, including animal welfare

WHAT IS NOT FUNDED No grants to individuals

WHO CAN BENEFIT Registered charities working in the areas outlined above

WHERE FUNDING CAN BE GIVEN UK

RANGE OF GRANTS £500–£18,500

FINANCES
- Year 1997
- Income £448,635
- Grants £158,900

TRUSTEES D G W Ballard, Rev C Curry, N J Armstrong

HOW TO APPLY In writing to the address under Who To Apply To

WHO TO APPLY TO N J Armstrong, FCA, Homelands Charitable Trust, Messrs Alliotts, 5th Floor, 9 Kingsway, London WC2B 6XF

CC NO 214322   **ESTABLISHED** 1962

■ The Homfray Trust

WHAT IS FUNDED To help certain charitable and other organisations, including animal welfare charities – usually in West Yorkshire, and particularly in Halifax and Sowerby Bridge

WHAT IS NOT FUNDED No grants to individuals or for expeditions, scholarships or further education

WHO CAN BENEFIT Organisations working in the area outlined above

WHERE FUNDING CAN BE GIVEN England, with preference for West Yorkshire

TYPE OF GRANT One-off donations, but this can often be made year after year in many instances. Core costs are also considered

RANGE OF GRANTS Normally £200–£400

Hornby's

Alphabetical register of grant making trusts

SAMPLE GRANTS £400 to RSPCA, Halifax Branch

FINANCES
- Year 1997
- Income £17,225
- Grants £14,182

TRUSTEES H J H Gillam, G S Haigh, D Murray Wells, M Hartley

NOTES Grants unlikely to be given to restore historic buildings or improve the environment

HOW TO APPLY Telephone calls not welcome. No application forms used. Sae from applicants useful, but not essential. No guidelines or deadlines

WHO TO APPLY TO G S Haigh, The Homfray Trust, Newlands House, Warley, Halifax, West Yorkshire HX2 7SW

CC NO 214503   **ESTABLISHED** 1928

■ Mrs E G Hornby's Charitable Settlement

WHAT IS FUNDED General charitable purposes, with particular interest in the field of animal welfare

WHO CAN BENEFIT Registered charities only

WHERE FUNDING CAN BE GIVEN UK

RANGE OF GRANTS £200–£10,000

SAMPLE GRANTS £10,000 to Countryside Foundation
£2,000 to People's Dispensary for Sick Animals

FINANCES
- Year 1997
- Income £56,287
- Grants £59,800

TRUSTEES Kleinwort Benson Trustees Limited, N J M Lonsdale, Mrs P M W Smith-Maxwell

NOTES New donations are normally considered only for national charities, and the Trustees usually only support charities already known to them

HOW TO APPLY Appeal in writing to the address under Who To Apply To. Only successful applications will be notified of the Trustees' decision

WHO TO APPLY TO Mrs E G Hornby's Charitable Settlement, Kleinwort Benson Trustees Limited, PO Box 191, 10 Fenchurch Street, London EC3M 3LB

CC NO 243516   **ESTABLISHED** 1965

■ The Geoffrey C Hughes Charitable Trust

WHAT IS FUNDED Rural conservation

WHAT IS NOT FUNDED No grants to individuals

WHO CAN BENEFIT Organisations working in the area of rural conservation

WHERE FUNDING CAN BE GIVEN UK

TYPE OF GRANT Small and large grants

FINANCES
- Year 1995
- Income £47,522

TRUSTEES J R Young, P C M Solon, A Reed

HOW TO APPLY Initial applications in writing, prefer details if possible

WHO TO APPLY TO P C M Solon, Trustee, The Geoffrey C Hughes Charitable Trust, Beachcroft Stanleys, 20 Furnival Street, London EC4A 1BN

CC NO 1010079   **ESTABLISHED** 1992

■ The Michael and Shirley Hunt Charitable Trust

WHAT IS FUNDED Relieving the suffering of animals

WHAT IS NOT FUNDED No grants for fines, bail and legal costs, etc

WHO CAN BENEFIT To benefit unwanted, sick or ill-treated animals of any species

WHERE FUNDING CAN BE GIVEN UK and overseas

TYPE OF GRANT One-off, buildings, endowments and start-up costs. Funding may be given for up to two years

RANGE OF GRANTS £200–£8,500, typical grant £2,000

SAMPLE GRANTS £2,000 to World Wildlife Fund
£2,000 to Celia Cross Greyhound Trust

FINANCES
- Year 1998–99
- Income £129,594
- Grants £35,764

TRUSTEES W J Baker, C J Hunt, S E Hunt, D S Jenkins, K D Pearson

HOW TO APPLY In writing to the address below

WHO TO APPLY TO Mrs D S Jenkins, Trustee, The Michael and Shirley Hunt Charitable Trust, Ansty House, High Street, Henfield, West Sussex BN5 9DA
Tel 01273 492233
Fax 01273 492273

CC NO 1063418   **ESTABLISHED** 1997

■ IFAW Charitable Trust (The International Fund for Animal Welfare Charitable Trust)

WHAT IS FUNDED (a) To educate the public in animal welfare; (b) to conserve and protect animals, including wildlife, and its habitats and the natural environment; and (c) the prevention of cruelty to and suffering of animals including wildlife. To give active consideration to all requests for assistance within the Trust's budget

WHO CAN BENEFIT Organisation working in the areas outlined above

WHERE FUNDING CAN BE GIVEN UK

FINANCES
- Year 1997
- Income £631,223
- Grants £209,536

TRUSTEES Gregory P McEwen, Frederick O'Regan, Eileen B Wilson

HOW TO APPLY In writing to the address under Who To Apply To

WHO TO APPLY TO Gregory P McEwen, Solicitor/Trustee, IFAW Charitable Trust, 55A Welbeck Street, London W1M 7HD

CC NO 1024806 **ESTABLISHED** 1992

■ INTACH (UK) Trust

WHAT IS FUNDED Conservation projects in India

WHAT IS NOT FUNDED No funding for expeditions, undergraduates, school projects or UK charities

WHO CAN BENEFIT Projects as outlined above

WHERE FUNDING CAN BE GIVEN India

TYPE OF GRANT One-off and recurring. Research is funded

RANGE OF GRANTS £500–£6,000

FINANCES
- Year 1996
- Income £87,616
- Grants £67,053

TRUSTEES Martand Singh (Chair), Sir B M Fielden, Sir J Thomson, R W Skelton, Cyrus Guzder, Dr D W MacDowell, Dr R Thapar

PUBLICATIONS Annual Report

NOTES INTACH stands for the Indian National Trust for Art and Cultural Heritage

HOW TO APPLY To the address under Who To Apply To in writing. Applications are considered in January and June each year

WHO TO APPLY TO Dr Philip Whitburn, Secretary, INTACH (UK) Trust, 10 Barley Mow Passage, London W4 4PH
Tel 0181-994 6477

CC NO 298329 **ESTABLISHED** 1987

■ The Idlewild Trust

WHAT IS FUNDED Preservation for the benefit of the public of waterways, woodlands and horticulture

WHAT IS NOT FUNDED The following categories are excluded: repetitive nationwide appeals, those where all or most of the beneficiaries are outside the UK, appeals in respect of buildings with no distinctive outstanding merit, parochial appeals, appeals for research projects, endowment and deficit funding, appeals received within 12 calendar months of a previous grant. No grants to individuals

WHO CAN BENEFIT Registered charities working in the areas outlined above

WHERE FUNDING CAN BE GIVEN UK

TYPE OF GRANT Buildings, core costs, endowments, feasibility studies, one-off, projects, research and start-up costs. Funding of up to three years will be considered

RANGE OF GRANTS Average grant £2,000

SAMPLE GRANTS £5,000 to Cotswolds Canal Trust for restoration of canal at Saul Junction

FINANCES
- Year 1996
- Income £188,623
- Grants £217,550

TRUSTEES Dr G W Beard (Chairman), Mrs F L Morrison-Jones, Mrs A C Grellier, Lady Goodison, M H Davenport, Mrs A S Bucks, J C Gale

PUBLICATIONS Guidelines leaflet available

NOTES Trustees regret it is impossible to acknowledge all applications because of the number and expense involved unless an sae is enclosed

HOW TO APPLY To the address under Who To Apply To. Considered in April, August and December each year. No formal application form. Full details of appeal and latest audited accounts required

WHO TO APPLY TO Angela Freestone, The Idlewild Trust, 54–56 Knatchbull Road, London SE5 9QY
Tel 0171-274 2266
Fax 0171-274 5222

CC NO 268124 **ESTABLISHED** 1974

Inland

■ The Inland Waterways Association

WHAT IS FUNDED Projects to restore and develop the inland waterways

WHAT IS NOT FUNDED No grants to individuals

WHO CAN BENEFIT Organisations involved in waterway restoration and development

WHERE FUNDING CAN BE GIVEN UK and Ireland

TYPE OF GRANT Waterway restoration projects – usually single grants for a specific purpose or interest-free loans. Funding may be given for up to three years

RANGE OF GRANTS Usually up to £1,000 maximum

FINANCES
- Year 1997
- Income £491,604
- Grants £132,326

TRUSTEES The Council of the Association

HOW TO APPLY To the address under Who To Apply To in writing, initially giving brief details and applicants latest Annual Reports and Accounts

WHO TO APPLY TO The Executive Director, The Inland Waterways Association, PO Box 114, Rickmansworth WD3 1ZY

CC NO 212342 **ESTABLISHED** 1946

■ Isle of Wight Gardens Trust

WHAT IS FUNDED To advance the education of the arts and sciences of garden law. To preserve and enhance garden land on the Isle of Wight for the pleasure of the public, particularly flora, lakes and landscapes.

WHO CAN BENEFIT Individuals and organisations

WHERE FUNDING CAN BE GIVEN Isle of Wight

TYPE OF GRANT Project. Funding is given for one year or less

FINANCES
- Year 1996–97
- Income £8,893
- Grants £543

TRUSTEES John Harrison, Hugh Noyes, Ron Smith

HOW TO APPLY On request of Trustees only

WHO TO APPLY TO P Marsden, Isle of Wight Gardens Trust, Lucerne, St Catherines Road, Niton Undercliff, Isle of Wight PO38 2NE *Tel* 01983 730289

CC NO 1047109 **ESTABLISHED** 1995

J

■ The Ruth & Lionel Jacobson Charitable Trust (No 2)

WHAT IS FUNDED Only such bodies of person and trust as are established for charitable purposes, including nature reserves

WHAT IS NOT FUNDED No individual cases. Registered charities only

WHO CAN BENEFIT Organisations only

WHERE FUNDING CAN BE GIVEN North East of England

TYPE OF GRANT One-off, buildings, project and research. Funding is available for one year or less

RANGE OF GRANTS £50–£10,000, typical grant £100–£500

FINANCES
- Year 1997
- Income £64,677
- Grants £37,357

TRUSTEES Mrs I R Jacobson, M D Jacobson

HOW TO APPLY In writing to the address below. Letters of application are considered bi-monthly

WHO TO APPLY TO Mrs I R Jacobson, The Ruth & Lionel Jacobson Charitable Trust, High Wray, 35 Montagu Avenue, Newcastle upon Tyne, Tyne and Wear NE3 4JH

CC NO 326665 **ESTABLISHED** 1984

■ The Johnson Foundation

WHAT IS FUNDED Environmental resources

WHAT IS NOT FUNDED No grants to individuals or students

WHO CAN BENEFIT Registered charities as outlined above

WHERE FUNDING CAN BE GIVEN Merseyside

TYPE OF GRANT One-off, recurrent, core costs, project and research. Funding is available for up to two years

RANGE OF GRANTS £100–£25,000, typical grant £500

FINANCES
- Year 1997–98
- Income £721,689
- Grants £76,208

TRUSTEES P R Johnson, S E Johnson, C W Johnson

PUBLICATIONS Annual Report

HOW TO APPLY To the address under Who To Apply To in writing at any time. Trustees meet monthly

WHO TO APPLY TO P R Johnson, The Johnson Foundation, Westmount, Vyner Road South, Birkenhead, Merseyside L43 7PN
Tel 0151-653 0566

CC NO 518660   **ESTABLISHED** 1987

K

■ The Kennel Club Charitable Trust

WHAT IS FUNDED The Trust supports research into canine diseases and disorders, and assists charities for disadvantaged dogs and disadvantaged humans aided by dogs

WHO CAN BENEFIT Registered charities benefiting dogs

WHERE FUNDING CAN BE GIVEN UK

TYPE OF GRANT One off and recurring for set periods

SAMPLE GRANTS £25,000 to Animal Health Trust for research
£25,000 to Royal School of Veterinary Surgeons for research
£25,000 to Bristol University for research
£8,050 to PDSA
£6,000 to Royal College of Veterinary Surgeons Trust Fund for veterinary Nursing Bursaries
£5,000 to Blue Cross
£2,500 to Justice for Dogs

FINANCES
- Year 1996–97
- Income £146,756
- Grants £108,050

TRUSTEES M T R Stockman, R J Clifford, B J Hall, W R Irwing, M Townsend

HOW TO APPLY To the address under Who To Apply To

WHO TO APPLY TO M C E Quirke, Clerk to the Trustees, The Kennel Club Charitable Trust, 1–5 Clarges Street, Piccadilly, London W1Y 8AB
Tel 0171-493 6651

CC NO 327802   **ESTABLISHED** 1988

■ The Graham Kirkham Foundation (385)

WHAT IS FUNDED Relief of the suffering of birds and animals; places of natural beauty

WHAT IS NOT FUNDED No grants to individuals

WHO CAN BENEFIT Organisations working in the areas outlined above

WHERE FUNDING CAN BE GIVEN UK, particularly South Yorkshire

TYPE OF GRANT One-off

FINANCES
- Year 1997
- Income £31,416
- Grants £360,609

Kirkham

TRUSTEES Sir G Kirkham, Lady P Kirkham

PUBLICATIONS Annual Report and Accounts

HOW TO APPLY In writing to the Secretary

WHO TO APPLY TO Barry Todhunter, Secretary, The Graham Kirkham Foundation, DFS Head Office, Bentley Moor Lane, Aldwick-Le-Street, Doncaster, South Yorkshire DN6 7BD
Tel 01302 330365
Fax 01302 330880

CC NO 1002390   **ESTABLISHED** 1991

Commentary

The Graham Kirkham Foundation was established in 1991 by Sir Graham Kirkham, Chairman of DFS, for general charitable purposes. The Foundation funds causes in which the Founder has a close personal interest particularly: education; relief of poverty and illness; relief of suffering of birds and animals; welfare of Armed Services personnel; help for people endangered by drug abuse; public recreation facilities; places of historic interest or rural beauty; the Duke of Edinburgh Award Scheme; and local activities.

The Foundation prefers to work independently. It does not fund statutory bodies or replace statutory funding, make loans, cover running costs or provide match-funding. Grants are usually one-off.

Applications should be made in writing to the Secretary. The Trustees decide which organisations they wish to assist, at regular meetings, and remain personally involved in the projects supported

SAMPLE GRANTS
The top ten grants made in 1997 were:
£100,000 to Gurkha Brigade Association Trust
£50,000 to Blue Cross
£40,000 to Wordsworth Trust
£39,109 to Animal Health
£25,000 to British Lung Foundation
£25,000 to Harrogate Grammar School
£25,000 to Alder Hey Hospital Appeal
£10,500 to MENCAP
£10,000 to Birmingham Children's Hospital
£10,000 to Northern Ballet Theatre

■ The Ernest Kleinwort Charitable Trust (93)

WHAT IS FUNDED There are no restrictions upon What Is Funded, although promotion of conservation and protection of the environment are areas in which the Trust has some concentration

WHAT IS NOT FUNDED Registered charities only. Local charities outside Sussex are normally excluded, no national appeals although exceptions are made for Sussex branches

WHO CAN BENEFIT Charities efficiently organised and managed by persons of proven business ability

WHERE FUNDING CAN BE GIVEN UK and overseas, with a preference for Sussex

TYPE OF GRANT Donations towards specific projects and annual subscriptions until further notice (mostly confined to Sussex)

FINANCES
- Year 1997
- Income £1,733,785
- Grants £2,697,616

TRUSTEES Kleinwort Benson Trustees Limited, The Earl of Limerick, KBE, Madeleine, Lady Kleinwort, Sir Richard Kleinwort, Bt, Miss M R Kleinwort, R M Ewing, Sir Christopher Lever, Bt

HOW TO APPLY In writing, although it should be noted that no reply is given to unsuccessful applicants

WHO TO APPLY TO The Secretary, The Ernest Kleinwort Charitable Trust, PO Box 191, 10 Fenchurch Street, London EC3M 3LB
Tel 0171-956 5478

CC NO 229665   **ESTABLISHED** 1963

Commentary

The Ernest Kleinwort Charitable Trust was set up in 1963 as a family trust with a wide remit, enabling the Trustees to give to any charitable cause that they chose. There are family connections with CHK Charities Limited, but they are kept completely separate in terms of their funds and their administration.

The Trustees concentrate on several fields of activity, namely medical research and care, conservation and the environment, disability, youth welfare, general welfare, hospices, family planning and associated healthcare, and welfare of the elderly. At present most support is given in the areas of medical research and care, conservation and the environment, disability and youth welfare, and this is not seen as likely to change significantly, although the Trustees do periodically review their priorities within the broad remit of what they will fund.

Preference is given to charities in Sussex. The conservation and family planning and associated healthcare programmes are spread all over the world wherever there is most need. That is not to say that projects fitting into the category of conservation in this country are overlooked; with a fairly even mixture of UK and overseas projects having been supported in past years.

The Trust has ongoing commitments to about 120 charities in Sussex which are 'subscribed' to annually – these are reviewed annually and reports are required. There is also a mini-committee that meets every two months to decide who in Sussex will be supported in addition to those that receive subscriptions. The bias towards Sussex is purely due to the fact that some members of the Kleinwort family live there and wish to benefit their local area as well as giving grants to major projects around the rest of the world.

The Trustees are not particularly proactive, preferring instead to rely on applications received. They set out to support many different types of charities within the areas that they fund; they do not want to be too rigid, feeling that this may lead them to miss out on supporting a really worthwhile cause or idea.

The Trust does not have a set policy on the replacing or augmenting of statutory funding, however there appears to be a bias against it. Match-funding has been undertaken in the past and, although the Trustees do not mind putting money towards the cost of part of a project if they think it seems to be worthwhile, they would much rather fund the whole thing.

The Trust has some preferences for the types of grant they like to give. Grants for start-up costs are favoured as they like to see a new charity able to establish itself. Most common are one-off grants of about £1,000 to £10,000, although grants of £100,000 and above have been made in the past. However they very rarely exceed £100,000. The Trust will normally only commit itself to a project for either a single grant or for funding over three to five years, and they never spend their capital in grants.

Applications should be in writing. When an application has been received, it is checked for eligibility by the Secretary of the Trust and applications that are unsuitable, such as national appeals, are weeded out. Those applications which are unsuccessful will not be acknowledged. Applications that are to receive further consideration are prepared by the Secretary of the Trust and copies are distributed to the Trustees prior to their main meetings in March and October, so that the Trustees are briefed in advance. The Trustees are then able to make much quicker decisions as to which charities will receive support.

After grants have been made progress reports are required annually, although for many of the larger grant recipients with whom a closer relationship has developed, there tends to be a more ongoing dialogue. Most of the projects receiving support of over £10,000 will be visited by one of the Trustees

SAMPLE GRANTS
The top ten grants made in 1997 were:
£115,000 to Tusk Trust
£100,000 to Crowborough Hospital
£100,000 to St Richard's Hospital Equipment Appeal
£90,000 to Intermediate Technology
£80,000 to Marie Stopes International
£60,000 to Diane Fossey Gorilla Fund
£50,000 to Ardingly College Sports Hall Appeal
£50,000 to Born Free Foundation
£50,000 to Cancer Relief Macmillan Fund
£50,000 to Chailey Heritage School

■ Sir James Knott Trust (160)

WHAT IS FUNDED To make grants to registered charities only, for the benefit of the community and particularly in the areas of: rural conservation; animal homes; animal welfare; wildlife parks; and agriculture

WHAT IS NOT FUNDED No grants to individuals

WHO CAN BENEFIT Registered charities only, except that the Trust is unable to make grants to Roman Catholic charities because of a clause in its original trust deed

WHERE FUNDING CAN BE GIVEN Northumberland, Durham and Tyne & Wear only

TYPE OF GRANT One-off and core costs for one year or less. Buildings, capital, project, recurring costs, running costs, salaries, and start-up costs for up to three years

RANGE OF GRANTS From £100 to over £10,000

FINANCES
- Year 1997
- Income £1,146,104
- Grants £1,153,256

TRUSTEES C A F Baker-Cresswell, OBE, TD, DL, M R Cornwall-Jones, Prof The Hon O F W James, Rt Hon The Viscount Ridley, KG, GCVO, TD

PUBLICATIONS Report and Accounts

NOTES The Trust supercedes the Sir James Knott Settlement (No 227333) which was removed from the Charity Commission Register in 1991

HOW TO APPLY A written application enclosing the most recent report and accounts is required. The Trustees usually expect applicants to have applied to the National Lottery as well

WHO TO APPLY TO Brigadier (Retd) J F F Sharland, Secretary, Sir James Knott Trust, 16–18 Hood Street, Newcastle-upon-Tyne NE1 6JQ
Tel 0191-230 4016

CC NO 1001363 **ESTABLISHED** 1990

Commentary

This Trust was established in 1990, originating from The Sir James Knott Settlement, which became The Sir James Knott 1990 Trust. Following a Deed of Change of Name by the Trustees the Trust became known as The Sir James Knott Trust in 1995.

Knott

Alphabetical register of grant making trusts

The Trust provides grants to registered charities which work to benefit the community. The Trust has no scales of preference as they support appeals across the board and the following information provides a summary of the percentage of grants given in the financial year of 1997–1998: education/expeditions (22.1); youth/children (20.8); community welfare (20.7); the disabled (6.4); service charities (6.4); heritage/museums (5.3); housing/homeless (4.4); conservation/horticultural (4.1); medical care and research (4.1); the arts (3.4) the elderly (1.2); and maritime charities (1.1). No changes in policy were introduced in this financial year. Funding is restricted to charities in the North East, particularly within Northumberland, Durham and Tyne & Wear, or to national charities whose work is expected to benefit this region. The funding these areas receive can be examined through the percentage of grants given: Tyne & Wear were given 42.2 per cent of funds; Durham received 24.4 per cent; Northumberland received 19.9 per cent; the North East in general received 12.5; and finally charities in other areas received 1.0 per cent.

The Trust subsidises statutory bodies through their support of schools in the area, although they do not donate to local authorities and do not replace statutory funding which has been withdrawn for whatever reason. The Trust does, however, part fund projects where the applicant has secured funds from additional sources.

Applications should be submitted in writing, stating the applicant's registered charity number and complete background details, including information about the connection with the North East of England, steps taken to raise funds and the sum already raised. Applications are considered by the Trustees who usually meet three times a year and the Trust monitors its distribution of funds through an independent assessor who conducts follow up visits to a random selection of recipients

SAMPLE GRANTS

The top ten grants given in 1997 were:
£50,000 to Community Council (Coalfield Project)
£50,000 to Newcastle University Development Trust Institute for the Health of the Elderly
£50,000 to North of England Cadet Forces Trust
£30,000 to Northern Counties School for the Deaf
£30,000 to Stanegate Inheritance Project
£25,000 to Newcastle University Development Trust Institute for the Health of the Elderly
£25,000 to St Oswald's Hospice: Newcastle
£25,000 to Citizens Advice Bureaux: NE
£20,000 to Cancer Relief Macmillan Fund: NE
£15,000 to Berwick Voluntary Forum

■ The Harry Kweller Charitable Trust

WHAT IS FUNDED Animal charities

WHAT IS NOT FUNDED The Trustees will not respond to applications from students, individuals or those seeking to join expeditions

WHO CAN BENEFIT Organisations working in the area outlined above

WHERE FUNDING CAN BE GIVEN UK and overseas

RANGE OF GRANTS £100–£1,000

FINANCES
- Year 1996–97
- Income £16,020
- Grants £11,100

TRUSTEES G J West, Ms V Z Brecher

HOW TO APPLY In writing to the address below

WHO TO APPLY TO Rhodes and Rhodes, The Harry Kweller Charitable Trust, 42 Doughty Street, London WC1N 2LY

CC NO 277474 **ESTABLISHED** 1979

L

■ The David Laing Charitable Trust

WHAT IS FUNDED Donations are given to bodies supporting the improvement of the environment and animal welfare

WHAT IS NOT FUNDED The Trustees do not make grants to individuals unless they act in a capacity representing a larger body for which a donation is applicable

WHO CAN BENEFIT Organisations working in the areas outlined above

WHERE FUNDING CAN BE GIVEN UK

TYPE OF GRANT Grants are not normally recurrent on a regular annual basis, unless forming phases of a larger donation. Some charities are closely associated with the Trust and would benefit more frequently. Starter finance, recurring expenses or single projects. Sometimes a small grant plus an interest free loan

RANGE OF GRANTS £250–£55,000

FINANCES
- Year 1995
- Income £126,983
- Grants £77,750

TRUSTEES D E Laing, R F D Barlow, J S Lewis, Mrs F M Laing

NOTES Where supporting larger charities, the support will be at both headquarters and local levels

HOW TO APPLY Applications will be considered by the Trustees at any time. Applications basically considered between March and September

WHO TO APPLY TO D E and Mrs F M Laing, The David Laing Charitable Trust, c/o Messrs Ernst & Young, Accountants, 400 Capability Green, Luton, Bedfordshire LU1 3LU

CC NO 278462   **ESTABLISHED** 1979

■ The Landale Charitable Trust

WHAT IS FUNDED This Trust will consider funding: rural conservation and agriculture

WHAT IS NOT FUNDED No grants to individuals or students

WHO CAN BENEFIT Registered charities working in the areas outlined above

WHERE FUNDING CAN BE GIVEN UK

TYPE OF GRANT Recurrent, buildings, capital, core costs, one-off, project and research. Funding is available for more than three years

FINANCES
- Year 1997
- Income £18,236
- Grants £31,594

TRUSTEES Sir David Landale, KCVO, William Landale, James Landale, Lady Landale, Peter Landale

PUBLICATIONS Annual Report

HOW TO APPLY In writing to the address below

WHO TO APPLY TO Jane Clark, The Landale Charitable Trust, Price Waterhouse Coopers, PO Box 90, Erskine House, 68–73 Queen Street, Edinburgh EH2 4NH

CC NO 274722   **ESTABLISHED** 1978

■ The Mrs F B Laurence 1976 Charitable Settlement

WHAT IS FUNDED Protection of the environment and wildlife

WHAT IS NOT FUNDED Applications for grants to individuals will not be considered

WHO CAN BENEFIT Organisations working in the areas outlined above

WHERE FUNDING CAN BE GIVEN UK and very occasionally, provided the donation is sought by a UK charity, overseas

TYPE OF GRANT Core costs, one-off, project and start-up costs. Funding is for one year or less

FINANCES
- Year 1997–98
- Income £110,217
- Grants £115,660

TRUSTEES G S Brown, D A G Sarre, M Tooth

NOTES Only applications supported by financial information will be considered

HOW TO APPLY To the address under Who To Apply To in writing

WHO TO APPLY TO The Trustees, The Mrs F B Laurence 1976 Charitable Settlement, c/o Payne Hicks Beach, 10 New Square, Lincoln's Inn, London WC2A 3QG
Tel 0171-465 4300

CC NO 296548   **ESTABLISHED** 1976

■ Raymond and Blanche Lawson Charitable Trust

WHAT IS FUNDED This Trust will consider funding: rural conservation, including environmental issues, and animal facilities and services

WHAT IS NOT FUNDED Registered charities only. Applications from individuals, including students, are not entertained

WHO CAN BENEFIT Registered charities working in the areas outlined above

WHERE FUNDING CAN BE GIVEN Whilst national charities are considered, local charities are favoured in East Sussex and Kent

TYPE OF GRANT Buildings, capital, core costs, one-off, project, research, recurring costs, running costs and start-up costs. Funding may be given for more than three years

RANGE OF GRANTS £100–£23,500. Typically £1,000

SAMPLE GRANTS £2,500 to English Heritage for general purposes
£2,000 to The National Trust

FINANCES
- Year 1998
- Income £85,338
- Grants £80,951

TRUSTEES J V Banks, J A Bertram, Mrs P E V Banks

HOW TO APPLY At any time, the Trustees hold regular meetings. Applications should include clear details of the need for which assistance is sought

WHO TO APPLY TO Mrs P E V Banks, Raymond and Blanche Lawson Charitable Trust, 28 Barden Road, Tonbridge, Kent TN9 1TX
Tel 01732 352183
Fax 01732 352621

CC NO 281269   **ESTABLISHED** 1980

■ The Eric and Dorothy Leach Charitable Trust

WHAT IS FUNDED Endangered species, environmental issues, and animal facilities and services

WHAT IS NOT FUNDED No grants to individuals

WHO CAN BENEFIT Organisations only

WHERE FUNDING CAN BE GIVEN UK

TYPE OF GRANT Capital, core costs, one-off, project, research, and recurring costs. Funding is given for one year or less

HOW TO APPLY In writing only

WHO TO APPLY TO R Chamberlain, The Eric and Dorothy Leach Charitable Trust, c/o Swayne, Johnson & Wight Solicitors, High Street, St Asaph, Denbighshire LL17 0RF
Tel 01745 582535
Fax 01745 584504

CC NO 1070041   **ESTABLISHED** 1998

■ The Leach Fourteenth Trust

WHAT IS FUNDED Charities working in the fields of: rural conservation; wildlife sanctuaries; and ornithology and zoology. Trustees mainly seek out their own ventures to support

WHAT IS NOT FUNDED Grants to UK-based registered charities only. No grants to individuals, for 'gap year' or similar projects or for sponsored bike rides, etc

WHO CAN BENEFIT Grants to registered charities only

WHERE FUNDING CAN BE GIVEN UK but the South West and London are favoured

TYPE OF GRANT Buildings, capital, core costs, one-off, project, research, running costs, recurring costs, and salaries will be considered. Funding may be given for one year or less or for more than three years

RANGE OF GRANTS £500–£5,000

SAMPLE GRANTS £4,000 to Countryside Restoration Trust
£3,000 to Jersey Wildlife Preservation Trust (SAFE)

FINANCES
- Year 1997
- Income £77,185
- Grants £87,000

TRUSTEES W J Henderson, M A Hayes, R Murray-Leach, Mrs J M M Nash

HOW TO APPLY No application forms. Not all applications acknowledged

WHO TO APPLY TO Mr and Mrs R Murray-Leach, The Leach Fourteenth Trust, Nettleton Mill, Castle Combe, Chippenham, Wiltshire SN14 7HJ

CC NO 204844   **ESTABLISHED** 1961

■ The Leche Trust

WHAT IS FUNDED Landscapes including the preservation of buildings

WHAT IS NOT FUNDED The Trustees do not make grants for religion, structural repairs to Church of England churches, any school buildings, public schools, social welfare, animals, medicine, expeditions, British students taking first degrees or postgraduate courses

WHO CAN BENEFIT Individuals and organisations

WHERE FUNDING CAN BE GIVEN UK

TYPE OF GRANT Grants for a specific purpose and not recurrent, including buildings

RANGE OF GRANTS £500–£5,000

FINANCES
- Year 1997
- Income £203,682

- Grants £158,000

TRUSTEES Mrs C J F Arnander (Chairman), Mrs Diana Hanbury, J Porteous, Sir John Riddell, I Bristow, S Jervis, S Wethered

HOW TO APPLY In writing to the address under Who To Apply To. The Trustees meet three times a year in October, February and June

WHO TO APPLY TO Mrs L Lawson, Secretary to the Trustees, The Leche Trust, 84 Cicada Road, London SW18 2NZ
Tel 0181-870 6233
Fax 0181-870 6233

CC NO 225659   **ESTABLISHED** 1963

■ The John Spedan Lewis Foundation

WHAT IS FUNDED To provide finance for charitable purposes and in the first instance reflecting the particular interests of John Spedan Lewis, namely horticulture, ornithology, entomology and associated educational and research projects

WHAT IS NOT FUNDED Objects must be exclusively charitable according to the law. No grants to individuals or to branches of national organisations or for medical research, welfare projects or building work

WHO CAN BENEFIT Preference is given to small projects and organisations dealing with the natural sciences

WHERE FUNDING CAN BE GIVEN UK

TYPE OF GRANT Mostly straight donations which may be repeated. Salaries not funded. Feasibility studies, one-off, project and research. Funding up to three years will be considered

FINANCES
- Year 1998
- Income £46,000
- Grants £50,000

TRUSTEES S Hampson, M K J Miller, W L R E Gilchrist, D R Cooper, Miss C Walton

HOW TO APPLY Write to Secretary giving full details and enclosing, where applicable, latest Annual Report and Accounts

WHO TO APPLY TO Ms B M F Chamberlain, Secretary, The John Spedan Lewis Foundation, 171 Victoria Street, London SW1E 5NN
Tel 0171-828 1000

CC NO 240473   **ESTABLISHED** 1964

■ The Enid Linder Foundation (273)

WHAT IS FUNDED Animal welfare

WHAT IS NOT FUNDED No grants to individuals

WHO CAN BENEFIT Registered charities benefiting animals

WHERE FUNDING CAN BE GIVEN UK

TYPE OF GRANT Capital, one-off, project, research and running costs. Funding is only given for one year

FINANCES
- Year 1998
- Income £622,655
- Grants £585,629

TRUSTEES M J C Butler, G S K Huntly, A A Ladeveze, J E Ladeveze, J S Stubbings

PUBLICATIONS Trustees Report and Financial Statements

HOW TO APPLY In writing to the Secretary to the Trustees at the address below

WHO TO APPLY TO B Billingham, Secretary to the Trustees, The Enid Linder Foundation, 35 Tranquil Vale, Blackheath, London SE3 0DB
Tel 0181-297 9884

CC NO 267509   **ESTABLISHED** 1974

Commentary

The Enid Linder Foundation was established by Enid Blanche Linder in 1974 to support medical research, teaching hospitals and universities and for general charitable purposes.

In 1998 support was given to organisations concerned with research into: diabetes, cancer, asthma, mental handicap and arthritis. Nearly one quarter of the Foundation's charitable expenditure was allocated to teaching hospitals, to help fund their medical students' electives, and to universities. The remainder was shared between a wide range of charitable organisations whose interests included: care for the disabled, elderly, children and animals; the arts; youth sports; and hospices. In the Foundation's scale of preference, therefore, medical research is the priority, followed by support for teaching hospitals. This funding policy was established in the Trust Deed and is upheld by the Trustees.

The Foundation funds UK based charities only; it does not fund statutory bodies, replace statutory funding, make loans, support infrastructure costs or participate in co-funding. Support, even for regular beneficiaries, is in the form of one-off grants, as funding can never be guaranteed into the following year.

Applications should be made in writing to the Secretary to the Trustees. The Trustees consider relevant applications, and allocate funding for the year, at a meeting held in February. Organisations which have received grants are expected to report

Lions

Alphabetical register of grant making trusts

on how the money has been used. The Trustees may also visit the Foundation's beneficiaries

SAMPLE GRANTS
The top ten grants made in 1998 were:
£35,000 to Royal College of Surgeons
£25,000 to Medicins sans Frontiéres
£15,000 to Victoria and Albert Museum
£12,000 to Cancer Research
£10,000 to Stroke Fund
£10,000 to Mandent
£10,000 to MENCAP
£10,000 to Brighton Society for the Blind
£10,000 to Intermediate Technology
£6,000 to Age Concern

■ Carterton Lions Charity Trust Fund

WHAT IS FUNDED Animal welfare; cats, catteries and other facilities for cats; and dogs, kennels and other facilities for dogs at the discretion of the Trustees

WHO CAN BENEFIT Individuals and organisations working in the areas outlined above

WHERE FUNDING CAN BE GIVEN Oxfordshire

TYPE OF GRANT One-off

FINANCES
- Year 1995–96
- Income £7,259
- Grants £5,745

TRUSTEES B Crossland, K I Tinner, D J Radburn

HOW TO APPLY In writing to the address below

WHO TO APPLY TO Carterton Lions Charity Trust Fund, 50 Davenport Road, Witney, Oxfordshire OX8 5EJ

CC NO 1021741   **ESTABLISHED** 1993

■ Mrs C M Livesley 1992 Charitable Trust

WHAT IS FUNDED Animal welfare

WHAT IS NOT FUNDED No grants to individuals, for expeditions or scholarships

WHO CAN BENEFIT Registered charities working in the areas outlined above

WHERE FUNDING CAN BE GIVEN UK and overseas

TYPE OF GRANT Core costs

RANGE OF GRANTS £1,000–£2,000

SAMPLE GRANTS £6,000 to Redwings Horse Sanctuary

FINANCES
- Year 1996
- Income £10,620

TRUSTEES A J Hawes, Miss S B J Livesley, Mrs P A Clare

HOW TO APPLY In writing. Trustees meet every six months

WHO TO APPLY TO A J Hawes, Mrs C M Livesley 1992 Charitable Trust, Blyth House, Rendham Road, Saxmudham, Suffolk IP17 1EA

CC NO 1014492   **ESTABLISHED** 1992

■ Longley Trust

WHAT IS FUNDED Charities working in the fields of: rural conservation; wildlife sanctuaries; and animal sciences. Preference for involvement of company staff

WHAT IS NOT FUNDED No grants to individuals or students

WHO CAN BENEFIT Small local projects

WHERE FUNDING CAN BE GIVEN West Sussex

TYPE OF GRANT One-off and recurrent grants of £1,000 or less. Funding is given for one year or less

RANGE OF GRANTS £50–£1,000

FINANCES
- Year 1997
- Income £15,080
- Grants £16,300

TRUSTEES P Longley, R P Longley, K F Bergin, J W Ebdon

NOTES National charities can be supported but the Trustees prefer to support local charities

HOW TO APPLY In writing at any time to the address below

WHO TO APPLY TO P Longley, Longley Trust, Longley House, East Park, Crawley, West Sussex RH10 6AP

CC NO 278615   **ESTABLISHED** 1979

■ Loraine Trust

WHAT IS FUNDED Improving the methods and practice of horticulture in areas where people live off the land in particular organic use of the land, soil conservation and local self-sufficiency and culture

WHO CAN BENEFIT Organisations working in the areas outlined above

WHERE FUNDING CAN BE GIVEN UK

TYPE OF GRANT Recurring

FINANCES
- Year 1996
- Income £8,277

TRUSTEES Joan B Loraine, Edward G Campbell Voullaire, Sir John C Palmer, James G Shute Harris

HOW TO APPLY In writing to the address below

WHO TO APPLY TO Miss J Loraine, Trustee and Secretary, Loraine Trust, Greencombe, Porlock, Somerset TA24 8NU

CC NO 299570   ESTABLISHED 1988

■ Lord Mayor of Chester Charitable Trust

WHAT IS FUNDED Local registered charities, particularly those working in the fields of: rural conservation and animal welfare

WHAT IS NOT FUNDED Non-registered charities are not funded

WHO CAN BENEFIT Registered charities working in the areas outlined above

WHERE FUNDING CAN BE GIVEN Chester only

TYPE OF GRANT One-off and capital grants will be considered

RANGE OF GRANTS £25–£1,000

FINANCES
- Year 1998
- Grants £6,205

TRUSTEES D Areld, E Plenderleath, P F Durham, M A Johnson

HOW TO APPLY In writing. Initial telephone calls are welcome. Deadline for applications is May of each year

WHO TO APPLY TO W Healiss, PA to the Lord Mayor, Lord Mayor of Chester Charitable Trust, Council of the City of Chester, Town Hall, Chester CH1 2HS
Tel 01244 402126

CC NO 513175   ESTABLISHED 1982

■ The Loseley & Guildway Charitable Trust

WHAT IS FUNDED Compassionate causes, mainly local or causes with which the family and members of the Firm are associated, including animal welfare

WHAT IS NOT FUNDED Registered charities only, not individuals

WHO CAN BENEFIT Organisations working in the area outlined above

WHERE FUNDING CAN BE GIVEN Surrey

RANGE OF GRANTS £25–£5,000. Typically £100

FINANCES
- Year 1998
- Income £58,986
- Grants £30,651

TRUSTEES J R More-Molyneux, Mrs S More-Molyneux, M G More-Molyneux, F R Gooch, L G Hodson

HOW TO APPLY Quarterly meetings. Due to current commitments, new applications for any causes are unlikely to be successful

WHO TO APPLY TO J R More-Molyneux, The Loseley & Guildway Charitable Trust, Loseley Park, Guildford, Surrey GU3 1HS
Tel 01483 304440
Fax 01483 302036

CC NO 267178   ESTABLISHED 1973

■ The C L Loyd Charitable Trust

WHAT IS FUNDED UK animal welfare charities

WHAT IS NOT FUNDED No local charities with which the Trust is not already closely associated and familiar

WHO CAN BENEFIT Charities working in the area outlined above

WHERE FUNDING CAN BE GIVEN UK, with a preference for Berkshire and Oxfordshire

TYPE OF GRANT One-off and recurring

FINANCES
- Year 1996–97
- Income £126,110
- Grants £167,375

TRUSTEES C L Loyd, T C Loyd

HOW TO APPLY To the address under Who To Apply To in writing

WHO TO APPLY TO C L Loyd, The C L Loyd Charitable Trust, Lockinge, Wantage, Oxfordshire OX12 8QL
Tel 01235 833265

CC NO 265076   ESTABLISHED 1973

■ Lyndhurst Settlement

WHAT IS FUNDED Protection of the environment including: rural conservation; bird sanctuaries and wildlife sanctuaries

WHAT IS NOT FUNDED Grants only made to registered charities. Grants to individuals are not given. The Trustees do not normally support medical or religious charities

WHO CAN BENEFIT Registered charities only

WHERE FUNDING CAN BE GIVEN Usually for work within the UK

TYPE OF GRANT Buildings, core costs, feasibility studies, one-off, projects, research, recurring costs, running costs, salaries and start-up costs. All funding is for one year or less. They are usually for the general purposes of the registered charities supported

SAMPLE GRANTS £3,000 to Save Britain's Heritage
£3,000 to Waste Watch

Lyndhurst

FINANCES
- Year 1997–98
- Income £89,314
- Grants £175,000

TRUSTEES Michael Isaacs, Anthony Skyrme, Kenneth Plummer

PUBLICATIONS Full accounts are on file at the Charity Commission

HOW TO APPLY Requests for grants or further information must be in writing (not by telephone) and include a brief description of the aims and objects of the charity. Unsuccessful applications are not acknowledged unless an sae is enclosed

WHO TO APPLY TO Bowker Orford, Chartered Accountants, Lyndhurst Settlement, 15–19 Cavendish Place, London W1M 0DD

CC NO 256063   **ESTABLISHED** 1968

M

■ The McCorquodale Charitable Trust

WHAT IS FUNDED Rural conservation; animal facilities and services; environmental and animal sciences; and other charitable purposes will be considered

WHERE FUNDING CAN BE GIVEN UK, Scotland

TYPE OF GRANT Buildings, core costs, project and research will be considered

RANGE OF GRANTS £100–£1,000

FINANCES
- Year 1996
- Income £14,082
- Grants £6,025

TRUSTEES C N McCorquodale, Coutts & Co

WHO TO APPLY TO Mrs R A A Iles, Senior Trust Officer, The McCorquodale Charitable Trust, Coutts & Co, Trustee Dept, 440 Strand, London WC2R 0QS

CC NO 297697   **ESTABLISHED** 1986

■ The R S Macdonald Charitable Trust

WHAT IS FUNDED Grants are made to charities which work to prevent cruelty to animals

WHO CAN BENEFIT Animals at risk of cruelty

WHERE FUNDING CAN BE GIVEN Scotland

TYPE OF GRANT One-off, recurring costs, project and research will be considered. Funding may be given for up to three years

FINANCES
- Year 1998
- Income £367,205
- Grants £177,000

TRUSTEES E D Buchanan, D W A Macdonald, S C Macdonald, D G Sutherland, R K Austin

PUBLICATIONS Information is available from the Trust

HOW TO APPLY Applications should be made in writing to the address under Who To Apply To

WHO TO APPLY TO R K Austin, The R S Macdonald Charitable Trust, 27 Cramond Vale, Edinburgh EH4 6RB
Tel 0131-312 6766

SC NO SCO 12710   **ESTABLISHED** 1978

■ Macfarlane Walker Trust

WHAT IS FUNDED Support for charities in the fields of: rural conservation; bird and wildlife sanctuaries; wildlife parks; and environmental issues

WHAT IS NOT FUNDED No grants are given for: expeditions; scholarships; fees for specialised training courses in higher or further education; medical expenses or nationwide appeals

WHO CAN BENEFIT Individuals, registered charities and institutions working in the areas outlined above

WHERE FUNDING CAN BE GIVEN Norfolk, Camden, Greenwich, Kensington and Chelsea, and Gloucestershire

TYPE OF GRANT Feasibility studies, one-off, project, research, running costs and start-up costs. Funding for up to and over three years will be considered

RANGE OF GRANTS £100–£3,000

FINANCES
- Year 1997
- Income £36,714
- Grants £28,191

TRUSTEES R F Walker, D F Walker, N G Walker

HOW TO APPLY By letter giving reason for appealing, and including outline of project with financial forecast. Sae must accompany initial application

WHO TO APPLY TO D A Launchbury, Secretary to the Trustees, Macfarlane Walker Trust, 32 Apple Orchard, Prestbury, Cheltenham GL52 3EH
Tel 01242 521438

CC NO 227890 **ESTABLISHED** 1963

■ The Helen Isabella McMorran Charitable Foundation

WHAT IS FUNDED Rural conservation, animal welfare and bird sanctuaries

WHAT IS NOT FUNDED No grants to individuals

WHO CAN BENEFIT Registered charities working in the areas outlined above

WHERE FUNDING CAN BE GIVEN UK and overseas

TYPE OF GRANT One-off

RANGE OF GRANTS £500–£2,000

FINANCES
- Year 1996–97
- Income £28,112
- Grants £14,350

TRUSTEES National Westminster Bank plc

HOW TO APPLY Applications by letter. Brief guidelines available. Closing date for applications February each year. Applications are considered annually

WHO TO APPLY TO National Westminster Bank plc, Helen Isabella McMorran Charitable Foundation, NatWest Investments, 67 Maple Road, Surbiton, Surrey KT6 4QT
Tel 0181-335 1762

CC NO 266338 **ESTABLISHED** 1973

■ Malachi (Family) Charitable Trust

WHAT IS FUNDED Rural conservation and other charitable purposes beneficial to the community

WHO CAN BENEFIT Ecological charities

WHERE FUNDING CAN BE GIVEN UK and overseas

TYPE OF GRANT One-off

RANGE OF GRANTS £50–£100

FINANCES
- Year 1997–98
- Income £9,013
- Grants £6,216

TRUSTEES Dr J W Heber, Mrs M L Heber, A J Heber

NOTES Funds are very limited and opportunities for non scheduled grants are rare

HOW TO APPLY By letter with full details of project and any official publication. If reply needed s.a.e essential

WHO TO APPLY TO J W Heber, Malachi (Family) Charitable Trust, Ravenhurst, Hope Bagot Lane, Knowbury, Ludlow, Shropshire SY8 3LG
Tel 01584 891434

CC NO 1006776 **ESTABLISHED** 1991

■ R W Mann Trustees Limited

WHAT IS FUNDED Charities working in the fields of nature reserves and woodlands. Other charitable purposes will be considered

WHAT IS NOT FUNDED No grants to individuals

WHO CAN BENEFIT Local activities or local branches of national charities

WHERE FUNDING CAN BE GIVEN Usually Tyne and Wear, occasionally beyond with a preference for North Tyneside

TYPE OF GRANT Recurrent expenditure, capital or single expenditure. Fixed grants out of income. Buildings, core costs, feasibility studies, interest free loans, one-off and project funding for one year or less will be considered

RANGE OF GRANTS £250–£7,000

Marchig

Alphabetical register of grant making trusts

SAMPLE GRANTS £7,000 to Rising Sun Farm Trust for consultancy for organic farm and countryside park

FINANCES
- Year 1997
- Income £128,915
- Grants £140,795

TRUSTEES The Directors: Mrs J Hamilton, Mrs A M Heath, G Javens

NOTES Please enclose an sae

HOW TO APPLY In writing to the address below at any time in the year subject to funds being available. Trustees' meetings are held approximately at intervals of three months. There are no application forms

WHO TO APPLY TO R W Mann Trustees Limited, PO Box 119, Gosforth, Newcastle upon Tyne NE3 4WF
Tel 0191-284 2158
Fax 0191-285 8617
E-mail John.Hamilton@onyx.octacon.co.uk

CC NO 259006   **ESTABLISHED** 1959

■ Marchig Animal Welfare Trust

WHAT IS FUNDED General animal welfare. Support of those engaged in work aimed at preventing or reducing animal suffering. Promotion of alternative methods to animal experimentation. Promotion and encouragement of practical work in preventing cruelty to animals. Periodic awards, known as the Marchig Animal Welfare Awards are made for outstanding work in the furtherance of the above aims. The awards are worth £8,000 and £16,000 and can be split. The following areas are also supported: animal homes; bird and wildlife sanctuaries; cats, catteries and other facilities for cats; dogs, kennels and other facilities for dogs; horses, stables and other facilities for horses; environmental issues, and wildlife parks

WHAT IS NOT FUNDED Applications from students attending courses, going on expeditions, study trips, travel bursaries, etc do not qualify for a grant from the Trust and will therefore not be considered

WHO CAN BENEFIT National and international organisations and individuals working for the protection of animals

WHERE FUNDING CAN BE GIVEN UK, Europe, Asia and Africa

FINANCES
- Year 1997
- Grants £9,590

TRUSTEES Jeanne Marchig, Trevor C Scott, Les Ward

HOW TO APPLY Applications assessed continuously. Trustees meet twice a year. Copy of applicant's Annual Accounts required

WHO TO APPLY TO Mrs Jeanne Marchig, Chairperson, Marchig Animal Welfare Trust, PO Box 14, 1223 Cologny, Geneva, Switzerland
Fax ++41 22 349 6458

CC NO 802133   **ESTABLISHED** 1989

■ The Earl of March's Trust Company Ltd

WHAT IS FUNDED Animal welfare and homes

WHAT IS NOT FUNDED No grants to individuals, students or overseas expeditions

WHO CAN BENEFIT Organisations working in the areas outlined above

WHERE FUNDING CAN BE GIVEN UK and overseas, with some preference for Sussex especially West Sussex

TYPE OF GRANT Largely one-off, some recurrent for core costs, feasibility studies, interest free loans, project, running costs, salaries and start-up costs. Funding is available for up to three years

RANGE OF GRANTS £250–£1,000

FINANCES
- Year 1996–97
- Income £19,000
- Grants £9,000

TRUSTEES Duke of Richmond and Gordon, FCA, Duchess of Richmond, Sir Peter Hordern, MP, Mrs C M Ward

NOTES Criteria are strictly adhered to

HOW TO APPLY Grants are only made to charities known personally to the Trustees

WHO TO APPLY TO Duke of Richmond, The Earl of March's Trust Company Ltd, Goodwood House, Chichester, West Sussex PO18 0PX
Tel 01243 755000
Fax 01243 755005

CC NO 220116   **ESTABLISHED** 1956

■ J and H Marsh and McLennan (Charities Fund) Ltd

WHAT IS FUNDED General charitable purposes including: rural conservation; animal facilities and services; and environmental and animal sciences

WHAT IS NOT FUNDED No grants to individuals or individual schools, churches or local scout groups, art organisations

WHO CAN BENEFIT National organisations and special appeals

WHERE FUNDING CAN BE GIVEN UK

TYPE OF GRANT Buildings, capital, core costs, one-off, project, research, running costs and salaries. Grants of one year or less will be considered

RANGE OF GRANTS £100–£500

FINANCES
- Year 1996
- Income £150,000
- Grants £150,000

TRUSTEES The Directors

HOW TO APPLY Letter with Annual Report and Accounts

WHO TO APPLY TO F R Rutter, Director, J and H Marsh and McLennan (Charities Fund) Ltd, Aldgate House, 33 Aldgate High Street, EC3N 1AQ
Tel 0171-357 3032

CC NO 261955 **ESTABLISHED** 1970

■ Michael D Martin Charitable Trust

WHAT IS FUNDED The environment

WHO CAN BENEFIT Individuals and organisations working in the area outlined above

WHERE FUNDING CAN BE GIVEN UK

FINANCES
- Year 1996
- Income £11,061
- Grants £9,095

TRUSTEES David M Berliand, Timothy M O'Donovan

HOW TO APPLY In writing to the address below

WHO TO APPLY TO M D Martin, Michael D Martin Charitable Trust, Hookway Farm, Pennymoor, Tiverton, Devon EX16 8LU

CC NO 288221 **ESTABLISHED** 1983

■ The Mayor of Torbay's Appeal Fund

WHAT IS FUNDED Animal health and welfare

WHO CAN BENEFIT Individuals and institutions working in the areas outlined above

WHERE FUNDING CAN BE GIVEN Torbay

FINANCES
- Year 1997
- Income £5,524

TRUSTEES The Town Clerk and Chief Executive Officer, Mayor of Torbay, Chairman of the Policy Committee

HOW TO APPLY To the address below in writing

WHO TO APPLY TO The Town Clerk, The Mayor of Torbay's Appeal Fund, Town Clerk's Department, Torbay Town Council, Torquay, Devon TQ1 3DR

CC NO 285492 **ESTABLISHED** 1982

■ Medical Equestrian Association

WHAT IS FUNDED To promote research into the use and development of safety equipment and clothing, the prevention and incidence of equestrian accidents and publish the useful results

WHO CAN BENEFIT Institutions and organisations working in the areas outlined above

WHERE FUNDING CAN BE GIVEN UK

HOW TO APPLY In writing to the address below

WHO TO APPLY TO Neville Sutton, Medical Equestrian Association, Lower Dean, Sparsholt, Winchester, Hampshire SO21 2LP

CC NO 328200 **ESTABLISHED** 1989

■ Melton Mowbray Building Society Charitable Foundation

WHAT IS FUNDED General charitable purposes for the benefit of persons resident within the counties of Rutland, Leicester, Lincoln and Nottingham, including environmental issues; lakes; landscapes; nature reserves; waterways; woodlands; animal welfare; and wildlife sanctuaries

WHAT IS NOT FUNDED No grants to political requests, extremist or unethical projects

WHERE FUNDING CAN BE GIVEN Rutland, Leicestershire, Lincolnshire and Nottinghamshire

TYPE OF GRANT One-off (may consider recurring), buildings, capital, core costs, feasibility studies, project, research, running costs and start-up costs. Funding is available for up to two years

RANGE OF GRANTS £1–£150, average grant £100

FINANCES
- Year 1998
- Income £6,254
- Grants £1,477

TRUSTEES R J Green, Canon D E B Law, C E I Thornton, D Twitchen, G F Wells

PUBLICATIONS Leaflet on display in all branches of the Building Society

HOW TO APPLY The Foundation is happy to receive initial telephone calls. There are no application forms, guidelines (except for geographical territory) or deadlines for applications. Sae is not required. The Trustees meet approximately every quarter

WHO TO APPLY TO Lisa Lound, Secretary, Melton Mowbray Building Society Charitable

Mersey

Foundation, 39 Nottingham Street, Melton Mowbray, Leicestershire LE13 1NR
Tel 01664 563937

CC NO 1067348   **ESTABLISHED** 1998

■ Mersey Basin Trust – ICI Green Action Grants

WHAT IS FUNDED The Trust awards ICI Green Action Grants for environmental projects carried out by voluntary groups and schools in the Runcorn and Northwich areas of Cheshire. The grant is part of the Weaver Valley Initiative. Charities working in the fields of: rural conservation; ecology; and natural history

WHAT IS NOT FUNDED No grants for repairs to buildings, etc

WHO CAN BENEFIT Voluntary and community organisations

WHERE FUNDING CAN BE GIVEN Runcorn and Northwich

TYPE OF GRANT Project grants paid retrospectively and funded for up to one year

RANGE OF GRANTS £100–£1,000

SAMPLE GRANTS £940 to Wallerscote Primary School for a wildlife and sensory garden
£910 to Little Leigh County Primary for an activity area
£859 to Frodsham Town Council for disabled access to riverside
£606 to Cloughwood School for renovation of Hartford Campus pond
£600 to Friends of Owley Wood for wildflower project

FINANCES
- Year 1997–98
- Income £600,000
- Grants £7,000

TRUSTEES Keith Noble, Derek Bullock, Michael O'Brian, Edgar Whewell, John Gittins, Charles Hamilton, Brian Lythgoe, Alan Howarth, Mrs Ann Gardiner, Dr Robin Henshaw, Frank Smith, Ben Williams, Anne Selby, Paul Christie, Anthony Bielderman, Roger Hutchins, David A Roydes, Frank Lythgoe, Cedric Selby, Mrs Diane Rhodes, Peter Glover, Bill Rhodes, John Ashworth, Bert Bowles

PUBLICATIONS *The Campaigner* quarterly newsletter

HOW TO APPLY Application should be made on a form available either by writing or telephone call. The awards panel meets quarterly

WHO TO APPLY TO Liz Allen, Mersey Basin Trust – ICI Green Action Grants, Weaver Valley Initiative, c/o North West Water, Winnington Avenue, Winnington, Northwich, Cheshire CW8 4EE
Tel 01606 79576
Fax 01606 871169

CC NO 1005305   **ESTABLISHED** 1991

■ Mersey Basin Trust – Stream Care Project

WHAT IS FUNDED The care and improvement of local watercourses through the action of the local community. The Trust offers advice and practical support to all local groups ranging from schools and anglers, to civic societies and tenants associations

WHAT IS NOT FUNDED No grants to individuals or for projects not designed for the improvement of waterways within the Mersey Basin

WHO CAN BENEFIT Waterside and waterway environments; community and local voluntary groups wishing to take action for improving their local watercourse

WHERE FUNDING CAN BE GIVEN Mersey Basin Campaign Area (Cheshire, part of Lancashire, Greater Manchester, Merseyside and part of Derbyshire)

TYPE OF GRANT One-off project support to enable volunteer action

RANGE OF GRANTS £25–£150; typical grant £50

FINANCES
- Year 1998
- Income £5,000
- Grants £2,500

TRUSTEES John Ashworth, Anthony Bielderman, Bert Bowles, Derek Bullock, Paul Christie, Ann Gardiner, Jon Gittins (Vice-Chair), Peter Glover, Charles Hamilton, Robin Henshaw, Alan Howarth, Roger Hutchins, Erica Jones, Brian Lythgoe, Frank Lythgoe, Frank Noble, Mike O'Brian, Keith Parry, Diane Rhodes, Bill Rhodes (Chairman), David Roydes, Cedric Selby, Anne Selby (Vice-Chair), Frank Smith, Henry West, Ben Williams, Edgar Whewall

PUBLICATIONS Waterside Safety leaflet

NOTES In 1998, Stream Care supported 40 groups carrying out practical projects and an additional 25 groups received advice and non-financial support

HOW TO APPLY Contact the name and address below detailing your plans, and/or telephone to arrange a site visit

WHO TO APPLY TO Sibongile Pradhan, Mersey Basin Trust – Stream Care Project, Sunley Tower, Piccadilly Plaza, Manchester M1 4AG

CC NO 1005305   **ESTABLISHED** 1991

■ Mersey Basin Trust – Waterside Revival Grants

WHAT IS FUNDED The conservation and improvement of waterside sites, open to the public by funding local voluntary groups to organise and carry out the improvement and management of such sites

WHAT IS NOT FUNDED No grants to individuals, or for projects which are not associated with a water course in the Mersey Basin

WHO CAN BENEFIT Voluntary groups and community organisations involved in waterside conservation

WHERE FUNDING CAN BE GIVEN Mersey Basin Campaign Area (Cheshire, part of Lancashire, Greater Manchester, Merseyside, High Peak in Derbyshire)

TYPE OF GRANT Feasibility studies, one-off and project for one year or less

RANGE OF GRANTS £446–£1,000; typical £850

SAMPLE GRANTS £1,000 to Rishton Prospects Panel for the improvement of land at the rear of the canal
£1,000 to Shropshire Union Canal Society
£1000 to Morts Astley Heritage Trust for pond and orchard restoration
£1,000 to Blackburn Groundwork Trust for renovating allotments for schools
£1,000 to Stacksteads Youth Club to improve access to park
£1,000 to Volunteer Angling Club for pathwork and tree planting
£1,000 to Langendale Heritage Trust for garden restoration

FINANCES
- Year 1997
- Income £20,060
- Grants £10,175

TRUSTEES John Ashworth, Anthony Bielderman, Bert Bowles, Derek Bullock, Paul Christie, Ann Gardiner, Jon Gittins (Vice-Chair), Peter Glover, Charles Hamilton, Robin Henshaw, Alan Howarth, Roger Hutchins, Erica Jones, Brian Lythgoe, Frank Lythgoe, Frank Noble, Mike O'Brian, Keith Parry, Diane Rhodes, Bill Rhodes (Chairman), David Roydes, Cedric Selby, Anne Selby (Vice-Chair), Frank Smith, Henry West, Ben Williams, Edgar Whewall

HOW TO APPLY Applications should be made on a form available from the address under Who To Apply To, whereupon a visit to the site will be made. At present, there is one grant panel per annum to consider applications, held in the summer. Telephone enquiries welcomed

WHO TO APPLY TO Caroline Downey, Mersey Basin Trust – Waterside Revival Grants, Sunley Tower, Piccadilly Plaza, Manchester M1 4AG
Tel 0161-228 6924

CC NO 1005305   **ESTABLISHED** 1991

■ The Methodist Relief and Development Fund

WHAT IS FUNDED Priorities for overseas development: agroforestry (organic farming, permaculture etc)

WHAT IS NOT FUNDED Applications from individuals and organisations without charitable status. Scholarships for studies or voluntary work overseas. Individual development education centres affiliated to the Development Education Association

WHO CAN BENEFIT Indigenous NGO's/religious organisations in the developing world and international NGO's who work with an indigenous partner to implement a project

WHERE FUNDING CAN BE GIVEN Overseas

TYPE OF GRANT Capital, core costs, feasibility studies, one-off, project, research, recurring costs, running costs and salaries. Funding for up to three years will be considered

RANGE OF GRANTS £100–£80,000. Average grants: £5,000–£15,000

SAMPLE GRANTS £60,300 (co-funded) to African Water and Agroforestry Programme (AWAP) for agroforestry, organic farming and water projects

FINANCES
- Year 1996–97
- Income £843,832
- Grants £628,468

TRUSTEES J Anderson, Rev G Barnard, Rev E Bellamy, K Cash, H Dalzell, Rev D Halstead, B Hindmarsh, J Hindson, Rev R Jacob, Rev Dr R Jones, Dr J Leitch, D Maidment, Rev F Munce, R Shackleton, S Veagra

PUBLICATIONS Annual Report. *MRDF Policy on Humanitarian Aid and Development. Funds in Focus* (quarterly publication). *Africa Link* (agroforestry publication)

HOW TO APPLY Applications should be sent to the address under Who To Apply To. Applicants should request a copy of the *MRDF Policy on Humanitarian Aid and Development* if they are unsure about their application to the MRDF. The MRDF does not issue guidelines or require applicants to complete a form. Applications must reach the Projects Co-ordinator one month prior to a quarterly Trustees meeting (dates available from the MRDF)

WHO TO APPLY TO Martin Watson, Projects Co-ordinator, The Methodist Relief and Development Fund, 1 Central Buildings, London SW1H 9NH
Tel 0171-222 8010
Fax 0171-799 2153
E-mail watson@mrdf.demon.co

CC NO 291691   **ESTABLISHED** 1985

Mickel Fund

WHAT IS FUNDED General charitable purposes including zoos

WHAT IS NOT FUNDED No grants to individuals

WHO CAN BENEFIT Mainly registered charities. Prefer local charities, but do give to UK charities

WHERE FUNDING CAN BE GIVEN East Lothian, East Renfrewshire, Edinburgh, Glasgow, Midlothian, North Ayrshire, North Lanarkshire, Renfrewshire, South Ayrshire, West Ayrshire and West Lothian

TYPE OF GRANT One-off and recurring funding. Buildings, capital, project and research. Funding is available for more than three years

FINANCES
- Year 1996–97
- Income £50,000
- Grants £124,000

TRUSTEES D W Mickel, D A Mickel, B G A Mickel, J C Craig, J R C Wark

HOW TO APPLY In writing from appropriate charities only

WHO TO APPLY TO J R C Wark, Mickel Fund, McTaggart & Mickel Ltd, 126 West Regent Street, Glasgow G2 2BH
Tel 0141-332 0001

SC NO SCO 03266   **ESTABLISHED** 1970

The Middleton Fund

WHAT IS FUNDED The preservation and improvement of the natural environment in the area Where Funding Can Be Given

WHO CAN BENEFIT Organisations working in the areas outlined above

WHERE FUNDING CAN BE GIVEN Humberside, North Yorkshire

FINANCES
- Year 1996
- Income £5,344
- Grants £2,395

TRUSTEES Lord Middleton, Lady Middleton, The Hon M C J Willoughby

HOW TO APPLY To the Secretary in writing

WHO TO APPLY TO The Secretary, The Middleton Fund, The Estate Office, Birdsall, Malton, North Yorkshire YO17 9NU

CC NO 505273   **ESTABLISHED** 1976

The Miller Foundation

WHAT IS FUNDED Organisations working for the welfare of animals

WHO CAN BENEFIT Organisations working in the area outlined above

WHERE FUNDING CAN BE GIVEN Scotland and occasionally other areas

TYPE OF GRANT Flexible

RANGE OF GRANTS £750–£7,500

FINANCES
- Year 1997
- Income £137,000
- Grants £130,000

TRUSTEES C Fleming Brown, G R G Graham, James Simpson, C C Wright

HOW TO APPLY Applications should be made in writing to the address under Who To Apply To

WHO TO APPLY TO G R G Graham, The Miller Foundation, Maclay Murray & Spens, 151 St Vincent Street, Glasgow G2 5NJ
Tel 0141-248 5019

SC NO SCO 08798   **ESTABLISHED** 1979

Mitsubishi Corporation Fund for Europe and Africa

WHAT IS FUNDED (a) To conserve and protect for the benefit of the public the environment as a whole and its animal, forest and plant life in particular and to educate the public in natural history and ecology and the importance of conservation of the environment; (b) to advance the education of the public and in particular to (i) promote education and research in the field of ecology and conservation of natural resources and the environment anywhere in the world and; (ii) to promote the study and appreciation of flora and fauna anywhere in the world with particular emphasis on endangered species; (iii) to promote the study and appreciation of agriculture, horticulture, silviculture, and land and estate management

WHERE FUNDING CAN BE GIVEN UK, Africa and Europe

FINANCES
- Year 1997–98
- Income £113,445
- Grants £80,468

TRUSTEES H Nemichi, S Inai, D Pownall, T Hanaoka, K Fujita

HOW TO APPLY In writing to the address below. However, it should be noted that funds are committed a year in advance

WHO TO APPLY TO Beatrice Garnett, Secretary to the Fund, Mitsubishi Corporation Fund for Europe and Africa, Bow Bells House, Bread

Street, London EC4M 9BQ
Tel 0171-822 1754

CC NO 1014621　　　**ESTABLISHED** 1992

■ The Monument Trust (64)

WHAT IS FUNDED　Rural conservation

WHAT IS NOT FUNDED　No grants direct to individuals, no grants overseas. Funding is not provided for animal welfare

WHO CAN BENEFIT　Registered charities only

WHERE FUNDING CAN BE GIVEN　UK

TYPE OF GRANT　One-off, capital, buildings, revenue costs and project. Funding may be given for up to three years

FINANCES
- Year 1997　　● Income £4,511,000
- Grants £3,671,000

TRUSTEES　S Grimshaw, R H Gurney, Mrs L Heathcoat-Amory, Sir Anthony Tennant

NOTES　Please note that the Trust is not seeking further applications for rural conservation. Their limited grantmaking in this area is pro-active, not reactive

HOW TO APPLY　Applications are not solicited but, if submitted, are considered at any time

WHO TO APPLY TO　M A Pattison, The Monument Trust, 9 Red Lion Court, London EC4A 3EF *Tel* 0171-410 0330

CC NO 242575　　　**ESTABLISHED** 1965

Commentary

The Monument Trust was established in 1965 and is one of the group of charities known collectively as the Sainsbury Family Charitable Trusts. Each of the Sainsbury Family Charitable Trusts supports areas in which the Settlors felt that they could make a particular impact. As with many of the other Family Trusts there is an interest in innovation and experiment, and in projects where funding is difficult to find, especially in the areas of social disadvantage and exclusion.

Most emphasis is placed upon the health and community care, and the social development programmes by the Trustees. Within these programmes there are concentrations upon AIDS and HIV funding as well as homelessness, social exclusion and the development of primary care. Some support will also be given to projects with new approaches for the rehabilitation of offenders and ex-offenders. An area that has diminished somewhat in importance with the advent of the National Lottery Heritage Funds is that of the built and natural environment. However, the Trust will still support well organised projects for preservation of both the natural environment and the built environment.

Perhaps more so than many of the other Sainsbury Trusts, there is concentration upon the arts, where there are generally a number of major grants given for a range of arts activities, primarily in areas where the Trustees have particular knowledge and interest. The Trustees review their policies annually but there have been no significant changes in the grant making policies of the Trust in recent years, and no major changes are expected.

The Trust makes grants within the United Kingdom, with some concentration upon London. Grants are not made overseas.

The Trust does not replace statutory responsibility, nor will it generally fund in areas where there is corporate sponsorship or local funding available. The Trustees do not generally involve themselves in organised partnership funding, although they may get involved where they have a particular interest and personal knowledge or experience. The Trust tends to make grants for projects over a number of years (rarely more than three), as well as grants for capital costs such as building and refurbishment, revenue costs for smaller organisations and one-off grants.

As with many of the other Sainsbury Trusts, the Monument Trust make few responses to unsolicited applications because they have Trustees who take a very pro-active stance; proposals are generally invited by the Trustees or initiated at their request. Therefore unsolicited applications are not likely to be successful, although all applications will receive a response. The Trustees may be more open to examine unsolicited applications in the field of the natural environment, although there remains no guarantee that a grant will result. Any applications made should be in the form of a letter at any time to the Director of the Trust and should include information on project objectives and costs, other likely sources of funds, the long-term funding position and background information on the organisation such as Annual Reports and Accounts. Applications of particular interest will be examined by the Trustees at one of the Trustee meetings.

The Trustees request reports from those who have received grants and also arrange periodic reviews of their major programmes, but do not have an assessment process whereby all organisations are visited

SAMPLE GRANTS

The top ten grants given in 1997 were:
£1,013,000 to the Royal Opera House Trust for redevelopment and current costs
£1,000,000 to the Royal National Theatre for redevelopment
£375,000 to the University of Cambridge over

Moore

five years towards bursaries for UK public and charitable sector workers to undertake MBA courses at the Judge Institute

£256,750 to the Wallace Collection towards the Centenary Scheme and other costs

£255,000 to Friends of Pallant House over two years towards expansion of the gallery facilities

£200,000 to King's Fund over two years for their intermediate care project

£168,000 to Waterville Project for Children and Young People over three years for support of young people aged 13 to 16 through two youth workers

£166,500 to the British Trust for Conservation Volunteers over three years for core funding

£150,000 to Phoenix House, St Mungo's and London Connection over three years towards developing joint services for homeless people with multiple needs

£125,000 to National Museums and Galleries on Merseyside over four years for research into laser cleaning

■ The Horace Moore Charitable Trust

WHAT IS FUNDED The Trust will consider funding: lakes and landscapes; nature reserves; waterways; woodlands; animal homes; dogs, kennels and other facilities for dogs; horses, stables and other facilities for horses; and agriculture

WHAT IS NOT FUNDED No grants to individuals. Donations only to registered charities, long waiting list, owing to small income

WHO CAN BENEFIT Organisations only

WHERE FUNDING CAN BE GIVEN The South East: including the London Boroughs of Kensington and Chelsea, Kingston upon Thames, and Richmond upon Thames. Gloucestershire; Wiltshire; Derbyshire; Nottinghamshire; Rutland; and Yorkshire and Humberside

FINANCES
- Year 1997
- Income £39,559

TRUSTEES J A G Leighton, J E A Leighton

NOTES Funds fully committed

HOW TO APPLY Donations are only given to charitable organisations and to those of personal interest to the Trustees

WHO TO APPLY TO J A G Leighton, Chairman, The Horace Moore Charitable Trust, Mallows Studio, Warreners Lane, Weybridge, Surrey KT13 0LH
Tel 01932 710250

CC NO 262545   **ESTABLISHED** 1962

■ The Peter Moores Foundation (50)

WHAT IS FUNDED Projects which come to the attention of the Patron or the Trustees, including the environment

WHAT IS NOT FUNDED No grants to individuals. Projects outside the areas that the Foundation supports and unsolicited applications

WHO CAN BENEFIT Organisations working in the area outlined above

WHERE FUNDING CAN BE GIVEN UK and Barbados

TYPE OF GRANT One-off or recurring, for buildings, revenue costs, capital costs, running costs

FINANCES
- Year 1997
- Income £3,205,498
- Grants £4,975,587

TRUSTEES Ludmilla Andrew, Trevor Conway, Peter Egerton-Warburton, Mrs Barbara D Johnstone

HOW TO APPLY This Trust states that it does not respond to unsolicited applications. General applications for grants are not encouraged. The Trustees have fully committed funds for a substantial future period and regret that they are unable to consider any direct applications for funds

WHO TO APPLY TO P A Saunders, The Peter Moores Foundation, c/o Wallwork Nelson & Johnson, Derby House, Lytham Road, Fulwood, Preston PR2 4JF

CC NO 258224   **ESTABLISHED** 1964

Commentary

The Peter Moores Foundation was established on 9 April 1964 by its Patron Peter Moores, CBE, DL. It supports projects which come to the attention of the Patron or the Trustees, through their interests or special knowledge. Preference is given to the following purposes: the raising of the artistic taste of the public, whether in relation to music, drama, opera, painting, sculpture or otherwise in connection with the fine arts; the promotion of education in the fine arts; the promotion of academic education; the promotion of the Christian religion; and the provision of facilities for recreation or other leisure-time occupation. In 1997, grants made fell into ten main areas: the performance and recording of music and training in music (9.57 per cent of the total grants made); fine art (79.87 per cent); heritage (0.31 per cent); youth (1.19 per cent); race relations (1 per cent); social (0.15 per cent); health (1.37 per cent); environment (0.10 per cent); Barbados (5.95 per cent); and one-off (0.49 per cent).

The Foundation will only support causes and organisations that come to be known to the Patron or the Trustees through their interests and special knowledge. Currently all the Foundation's funds are committed in such a way and, as a result, applications for grants from outside sources cannot be considered and are not encouraged.

The funding policies of the Foundation were set in the Trust Deed, but the Trustees take account of the preferences of the Patron. Only the Patron has the power to appoint Trustees, whose investment powers are unrestricted, but must have written consent of the Patron. The Foundation supports causes throughout the UK and in Barbados. It helps some UK based people, for example young opera singers, to study in Europe.

The Foundation supports statutory bodies in the sense that it makes grants to schools, colleges and universities, but it does not appear to be prepared to replace statutory funding. Nor does it appear to participate in co-funding projects. Grants made are usually one-off or recurring, and are for a variety of purposes, which include: building work, conversion and restoration, revenue costs and capital grants for purchasing works of art, such as in the case of the Compton Verney House Trust; the production of recordings of rare pieces of music, with Opera Rara; scholarships for promising young opera singers to the Royal Northern School of Music; helping young opera singers to study abroad; the Peter Moores Barbados Trust, which works to improve agriculture, protect the environment, provide employment and help farmers to become more self-sufficient in Barbados; and the provision of therapy and information to AIDS sufferers. Loans were not made in 1997, but infrastructure costs are supported.

There is no applications procedure, because, as already stated, unsolicited applications are not considered or welcomed. Only projects already known to the Trustees and Patron are supported

SAMPLE GRANTS
The top ten grants made in 1997 were:
£3,953,500 to Compton Verney House Trust for the conservation and restoration of the house, the purchasing of works of art to be displayed there and their revenue costs for ten years
£245,026 to Peter Moores Barbados Trust for the Scotland Project, which works to improve agriculture, protect the environment, provide employment and help farmers to become more self-sufficient in Barbados
£59,142 to Opera Rara for the recording of Three Rossini Tenors
£50,000 to Almeida Theatre for the Almeida Opera Festival
£50,000 to the Rossini Opera Festival which teaches talented singers to understand the style of Rossini
£48,053 to University of West Indies to establish a Chair in Tropical Horticulture, which will be funded for three years by the Foundation and will also provide courses for local people in horticulture
£46,035 to Opera Rara for the recording of Rosmonda d'Inghilterra
£36,000 to the Royal Northern School of Music for the scholarships for nine promising young opera singers
£33,377 to Opera Rara for the recording of Maria d'Inghilterra
£15,000 to Immune Development Trust

■Edith Murphy Foundation

WHAT IS FUNDED To provide relief of suffering of animals and provision for the care of unwanted or sick animals

WHO CAN BENEFIT Organisations working in the areas outlined above

WHERE FUNDING CAN BE GIVEN UK

RANGE OF GRANTS £28,591–£150,000

FINANCES
- Year 1997
- Grants £178,591
- Income £133,191

TRUSTEES Mrs E A Murphy, D L Tams, Ms P M Breakwell, Ms F Kesterton, J Kesterton

HOW TO APPLY To the address under Who To Apply To in writing

WHO TO APPLY TO D L Tams, Solicitor, Edith Murphy Foundation, Crane & Walton, 113–117 London Road, Leicester, Leicestershire LE3 0RG

CC NO 1026062   **ESTABLISHED** 1993

Nabarro

■ The Kitty and Daniel Nabarro Charitable Trust

WHAT IS FUNDED Rural conservation; particularly endangered species and environmental issues

WHAT IS NOT FUNDED No grants to individuals

WHO CAN BENEFIT Registered charities only

WHERE FUNDING CAN BE GIVEN UK; particularly Barnet

TYPE OF GRANT One-off and project

FINANCES
- Year 1997
- Income £24,032
- Grants £36,475

TRUSTEES D J N Nabarro, Mrs K Nabarro, E Cohen

HOW TO APPLY To the address under Who To Apply To in writing. The Trustees allocate grants on an annual basis to an existing list of charities. The Trustees do not at this time envisage giving grants to charities which are not already on the list. **This Trust states that it does not respond to unsolicited applications**

WHO TO APPLY TO D J N Nabarro, The Kitty and Daniel Nabarro Charitable Trust, PO Box 7491, London N20 8LY

CC NO 1002786   **ESTABLISHED** 1991

■ National Animal Sanctuaries Support League

WHAT IS FUNDED Animal welfare

WHAT IS NOT FUNDED No grants for students

WHO CAN BENEFIT New organisations and innovative projects

WHERE FUNDING CAN BE GIVEN UK

RANGE OF GRANTS £1,000 or less

FINANCES
- Year 1996–97
- Income £19,420
- Grants £195

TRUSTEES Mrs P A Wilson, R Mackinlay, Mrs B Lambert

PUBLICATIONS Annual Report

HOW TO APPLY In writing to the address below

WHO TO APPLY TO Mrs P A Wilson, National Animal Sanctuaries Support League, PO Box 42, Newton Aycliffe, Co Durham DL5 5JA

CC NO 1024884   **ESTABLISHED** 1993

■ National Lottery Charities Board (1)

WHAT IS FUNDED Projects submitted from registered charities and/or voluntary sector organisations which are charitable, philanthropic or benevolent and based in the UK; including those working in the fields of endangered species and environmental issues. Organisations must be legally eligible to apply for a grant from the Board. The Board publishes a leaflet called 'Guide to Eligibility'. Awards are currently being offered through a series of main grants programmes (community involvement, and poverty and disadvantage), Small Grants or Awards For All, International Grants and a specialist Health and Social Research programme

WHAT IS NOT FUNDED Duplication of existing services or replacement of statutory provision. The Board is not able to make grants to local authorities, local education Trusts, to schools or to charities set up to support statutory bodies. Applications will not be accepted from professional fundraisers. The Board does not make emergency awards. All grants must be additional to public expenditure

WHO CAN BENEFIT Charitable, benevolent and philanthropic organisations which run projects that help to meet the Board's mission statement; namely to meet the needs of those at greatest disadvantage in society. There are no restrictions on the age; family situation; religion and culture; and social circumstances of; or disease or medical condition suffered by, the beneficiaries

WHERE FUNDING CAN BE GIVEN UK-wide through main grants programmes

TYPE OF GRANT Capital grants, revenue grants or a combination of both. Also buildings, core costs, feasibility studies, one-off, project, research, recurring and running costs, salaries and start-up costs. Grants are awarded for projects for up to three years for the main grants programmes. Re-applications can be considered

RANGE OF GRANTS £500 minimum (in main and small grants programmes); no maximum though the largest grants have been £1.1 million. Average size of grant is £48,700

FINANCES
- Year 1997–98
- Income £333,000,000
- Grants £366,000,000

TRUSTEES David Sieff (Chairman), Sir Adam Ridley (Deputy Chairman), Tessa Baring, CBE, Amir Bhatia, OBE, Steven Burkeman, Jeff Carroll, June Churchman, OBE, DL, Stella Clarke, CBE, Anne Clark, Kay Hampton, Tom

Jones, OBE, Amanda Jordan, Barbara Lowndes, MBE, Sheila Jane Malley, Richard Martineau, Garth Morrison, CBE, DL, William Osborne, Ron Partington, John Simpson, OBE, Noel Stewart, OBE, Sir Eric Stroud, Elisabeth Watkins

PUBLICATIONS Range of materials and guidance on applications to the Board available from all Board Offices

HOW TO APPLY New telephone numbers apply from 1 July 1999. Application packs for each of the main programmes may be obtained by calling a 24-hour central mailing number: 0845 791 9191. Welsh speakers can ring 0845-627 3273 (including Small Grants). Application packs for the Awards For All England programme are available on 0845 600 2040 and for the Awards For All Scotland programme on 0645 700777. Application forms for Community Involvement, Poverty and Disadvantage and Small Grants (Northern Ireland) are also available at the NLCB's website: www.nlcb.org.uk. Completed applications should be returned to the office indicated on the pack

WHO TO APPLY TO **UK-wide Office:** Gerald Oppenheim, Director UK and Corporate Planning, National Lottery Charities Board, St Vincent House, 16 Suffolk Street, London SW1Y 4NL
Tel 0171-747 5315
Textphone 0171-747 5347
Fax 0171-747 5307
E-mail enquiries@nlcb.org.uk
Web Site http://www.nlcb.org.uk

REGIONAL OFFICES **International grants office:**
St Vincent House, 16 Suffolk Street, London SW1Y 4NL
Tel 0171-747 5294
Textphone 0171-747 5347
Fax 0171-747 5307
E-mail mday@nlcb.org.uk

Country Offices:
Wales Office: Roy Norris, Director for Wales, Ladywell House, Newtown, Powys SY16 1JB
Tel 01686 621644
Textphone 01686 610205
Fax 01686 621534
E-mail enquiries@wales.nlcb.org.uk

Northern Ireland Office: Ann McLaughlin, Director for Northern Ireland, 2nd Floor, Hildon House, 30-34 Hill Street, Belfast BT1 2LB
Tel 01232 551455
Textphone 01232 551431
Fax 01232 551444
E-mail enquiries@ni.nlcb.org.uk

Scotland Office: John Rafferty, Director for Scotland, Norloch House, 36 Kings Stables Road, Edinburgh EH1 2EJ
Tel 0131-221 7100
Textphone 0131-221 7122
Fax 0131-221 7120
E-mail enquiries@scotland.nlcb.org.uk

Awards for All Scotland Office: Stephen Shields, Programme Manager, 4 Shore Place, Leith, Edinburgh EH6 6UU
Tel 0131-622 7600
Textphone 0131-221 7122
Fax 0131-622 7311

England Head Office: Janet Paraskeva, Director for England, Readson House, 96-98 Regent Road, Leicester LE1 7DZ
Tel 0116-258 7000
Textphone 0116-255 5162
Fax 0116-255 7398
E-mail enquiries@englandhq.nlcb.org.uk

England Regional Offices:
London: Janice Needham, Regional Manager, 3rd Floor, Whittington House, 19-30 Alfred Place, London WC1E 7EZ
Tel 0171-291 8500
Textphone 0171-291 8526
Fax 0171-291 8503
E-mail enquiries@lon.nlcb.org.uk

South East: Dorothy Buckrell, Regional Manager, 3rd Floor, Dominion House, Woodbridge Road, Guildford, Surrey GU1 4BN
Tel 01483 462900
Textphone 01483 568764
Fax 01483 569893
E-mail enquiries@se.nlcb.org.uk

South West: John de la Cour and Pippa Warin, Regional Managers, Beaufort House, 51 New North Road, Exeter EX4 4EQ
Tel 01392 849700
Textphone 01392 490633
Fax 01392 491134
E-mail enquiries@sw.nlcb.org.uk

Eastern: Lynn Morgan, Acting Regional Manager, Great Eastern House, Tenison Road, Cambridge CB1 2TT
Tel 01223 449000
Textphone 01223 352041
Fax 01223 312628
E-mail enquiries@ea.nlcb.org.uk

East Midlands: Leonie Lupton, Regional Manager, 3rd Floor, 33 Park Row, Nottingham, NG1 6NL
Tel 0115-934 9300
Textphone 0115-948 4436
Fax 0115-948 4435
E-mail enquiries@em.nlcb.org.uk

West Midlands: Fran Jones, Regional Manager, 4th Floor, Edmund House, 12-22 Newhall Street, Birmingham B3 3NL
Tel 0121-200 3500
Textphone 0121-212 3523
Fax 0121-212 3081
E-mail enquiries@wm.nlcb.org.uk

Yorkshire and Humberside: Helen Wollaston, Regional Manager, 3rd Floor, Carlton Tower, 34 St Paul's Street, Leeds LS1 2AT
Tel 0113-224 5300
Textphone 0113-245 4104
Fax 0113-244 0363
E-mail enquiries@yh.nlcb.org.uk

North West: Andrew Freeney, Regional Manager, Dallam Court, Dallam Lane, Warrington WA2 7LU

National

Tel 01925 626800
Textphone 01925 231241
Fax 01925 234041
E-mail enquiries@nw.nlcb.org.uk

North East: Peter Deans, Regional Manager, Ground Floor, Bede House, All Saints Business Centre, Broad Chare, Newcastle Upon Tyne NE1 2NL
Tel 0191-255 1100
Textphone 0191-233 2099
Fax 0191-233 1997
E-mail enquiries@ne.nlcb.org.uk

ESTABLISHED 1994

Commentary

The National Lottery Charities Board is one of the six good causes and one of the twelve Distributing Bodies set up to distribute Lottery funds. The Board is a Non-Departmental Public Body, sponsored by the Department for Culture, Media and Sport but is independent of Government. Since the launch of the Board in August 1994 grants totalling more than £1 billion have been made through over 20,000 awards. The Board is the largest, all-purpose grantmaker in the UK with a grant-making approach designed to provide the greatest opportunity for voluntary sector and charitable organisations to apply for grants. The Board's grant-making procedures are made as transparent as possible, especially as it operates in the glare of public scrutiny to a far greater extent than most other grant-making trusts.

The Board makes grants in a variety of ways. These comprise: (a) UK-wide main grants programmes; (b) Small Grants programmes or Cross-Distributor programmes through Awards For All across the UK; (c) International programmes; (d) Specialist programmes to do with Health and Social Research.

The Board funds projects which help those at greatest disadvantage in society. The main grants programmes run so far include: (a) poverty; (b) youth issues/low income; (c) health, disability and care; (d) new opportunities and choices/voluntary sector development; (e) improving people's living environment/voluntary sector development. Those running at present are (f) community involvement/voluntary sector development; (g) poverty and disadvantage. The Small Grants programme, which currently operates in England, Wales and Northern Ireland, will cease taking applications in 1999, when the cross-distributor grants programme Awards For All will be extended from Scotland and the East Midlands to the rest of England and, in slightly different forms, to Wales and Northern Ireland respectively.

The International Grants programmes make grants to UK organisations working overseas in the following geographical areas: Africa; Asia (including the pacific, the Caucasus and Central Asian Republics); the Middle East, South and Central America; the Caribbean; Central and Eastern Europe.

A specialist programme for Health and Social Research was run in 1998–99 (awards due to be announced in June 1999).

The Board is committed to meeting the widest possible range of need in a fair and equitable way. Its grant programmes are designed with this in mind. Part of the commitment to meeting need is reflected in the way programmes are run. The main grants programmes, Community Involvement and Poverty & Disadvantage, are being run continuously, replacing the system of timelimited grant rounds which applied before. Applicants no longer have to submit applications to deadlines. Small Grants and Awards For All are also run continuously.

In addition, the Board has consulted widely with the Voluntary Sector in order to inform the development of its Strategic Plan required by the National Lottery Act 1998. This shows the Board's commitment to meeting needs and how future grant programmes will reflect this at country level, regional level in England and across all four countries of the UK. All applications are assessed on merit against clear criteria and policies set out in the application pack.

Decisions on awards are taken by the five grant-making Committees: England, Scotland; Wales; Northern Ireland and the UK (which also decides on awards under the International and Health and Social Research programmes); and from spring/summer 1999 decisions on awards will also be made by the nine England Regional Awards Committees. Committees are made up of members of the Board who are appointed by the Secretary of State for Culture, Media and Sport. Grants Officers (or assessors for the International and research grant programmes) undertake the assessment of grant applications.

Applications can only be made by application form. Those for Community Involvement, Poverty and Disadvantage, Small Grants in Northern Ireland and Millennium Small Grants in Northern Ireland, International Grants, Health and Social Research programmes are available by calling a 24 hour request line on 0845 794 9191. Welsh speakers can apply for application forms for these by telephoning 0845 627 3273. Application forms for the Awards For All England are available on 0845 600 2040 and Awards For All Scotland on 0645 700777. Application forms may also be downloaded from the Internet at www.nlcb.org.uk.

The Board is also under contract to the New Opportunities Fund (NOF) to process applications to NOF's Out of School Childcare Scheme. Application forms for this programme can be obtained on the following numbers: 0845 604 0555 (England); 0845 606 1199 (Scotland); 0845 600 4848 (Northern Ireland); and 0845 606 4567 (Wales).

Application packs contain detailed guidance on how to fill in the form, and applicants are advised to read these carefully before applying.

For projects costing over £200,000 a comprehensive Business Plan must be included with the application form. Copies of audited, or approved accounts are required. Details of an independent referee must be provided, someone who is not part of the applicant organisation but who know its work and the project well. General information about eligibility to apply and the work of the Board is available from Country and Regional offices as well as on the Internet at www.nlcb.org.uk.

During the assessment process the applicant may be contacted for clarification on the details of a bid and may be visited. For large bids over £500,000, second-level assessment will also take place using expert opinion from surveyors or accountants as necessary. At the end of the assessment process a detailed portfolio of recommended grants is put forward for decision at Committee level.

The Board monitors all projects which receive grants. Successful applicants are required to complete end of year and end of grant project reports to satisfy the Board that the objectives of the project are being met, how they have been achieved and who has benefited. Monitoring visits are made to all projects which have received funding of over £150,000 and to a 2 per cent sample of those receiving less. The Board continues to monitor its own performance in grant-making and has an independent complaints review system. Annual Reports are available on request.

The Board cannot fund statutory bodies and does not replace statutory funding.

Awards are made for projects. The Board does not require matching funding and awards can be for the full cost of projects. Awards are made for capital costs, revenue costs and a combination of capital and revenue costs. Awards are made over one, two or three years and are made to registered charities or those organisations which are charitable, benevolent or philanthropic. The Board can not make grants to statutory bodies or individuals and cannot make loans

SAMPLE GRANTS
At April 1999 some of the largest grants awarded to date were:
£1,106,991 to Shelter
£1,092,838 to ACTIONAID
£1,007,762 to Save the Children (UK)
£1,000,000 to St Gemma's Hospice
£1,000,000 to Northern Ireland Hospice
£999,504 to Oxfam
£973,564 to St Christopher's Hospice
£943,000 to Fairbridge
£917,717 to Save the Children (UK)
£889,000 to National Council on Ageing

■ The New Horizons Trust

WHAT IS FUNDED Charities working in the field of rural conservation will be considered

WHO CAN BENEFIT Neighbourhood-based community projects. Groups must consist of at least ten people, at least half of whom must be aged 60 or more. Proposed project must be new and use the knowledge and experience of the group members

WHERE FUNDING CAN BE GIVEN UK

TYPE OF GRANT Core costs, one-off, project running costs for up to 18 months, buildings and start-up costs will be considered. Funding may be given for up to two years

RANGE OF GRANTS £500–£5,000

FINANCES
- Year 1995–96
- Income £50,150
- Grants £25,575

TRUSTEES A M Pilch, CBE, Mrs B C Pilch, A R Neale, P Miles, Ms K Dibley

PUBLICATIONS Leaflet, Annual Report

HOW TO APPLY On a form available from the Administrator. Callers are asked to contact the appropriate Area Officer, details given, who will issue application forms, offer advice and guidance. Send completed forms to Trustees. Do not require sae

WHO TO APPLY TO The Administrator, The New Horizons Trust, Paramount House, 290–292 Brighton Road, South Croydon, Surrey CR2 6AG
Tel 0181-666 0201
Fax 0181-667 0037

CC NO 293777   **ESTABLISHED** 1985

■ The Joseph Nickerson Charitable Foundation

WHAT IS FUNDED Mainly to support or engage in charitable purposes which are of primary benefit to the old County of Lincolnshire parts of Lindsey, including agriculture and rural conservation

WHO CAN BENEFIT Applications should only be made if in accordance with What is Funded and only if exceptionally meritorious

WHERE FUNDING CAN BE GIVEN Mainly Lincolnshire

TYPE OF GRANT The Trustees will normally decide which grants to make themselves

FINANCES
- Year 1997
- Income £35,923
- Grants £21,969

TRUSTEES M S Edmundson, M Kerrigan, P R C Braithwaite, Lady Nickerson

HOW TO APPLY To the address under Who To Apply To in writing

WHO TO APPLY TO Mrs L E Thompson, The Joseph Nickerson Charitable Foundation, Villa Office, Rothwell, Market Rasen, Lincolnshire LN7 6BJ
Tel 01472 371371
Fax 01472 371545

CC NO 276429 **ESTABLISHED** 1978

■ The Nikeno Trust

WHAT IS FUNDED General charitable purposes in East Sussex including: environmental issues: fauna; flora; nature reserves; and woodlands

WHAT IS NOT FUNDED No grants to individuals

WHO CAN BENEFIT Organisations only

WHERE FUNDING CAN BE GIVEN Wadhurst and surrounding area in East Sussex, and West Sussex

TYPE OF GRANT Buildings, project, research, recurring costs and salaries. Funding may be given for up to three years

RANGE OF GRANTS £500–£30,000

FINANCES
- Year 1996
- Income £19,000
- Grants £138,430

TRUSTEES A L K Koerner, E L Rausing, M M E Rausing, S M E Rausing

HOW TO APPLY By letter to the Trust Secretary at the address below

WHO TO APPLY TO The Trust Secretary, The Nikeno Trust, PO Box 216, Wadhurst, East Sussex TN5 6LW
Tel 0171-259 9466

CC NO 1043967 **ESTABLISHED** 1995

■ The Norman Family Charitable Trust

WHAT IS FUNDED To support the relief of suffering and the provision of a better way of life for animals needing help

WHAT IS NOT FUNDED No support will be given to projects involving experiments on live animals or the maintenance of churches, ancient monuments, etc or to overseas projects. No grants to individuals

WHO CAN BENEFIT Organisations working in the areas outlined above

WHERE FUNDING CAN BE GIVEN Devon, Cornwall and Somerset

TYPE OF GRANT One-off, interest free loans, project, research and start-up costs will be considered. Funding may be given for up to one year

RANGE OF GRANTS £250–£10,000

SAMPLE GRANTS £4,000 to Celia Hammond Trust for animal welfare

FINANCES
- Year 1997
- Income £252,979
- Grants £215,000

TRUSTEES W K Norman, R J Dawe, Mrs M H Evans, M B Saunders, Mrs N J Webb

HOW TO APPLY In writing to the address below stating the registration number of the applicant with the Charity Commissioners. No initial telephone calls are welcome. There is an application form available. Sae required

WHO TO APPLY TO W K Norman, The Norman Family Charitable Trust, Rosemerrin, 5 Coastguard Road, Budleigh Salterton, Devon EX9 6NU
Tel 01395 445177

CC NO 277616 **ESTABLISHED** 1979

■ The Norman Trust

WHAT IS FUNDED To benefit the environment

WHO CAN BENEFIT Large national charities and organisations

WHERE FUNDING CAN BE GIVEN UK and overseas

RANGE OF GRANTS Range of grants of £1,000 or more

FINANCES
- Year 1997
- Income £189,201

TRUSTEES T P A Norman, Mrs E A Norman, K C Barlow, FCA

HOW TO APPLY In writing to the address below

WHO TO APPLY TO T Norman, The Norman Trust, 62 Gloucester Crescent, London NW1 7EG

CC NO 327288 **ESTABLISHED** 1986

O

■ The Oakdale Trust

WHAT IS FUNDED The Trust gives preference to Welsh charities including those working in the fields of rural conservation; animal facilities and services; and animal sciences

WHAT IS NOT FUNDED The Trust does not normally give grants to individuals, holiday schemes, sports activities and expeditions or church restoration

WHO CAN BENEFIT Organisations working in the areas outlined above

WHERE FUNDING CAN BE GIVEN Wales, with occasional help to UK and overseas organisations

TYPE OF GRANT Single outright grants averaging £500. Buildings, capital, core costs, project, research, running costs and salaries will be considered. Funding may be given for up to two years

RANGE OF GRANTS Typical grant £500

SAMPLE GRANTS £1,000 to RSPB
£500 to Radnorshire Wild Life Trust
£500 to Devon Wildlife Trust
£500 to International Gorilla Crisis Programme
£200 to PDSA
£200 to National Canine Defence League

FINANCES
- Year 1998–99
- Income £160,000
- Grants £130,000

TRUSTEES B Cadbury, Mrs F F Cadbury, R A Cadbury, F B Cadbury, Dr R C Cadbury, Mrs O H Tatton-Brown

HOW TO APPLY No application form is necessary, but requests should be concise, quoting their charity's registration number, a summary of their achievements, plans and needs, and a copy or summary of their most recent Annual Accounts. The six Trustees meet twice yearly, usually in April and September, and requests should be submitted if possible before the start of these months. Owing to a lack of secretarial help and in view of the numerous requests we receive, no applications are acknowledged even when accompanied by a sae

WHO TO APPLY TO Brandon Cadbury, The Oakdale Trust, Tan y Coed, Pantydwr, Rhayader, Powys LD6 5LR

CC NO 218827   **ESTABLISHED** 1950

■ The Oakley Charitable Trust

WHAT IS FUNDED Funding may be given for rural conservation; animal homes; animal welfare; bird sanctuaries; cats, catteries and other facilities for cats; dogs, kennels and other facilities for dogs

WHAT IS NOT FUNDED No grants to individuals will be considered

WHO CAN BENEFIT Organisations working in the areas outlined above

WHERE FUNDING CAN BE GIVEN West Midlands, South West and Channel Islands

TYPE OF GRANT Buildings and core costs for one year or less

RANGE OF GRANTS Average grant £500–£1,000

FINANCES
- Year 1998
- Income £71,200
- Grants £51,330

TRUSTEES Mrs H L Oakley, G M W Oakley, Mrs C M Airey

HOW TO APPLY Applications by letter only to the address below

WHO TO APPLY TO G M W Oakley, The Oakley Charitable Trust, 3rd Floor, York House, 38 Great Charles Street, Birmingham B3 3JU

CC NO 233041   **ESTABLISHED** 1963

■ Oldham Foundation

WHAT IS FUNDED Charities working in the fields of: rural conservation; animal facilities and services; and environmental and animal sciences will be considered

WHAT IS NOT FUNDED Applications from individuals, including students, are ineligible with the exception of those already selected for schemes like Operation Raleigh. No grants to general appeals from national bodies. Inappropriate appeals are not acknowledged

WHO CAN BENEFIT Organisations working in the areas outlined above

WHERE FUNDING CAN BE GIVEN North West and South West of England. Charities aided in the area may have objectives overseas

TYPE OF GRANT Grants usually one-off. Does not provide core funding. General charitable grants with bias towards active participation by Trustees

RANGE OF GRANTS £40–£5,000; typical grant £250/£500/£1,000

FINANCES
- Year 1998
- Income £77,693
- Grants £96,892

Onaway

TRUSTEES J Bodden, Mrs D Oldham, J Oldham (Chairman), S Roberts, Prof R Thomas, J Sharpe

HOW TO APPLY Any time. Trustees meet twice a year. Applications should include clear details of projects, budgets, and/or accounts where appropriate. Telephone submissions not accepted

WHO TO APPLY TO Mrs D Oldham, Oldham Foundation, King's Well, Douro Road, Cheltenham, Gloucestershire GL50 2PF

CC NO 269263   **ESTABLISHED** 1974

■The Onaway Trust

WHAT IS FUNDED The Trustees concentrate mainly on native Americans. The Onaway Trust's wide remit includes animal welfare and the environment

WHAT IS NOT FUNDED No grants for administration

WHO CAN BENEFIT Registered charities working in the areas outlined above

WHERE FUNDING CAN BE GIVEN UK and overseas

SAMPLE GRANTS £11,118 to Rainy Mountain Foundation for Land Claim for Native American Peoples
£7,683 to Alaska Wildlife Alliance to prevent killing of wild animals
£6,000 The Woodland Trust for woodland management and research
£5,122 to Environmental Magazine for promotion of environmental issues
£5,000 to Oxfam for funds for seeds, medicines and tools
£3,250 to Zoo Animal Rescue for animal sanctuary

FINANCES
- Year 1996
- Income £135,352
- Grants £100,739

TRUSTEES J Morris, B J Pilkington, A Breslin

PUBLICATIONS Annual Report to members

HOW TO APPLY Funds are fully committed and we regret that no further applications can be considered

WHO TO APPLY TO J Morris, 275 Main Street, Shadwell, Leeds LS17 8LH
Tel 0113-265 9611

CC NO 268448   **ESTABLISHED** 1974

■The Owen Family Trust (formerly New Hall Charity Trust)

WHAT IS FUNDED Mainly support for projects known personally by Trustees, including rural conservation

WHAT IS NOT FUNDED Grants to individuals are unlikely

WHO CAN BENEFIT Organisations working in the area outlined above

WHERE FUNDING CAN BE GIVEN UK, but preference for Midlands, and Gwynedd and Wrexham

TYPE OF GRANT Buildings, capital, and recurring costs will be considered. Funding may be given for more than three years

RANGE OF GRANTS £50–£25,000

FINANCES
- Year 1997
- Income £48,008
- Grants £42,350

TRUSTEES Mrs H G Jenkins, A D Owen

NOTES The Trust is only able to consider about 15 new projects each year. Due to cost it is regretted not all applications will be acknowledged

HOW TO APPLY Send brochures with explanatory letter to the address below

WHO TO APPLY TO A D Owen, The Owen Family Trust, Mill Dam House, Mill Lane, Aldridge, Walsall WS9 0NB

CC NO 251975   **ESTABLISHED** 1967

■ PF Charitable Trust (155)

WHAT IS FUNDED Rural conservation and animal facilities and services, and other charitable purposes

WHAT IS NOT FUNDED Grants are not made for the restoration of individual churches, instead large donations are made to: Historic Churches Preservation Fund; Methodist Church Home Missions Division; and Scottish Churches Architectural Heritage. Likewise, grants are not made to individual hospices; instead a large donation is made to Help the Hospices. Individual Scout Troops or Boys Brigade Companies are not supported because donations are made to their head organisations. Individuals are not considered, neither are unregistered bodies

WHO CAN BENEFIT Charitable organisations

WHERE FUNDING CAN BE GIVEN UK

TYPE OF GRANT One-off and recurring, buildings, core costs, project, research and running costs. Funding may be given for up to three years

FINANCES
- Year 1997
- Income £1,473,201
- Grants £1,195,035

TRUSTEES Philip Fleming, Robert Fleming, Rory D Fleming, Valentine P Fleming

HOW TO APPLY To the Secretary at any time, in writing with full information. Replies will be sent to unsuccessful applications only if a sae is provided

WHO TO APPLY TO The Secretary, PF Charitable Trust, 25 Copthall Avenue, London EC2R 7DR

CC NO 220124   **ESTABLISHED** 1951

Commentary

The PF Charitable Trust was established in 1951 by the late Phillip Fleming, father of the current senior Trustee, Robin Fleming. The Trust has always been a family concern, quite separate from their business interests in Flemings the bankers. All Trustees of the PF Charitable Trust are family members, and the Trust remains an entirely independent family concern, with no connection to the Flemings Company. The Flemings company has its own charity, the Flemings Charity, and occasionally the PF Charitable Trust will work with the Charity on certain projects. The Trust also occasionally works with the Save & Prosper Educational Trust (Save & Prosper is a member of Flemings). The Trust has recently forged a link with the Caledonian Foundation, who are to administer £170,000 for the Trust over three years to charities on the West Coast of Scotland. In addition, the Charities Aid Foundation distributes approximately £70,000 each year on behalf of the Trust in areas that the Trust specifies.

The PF Trust supports general charitable purposes. For convenience these have been separated into 15 different categories, but they do not reflect any funding preferences. Any application received will fit into one of these categories. The categories are: medical research; hospitals and associated organisations; blind and deaf; animals, birds, fish, etc; conservation, preservation and restoration; youth clubs and youth associated entities; welfare – old folks, including housing; welfare – youth; welfare – rehabilitation, including specialised housing; welfare – miscellaneous; welfare – settlements; welfare – housing associations, excluding old peoples' homes and housing; universities and schools; music, theatre and arts; and miscellaneous. These categories are to be revised in the future.

The Trustees have no scales of preference within the causes that they support and every application is given equal consideration. The Trust is, however, very clear about what it will not fund: individual churches for restoration, because large donations are now made to the Historic Churches Preservation Trust, the Methodist Church Home Missions Division and Scottish Churches Architectural Heritage; individual hospices because a large donation is made to Help the Hospices instead; individual Scout Troops or Boys Brigade Companies because large donations are made to their head organisations; and individuals. Applicants must have charitable status in order to receive a donation from the Trust.

The funding policies of the Trust are at the Trustees' discretion. The policies do not significantly change, but the focus may change throughout the year, for example at the start of the last quarter of the year the Trustees will check whether they have overly favoured any one category, whilst neglecting another and then try to redress the balance.

The Trust will make grants to organisations throughout the whole UK, but it will not make grants to overseas charities. The Caledonian Foundation receives grants on behalf of the Trust for the West Coast of Scotland and the Fleming family has very strong links with this area.

The Trust will make grants to statutory bodies, in the sense that it supports schools and universities, etc, but it will not replace statutory funding. It is sometimes prepared to give over and above to organisations that receive statutory funding, but not to replace it, because the

Trustees feel that other organisations without that source of funding need the money more.

The Trust has a formal co-funding link with the Fleming Charity and the Save & Prosper Educational Trust, where they work together to fund certain projects, for example, all three are currently working together to provide a Chair of the History of Scottish Art at Dundee University. The Trust is working more loosely with the Caledonian Foundation who are administering some funds on behalf of the Trust in the area of the West Coast of Scotland. Other than these two associations though, the Trust has no formal links as far as co-funding is concerned, and it is up to each applicant to obtain all the funding that they require, on their own behalf. The Trust has no concerns if an applicant has additional funding from the National Lottery Charities Board.

The Trust prefers to make one-off donations or commitments of a certain amount for up to three years. Such commitments are occasionally made for up to five years, but this is generally only in the case of medical research. The commitments may be renewed after the first period, eg three years, is completed. Loans have not been made or considered in the past. Infrastructure costs are met, as are running costs, but the Trust is not keen to support salaries of staff members of organisations. The Trust does not stipulate how the grants it awards are to be spent, and therefore charities do not have to identify specific projects for funding. Some charities do identify specific projects and the Trust is equally happy to support them.

Applications should be by letter to the Secretary of the Trust. If applicants wish to be informed if they are unsuccessful, they must provide a sae, because normally only successful applicants are contacted. This is due to the fact that the Trustees feel that the money required for postage if all applications were to be acknowledged can be better spent as grants to organisations that need it. Telephone enquiries are not welcomed.

All applications are read by the Secretary, then passed on to the Trustees. The Trustees meet once a month (except in August) to consider each application in turn. There is a fairly quick turnaround: from receipt of application to release of grant if it is successful, normally takes only a couple of months. The speed with which an application is dealt depends on when it arrives in relation to the next Trustees' meeting. If it just misses the latest meeting, it may have to wait more than a month for the next one. Grants are awarded throughout the year, after each Trustees' meeting.

Visits to applicants are rarely made, except in the case of the Caledonian Foundation which does visit and assess applicants, in order to distribute grants on behalf of the PF Charitable Trust. The Trust occasionally visits grant recipients, but there is no structured visiting programme.

Potential applicants should make particular note of the restrictions that the Trust has and ensure that their applicants clearly fit into What Is Funded by the Trust. The Trust also feels that charities should do more to ensure that their administration is as efficient as possible. This is particularly important when the Trust makes, for example, a three year commitment to provide a certain amount each year, because frequently they make such commitments and after the first year they receive letters asking for a repeat donation, when it has already been promised. They also frequently receive more than one letter from the same organisation requesting the same thing, but from different people, and this is something that the Trust wishes to avoid

SAMPLE GRANTS

The top ten grants awarded in 1997 were:
£34,250 to St Mary's Church – Steeple Barton
£30,000 to Guideposts Trust
£28,000 to Cancer Research Campaign
£25,000 to Almshouse Association – Golden Jubilee Appeal
£25,000 to Children's Trust
£25,000 to Help the Hospices
£25,000 to Royal Hospital Neurosurgical Research Fund
£25,000 to St Thomas' Charitable Trust
£25,000 to Tate Gallery
£20,000 to Museum of Scotland Project

■ **The Paget Trust** (also known as the Joanna Herbert-Stepney Charitable Settlement)

WHAT IS FUNDED Sheer need is paramount – and in practice, nothing else can be considered. Preference for the unglamorous, for much achievement with minimal resources. Priorities include 'green' projects, animal welfare, organic projects and rural conservation. We do sometimes give on-going support, thus leaving fewer funds for new applicants

WHAT IS NOT FUNDED Registered British charities only. We cannot help individuals, students, mental disability, medical research or youth clubs

WHO CAN BENEFIT Those whose need is greatest. Normally only British registered charities benefiting animals and countryside

WHERE FUNDING CAN BE GIVEN UK and overseas, with preference for Loughborough in Leicestershire. We cannot usually fund 'local' type projects beyond Leicestershire

TYPE OF GRANT Generally one-off, sometimes recurring

RANGE OF GRANTS £200–£7,000; typically £500–£1,000

SAMPLE GRANTS £2,000 to Compassion in World Farming Trust for farm animal welfare

FINANCES
- Year 1998
- Income £170,934
- Grants £134,345

TRUSTEES Joanna Herbert-Stepney, Lesley Blood, Joy Pollard

HOW TO APPLY Any time – Trustees meet spring and autumn. No application form. Regret we cannot respond to all applications

WHO TO APPLY TO Miss J Herbert-Stepney, The Paget Trust, 41 Priory Gardens, London N6 5QU
Tel 01252 850253

CC NO 327402   **ESTABLISHED** 1986

■The Peacock Charitable Trust (112)

WHAT IS FUNDED Charities of which the Trustees have special knowledge, interest or association in the field of conservation, particularly the conservation of birds and their environment

WHAT IS NOT FUNDED No grants are given to individuals, no response will be made to unsolicited applications

WHO CAN BENEFIT Registered charities working in the above areas

WHERE FUNDING CAN BE GIVEN UK, although some grants are made to major UK charities to be used overseas

TYPE OF GRANT Capital, project and some recurring

RANGE OF GRANTS £200–£120,000; average size of grants £10,000

FINANCES
- Year 1998
- Income £3,043,339
- Grants £2,094,720

TRUSTEES W M Peacock, Mrs S Peacock, C H Peacock

HOW TO APPLY In writing, including a clear description of the aims of the projects and a set of the most recent Accounts. However, charities already being supported on a regular basis are now taking most of the available income so only in exceptional cases are fresh causes likely to receive help

WHO TO APPLY TO Mrs Janet D Gilbert, Secretary to the Trustees, The Peacock Charitable Trust, PO Box 902, London SW20 0XJ

CC NO 257655   **ESTABLISHED** 1968

Commentary

The Peacock Charitable Trust was set up in 1968 by W M Peacock and his wife. The purpose was to enable them to support in a flexible and efficient way causes about which they feel strongly.

The Trust's giving is spread over a wide range of causes, including: medical research, primarily in cancer; care-giving, especially for sufferers of cancer, arthritis, Alzheimer's disease, mental illness, and heart and lung disease; disability, including disabilities ranging from asthma, deafness and back pain to multiple sclerosis; youth work – particularly for young people at risk and young people's groups and organisations; drug addiction; ex-armed forces organisations; and ex-offenders. The Trustees are also very keen on conservation, especially the conservation of birds and their environment, and on projects connected with sailing – for example projects giving disabled people the opportunity to sail.

The Trust gives to organisations throughout the UK, however some grants are made to major UK charities to be used overseas. These grants tend to go to major organisations like Sightsavers and Orbis, although charities benefiting deaf people in the third world have also received funding in the past. The organisations chosen to receive funding are those that are able to improve the quality of life of people in third world countries, especially those charities that work in a particularly cost effective way, rather than general relief appeals. There are no real overall preferences with the projects that are likely to be favoured within the UK; each one receives consideration upon its own merits. There are, however, some preferences in terms of where the Trust will fund in this country, with a certain concentration upon Surrey and Sussex for most of the local projects.

The Trustees are not concerned about the issue of assisting organisations that are primarily government-funded, and have given to NHS Trusts and hospitals in the past. The view seems to be that if a project is worthwhile and requires funding that is not being received from elsewhere, it should be given consideration for a grant. The Trust is not afraid to be the first to give a project money in order that others may follow.

Grants are generally made in the region of £10,000, although some smaller ones are made to local projects and some larger ones may also be made. These larger grants are generally for capital costs, while the smaller grants may be for ongoing projects.

Applications should include clear details of the need the intended project is designed to meet plus an outline budget. Only applications from eligible bodies are considered, when further information may be requested. **To maximise the use of funds beneficially, only applications being considered will receive replies.** Applications are considered as part of a rolling process, with those

Peartree

Alphabetical register of grant making trusts

receiving further consideration going forward to full Trustee meetings. After a grant has been given, there is no formal system of assessment of how it has been used. The Trust feels that with the care taken when choosing which organisations should receive grants, there is actually very little need to monitor them. Having said this, ongoing projects supported by the Trust are required to send in their Annual Reports and Accounts, and some organisations will receive personal visits from one of the Trustees

SAMPLE GRANTS
The top ten grants made in 1998 were:
£120,000 to Cancer Research Campaign
£81,400 to Royal Hospital for Neuro Disability
£80,000 to Marie Curie Cancer Care
£77,000 to Macmillan Cancer Relief Fund
£55,000 to Queen Elizabeth's Foundation for the Disabled
£54,000 to Youth at Risk
£50,000 to Alzheimer's Research Trust
£50,000 to Bacup
£50,000 to Fairbridge Drake Society
£50,000 to Jubilee Sailing Trust

■The Peartree Trust

WHAT IS FUNDED Flora

WHO CAN BENEFIT Organisations only

WHERE FUNDING CAN BE GIVEN UK and overseas

TYPE OF GRANT Recurring and one-off

FINANCES
- Year 1997
- Income £10,037

TRUSTEES P J Baker, T D Baker, H E Knowles

HOW TO APPLY In writing to the address below

WHO TO APPLY TO T D Baker, The Peartree Trust, Oakshade, Bicknacre Road, Danbury, Chelmsford, Essex CM3 4ES

CC NO 278235   **ESTABLISHED** 1979

■The J B Pelly Charitable Trust
(formerly The Joanne Pelly Charitable Settlement)

WHAT IS FUNDED Tree planting; organic gardening; nature conservation and environment

WHAT IS NOT FUNDED No grants to individuals. No grants for illness, disease and Church of England

WHO CAN BENEFIT Organisations working in the areas outlined above

WHERE FUNDING CAN BE GIVEN South Devon

TYPE OF GRANT One-off, project, research, and start-up costs. Funding is available for up to three years

RANGE OF GRANTS £50–£1,000

SAMPLE GRANTS £2,000 to Friends of the Earth Trust

FINANCES
- Year 1997
- Income £65,260
- Grants £45,800

TRUSTEES Miss H G Pelly, A J R Pelly

HOW TO APPLY Written applications (with supporting information if available) to the address below

WHO TO APPLY TO The J B Pelly Charitable Trust, c/o Bromhead & Co, Britton House, 10 Fore Street, Kingsbridge, Devon TQ7 1NY
Tel 01548 852599
Fax 01548 854082

CC NO 285565   **ESTABLISHED** 1987

■Personal Assurance Charitable Trust

WHAT IS FUNDED Environmental resources including; rural conservation; animal facilities and services; and animal sciences

WHERE FUNDING CAN BE GIVEN Mainly UK, will consider overseas

TYPE OF GRANT Buildings, capital, core costs, project, research, running costs, recurring costs, salaries and start-up costs. Funding is for up to three years

FINANCES
- Year 1998
- Income £92,856
- Grants £101,853

TRUSTEES C W T Johnston, J Barber

NOTES Applications restricted to policyholders of Personal Assurance plc or their employers

HOW TO APPLY In writing to the address below

WHO TO APPLY TO Dr J Barber, Personal Assurance Charitable Trust, Personal Assurance plc, Bank House, 171 Midsummer Boulevard, Central Milton Keynes MK9 1EB

CC NO 1023274   **ESTABLISHED** 1993

■The Persula Foundation

WHAT IS FUNDED Support of (particularly small) groups working in the field of animal welfare

WHAT IS NOT FUNDED No grants to individuals, for buildings/building works or to statutory bodies

WHO CAN BENEFIT Organisations, preferably local, working in the area outlined above

WHERE FUNDING CAN BE GIVEN Internationally, but predominantly UK

TYPE OF GRANT Grants for all requirements considered, core costs, one-off projects, recurrent, etc

FINANCES
- Year 1996
- Income £120,236

TRUSTEES Julian Richer, John Currier, David Robinson, David Highton, David Clark, Mrs R Richer, Mrs H Oppenheim, Rev Peter Timms, Miss Nicola Phillips

PUBLICATIONS Information leaflet, Annual Report, Financial Accounts

HOW TO APPLY Flexible and varied

WHO TO APPLY TO John Currier, Company Secretary, Persula Foundation, Richer House, Hankey Place, London SE1 4BB

CC NO 1044174   **ESTABLISHED** 1994

■ Pet Plan Charitable Trust

WHAT IS FUNDED Animal homes; animal welfare; cats, catteries and other facilities for cats; dogs, kennels and other facilities for dogs; and horses, stables and other facilities for horses

WHAT IS NOT FUNDED No grants for scholarships or on-going costs

WHO CAN BENEFIT Animal charities and organisations

WHERE FUNDING CAN BE GIVEN UK

TYPE OF GRANT Buildings, capital, one-off, project, research, recurring costs and salaries. Funding may be given for up to three years

RANGE OF GRANTS £1,000–£150,000

SAMPLE GRANTS £109,776 to Royal Veterinary College over three years for canine internerfibral disc herniation
£47,888 to University of Glasgow Veterinary School over three years for markers for FIV infection
£5,950 to Skye View Animal Home for isolation unit for cats and kittens
£5,900 to Animal Health Trust for blood flow to equine front foot
£5,245 to Cambridge Veterinary School for oxygen tensions in dogs with upper respiratory obstructions
£5,000 to Hull Animal Welfare Trust for purpose built cattery
£5,000 to VIGIL German Shepherd Rescue for replacement rescue vehicle
£5,000 to Cat Welfare Sussex for neutering and veterinary assistance
£4,500 to Cambridge Veterinary School for joint disease in the horse
£4,500 to Feline Advisory Bureau for contribution to production of feral cat manual

FINANCES
- Year 1996
- Income £406,013

- Grants £245,161

TRUSTEES Patsy Bloom (Chairman), Clarissa Baldwin, John Bower, I Brecher, Dr Andrew Higgins, David Simpson, George Stratford

NOTES Help is limited to dogs, cats and horses only, those being the species insured by Pet Plan. Rabbits will be considered

HOW TO APPLY To the address under Who To Apply To in writing. An initial telephone call is welcome to request an application form and guidelines

WHO TO APPLY TO Roz Hayward-Butt, Administrator, Pet Plan Charitable Trust, Great West Road, Brentford, Middlesex TW8 9EG
Tel 0181-580 8013
Fax 0181-580 8186

CC NO 1032907   **ESTABLISHED** 1994

■ Pewterers' Charity Trust

WHAT IS FUNDED This Trust will consider funding a wide range of charitable bodies including those in the fields of: rural conservation, animal facilities and services; and animal sciences

WHAT IS NOT FUNDED Expeditions and further education for individuals will not be funded

WHO CAN BENEFIT Organisations working to preserve the countryside and animal welfare organisations

WHERE FUNDING CAN BE GIVEN UK

TYPE OF GRANT One-off grants

RANGE OF GRANTS £500 for one to three years

FINANCES
- Year 1997–98
- Income £15,300

TRUSTEES The Worshipful Company of Pewterers

HOW TO APPLY At any time. Trustees meet half yearly in June and November. This Trust passes on the bulk of claims to the Company's general charity Trustees who can disburse donations of a few hundred pounds. The Seahorse Trustees, another charity run by the Worshipful Company of Pewterers, select a few charities for support for three or more years with £1,000–£3,000 per annum

WHO TO APPLY TO The Clerk to the Trustees, Pewterers' Charity Trust, Pewterers Hall, Oat Lane, London EC2V 7DE

CC NO 261889   **ESTABLISHED** 1974

Philanthropic

Alphabetical register of grant making trusts

■ The Philanthropic Trust

WHAT IS FUNDED The Trust has an interest in endangered species, environmental issues, fauna, animal welfare and wildlife sanctuaries

WHAT IS NOT FUNDED No grants to individuals

WHO CAN BENEFIT Registered charities working in the areas outlined above. Overseas projects must apply through UK registered charities

WHERE FUNDING CAN BE GIVEN UK and overseas

TYPE OF GRANT Project grants. Funding may be given for up to three years

RANGE OF GRANTS £500–£2,000

FINANCES
- Year 1997
- Income £239,672
- Grants £109,000

TRUSTEES Paul H Burton, Jeremy J Burton, Amanda C Burton

HOW TO APPLY To the address under Who To Apply To in writing, there are no application forms or guidelines, no application deadlines and sae is not required. No telephone calls please

WHO TO APPLY TO Trust Administrator, The Philanthropic Trust, Trustee Management Limited, 27 East Parade, Leeds LS1 5SX

CC NO 1045263   **ESTABLISHED** 1995

■ Claude & Margaret Pike Woodlands Trust

WHAT IS FUNDED (a) To protect, improve or foster an appreciation of the landscape, natural beauty and amenity of woodlands, copses or other areas of land in the UK and the flora and fauna therein for the benefit of the public. (b) To foster the growth of specimen trees and shrubs and the establishment of woodlands or copses which by their location will be an inspiration to man in the environment in which he lives and a demonstration of man's faith in nature

WHAT IS NOT FUNDED No appeals from outside Devon will be considered

WHERE FUNDING CAN BE GIVEN Devon only

SAMPLE GRANTS £5,000 to The Royal Horticultural Society Appeal for the Woods at Rosemoor
£2,500 to Craigencalt Farm Ecology Centre
£1,000 to Devon County Agricultural Association
£500 to RSPB

FINANCES
- Year 1998
- Income £94,543
- Grants £17,631

TRUSTEES C D Pike, J D Pike, Dr P A D Holland

NOTES The Trust has complete flexibility in Devon where applications are supported depending upon the nature of the appeal

HOW TO APPLY This Trust states that it will not respond to unsolicited applications from outside Devon

WHO TO APPLY TO C D Pike, OBE, DL, Claude & Margaret Pike Woodlands Trust, Dunderdale Lawn, Penshurst Road, Newton Abbot, Devon TQ12 1EN

CC NO 266072   **ESTABLISHED** 1973

■ The Cecil Pilkington Charitable Trust

WHAT IS FUNDED Environmental and conservation projects; advancement of education in agriculture and forestry. Other charitable purposes will be considered

WHAT IS NOT FUNDED Religious or sporting projects will not be considered. No grants to individuals

WHO CAN BENEFIT Registered charities only. No restrictions as to size. Support may be given to agricultural students

WHERE FUNDING CAN BE GIVEN UK, though some third world projects considered

TYPE OF GRANT Mostly project grants. Some of these may be recurring

SAMPLE GRANTS £25,818 to Forestry Commission
£20,000 to Royal Botanical Gardens
£3,000 to Groundwork Trust
£2,000 to Landlife
£2,000 to Woodland Heritage
£2,000 to Woodland Trust

FINANCES
- Year 1997
- Income £194,001
- Grants £79,418

TRUSTEES Sir Anthony Pilkington, A P Pilkington, R F Carter Jonas

HOW TO APPLY This Trust states that it does not respond to unsolicited applications

WHO TO APPLY TO The Administrator, The Cecil Pilkington Charitable Trust, 9 Greyfriars Road, Reading, Berkshire RG1 1JG

CC NO 249997   **ESTABLISHED** 1966

■ The Pittecroft Trust

WHAT IS FUNDED General charitable purposes including the environment

WHO CAN BENEFIT Individuals and organisations

WHERE FUNDING CAN BE GIVEN UK

TYPE OF GRANT One-off

FINANCES
- Year 1996
- Income £8,907

TRUSTEES C Beney, H Beney

NOTES Grants normally at the Trustee's initiative. Very rare to respond to external requests

HOW TO APPLY See Notes above

WHO TO APPLY TO C Beney, The Pittecroft Trust, 12 Woodlands Road, Bushey, Hertfordshire WD2 2LR

CC NO 294174   **ESTABLISHED** 1986

■ The Portrack Charitable Trust

WHAT IS FUNDED Charities working in the fields of: rural conservation and wildlife sanctuaries. Grants are only made to charities or individuals known to the Trustees

WHO CAN BENEFIT Organisations working in the areas outlined above

WHERE FUNDING CAN BE GIVEN England and Scotland

TYPE OF GRANT Buildings, core costs, one-off, research and recurring costs. Funding of up to three years will be considered

RANGE OF GRANTS £50–£4000

FINANCES
- Year 1995
- Income £26,979
- Grants £25,004

TRUSTEES Clare, Lady Keswick, C A Jencks

HOW TO APPLY Trustees consider applications in June and December

WHO TO APPLY TO The Portrack Charitable Trust, Matheson Bank Ltd, Jardine House, 6 Crutched Friars, London EC3N 2HT

CC NO 266120   **ESTABLISHED** 1973

■ The Prince's Trust - BRO (170)

WHAT IS FUNDED Environmental improvements including: environmental issues; flora; landscapes; lakes; nature reserves; waterways and woodlands

WHAT IS NOT FUNDED Grants are limited to projects being carried out by voluntary groups

WHO CAN BENEFIT Welsh voluntary groups who are carrying out practical projects that make communities more sustainable

WHERE FUNDING CAN BE GIVEN Wales

TYPE OF GRANT Project grants and feasibility studies. Also buildings, capital, one-off, research and start-up costs. Funding may be given for up to three years

FINANCES
- Year 1998
- Income £1,186,854
- Grants £1,053,075

TRUSTEES William Castell (Chairman), Sir Christopher Harding, John Jarvis, Stephen Lamport, Peter Mimpriss, Rt Hon Angus Ogilvy, KCVO, John Rose, Mrs Kate Thomas, JP, DL, Ronald Woodhouse

PUBLICATIONS Newsletter – approximately three times a year, seminar reports

HOW TO APPLY Through the Development Officers at the address below

WHO TO APPLY TO Development Officers, The Prince's Trust - BRO, 4th Floor, Empire House, Mount Stuart Square, Cardiff CF1 6DN
Tel 01222 471121
Fax 01222 482086
E-mail hq@bro.cymru.net

CC NO 1053960   **ESTABLISHED** 1996

Commentary

On 1 April 1996, the activities and assets of the Prince of Wales' Committee were transferred to a new charitable company, registered as the Prince's Trust – BRO. The Prince of Wales' Committee was originally established in 1971 by His Royal Highness The Prince of Wales, the President of the Prince's Trust – BRO. The Prince's Trust is the holding company and charity that provides common services and support, strategic co-ordination, research and innovation functions for the member charities, which also includes the Prince's Trust – Action, the Prince's Trust – Volunteers and the Prince's Youth Business Trust. The four charities in Wales will come together to form The Prince's Trust Cymru on 1 April 1999.

The Prince's Trust – BRO aims to champion local environmentally and socially sustainable development in Wales, by assisting local authorities with the processes involved in drawing up and implementing Local Agenda 21 strategies. The idea of a 'Local Agenda 21' – a document setting out a local community's vision for an environmentally and socially sustainable and desirable future, and the actions to be taken towards it – springs from chapter 28 of 'Agenda 21', a blueprint for sustainable development endorsed by world leaders at the 1992 Earth Summit. The other aims of the Trust include involving young people in designing and delivering

Prince's

Local Agenda 21 targets, and to seek to benefit them through these activities; to work in partnership with local communities, voluntary bodies, businesses, and national agencies in the planning and implementation of LA21 strategies and local sustainable development projects throughout Wales. The Trust works to further these objectives by: (a) co-ordinating and administering formal partnerships both locally and nationally that promote understanding and the implementation of local sustainable developments and LA21; (b) deploying a team of Development Officers to work with community-based voluntary organisations to help them to carry out practical environmental projects that also address social, cultural and economic needs; and (c) making grants in support of such projects.

These objectives are the result of a thorough review of the organisation and the drawing up of a new agenda, when the Trust was still working under the title of the Prince of Wales' Committee. This review identified the need to advance the mission and the objectives of the Committee through the formation of a new charitable company registered as the Prince's Trust – BRO. The Company takes advantage of a new strategic approach, marketing strategy and organisational structure resulting from its membership of the Prince's Trust group.

In the year to the end of March 1998, the Trust co-ordinated the Welsh Office's Environment Wales Partnership and met its grant programme targets. The Trust also administered grants programmes on behalf of the Welsh Development Agency, the Development Board for Rural Wales and the Wales Tourist Board, as well as providing enabling support to 300 community-based organisations throughout Wales and running its grants programme. Grants are given exclusively within Wales for environmental projects.

The Trust will not replace government responsibilities, but it will work in partnership with the Welsh Office. It is especially keen to work in partnership with local communities, voluntary bodies and national agencies throughout Wales working in the same field. Grants are made for environmental projects, hence they are generally over a period of more than one year. Applications should only be made on the forms available from the Director. Applications are looked at by the Grants Committee of the Board, before recommendations are made to the Director for projects to receive a grant. The Trust is largely reactive in its grant making, relying on applications received for its local community-based schemes, although the major partnership schemes tend to be pro-active

SAMPLE GRANTS
The top ten grants made in 1998 are not known

■ The Ronald & Kathleen Pryor Charity

WHAT IS FUNDED Charities working in the fields of: environmental issues; nature reserves; zoos; ornithology and zoology

WHAT IS NOT FUNDED No grants to individuals

WHO CAN BENEFIT Registered charities only

WHERE FUNDING CAN BE GIVEN Sheffield and surrounding area

TYPE OF GRANT One-off and research funding for more than three years will be considered

RANGE OF GRANTS £250–£5,000

FINANCES
- Year 1998
- Income £33,500
- Grants £38,500

TRUSTEES P W Lee, CBE, Miss M Upton, J D Grayson

NOTES Trustees meet in January and July each year

HOW TO APPLY By letter to Miss M Upton at the address below. Sae not required

WHO TO APPLY TO Miss M Upton, The Ronald & Kathleen Pryor Charity, Edward Pryor & Son Ltd, Egerton Street, Sheffield S1 4JX
Tel 0114-276 6044
Fax 0114-276 6890
E-mail enquiries@Pryormarking.com

CC NO 276868   **ESTABLISHED** 1979

■ Mr and Mrs J A Pye's No 1 Charitable Settlement (383)

WHAT IS FUNDED General charitable purposes at the Trustees' discretion. Of particular interest are charities involved with rural conservation, as well as national and local needs in various fields

WHAT IS NOT FUNDED Grants are not given to individuals, non-charitable organisations, for endowment funds, government projects or animals

WHO CAN BENEFIT Organisations working in the areas outlined above

WHERE FUNDING CAN BE GIVEN UK, especially London, Northern Ireland, Oxfordshire, Bristol and South Gloucestershire

TYPE OF GRANT One-off, core costs, projects, research, recurring, running and start-up costs, and salaries. Capital costs may be considered. Funding may be given for up to or more than three years. Also interest free loans

RANGE OF GRANTS £250–£25,000

FINANCES
- Year 1998
- Grants £368,901
- Income £483,983

TRUSTEES G C Pye, J S Stubbings, D S Tallon

PUBLICATIONS Guidelines for Applicants

HOW TO APPLY Telephone calls are discouraged. There is no application form, but guidelines for applicants are available

WHO TO APPLY TO Mr and Mrs J A Pye's No 1 Charitable Settlement, c/o Sharp Parsons Tallon, 167 Fleet Street, London EC4A 2EA

CC NO 242677   **ESTABLISHED** 1965

Commentary

The Mr and Mrs Pye No 1 Charitable Settlement was established on 5 March 1965 by the late Mr J A Pye and his wife Mrs M E Pye, for general charitable purposes.

The Settlement supports general charitable purposes, with particular interest in organisations involved with the following areas: nutritional and medical research; mental health; education; youth and child welfare; conservation and the environment; and the arts. Also supported are national and local needs in various fields.

The funding policies of the Settlement were set out in the Deed of Trust in 1965 and they have not changed since. Grants are made throughout the UK. The Settlement will not fund statutory bodies. However, its attitude to co-funding is not known. The Settlement will consider a wide range of grant types and will make interest free loans. In 1998 the largest loan amounted to £104,000 and the smallest to £3,000. The total of loans made amounted to £300,730. Infrastructure costs are supported by the Trust.

Applications should include: the registered charity number or evidence of an organisation's tax exempt status; a brief description of the activities of the charity; details of the project for which the grant is sought; details of the overall cost of the project including a breakdown and details of funds already raised; the latest Trustees' Report and full audited or independently examined Accounts. The assessment procedure is not known

SAMPLE GRANTS
The top ten grants made in 1998 were:
£120,551 to Elm Farm Research Centre for organic farming development
£35,000 to Elm Farm Research Centre for diesel emission research
£30,000 to Parnham Trust (Hooke Park College)
£22,500 to The British Trust for conservation volunteers
£22,000 to Association for Post-Natal Illness
£15,000 to London Immunotherapy Cancer Trust
£15,000 to Radcliffe Medical Foundation
£14,000 to Magdalene College School
£12,000 to Harris Manchester College
£10,000 to Music at Oxford

R

■ The RAC Foundation for Motoring and the Environment Ltd

WHAT IS FUNDED Environmental issues. Research programme undertaken to examine the impacts of the Okehampton Bypass

WHO CAN BENEFIT Organisations working in the area outlined above

WHERE FUNDING CAN BE GIVEN UK

TYPE OF GRANT Research

FINANCES
- Year 1996
- Income £47,187

TRUSTEES J D Rose, N A Johnson, Sir D G T Williams, Sir Christopher Foster, Prof T M Ridley

NOTES Charitable expenditure concerns consultancy fees for the research projects. No grants were given in 1995

HOW TO APPLY To the address under Who To Apply To in writing

WHO TO APPLY TO The RAC Foundation for Motoring and the Environment Ltd, RAC House, 1 Forest Road, Feltham TW13 7RR

CC NO 1002705   **ESTABLISHED** 1991

■ RSPCA – Winchester and Romsey Branch

WHAT IS FUNDED The promotion of kindness and prevention of cruelty to animals

WHO CAN BENEFIT Animals

WHERE FUNDING CAN BE GIVEN Winchester and Romsey

FINANCES
- Year 1997
- Income £9,646

HOW TO APPLY In writing to the address below

WHO TO APPLY TO Mrs Dulcie A Eridge, RSPCA – Winchester and Romsey Branch, The Old Post Office, Cheriton, Alresford, Hampshire SO24 0QA

CC NO 270576   **ESTABLISHED** 1976

■ Radley Charitable Trust

WHAT IS FUNDED To help small organisations that are unlikely to have wide appeal or support including those working in the fields of: landscapes; nature reserves; woodlands; ecology; organic food production; and rural conservation

WHAT IS NOT FUNDED No grants for electives, for doctorates, for travel bursaries or for expeditions

WHO CAN BENEFIT Organisations working in the areas outlined above

WHERE FUNDING CAN BE GIVEN UK, with preference for Cambridgeshire, and overseas

TYPE OF GRANT Normally one-off grants. Buildings, capital, core costs, project, research, running costs, recurring costs and start-up costs. Funding of one or less will be considered

RANGE OF GRANTS £50–£1,300, typically £150–£500

SAMPLE GRANTS £500 to Manor House Agricultural Fund for aid for education in farming in Kenya

FINANCES
- Year 1996–97
- Income £22,568
- Grants £17,580

TRUSTEES C F Doubleday, I R Menzies, I O Palmer, P F Radley, J J Wheatley

NOTES Meetings of the Trustees to consider applications are held at two-monthly intervals

HOW TO APPLY Letters with details, enclosing sae, to the address below. The name of a referee who is in a position to support the application should be included. Priority will normally be given to individual applications

WHO TO APPLY TO Patrick Radley, Radley Charitable Trust, 12 Jesus Lane, Cambridge CB5 8BA

CC NO 208313   **ESTABLISHED** 1951

■ The Edward Ramsden Charitable Trust

WHAT IS FUNDED Animal welfare

WHO CAN BENEFIT Institutions and organisations working in the area outlined above

WHERE FUNDING CAN BE GIVEN North and West Yorkshire

RANGE OF GRANTS £50–£250

FINANCES
- Year 1997
- Income £11,316

TRUSTEES G E Ramsden, T J P Ramsden

HOW TO APPLY To the address below in writing

WHO TO APPLY TO T J P Ramsden, Trustee, The Edward Ramsden Charitable Trust, Breckamore, Ripon, North Yorkshire HG4 3JX

CC NO 502611   **ESTABLISHED** 1973

■The Rank Foundation (32)

WHAT IS FUNDED Grants have been made in the fields of rural conservation and animal welfare. However, such contributions have been made on a pro-active, rather than a reactive, basis

WHAT IS NOT FUNDED The Directors have decided that, in general, they will no longer make grants in the following areas: agriculture and farming; cathedrals; churches (except where community facilities are involved); cultural projects; university and school building; bursary funds; and medical research. Existing commitments in these areas will however be met. Appeals from individuals or appeals from registered charities on behalf of named individuals will not be considered, neither will appeals from overseas or from UK based organisations where the object of the appeal is overseas

WHO CAN BENEFIT Organisations working in the areas outlined above

WHERE FUNDING CAN BE GIVEN UK

TYPE OF GRANT One-off, recurrent, core costs, capital, research, salaries, buildings

RANGE OF GRANTS For unsolicited appeals: £250–£10,000

FINANCES
- Year 1997
- Income £8,479,000
- Grants £7,530,000

TRUSTEES Directors: R F H Cowen, CBE (Chairman), M D Abrahams, CBE, DL, Lord Charteris of Amisfield, GCB, GCVO, QSO, OBE, The Hon Mrs S M Cowen, M E T Davies, Mrs L G Fox, JP, J R Newton, F A R Packard, D R Peppiatt, V A L Powell, FCA, Sir Michael Richardson, Lord Shuttleworth, JP, D R W Silk, CBE, MA, M J M Thompson, MA, FRICS

NOTES In general, the Directors are active in identifying initiatives where they provide substantial support and the vast majority of unsolicited appeals do not receive a grant

HOW TO APPLY In writing as there is no formal application form. **However, it should be noted that the Directors only make grants for rural conservation and animal welfare on a pro-active basis, and unsolicited applications will not be considered.** There are strict guidelines for the application letter – see Commentary for details

WHO TO APPLY TO S J B Langdale, Director of Grants and Special Projects, The Rank Foundation Ltd, 4–5 North Bar, Banbury, Oxfordshire OX16 0TB
Tel 01295 272337
Fax 01295 272336

CC NO 276976   **ESTABLISHED** 1953

Commentary

The Rank Foundation was established in 1953 by the late Lord and Lady Rank. Lord and Lady Rank founded several charities and companies at this time, using their controlling interest in the Rank Organisation plc, and sharing this interest between each of the new companies and charities, thereby providing financial backing. The Rank Foundation has a very strong association with the Foundation for Christian Communication Ltd, (FCCL), which aids their work in promoting the Christian religion. It works with various other organisations on its different initiatives, for example with the University of Kent and Christ Church College Canterbury, to provide a degree course, training experienced, but unqualified local youth leaders.

The Foundation has three main aims: (i) to promote the Christian religion, Christian principles, Christian religious education and the study of the Christian faith, by the exhibition of religious videos and other lawful means; (ii) to promote education, including youth work; and (iii) to promote and support other purposes which are exclusively charitable according to the laws of England in force at any time.

Various projects and causes are supported within the three main areas that the Foundation supports. Its work in promoting the Christian religion is limited to the support it gives to FCCL, because their commitment is very substantial and continues long-term. FCCL provides Christian-based training courses and audio-visual production facilities. The latter, when not in use by FCCL, are available for commercial hire, the proceeds of which are used to subsidise FCCL's charitable work.

Many different projects are supported within the aim of promoting education, because the Directors take a broad interpretation of the aim and include work with young people in this area. The Directors wish to involve young people in decisions that affect their future and to encourage attitudes in them that will make them useful members of society. The Foundation supports boys and girls in their last two to three years at independent school, who either show great potential for leadership, or who have financial difficulties which mean that they would otherwise have to move school. All pupils supported in these ways are monitored whilst still at school and afterwards in later life. Such pupils must be nominated by the Head of their school, and applications from parents or guardians will not be considered. More generally, the Foundation currently supports the Learning Through Action programme in schools, which works on behaviour such as bullying, and the Humberside Probation Service Supervised Options and Activities Scheme, which identifies local educational and recreational opportunities for youngsters on probation.

The Directors wish to help young people develop to their full potential, and to this end the Foundation supports a number of projects on a long-term basis. The work falls into three main programmes: 'Youth or Adult?'; 'Investing in Success'; and the 'Gap Scheme'. The 'Youth or Adult?' scheme supports projects for five years and involves the training of local experienced, but unqualified youth workers, leading to a degree from the University of Kent. It also involves young people in the design and implementation of an active programme, reflecting their real commitment and responsibility. The 'Investing in Success' scheme enables organisations with an existing relationship with the Foundation to develop their services to young people, with a commitment lasting five years. Key worker posts in organisations, such as for the homeless and conservation, are supported, and up to 15 apprentice positions are supported under the initiative. The 'Gap Scheme' encourages full time volunteering by the unemployed or students wishing to take a gap year from their studies. It also provides a Certificate in Foundation Studies course in informal and community education, which is equivalent to one and a half A-Levels. Various other projects are being initiated and supported in Northern Ireland, Wales, Scotland and England. The Foundation will support unsolicited appeals that involve imaginative work at a local level, and that will benefit from a small amount of financial help from an external source.

The general charitable work that the Foundation supports falls into various areas, which have been outlined above, and many different types of project are supported within each. Grants for the elderly made up the largest share of the total grants awarded for general charitable purposes in 1997, with 10.15 per cent of the total. Disability received 7.04 per cent; community service received 6.74 per cent; medicine/healthcare received 5.85 per cent; animal conservation/welfare received 0.74 per cent; and cultural causes received 0.42 per cent. No grants were made in the categories of religion-fabric, or research in 1997.

There are no stated scales of preference within the areas that are funded by the Foundation. Due to the long term commitments that the Foundation has to certain organisations, only around one third of the total funds available for grant making are in reality open to external application.

The funding policies of the Foundation are agreed by the Directors, implemented by the executive staff and monitored by the committees. There are three committees: the Appeals and Community Care Committee meets four times each year and considers all unsolicited applications, plus any initiatives they are informed of by the executive staff. The committee has limited discretionary powers to make grants, but larger grants must be put forward as recommendations to the Board and be considered by all the Directors. The Education Committee and Youth Committee both meet three times each year to consider initiative recommendations in their area. They aim to provide bursary support to selected schools and to encourage leadership in young people, by making them responsible for their own decisions. The Finance Committee meets four times each year and is responsible for the overall financial management of the Foundation.

Funding can be given to any registered charity based and working in the UK. Appeals from overseas or from UK based organisations where the object of the appeal is overseas are not considered. Grants are not made to statutory bodies and the Foundation will not replace statutory funding. The Foundation occasionally works with other organisations for co-funding purposes, for example, £50,000 was given to Oxford University in 1996 as support for a Chair in Electro-Optic Engineering, and was part of a joint initiative with the Rank Prize Fund. The Foundation makes a wide range of grants to organisations, which in 1997 ranged from under £500 up to £1,990,000. Many different types of grant are made, including one-off, recurrent, capital, building, core costs, research and salaries. Interest free loans are made by the Foundation. Infrastructure costs such as for building work are also supported.

There is no formal application form but for administrative purposes it is helpful if the actual appeal letter can be kept to one or two sides of A4, which can be supported by reports etc. General appeals, including unsolicited appeals relating to youth, educational and community care projects, should be addressed to S J B Langdale, Director of Grants and Special Projects, at the Banbury Office and should include: (i) charity registration number; (ii) details of project and funding sought; (iii) details of funds already available, indicating the degree of local support within the total; (iv) copy of last audited Accounts. The unsolicited appeals are considered quarterly. All appeals are acknowledged and applicants are advised as to when a decision can be expected. Applications are passed on to the relevant committee, where it is considered. The Appeals and Community Care Committee has limited powers to authorise grants, but most grants need to be referred to the Board of Directors. Assessors visit disabled applicants in particular, to assess their degree of disability

SAMPLE GRANTS

The top ten grants made in 1997 were: £1,990,000 to Foundation for Christian Communication Ltd for the production of religious programmes, training in the use of

media and building adaptation costs
£224,696 to Gap Project for the costs involved in the 'Gappers' scheme operated by the Foundation
£158,732 to University of Glasgow as part of a joint initiative with The Rank Prize Funds to provide core funding over ten years for Rank Departments of Human Nutrition
£136,664 to Carers' National Association supporting the development of initiatives and networks supporting carers
£121,457 to Queen Mary & Westfield College as part of a joint initiative with The Rank Prize Funds to provide core funding over ten years for Rank Departments of Human Nutrition
£110,000 to Alzheimer Scotland Action on Dementia to develop initiatives to help sufferers of Alzheimer's disease and their families
£80,871 to Cheshire and Wirral Federation of Youth Clubs
£80,365 to People and Work Unit
£77,984 to Age Concern Scotland to develop initiatives benefiting the elderly in mostly rural areas
£77,759 to YouthLink Scotland

■ The Raptor Trust

WHAT IS FUNDED To help care for injured birds of prey, conserve their habitat and advance the publics' awareness of conservation issues. The Trust will consider funding: endangered species; environmental issues; fauna; nature reserves; woodlands; animal homes; animal welfare; bird sanctuaries; wildlife sanctuaries; and ornithology and zoology

WHAT IS NOT FUNDED Anyone who has been convicted of an offence under the Wildlife and Countryside Act 1981, or other animal welfare legislation

WHO CAN BENEFIT Individuals and organisations involved in birds of prey welfare and conservation

WHERE FUNDING CAN BE GIVEN Mainly Norfolk and Suffolk. Grants are sometimes available for worldwide projects

TYPE OF GRANT One-off grant for specific projects. Funding may be given for up to two years

RANGE OF GRANTS Not more than £500

SAMPLE GRANTS £270 for Philippine Project run by the Owl Taxonomy Group

FINANCES
- Year 1998
- Income £8,481

TRUSTEES Monica Barton, Clive Britcher, Chris Britcher, Julie Finnis, Sheila Fish, Colin Fish, Bob Kerry, Carrie Kerry, Nigel Middleton, Ivan Prior, Paul Raby, April Wright

PUBLICATIONS Bi-annual newsletter, various leaflets

HOW TO APPLY Written application required giving full details of grant requested, including full estimated cost of project and its aim

WHO TO APPLY TO Robert J Kerry, The Raptor Trust, Oak Villa, Helington Corner, Bergh Apton, Norwich, Norfolk NR15 1BE
Tel 01508 480661

CC NO 1036884   **ESTABLISHED** 1983

■ Marit and Hans Rausing Charitable Foundation

WHAT IS FUNDED The conservation of fauna, flora and nature reserves are considered for funding

WHAT IS NOT FUNDED No grants to individuals

WHO CAN BENEFIT Organisations working in the areas outlined above

WHERE FUNDING CAN BE GIVEN Brighton and Hove, Sussex and Kent

TYPE OF GRANT Project and research. Funding may be given for up to three years

SAMPLE GRANTS £50,000 to European Science and Environment Forum for independent scientific debate
£3,540 to Sussex Wildlife Trust for nature preservation

FINANCES
- Year 1997
- Income £200,000
- Grants £100,000

HOW TO APPLY By letter to the Trustees at the address below

WHO TO APPLY TO Mrs E Owen, Marit and Hans Rausing Charitable Foundation, 132 Sloane Street, London SW1X 9AR
Tel 0171-259 9466

CC NO 1059714   **ESTABLISHED** 1996

■ The Ruben and Elizabeth Rausing Trust

WHAT IS FUNDED Charities working in the fields of: environmental issues and waterways

WHAT IS NOT FUNDED No grants to individuals

WHERE FUNDING CAN BE GIVEN UK and preference for overseas

TYPE OF GRANT Project and research

RANGE OF GRANTS £250–£500,000, average grant £20,000

SAMPLE GRANTS £75,000 to International Rivers Network for environmental organisation

Rawdon-Smith

FINANCES
- Year 1997
- Income £2,845,995
- Grants £2,314,239

TRUSTEES L Koerner, S Rausing, J Mailman, T Kaufman

NOTES Trustees meet in June to consider existing donations and in September to consider new applications and proposals

HOW TO APPLY By invitation from individual Trustees only

WHO TO APPLY TO Mrs Elaine Owen, Administrator, The Ruben and Elizabeth Rausing Trust, 132 Sloane Street, London SW1X 9AR
Tel 0171-259 9466

CC NO 1046769 **ESTABLISHED** 1995

■ The Rawdon-Smith Trust

WHAT IS FUNDED The preservation of the area called the 'Bed of Coniston Water' for the benefit of the public; other charitable purposes including lakes and woodlands

WHAT IS NOT FUNDED Applications for grants for individuals will not be supported

WHO CAN BENEFIT Local organisations

WHERE FUNDING CAN BE GIVEN Coniston and the five parishes surrounding Coniston Water

TYPE OF GRANT Buildings, capital, core costs and one-off grants. Funding is given for one year or less

FINANCES
- Year 1996
- Income £94,394
- Grants £28,797

HOW TO APPLY To the address under Who To Apply To in writing. The Trustees meet to consider applications in February, May and November

WHO TO APPLY TO I Stancliffe, Secretary, The Rawdon-Smith Trust, Campbell House, Coniston, Cumbria LA21 8EF

CC NO 500355 **ESTABLISHED** 1964

■ Sir James Reckitt Charity (317)

WHAT IS FUNDED Charitable organisations submitting applications working in the following areas: fauna; flora; lakes; landscapes; nature reserves; waterways; and woodlands

WHAT IS NOT FUNDED No grants to associations not based in the UK or registered under the Charities Act. No grants to individuals, other than individual Quakers or residents of Hull and the East Riding of Yorkshire or for specific events such as geographical expeditions. No support for causes of a warlike nature nor to smaller bodies working in areas other than those set out above

WHO CAN BENEFIT Registered charities working in the areas outlined under What is Funded

WHERE FUNDING CAN BE GIVEN Priority given in descending order to: Hull and the East Riding of Yorkshire, excluding York; nationally; regionally, where work extends to include the Hull area; and internationally

TYPE OF GRANT Annual subscription and/or donation for special projects or towards running costs. Innovatory or long established projects receive equal consideration

RANGE OF GRANTS £50–£20,000, typical grant £500

FINANCES
- Year 1997
- Income £666,831
- Grants £484,302

TRUSTEES Mrs G M Atherton, R A Bellingham, J R Clayton, J M Green, J H Holt (Vice Chairman), J B Hughes-Reckitt, Mrs C J Jennings, Miss C Pollock (Chairman), W N Russell, J E Upton, J N Upton, R J Upton, Mrs J Wilson

PUBLICATIONS *A History of the Sir James Reckitt Charity 1921–1979* by B N Reckitt

HOW TO APPLY At any time in writing only, for consideration by the Trustees at meetings in the spring and autumn of each year. There is no application form. Letters should be brief but include full financial information, with a copy of the latest Annual Report and Accounts attached where appropriate. All applications are acknowledged and further information sought if necessary, but no further correspondence can be entered into

WHO TO APPLY TO I Gillespie, The Sir James Reckitt Charity, 233 Carr Lane, Willerby, East Yorkshire HU10 6JF

CC NO 225356 **ESTABLISHED** 1921

Commentary

The Sir James Reckitt Charity was founded in 1921 by Sir James Reckitt, Bart, with the aim of supporting general charitable purposes. His connections with the Society of Friends (Quakers) and his family's business interests in the Hull area have always guided the distribution of grants by the Trust. In 1996 the Trust celebrated its 75th anniversary and marked it by encouraging the formation of a consortium of grant giving trusts in Hull and the East Riding of Yorkshire areas. The consortium's aim is to improve co-operation between the local trusts.

The Trust will support general charitable purposes in eight main areas: social work, education, medical, religion, youth, children, the elderly and the environment. Social work receives the largest proportion of the total value of grants in 1997, approximately 36 per cent. Education received 17 per cent, medical 13 per cent, religion 12 per cent, youth 9 per cent, children 5 per cent, elderly 4 per cent and environment 4 per cent. The Trust favours projects relating to the Society of Friends (Quakers) and projects within the Hull and East Riding of Yorkshire areas, due to the connections of Sir James Reckitt. Also favoured are national charities whose work affects the nation as a whole, regional charities whose work affects those in the Hull area and finally international work in special circumstances such as major disasters. The Trust therefore has a scale of preference within its priorities for grant giving, with the Quakers and the Hull/East Riding areas as the highest preference. The Trust will consider applications from individuals and made approximately 50 grants to individuals in 1997.

A Trust Deed in 1921 governs the funding policies of the Trust and requires that the income of the Trust is used for general charitable purposes at the Trustees' discretion. The policies change only to the extent that the Trustees have discretion to do so.

Funding can only be given to UK based organisations and individuals, with priority given to Quakers or those in the Hull area, as explained above. The Trust does not fund statutory bodies and will not replace statutory funding. The Trust does not believe itself large enough to consider co-funding with large organisations such as the Lottery or with Europe. However the Trust would consider joint projects with other small organisations.

Approximately 60 per cent of the Trust's income is distributed in the form of subscriptions, offering annual support which may continue for many years. This support is sometimes offered for limited periods. The remaining 40 per cent is distributed as grants to approximately 100 applicants, at the May and November Trustees meetings. The Trust will never make loans, but are prepared to support infrastructure costs of organisations based in Hull and the East Riding of Yorkshire.

Applications should be made in writing to the Administrator. There is no application form. Applications are assessed by one of several methods: (a) urgent applications that clearly fit the Trust's Objects and require only limited funding are assessed by the Administrator, then passed directly to the Chairman and can be dealt with very rapidly; (b) less urgent applications or those which do not so clearly meet the Objects and therefore need further consideration are held and passed to the Trustees at their bi-annual meetings. Further information will be requested as necessary.

Trust representatives will visit subscriber organisations at least once every five years. Occasionally visits are made to applicants, by the Administrator or a Trustee, if their work is of particular interest to the Trustees

SAMPLE GRANTS
> The top ten grants awarded in 1997 were:
> £28,900 to Britain Yearly Meeting
> £20,000 to Quaker Social Responsibility and Education
> £15,220 to Ackworth School
> £12,750 to Leighton Park School
> £12,700 to North Humberside Hospice Project
> £11,500 to The Retreat
> £10,000 to Elizabeth Fry Young Offenders Trust
> £10,000 to Humberside Police – Action Against Drugs
> £10,000 to Quaker Peace and Service
> £9,070 to Woodbrook Council

■ R A & V B Reekie Trust

WHAT IS FUNDED Donations are only given to registered charitable organisations. We like to support organisations concerned with rural conservation

WHAT IS NOT FUNDED No individual applicants

WHO CAN BENEFIT Headquarters organisations plus local branches

WHERE FUNDING CAN BE GIVEN UK, with preference for Wiltshire

TYPE OF GRANT One-off. In exceptional circumstances grant commitments may be recurring

FINANCES
- Year 1998
- Income £24,216
- Grants £23,857

TRUSTEES Mrs V B Reekie, R A Reekie, J A J Reekie

PUBLICATIONS Annual Report and Accounts

HOW TO APPLY None required. Applications will not be acknowledged

WHO TO APPLY TO Mrs V B Reekie, R A & V B Reekie Trust, c/o Roger Harriman, New Guild House, 45 Great Charles Street, Queensway, Birmingham B3 2LX
Tel 0121-212 2222

CC NO 274388   **ESTABLISHED** 1977

■ The Reuter Foundation

WHAT IS FUNDED Charities working in the field of rural conservation, including environmental issues

WHAT IS NOT FUNDED Will not support political, religious, sports or animal causes. No grants to individuals

WHO CAN BENEFIT Registered charities working in the areas outlined above

WHERE FUNDING CAN BE GIVEN UK and overseas

TYPE OF GRANT One-off, recurring costs, project, research and start-up costs will be considered

FINANCES
- Year 1997
- Income £3,121,555
- Grants £2,794,150

TRUSTEES P Job, D G Ure, M W Wood

PUBLICATIONS *Annual Review, Reuterlink, Reuterlink Extra, Contacts Directory*

NOTES Applications must be supported by a member of Reuters staff

HOW TO APPLY In writing at any time. Application form available

WHO TO APPLY TO S Somerville, The Reuter Foundation, 85 Fleet Street, London EC4P 4AJ
Tel 0171-542 7015
Fax 0171-542 8599
E-mail rtrfoundation@easynet.co.uk
Web Site http://www.foundation.reuters.com

CC NO 803676   **ESTABLISHED** 1982

■ Joan K Reynall Charitable Trust

WHAT IS FUNDED Nature reserves, woodlands, animal welfare and agriculture

WHAT IS NOT FUNDED No grants to individuals

WHO CAN BENEFIT Registered charities working in the areas outlined above

WHERE FUNDING CAN BE GIVEN UK and overseas

TYPE OF GRANT One-off and project, up to one year

RANGE OF GRANTS Up to £500

FINANCES
- Year 1998
- Income £17,000

TRUSTEES Midland Bank Trust Company Ltd, J K Reynell, A C Reynell

HOW TO APPLY In writing to the address under Who To Apply To

WHO TO APPLY TO The Trust Manager, Joan K Reynall Charitable Trust, Midland Bank Private Banking, Cumberland House, 15–17 Cumberland Place, Southampton, Hampshire SO15 2UY
Tel 01703 531396
Fax 01703 531341

CC NO 1069397   **ESTABLISHED** 1997

■ Miss Maria Susan Rickard Animals' Charity

WHAT IS FUNDED Animal welfare charities

WHO CAN BENEFIT Registered charities working in the areas mentioned above

WHERE FUNDING CAN BE GIVEN UK and overseas

RANGE OF GRANTS £10–£550

SAMPLE GRANTS £550 to West Norfolk Seal Rescue
£300 to Cares Wildlife Hospital
£250 to Wood Green Animals Shelter
£209 to British Chelonia Group
£200 to Donkey Sanctuary
£200 to Withers Mill Wild Animal Sanctuary
£175 to Exotic Pet Refuge
£155 to Cambridge University Veterinary School Trust
£100 to Animal Helpline Sanctuary
£100 to Millhouse Animal Sanctuary

FINANCES
- Year 1996
- Income £14,130
- Grants £4,375

TRUSTEES Miss M S Rickard, G E Smart, J T Dean

WHO TO APPLY TO J Dean, Miss Maria Susan Rickard Animals' Charity, H W Dean & Son, 57 Regent Street, Cambridge CB2 1AQ

CC NO 281303   **ESTABLISHED** 1980

■ Rivington Heritage Trust

WHAT IS FUNDED To conserve, preserve, maintain, protect and enhance all aspects and features of the environment, including flora and fauna

WHO CAN BENEFIT Organisations working in the areas outlined above

WHERE FUNDING CAN BE GIVEN UK

HOW TO APPLY In writing to the address below

WHO TO APPLY TO Ms P Roscoe, Managing Agent, Rivington Heritage Trust, 183 Town Lane, Whittle-Le-Woods, Chorley, Lancashire PR6 8AG

CC NO 1064700   **ESTABLISHED** 1997

■ The E E Roberts Charitable Trust

WHAT IS FUNDED Farming and wildlife, including environmental issues

WHAT IS NOT FUNDED No support for large national charities, church or village appeals outside the area or for animal charities

Alphabetical register of grant making trusts   **Rollit**

WHO CAN BENEFIT Registered charities working in the areas outlined above

WHERE FUNDING CAN BE GIVEN East Sussex and Kent

TYPE OF GRANT Chiefly recurring payments from income. Occasional one-off capital grants and research. Funding is available for more than three years

RANGE OF GRANTS Capital grants: £2,000; recurring grants: £1,000pa

FINANCES
- Year 1997
- Grants £36,603
- Income £34,617

TRUSTEES Mrs E E Roberts, C S Hall, N B C Evelegh

HOW TO APPLY In writing to the address under Who To Apply To. The Trustees meet twice a year in January and July. Applications will not be acknowledged

WHO TO APPLY TO C Hall, The E E Roberts Charitable Trust, Messrs Cripps Harries Hall, Solicitors, 6–10 Mount Ephraim Road, Tunbridge Wells, Kent TN1 1EE
Tel 01892 515121

CC NO 273697   **ESTABLISHED** 1977

■ The J C Robinson Trust No 3

WHAT IS FUNDED Rural conservation

WHAT IS NOT FUNDED No grants made for historic buildings or village halls except in Sussex, Bristol and South Gloucestershire. No grants to animal charities

WHO CAN BENEFIT Individuals and organisations working in the areas outlined above

WHERE FUNDING CAN BE GIVEN East Sussex, Bristol and South Gloucestershire

TYPE OF GRANT Recurrent or one-off. Buildings, capital, project, running costs, salaries and start-up costs. Funding may be given for up to two years

RANGE OF GRANTS £50–£1,000

FINANCES
- Year 1997
- Grants £18,973
- Income £17,771

TRUSTEES Miss C M Howe, Dr C J Burns-Cox

HOW TO APPLY By post only to the address below

WHO TO APPLY TO Dr C Burns-Cox, The J C Robinson Trust No 3, Southend Farm, Wotton-under-Edge, Gloucestershire GL12 7PB

CC NO 207294   **ESTABLISHED** 1931

■ The Rochester Bridge Trust

WHAT IS FUNDED The maintenance of the Rochester bridges, also any other crossings of the River Medway. Other charitable purposes including rural conservation; animal facilities and services; and animal sciences

WHAT IS NOT FUNDED Revenue

WHO CAN BENEFIT Charitable bodies

WHERE FUNDING CAN BE GIVEN Kent

TYPE OF GRANT Capital including equipment, buildings and one-off. Funding is available for one year or less

RANGE OF GRANTS Largest grant £50,000

FINANCES
- Year 1995–96
- Grants £125,000
- Income £1,800,000

TRUSTEES The Court of Wardens and Assistants of Rochester Bridge; 17 members who hold office for three year terms

PUBLICATIONS Policy synopsis available on request

HOW TO APPLY To the address under Who To Apply To in writing. Applications considered annually only in June and July. Determined in October

WHO TO APPLY TO Michael Lewis, Bridge Clerk, The Rochester Bridge Trust, The Bridge Chamber, 5 Esplanade, Rochester, Kent ME1 1QE
Tel 01634 846706/843457

CC NO 207100   **ESTABLISHED** 1399

■ The Vera Kaye Rollit Trust

WHAT IS FUNDED Animal homes; animal welfare charities; cats, catteries and other facilities for cats; dogs, kennels and other facilities for dogs; and horses, stables and other facilities for horses

WHO CAN BENEFIT Local organisations, local branches of national organisations

WHERE FUNDING CAN BE GIVEN Hull and East Riding of Yorkshire

TYPE OF GRANT Buildings, capital, core costs, endowments, feasibility studies, one-off, project, research, recurring costs, running costs, salaries and start-up costs. Funding from less than one year to more than three will be considered. No loans

RANGE OF GRANTS £500–£5,000, typical £500–£1,000

SAMPLE GRANTS £5,000 to PDSA for equipment/refurbishment of clinic
£2,000 to Hull Animal Welfare Club for general

Does the trust you have chosen match your needs? Haphazard applications waste postage and time   **155**

Rotaract

purposes
£1,000 to Cats Protection League for general purposes
£1,000 to Hessle Dog Rescue Services for general purposes

FINANCES
- Year 1997–98
- Income £19,650
- Grants £12,000

TRUSTEES J W Brennand, D J Bowes, S J Trynka

HOW TO APPLY To the address under Who To Apply To in writing. No formal application form is available

WHO TO APPLY TO The Vera Kaye Rollit Trust, Wilberforce Court, High Street, Hull HU1 1YJ
Tel 01482 323239
Fax 01482 326239

CC NO 500391 **ESTABLISHED** 1970

■Bristol North West Rotaract Club

WHAT IS FUNDED Rural conservation; animal facilities and services; and environmental and animal sciences

WHO CAN BENEFIT Individuals and institutions working in the areas outlined above

WHERE FUNDING CAN BE GIVEN UK

TYPE OF GRANT One-off, buildings, capital, core costs, project, running costs, start-up costs

FINANCES
- Year 1996–97
- Income £4,619
- Grants £1,833

HOW TO APPLY In writing to the address below

WHO TO APPLY TO Fiona Campbell, Bristol North West Rotaract Club, 6 Aust Lane, Westbury-on-Trym BS9 3HB

CC NO 1035486 **ESTABLISHED** 1994

■Rotary Club of Arbury Charity Trust Fund

WHAT IS FUNDED Animal facilities and services; endangered species; and environmental issues ,

WHO CAN BENEFIT Institutions, organisations and individuals

WHERE FUNDING CAN BE GIVEN UK and overseas

TYPE OF GRANT One-off, capital, core costs, project and start-up costs. Funding may be given for up to two years

FINANCES
- Year 1996
- Income £9,613

TRUSTEES President, President Elect, Secretary, Treasurer

HOW TO APPLY In writing to the address below

WHO TO APPLY TO M Larder, Treasurer, Rotary Club of Arbury Charity Trust Fund, 4 Brookfield Drive, Wolvey, Hinckley, Leicestershire LE10 3LT

CC NO 1033087 **ESTABLISHED** 1994

■Rotary Club of Ashtead Trust Fund

WHAT IS FUNDED Local rural conservation and other charitable purposes, institutions, societies or objects as the Club directs

WHAT IS NOT FUNDED No grants for large national organisations using professional fund raisers

WHO CAN BENEFIT Institutions and societies

WHERE FUNDING CAN BE GIVEN Ashtead, Surrey and West Sussex

TYPE OF GRANT Recurring and one-off. Also buildings, capital, core costs, project, running costs, salaries and start-up costs. Funding may be given for one year or less

RANGE OF GRANTS £25–£1,000

FINANCES
- Year 1997–98
- Income £13,854
- Grants £6,953

TRUSTEES R W Bracher, A Combeer, M G Goulder, J D G Jones

HOW TO APPLY By letter with full particulars to the address below

WHO TO APPLY TO R W Bracher, Rotary Club of Ashtead Trust Fund, Larchmont, Skinners Lane, Ashtead, Surrey KT21 2NN
Tel 01372 815448
Fax 01372 815448

CC NO 285254 **ESTABLISHED** 1982

■Rotary Club of Eastleigh Trust Fund

WHAT IS FUNDED Rural conservation; animal facilities and services; and environmental and animal sciences

WHAT IS NOT FUNDED No religion or politics

WHO CAN BENEFIT Individuals and institutions working in the areas outlined above

WHERE FUNDING CAN BE GIVEN Eastleigh and overseas

TYPE OF GRANT One-off and project

FINANCES
- Year 1996–97
- Income £6,715
- Grants £7,753

TRUSTEES Fred Coalbran, Arnold Clegg, Jonathan Kane, John Stephens

WHO TO APPLY TO R J Stephens, Rotary Club of Eastleigh Trust Fund, Pathways, Wychwood Grove, Chandlers Ford, Eastleigh, Hampshire SO53 1FQ

CC NO 1003784   **ESTABLISHED** 1991

■ Folkestone Rotary Club Samaritan Fund Trust

WHAT IS FUNDED Environmental issues at the discretion of the Trustees

WHAT IS NOT FUNDED No purely religious and political organisations

WHO CAN BENEFIT National schemes and local organisations working in the areas outlined above

WHERE FUNDING CAN BE GIVEN Folkestone or the surrounding district

TYPE OF GRANT Recurring and one-off. Also start-up costs. Funding may be given for up to two years

FINANCES
- Year 1995–96
- Income £11,024
- Grants £10,167

TRUSTEES B G Oclee, B J Booth, H Wald, E Elliott, A W Ruderman

HOW TO APPLY In writing to the address below

WHO TO APPLY TO H Wald, Folkestone Rotary Club Samaritan Fund Trust, 10 Cornwallis Close, Folkestone, Kent CT19 5JD

CC NO 266883   **ESTABLISHED** 1973

■ Rotary Club of Hadleigh Charitable Trust Fund

WHAT IS FUNDED Landscapes, nature reserves, woodlands, animal welfare, bird sanctuaries, and wildlife sanctuaries

WHAT IS NOT FUNDED Endowments, research and on-going projects will not be considered for funding

WHO CAN BENEFIT Individuals and organisations working in the areas outlined above

WHERE FUNDING CAN BE GIVEN Mainly Hadleigh (within a 10 mile radius). Also limited funds for worldwide charitable causes

TYPE OF GRANT One-off and capital. Funding is available for up to one year

RANGE OF GRANTS £20–£3,000, typical grant £100–£300

FINANCES
- Year 1998
- Income £10,591
- Grants £6,676

TRUSTEES D P Stokes, W D Yorke Edwards, I M Burne

HOW TO APPLY By letter giving full details of requirement

WHO TO APPLY TO D P Stokes, Rotary Club of Hadleigh Charitable Trust Fund, Ravenbank, Upper Street, Layham, Ipswich IP7 5JZ
Tel 01473 827226

CC NO 1049781   **ESTABLISHED** 1995

■ The Rotary Club of Thornbury Trust Fund

WHAT IS FUNDED Rural conservation; animal facilities and services; and environmental and animal sciences

WHO CAN BENEFIT Individuals and organisations working in the areas outlined above

WHERE FUNDING CAN BE GIVEN South Gloucestershire, UK and overseas

TYPE OF GRANT One-off and start-up costs will be considered

RANGE OF GRANTS £25–£5,000

FINANCES
- Year 1997
- Income £19,883
- Grants £10,619

TRUSTEES L Hales, J Massie, S Crawford, J Gibbon

HOW TO APPLY Only applications brought to our attention by our members or other Rotary organisations will be considered

WHO TO APPLY TO S Crawford, The Rotary Club of Thornbury Trust Fund, 30 Cleveland Close, Thornbury, Bristol BS35 2YD
Tel 01454 413106
Fax 01454 413406

CC NO 1035557   **ESTABLISHED** 1982

■ The Charitable Fund of the Rotary Club of Wallasey

WHAT IS FUNDED Animal welfare and other charitable purposes

WHO CAN BENEFIT Individuals and organisations working in the areas outlined above

WHERE FUNDING CAN BE GIVEN Wirral

TYPE OF GRANT One-off

FINANCES
- Year 1995–96
- Income £8,804
- Grants £12,451

TRUSTEES President, Vice President, Secretary and Treasurer of the Wallasey Rotary Club

HOW TO APPLY In writing to the address below

WHO TO APPLY TO David Foster, Charitable Fund of Rotary Club of Wallasey, 23 Warrenhurst, Montpellier Crescent, New Brighton, Wirral L45 9JZ

CC NO 515323   **ESTABLISHED** 1984

■ The Rowan Charitable Trust (304)

WHAT IS FUNDED Overseas: agriculture; environment. UK: environmental improvement

WHAT IS NOT FUNDED No individuals, buildings or building works, or academic research; charitable organisations only

WHO CAN BENEFIT Organisations working in the areas outlined above

WHERE FUNDING CAN BE GIVEN Overseas – Africa, Asia, Middle East, Pacific Islands, South and Central America; and UK, particularly Merseyside

TYPE OF GRANT One-off, recurring

FINANCES
- Year 1997
- Income £347,069
- Grants £542,915

TRUSTEES Mrs H Russell, C R Jones

PUBLICATIONS Annual Report and Accounts, Guidelines for Applicants

HOW TO APPLY In writing to the Administrator. No application forms are issued. Guidelines are issued. Deadline for applications for consideration at February and August Trustees' meetings is December and June respectively

WHO TO APPLY TO The Administrator, The Rowan Charitable Trust, 9 Greyfriars Road, Reading, Berkshire RG1 1JG
Tel 0118-959 7111
Fax 0118-960 7700

CC NO 242678   **ESTABLISHED** 1964

Commentary

The Rowan Charitable Trust was established in 1964 for general charitable purposes. The Trust's focus is on projects, both overseas and in the UK, which will benefit disadvantaged groups and communities. It will also support advocacy and challenges to powerful economic forces on behalf of the poor or powerless. Two-thirds of the funds available are given as grants each year to charitable organisations overseas; the remaining third is allocated within the UK, with a strong preference for Merseyside.

Overseas, the Trust focuses on projects in the fields of: agriculture – crop and livestock production and settlement schemes; community development – appropriate technology and village industries; health – preventative medicine, water supplies and blindness; education – adult education and materials; environmental – protecting and sustaining ecological systems at risk; human rights – of women, children, and the disabled; fair trade – for primary producers and workers. Overseas project proposals should involve the local community in the planning and implementation; invest in people through training and enabling; have a holistic concern for all aspects of life and a respect for local cultural patterns and beliefs.

In the UK, the Trust supports projects for: housing and homelessness; social and community care; education; employment; after-care; welfare rights; community development; and environment improvement. UK project proposals should demonstrate: an element of self-help; user and community involvement in the planning and delivery of the project; a multi-disciplinary approach; and emphasis on empowerment.

The Trust's funding policies are set by the Trustees. The Trust is prepared to give core-funding, but does not fund statutory bodies, replace statutory funding, cover building costs or make loans. The Trust rarely funds a project in its entirety, participating instead in co-funding with other charitable organisations and the National Lottery.

The Trust makes one-off grants and recurring grants; recurring grants are made to a few large, national organisations and development agencies, including: Christian Aid, UNICEF, Intermediate Technology, and Barnados. It also gives smaller grants to much smaller organisations and locally-based projects.

Guidelines for applicants are available from the Correspondent. Applications should be made in writing to the Correspondent and should include a brief description of the project (two sides of A4 paper), a budget and the latest Annual Report and Accounts. Unsuccessful applicants will only be notified if an sae is enclosed.

The Trustees meet to allocate grants in February and August each year. Reports are requested from organisations which have received grants

SAMPLE GRANTS
The top ten grants made in 1997 were:
£55,000 to Christian Aid
£52,000 to Intermediate Technology
£22,000 to UNICEF
£15,000 to Barnados
£15,000 to Children's Society
£13,000 to UNA International Service
£12,500 to Tools for Self Reliance
£12,000 to International Child Care Trust

£10,000 to LEPRA
£10,000 to Fairtrade Foundation

■ The Royal Botanical & Horticultural Society of Manchester and the Northern Counties

WHAT IS FUNDED Financial assistance to local gardens or projects of horticultural interest and local horticultural societies in the North West

WHAT IS NOT FUNDED No grants to individual students. Grants may only be awarded through a college/university

WHO CAN BENEFIT Horticultural societies, shows and gardens of horticultural interest

WHERE FUNDING CAN BE GIVEN North West

TYPE OF GRANT Cash payment towards prize money or specific expenditure

RANGE OF GRANTS Grants given for prizes in open competition classes from £45–£65. Larger grants given to horticulture ranging from £200–£2,000

SAMPLE GRANTS £2,000 to University of Liverpool – New Botanic Gardens for student bursary
£1,500 to North West Counties Chrysanthemum League for Manchester Town Hall Shows
The following grants were given for horticultural projects:
£1,000 to Dorothy Clive Garden, Willoughbridge
£750 to Tatton Garden Society
£500 to University of Liverpool Centenary Conference
£500 to Caring for Life
£500 to Lakeland Horticultural Society
£500 to Houghton Green Gardening Society
£500 to Royal School for the Deaf
£400 to Denton Chrysanthemum and Dahlia Society

FINANCES
- Year 1998
- Income £21,893
- Grants £12,410

TRUSTEES Incorporated Governors of the Society

HOW TO APPLY Meetings are held in March and November. Application forms can be obtained from the address detailed below for the grants awarded for prizes in open competition classes

WHO TO APPLY TO A Pye, MA, FCA, The Royal Botanical & Horticultural Society, PO Box 500, 201 Deansgate, Manchester M60 2AT
Tel 0161-455 8380
Fax 0161-829 3803

CC NO 226683   **ESTABLISHED** 1827

■ Rufford Foundation (114)

WHAT IS FUNDED General charitable purposes with a particular interest in ecology/conservation including: endangered species; environmental issues; fauna; flora; woodlands; animal welfare; wildlife parks; and wildlife sanctuaries

WHAT IS NOT FUNDED Grants for building costs or salaries are unlikely to be considered. No grants to individuals. Registered charities only

WHO CAN BENEFIT Charities working in the areas outlined above

WHERE FUNDING CAN BE GIVEN UK and primarily outside of first world countries

TYPE OF GRANT One-off and project. No loans available

RANGE OF GRANTS Minimum £500; no maximum. However, there are very limited funds available in the near to medium future due to existing commitments

FINANCES
- Year 1997
- Income £1,726,333
- Grants £2,085,032

TRUSTEES C R F Barbour, A Gavazzi, A J Johnson, J H Laing, K W Scott, M I T Smailes, V Lees

NOTES Very limited funds available in the near to medium future due to existing commitments

HOW TO APPLY At any time, enclosing budgets, Annual Report and Accounts if available

WHO TO APPLY TO T Kenny, Trust Director, Rufford Foundation, 15a Old Church Street, London SW3 5DL
Web Site http://www.rufford.org

CC NO 326163   **ESTABLISHED** 1982

Commentary

The Rufford Foundation was founded in 1982 by J H Laing, with the purpose of giving to various worthwhile charitable causes at his and the other Trustees' discretion.

There is a strong interest in conservation and the environment, with perhaps two thirds of the Foundation's funding going to these areas. Many other causes are supported, especially in the field of social welfare. The Trustees try to help organisations where they feel that their intercession will make a positive difference.

The Foundation tends to concentrate upon conservation in non-first world or 'developing' countries where funds are more scarce and there is much greater difficulty in raising the required funding, rather than projects within the UK where there is generally more access to fundraising possibilities.

There is a definite and conscious attempt to avoid replacing statutory funding The Foundation does not give grants to individuals, but only to registered charities. The Rufford Foundation tends to avoid making recurring grants on a long term basis. The Trustees tend not to give grants for building costs or salaries, or for other infrastructure costs. The Foundation does not make loans.

Applications can be made at any time throughout the year and should include a full proposal, a copy of the latest Accounts and Annual Report if available, as well as budgets for the proposed project. All applications are responded to. For the smaller grant applications under £5,000 there is a rolling programme which allows a relatively quick response, while larger grants, those above £10,000, must go forward to Trustee meetings.

After a grant has been made, many of the organisations running a project will be asked for a progress report. Visits may also be made to some of the larger organisations, although there is a tendency not to visit organisations to whom grants of less than £10,000 have been made

SAMPLE GRANTS
The top ten grants given in 1997 were:
£553,000 to the World Wildlife Fund
£125,000 to EIA Charitable Trust
£90,000 to Compassion in World Farming Trust
£85,000 to Health Unlimited
£79,333 to the Salvation Army
£50,000 to the Royal Botanic Gardens, Kew
£50,000 to the World Development Movement
£47,336 to Conservation International
£45,224 to VSO
£31,000 to CRUSAID

S

■ Jean Sainsbury Animal Welfare Trust (formerly Jean Sainsbury Charitable Trust)

WHAT IS FUNDED To support smaller charities concerned with animal welfare and wildlife

WHAT IS NOT FUNDED No grants to non-registered charities or individuals

WHO CAN BENEFIT National and international animal welfare organisations

WHERE FUNDING CAN BE GIVEN UK, Europe and Africa

TYPE OF GRANT Buildings, capital, core costs, one-off, project, running costs and recurring costs. Funding for up to three years is available

RANGE OF GRANTS £250–£10,000, typical grant £500

SAMPLE GRANTS £11,000 to Brent Lodge Bird and Wildlife Trust to set up new charity shop
£10,000 to Manchester Home for Lost Dogs for renovating puppy unit
£10,000 to North Staffordshire Spaying Trust for new clinic
£10,000 to Animals in Distress, Manchester (annual donation)
£9,500 to Royal Vet College for fund to assist poor owners
£6,000 to Horse Rescue Fund (annual donation)
£6,000 to North Clwyd Animal Rescue (annual donation)
£6,000 to Three Owls Bird Sanctuary (annual donation)
£6,000 to Wildlife Hospital Trust (annual donation)
£5,000 to Clacton Animal Aid for fencing exercise area for dogs

FINANCES
- Year 1998
- Income £289,562
- Grants £208,963

TRUSTEES Mrs J Sainsbury, C H Sainsbury, C P Russell, Mrs G Tarlington, J A Keliher, M Spurdens, MRCVS, Miss J Winship, SRN, Mrs A Lowrie

PUBLICATIONS Accounts prepared to December 31, 1998

HOW TO APPLY Three Trustees' meetings yearly. Approximately March, July and November (submissions eight weeks earlier)

WHO TO APPLY TO Miss A Dietrich, Administrator, Jean Sainsbury Animal Welfare Trust, PO Box 469, London W14 8PJ
Fax 0171-371 4918

CC NO 326358   ESTABLISHED 1982

■ The St John's Wood Trust

WHAT IS FUNDED Promotion of research in biological husbandry and alternative technology, particularly the advancement of organic and experimental farming. Income is currently wholly committed

WHO CAN BENEFIT Organisations working in the areas outlined above

WHERE FUNDING CAN BE GIVEN UK

TYPE OF GRANT Research grants

SAMPLE GRANTS £63,600 to Progressive Farming Trust Ltd for organic farming research

FINANCES
- Year 1997
- Income £41,269
- Grants £63,600

TRUSTEES S G Kemp, Hon F D L Astor, Mrs B A Astor, R D L Astor

HOW TO APPLY Since all income is committed for the foreseeable future, no applications can be considered

WHO TO APPLY TO S G Kemp, The St John's Wood Trust, Sayers Butterworth, Chartered Accountants, 18 Bentinck Street, London W1M 5RL

CC NO 281897   ESTABLISHED 1980

■ The Salisbury Pool Charity

WHAT IS FUNDED Rural conservation; animal facilities and services; and environmental and animal sciences, and other charitable purposes

WHAT IS NOT FUNDED No grants to individuals and most national charities

WHO CAN BENEFIT Local organisations working in the areas outlined above

WHERE FUNDING CAN BE GIVEN Primarily Hertfordshire and Dorset

TYPE OF GRANT One-off and recurring costs may be considered. Funding is given for one year or less

FINANCES
- Year 1995–96
- Income £16,500
- Grants £10,900

TRUSTEES The Marquess of Salisbury, Viscount Cranborne

HOW TO APPLY To the address under Who To Apply To in writing. Sae from applicants required

WHO TO APPLY TO M R Melville, The Salisbury Pool Charity, Hatfield House, Hatfield, Hertfordshire AL9 5NF

CC NO 272626   ESTABLISHED 1976

■ Sarnia Charitable Trust

WHAT IS FUNDED Interest in wildlife and conservation projects in the Channel Islands especially Guernsey

WHAT IS NOT FUNDED Expeditions and scholarships. No grants to individuals

WHO CAN BENEFIT Registered charities only

WHERE FUNDING CAN BE GIVEN UK and the Channel Islands, especially Guernsey

RANGE OF GRANTS £100–£10,000

SAMPLE GRANTS £10,000 to George Adamson Wildlife Trust
£10,000 to Norfolk Naturalists Trust
£5,000 to Norfolk and Norwich Naturalists Trust
£5,000 to SOF Guernsey Meeting

FINANCES
- Year 1998
- Income £30,401
- Grants £37,500

TRUSTEES Dr T N D Peet, R Harriman, Mrs C V E Benfield

HOW TO APPLY As it is currently fully committed, this Trust states that it does not respond to unsolicited applications

WHO TO APPLY TO R Harriman, Sarnia Charitable Trust, New Guild House, 45 Great Charles Street, Queensway, Birmingham B3 2LX
Tel 0121-212 2222

CC NO 281417   ESTABLISHED 1979

■ The Schuster Charitable Trust

WHAT IS FUNDED General charitable purposes. Preference for small, local charities working in the following areas: rural conservation; endangered species; various animal facilities and services; agriculture and animal breeding

WHAT IS NOT FUNDED No grants to individuals. This includes students on award schemes; expeditions; scholarships

WHO CAN BENEFIT Registered charities benefiting endangered species and wildlife

WHERE FUNDING CAN BE GIVEN UK and overseas, though principally UK and especially Oxfordshire, Buckinghamshire, Gloucestershire and Argyll and Bute

TYPE OF GRANT Mainly one-off grants, buildings, capital, core costs, project and research

Schweitzer's

Alphabetical register of grant making trusts

grants. Funding can be for up to and over three years

RANGE OF GRANTS £250–£3,000. Average grant £500–£1,000

FINANCES
- Year 1997–98
- Income £20,959
- Grants £23,800

TRUSTEES Mrs J V Clarke, P J Schuster, R D Schuster

HOW TO APPLY At all times, no application form used. Trustees meet twice annually, normally June and December. Sae required

WHO TO APPLY TO Mrs J V Clarke, The Schuster Charitable Trust, Nether Worton House, Middle Barton, Chipping Norton, Oxfordshire OX7 7AT

CC NO 234580   **ESTABLISHED** 1964

■ Dr Schweitzer's Hospital Fund

WHAT IS FUNDED Animal welfare administered on Dr Schweitzer's principles

WHO CAN BENEFIT Individuals and institutions working in the areas outlined above

WHERE FUNDING CAN BE GIVEN UK and overseas

TYPE OF GRANT Recurring

FINANCES
- Year 1995–96
- Income £9,419
- Grants £7,629

TRUSTEES Percy Mark, DipArch, ARIBA, Dr J R Witchalls, MB, FAW, Frank Schweitzer, MS, FRCS

HOW TO APPLY By letter to the address below

WHO TO APPLY TO Percy Mark, Dr Schweitzer's Hospital Fund, Kenwood Cottage, Croydon, Royston, Hertfordshire SG8 0DR

CC NO 210124   **ESTABLISHED** 1959

■ The Frieda Scott Charitable Trust

WHAT IS FUNDED A very wide range of registered charities concerned with lakes; landscapes; nature reserves; woodlands; animal homes; animal welfare; bird sanctuaries; cats, catteries and other facilities for cats; and dogs, kennels and other facilities for dogs

WHAT IS NOT FUNDED No grants to individuals or school appeals. No grants to charities outside the stated geographical area

WHO CAN BENEFIT Small local charities and occasionally locally based work of larger charities

WHERE FUNDING CAN BE GIVEN The old County of Westmorland and the area covered by South Lakeland District Council

TYPE OF GRANT Buildings, capital, one-off, project, running costs and start-up costs. Funding of up to three years will be considered

RANGE OF GRANTS £200–£5,000 with occasional much larger grants

FINANCES
- Year 1998
- Income £252,712
- Grants £254,712

TRUSTEES Mrs C Brockbank (Chairman), Mrs J H Barker, Mrs O Clarke, OBE, R A Hunter, Miss C R Scott, P R W Hensman, Mrs M G Wilson

PUBLICATIONS Grants guide leaflet available

HOW TO APPLY Applications by letter with accompanying Accounts considered three times a year in February, May and October. Initial telephone calls about applications are welcome

WHO TO APPLY TO D J Harding, Secretary, The Frieda Scott Charitable Trust, Sand Aire House, Kendal, Cumbria LA9 4BE *Tel* 01539 723415

CC NO 221593   **ESTABLISHED** 1962

■ The Sedgwick Trust

WHAT IS FUNDED Small scale agricultural projects in developing nations, especially Madagascar

WHAT IS NOT FUNDED No grants made to individuals

WHO CAN BENEFIT Non-governmental development and aid agencies in Madagascar and Africa

WHERE FUNDING CAN BE GIVEN For the present, only projects in Madagascar will be considered

TYPE OF GRANT Recurring, project

FINANCES
- Year 1996
- Income £10,898
- Grants £9,267

TRUSTEES J E M Gilbey, A W Pottinger, Mrs K E Pottinger, D I Pottinger, J I Pottinger

HOW TO APPLY In writing to the address below

WHO TO APPLY TO John Gilbey, The Sedgwick Trust, 2 Westfield Terrace, Wakefield WF1 3RD

CC NO 328489   **ESTABLISHED** 1990

■ The Dr N K Shah Trust

WHAT IS FUNDED Activities to promote Jain values of ecology and animal welfare

WHAT IS NOT FUNDED Empirical education not funded, only theological and spiritual studies

WHO CAN BENEFIT Any person or organisation

WHERE FUNDING CAN BE GIVEN Mainly UK, but overseas also considered

TYPE OF GRANT May be project related

RANGE OF GRANTS Depends on the project

FINANCES
- Year 1997
- Income £15,482
- Grants £22,719

TRUSTEES Dr N K Shah, Mrs B N Shah, Dr S N Shah, L N Shah

NOTES Only persons studying theology, spiritual education or research and study related to Jain values may apply

HOW TO APPLY In writing to the address below

WHO TO APPLY TO Dr N K Shah, The Dr N K Shah Trust, 20 James Close, London NW11 9QX

CC NO 327291 **ESTABLISHED** 1986

■ The Shark Trust

WHAT IS FUNDED The advancement for the public benefit of the conservation of sharks, rays and chimaeras in the UK, European and International waters through education and the promotion and dissemination of research into such conservation

WHAT IS NOT FUNDED No grants for expeditions, scholarships, meetings or training

WHO CAN BENEFIT Individuals and organisations working with and benefiting sharks, rays and chimaeras

WHERE FUNDING CAN BE GIVEN UK and overseas

TYPE OF GRANT One-off and recurring for projects and research

RANGE OF GRANTS £100–£500

FINANCES
- Year 1997–98
- Income £60,000

TRUSTEES G S Croft, I K Fergusson, J Stafford-Deitsch, G Swinney

PUBLICATIONS *Shark Focus* – newsletter

HOW TO APPLY To the address under Who To Apply To in writing

WHO TO APPLY TO Ms S Fowler, Secretary, The Shark Trust, 36 Kingfisher Court, Hambridge Road, Newbury, Berkshire RG14 5SJ
Tel 01635 551150

CC NO 1064185 **ESTABLISHED** 1997

■ The Shears Charitable Trust

WHAT IS FUNDED Funding may be given to rural conservation; animal facilities and services; and environmental and animal sciences

WHAT IS NOT FUNDED No grants for domestic animal welfare

WHO CAN BENEFIT Organisations working in the areas outlined above

WHERE FUNDING CAN BE GIVEN Northumberland, Tyne and Wear, Durham, West Yorkshire, Dorset and Isle of Wight

TYPE OF GRANT One-off

RANGE OF GRANTS Up to £5,000, typical grant £1,000

SAMPLE GRANTS £250 to The National Trust

FINANCES
- Year 1997
- Income £49,316
- Grants £31,150

TRUSTEES Ms L G Shears, T H Shears, P J R Shears

HOW TO APPLY In writing to the address below

WHO TO APPLY TO T H Shears, Trustee, The Shears Charitable Trust, 35 Elmfield Road, Gosforth, Newcastle upon Tyne NE3 4BA

CC NO 1049907 **ESTABLISHED** 1994

■ The David Shepherd Conservation Foundation

WHAT IS FUNDED The conservation of endangered mammals worldwide. Particular focus is given to direct funding for field work for tigers, elephants and rhinos in Africa and Asia. The Foundation assists official law enforcement agencies to combat wildlife crime

WHAT IS NOT FUNDED No grants to anything unrelated to critically endangered mammals

WHO CAN BENEFIT Endangered wild flora and fauna and their dependent species

WHERE FUNDING CAN BE GIVEN UK and overseas. Any area in which endangered mammals occur is considered

TYPE OF GRANT Direct grants to field projects

RANGE OF GRANTS £200–£20,000

FINANCES
- Year 1996
- Income £261,651
- Grants £219,473

Sheringham

TRUSTEES Sir Robert Clark, Anthony Athaide, Peter Giblin, David Gower, OBE, Avril Shepherd, David Shepherd, OBE, FRSA

PUBLICATIONS Bi-annual membership magazine *Wildlife Matters*

HOW TO APPLY In writing to the address below

WHO TO APPLY TO Melanie Shepherd, Director, The David Shepherd Conservation Foundation, 61 Smithbrook Kilns, Cranleigh, Surrey GU6 8JJ

CC NO 289646   **ESTABLISHED** 1984

■ Sheringham and District Preservation Society

WHAT IS FUNDED To promote high standards of planning and architecture; to preserve and develop features of historic interest and to stimulate public interest in the Parishes of Sheringham and Beeston Regis. Particularly environmental issues; landscapes and nature reserves

WHO CAN BENEFIT Individuals and organisations

WHERE FUNDING CAN BE GIVEN Sheringham and Beeston Regis

TYPE OF GRANT Buildings, capital and project

FINANCES
- Year 1996–97
- Income £4,192
- Grants £2,500

HOW TO APPLY In writing to the address below

WHO TO APPLY TO Joan Long, Sheringham and District Preservation Society, 5C Weybourne Road, Sheringham, Norfolk NR26 8HF
Tel 01263 824448

CC NO 280951   **ESTABLISHED** 1980

■ The Shetland Islands Council Charitable Trust (42)

WHAT IS FUNDED Endangered species; environmental issues; fauna; flora; nature reserves; wildlife parks; and wildlife sanctuaries

WHAT IS NOT FUNDED Funding is restricted to Shetland

WHO CAN BENEFIT Self-help organisations and voluntary organisations benefiting the inhabitants of Shetland

WHERE FUNDING CAN BE GIVEN Shetland

TYPE OF GRANT Project, one-off, capital, running and recurring costs, agricultural Ten Year Loan Scheme,

FINANCES
- Year 1997
- Income £10,102,000
- Grants £5,985,000

TRUSTEES R I Black, M U Colligan, J W Easten, C B Eunson, M L Flaws, J R Gear, A C Goodlad, F B Grains, B P Gregson, L G Groat, I Hawkins, L Hutchison, J C Irvine, R L Johnson, W H Manson (Chairman), G M McElvogue, P Malcolmson, J P Nicolson, W A Ratter, J H Scott, T H Scott, J L B Smith, L S Smith, L S Smith, W A Smith, I W Spence, W N Stove, W Tait (Vice-Chairman)

PUBLICATIONS Annual Report

NOTES The Trust has a policy of only accepting recommendations from the Shetland Islands Council, other applications will be not considered

HOW TO APPLY The Trust can be approached through either the appropriate council department or through one of the specialist trusts

WHO TO APPLY TO The Shetland Islands Council Charitable Trust, Breiwick House, 15 South Road, Lerwick, Shetland ZE1 0RB
Tel 01595 744681
Fax 01595 744667

SC NO SCO 27025   **ESTABLISHED** 1976

Commentary

The Shetland Islands Council Charitable Trust was founded in 1976 by the Shetland Islands Council to benefit Shetland and its inhabitants. The Trust has connections with five specialist trusts which it funds: (a) Shetland Amenity Trust; (b) Shetland Arts Trust; (c) Shetland Field Studies Trust; (d) Shetland Recreational Trust; and (e) Shetland Welfare Trust.

The Trust was set up to fund general charitable purposes, supporting the needs of the community it serves. There are only two limits within which the Trust must make grants – the purposes must be charitable and solely in the interests of Shetland and its inhabitants. However, the Trustees have a preference for (a) improving the quality of life for the inhabitants of Shetland, especially in the areas of social need, leisure, environment and education; (b) building on the energy and initiatives of local self-help groups, and assisting them to achieve their objectives, without destroying the independence and enterprise which brought them into being; (c) utilising the available funds in order to provide large scale facilities which would be of long-term benefit to the inhabitants of Shetland; (d) supporting traditional industries and assisting in the introduction of new ones, in ways where a charity and a trust might usefully assist, particularly in the areas of agriculture, fishing, knitwear and aquaculture; and (e) maintaining flexibility for the Trust's funds, in order to be able to meet new situations and priorities, but to do so against the background of a published framework of plans. All funding is provided solely for Shetland.

The Trust has not stated whether or not it has any scales of preference in it's funding policies; however, in 1997 the Trust gave 39 per cent of it's total grants to both Social Work and Community Services, 10 per cent to Policy and Resources, 7 per cent to Planning, 2 per cent to both Housing and Education, and 1 per cent to Environmental Services and Development.

The Trust was reconstituted in 1997, taking over much of the previous Trust's activities and all new projects. It is similarly constituted and has the same aims and objectives.

The Trust assists projects which are government grant maintained; an example of this is through the Agricultural Bridging Loan Scheme through which the Trust assists with projects which are grant-aided by the Scottish Office Agriculture and Fisheries Department. Projects which also qualify for co-funding are supported.

The Trust provides funding through a variety of methods including: one-off grants; running cost grants; and capital and building project grants. When the Trust is considering whether to contribute to any capital costs, the Trustees look beyond the initial construction phase, to a time when the project would be running, and in need of continued funding. Often the Trust will be asked not only for construction costs, but also for annual running costs. Farmers and crofters can benefit from the Agricultural Ten Year Loan Scheme, under the terms of which loans are repayable over a ten-year period. The Trust operates an Agricultural Bridging Loan Scheme (see above for details) where the grant is not paid until the project has been completed; and also provides hire purchase finance, loan and equity finance and provision of leasehold premises through subsidiary companies.

Applicants are requested to contact the Trust either through the relevant Council department or through one of the following specialist trusts, whichever route seems relevant to their needs: (a) Shetland Amenity Trust whose priorities are the protection, improvement and enhancement of buildings and artefacts of architectural, historical, educational or other interest; and the provision, development, and improvement of facilities for the enjoyment by the public of the Shetland countryside, and its flora and fauna. (b) Shetland Arts Trust whose priorities are the encouragement, stimulation and promotion of interest and participation in, and understanding of, artistic pursuits among the inhabitants of the Shetland Islands. (c) Shetland Field Studies Trust whose priorities are the promotion of the enjoyment and understanding of the human and natural history of Shetland; spreading knowledge of and concern for Shetland's natural species and habitats and helping in their long-term conservation; running and/or supporting a Field Studies Resource Centre and service; providing an educational service to schools, groups and individuals; and assisting in special projects and school projects. (d) Shetland Recreational Trust whose priorities are the provision, or assistance in the provision of, facilities in the interest of social welfare for recreation and leisure time occupation with the object of improving the condition of life for the inhabitants of the Shetland Islands. (e) Shetland Welfare Trust whose priorities are the provision of facilities in the interest of the welfare of the inhabitants of the Shetland Islands, with the objects of improving the condition of life for such inhabitants, and in particular to secure the establishment, maintenance and management of care centres in the Shetland Islands.

The Shetland Islands Council review the applications before the Trust receives them, generally preferring to give funds to groups rather than individuals, although individuals do receive grants in cases such as social work. Once allocated funds, projects are monitored by the Trust

SAMPLE GRANTS

The top ten grants given in 1997 were:
£1,948,419 to Clickimin Pool/Bowls Hall
£600,000 for a Christmas grant to pensioners (Social Welfare)
£451,543 to Independence at Home Scheme (Social Work)
£277,839 to Overtonlea Care Centre, Levenwick (Social Work)
£276,296 to Westview Care Centre, Walls (Social Work)
£272,803 to North Haven Care Centre, Brae (Social Work)
£253,496 to Femlea Care Centre, Whalsay (Social Work)
£212,568 to Shetland Amenity Trust Development Scheme (Planning)
£195,926 for Shetland Amenity Trust Administration (Planning)
£119,667 to Unst Leisure Centre (Community Services)

■ The Andre Simon Memorial Fund

WHAT IS FUNDED Agriculture will be considered to relieve famine and undernourishment in any part of the world. Also environmental issues

WHO CAN BENEFIT Individuals and institutions working in the areas outlined above

WHERE FUNDING CAN BE GIVEN UK and overseas

FINANCES
- Year 1995–96
- Income £9,793
- Grants £15,039

TRUSTEES J J Cotterell, J Avery, Lady Higgs, N Lander, M A Scheiderman

Skells

Alphabetical register of grant making trusts

NOTES Please note that, at the moment, the Trust's funds are committed to their established awards

HOW TO APPLY In writing to the address below

WHO TO APPLY TO Tessa Hayward, Secretary to the Trustees, The Andre Simon Memorial Fund, 5 Sion Hill Place, Lansdown, Bath BA1 5JJ

CC NO 265427   **ESTABLISHED** 1972

■ Bequest of Harry Skells

WHAT IS FUNDED Charities working in the fields of landscapes, nature reserves and woodlands

WHAT IS NOT FUNDED Generally no grants to individuals. No grants for running expenses or equipment

WHO CAN BENEFIT Local organisations

WHERE FUNDING CAN BE GIVEN Stamford

TYPE OF GRANT One-off grants given for approved projects. Funding may be given for up to three years

RANGE OF GRANTS £250–£20,000

FINANCES
- Year 1997–98
- Income £23,293
- Grants £14,111

TRUSTEES Stamford Town Council

HOW TO APPLY Application forms are available from the address under Who To Apply To

WHO TO APPLY TO Mrs M Paterson, Clerk, Bequest of Harry Skells, Town Hall, Stamford, Lincolnshire PE9 2DR
Tel 01780 753808

CC NO 239573   **ESTABLISHED** 1965

■ The Peter Smith Charitable Trust for Nature

WHAT IS FUNDED Although set up with wide charitable purposes, there is a concentration on nature including rural conservation and animal welfare

WHO CAN BENEFIT Organisations working in the areas outlined above

WHERE FUNDING CAN BE GIVEN UK

FINANCES
- Year 1996
- Income £5,085

HOW TO APPLY In writing to the address below

WHO TO APPLY TO P Smith, Secretary to the Trustees, The Peter Smith Charitable Trust for Nature, The Old Rectory, Hills End, Eversholt, Milton Keynes, Buckinghamshire MK17 9DR

CC NO 328458   **ESTABLISHED** 1990

■ The Leslie Smith Foundation

WHAT IS FUNDED Preference to charities in which the Trust has special interest, knowledge or association. Funding may be given for nature reserves

WHAT IS NOT FUNDED Registered charities. Applications from individuals are not normally eligible

WHO CAN BENEFIT Small, local charities

WHERE FUNDING CAN BE GIVEN UK

TYPE OF GRANT Capital, one-off, research and recurring costs. Funding is available for up to one year

RANGE OF GRANTS £1,000–£100,000, typical grant £3,000–£5,000

SAMPLE GRANTS £4,000 to Suffolk Wildlife Trust

FINANCES
- Year 1998
- Income £221,000
- Grants £130,000

TRUSTEES M D Willcox, Mrs E A Furtek

HOW TO APPLY At any time. Only successful appeals will be acknowledged

WHO TO APPLY TO M D Willcox, The Leslie Smith Foundation, The Old Coach House, Bergh Apton, Norwich, Norfolk NR15 1DD

CC NO 250030   **ESTABLISHED** 1964

■ The Martin Smith Foundation

WHAT IS FUNDED General charitable purposes which may include ecology or environmental issues

WHAT IS NOT FUNDED No grants for travel expenses

WHO CAN BENEFIT Individuals and organisations working in the areas outlined above

WHERE FUNDING CAN BE GIVEN UK

TYPE OF GRANT Capital, core costs, one-off, project, and research grants will be considered. Grants are typically one-off

RANGE OF GRANTS Typically £2,500

TRUSTEES E Buchanan, M MacFadyen, E B Smith, J Smith, K Smith, M G Smith

HOW TO APPLY Write to the Administrator with brief description of purpose of application and a form will be sent. Trustees meet once a quarter

WHO TO APPLY TO Mrs G Goodrich, The Martin Smith Foundation, PO Box 22507, London W8 7ZF

CC NO 1066587 **ESTABLISHED** 1997

■ Stanley Smith (UK) Horticultural Trust

WHAT IS FUNDED Grants are made to individual projects which involve the advancement of amenity horticulture and horticultural education. In the past assistance has been given to the creation, preservation and development of gardens to which the public is admitted, to the cultivation and wider distribution of plants derived by breeding or by collection from the wild, to research and to the publication of books with a direct bearing on horticulture

WHAT IS NOT FUNDED Grants are not made to individual students for fees, subsistence, etc relating to any academic or diploma course

WHO CAN BENEFIT Grants are made to individuals or to institutions benefiting students of botany and horticulture, as appropriate

WHERE FUNDING CAN BE GIVEN UK and overseas

TYPE OF GRANT Buildings, capital, core costs, feasibility studies, interest free loans, one-off, research and start-up costs. Grants are normally made as a contribution to cover the costs of identified projects. In exceptional cases grants are made over a three-year period

RANGE OF GRANTS £500–£2,000–£10,000

FINANCES
- Year 1997
- Income £142,439
- Grants £63,280

TRUSTEES C D Brickell, J J Dilger, J L Norton, Lady J Renfrew, J B E Simmons

HOW TO APPLY To the Director (address below). Applications are considered twice a year: spring (closing date for the receipt of applications 15 February) and autumn (closing date 15 August). Copies of annual accounts are generally required. Guidelines for applicants are available from the Director

WHO TO APPLY TO James Cullen, DSc, Director, Stanley Smith (UK) Horticultural Trust, Cory Lodge, PO Box 365, Cambridge CB2 1HR
Tel 01223 336299
Fax 01223 336278

CC NO 261925 **ESTABLISHED** 1970

■ South East Wales Community Foundation

WHAT IS FUNDED The promotion of any charitable purposes for the benefit of Mid and South Glamorgan and its immediate neighbourhood. Particularly voluntary groups working with environmental issues including: rural conservation; animal facilities and services; and environmental and animal sciences

WHAT IS NOT FUNDED No grants to individuals

WHO CAN BENEFIT Organisations working in the areas outlined above

WHERE FUNDING CAN BE GIVEN South East Wales

TYPE OF GRANT One-off, capital and start-up grants

RANGE OF GRANTS £50–£165,000

FINANCES
- Year 1997–98
- Income £567,701

TRUSTEES Keith Arnold, OBE, John Curteis, RD, DL, Jeff Lane, Charles Middleton, John Pathy, OBE, Don Ramsay, Andrew Reid, Tony Roberts, OBE, D Hugh Thomas, CBE, CStJ, DL, MA, R T John Tree, MBE, DL

PUBLICATIONS Brochure *Making More Out of Giving*

HOW TO APPLY Initial enquiries by telephone or letter. Application forms and guidelines available. No deadline. Sae not required

WHO TO APPLY TO Irene John, South East Wales Community Foundation, 14–16 Merthyr Road, Whitchurch, Cardiff CF4 1DG
Tel 01222 520250
Fax 01222 521250

CC NO 519795 **ESTABLISHED** 1987

■ South Square Trust

WHAT IS FUNDED Registered charities working in the fields of: rural conservation; animal welfare; bird sanctuaries; dogs, kennels and other facilities for dogs; wildlife sanctuaries; and animal breeding

WHAT IS NOT FUNDED No grants made for expeditions and travel bursaries. No courses outside the UK will be funded

WHO CAN BENEFIT Registered charities working in the areas outlined above

WHERE FUNDING CAN BE GIVEN UK

TYPE OF GRANT Buildings, capital, core costs, project and research will be considered. Funding may be given for one year or less

RANGE OF GRANTS £100–£1,000

FINANCES
- Year 1996–97
- Income £188,264
- Grants £222,000

TRUSTEES C R Ponter, A E Woodall, W P Harriman, C P Grimwade, D B Inglis

HOW TO APPLY Charities apply by letter, enclosing accounts. General donations considered three times a year

WHO TO APPLY TO Mrs N Chrimes, Clerk to the Trustees, South Square Trust, PO Box 67, Heathfield, East Sussex TN21 9ZR
Tel 01435 830778
Fax 01435 830778

CC NO 278960   **ESTABLISHED** 1979

■ W W Spooner Charitable Trust

WHAT IS FUNDED The Trustees invite appeals which broadly fall within the following selected field: the countryside – protection and preservation of the environment including rescue and similar services

WHAT IS NOT FUNDED No grants for high profile appeals seeking large sums, most donations made are less than £500

WHO CAN BENEFIT Preference for local activities

WHERE FUNDING CAN BE GIVEN The County of Yorkshire

TYPE OF GRANT Recurring annual donations to a hard core list of charities. One-off response to 25–30 single appeals

RANGE OF GRANTS £200–£2,000, average £200–£500

FINANCES
- Year 1997
- Income £60,004
- Grants £52,400

TRUSTEES M H Broughton, Sir James F Hill, Bt, T J P Ramsden, R Ibbotson, J H Wright, Mrs J M McKiddie

NOTES Preference given to Yorkshire-based appeals

HOW TO APPLY By letter to the address under Who To Apply To

WHO TO APPLY TO Messrs Addleshaw Booth & Co, W W Spooner Charitable Trust, Sovereign House, PO Box 8, Sovereign Street, Leeds LS1 1HQ

CC NO 313653   **ESTABLISHED** 1961

■ Stanhope-Palmer Charity

WHAT IS FUNDED Charities working in the field of rural conservation

WHAT IS NOT FUNDED No grants to individuals

WHO CAN BENEFIT Registered UK charities working in the areas outlined above

WHERE FUNDING CAN BE GIVEN UK and overseas

TYPE OF GRANT One-off, core costs and research grants will be considered. Funding may be given for up to three years

RANGE OF GRANTS £250–£15000

FINANCES
- Year 1998
- Income £18,236
- Grants £27,675

TRUSTEES Stanhope-Palmer Charity Trustees Ltd

HOW TO APPLY Please include latest Annual Report and Accounts with application

WHO TO APPLY TO A B V Hughes, Stanhope-Palmer Charity, 27–56 Vincent Square, London SW1P 2NE
Tel 0171-834 0403

CC NO 326447   **ESTABLISHED** 1983

■ Staples Trust (259)

WHAT IS FUNDED Rural conservation

WHAT IS NOT FUNDED No grants to individuals, for expeditions or scholarships. Funding is not given for animal welfare

WHO CAN BENEFIT Environmental organisations

WHERE FUNDING CAN BE GIVEN UK and overseas

TYPE OF GRANT One-off and recurring for up to three years

FINANCES
- Year 1997
- Income £500,460
- Grants £613,001

TRUSTEES Miss J M Sainsbury, A J Sainsbury, T J Sainsbury, Miss J S Portrait, P Frankopan

NOTES Please note that the Trust is not seeking further applications for rural conservation. Their limited grantmaking in this area is pro-active, not reactive

HOW TO APPLY In writing, but unsolicited applications are rarely successful. All applications are acknowledged. Guidelines are not issued by the Trust

WHO TO APPLY TO M A Pattison, The Staples Trust, 6 Red Lion Court, London EC4A 3EB
Tel 0171-410 0330

CC NO 1010656   **ESTABLISHED** 1992

Commentary

The Staples Trust was established by a Trust Deed in March 1992, making it one of the most recently formed of the group of charities known collectively as the Sainsbury Family Charitable Trusts. Each of the Sainsbury Family Charitable Trusts represents an area in which the settlor felt that they could make a particular impact and, although the Trust was set up with general charitable objectives, it applies itself in a few areas of concentration. There is an interest in innovation and experiment common to the majority of the Sainsbury Family Trusts, with the Trustees keen to support schemes that can be replicated successfully or become self-sustaining.

The foremost of the Trust's areas of concentration is in Overseas Development, for which the Trust made grants totalling £296,576 in 1997. Funding in this category covers a wide range of activities, especially: income generation projects, with a particular emphasis on the empowerment of women; shelter and housing; sustainable agriculture and forestry; and the rights of indigenous people. The Trustees are particularly interested in supporting development projects in East and South Africa, South and South East Asia, and South America which take account of environmental sustainability. In many cases, the environmental and developmental benefits of the projects are of equal importance. It is no surprise then, that the second largest area of concentration of the Trust is Environmental Issues, for which grants totalling £133,324 were made in 1997. Funding is given for renewable energy technology, training and skills upgrading, and occasionally research. Projects are supported in: (a) Central and Eastern Europe, where the Trustees are interested in providing training opportunities for community/business leaders and policy makers and in contributing to the process of skill sharing and information exchange; and (b) the UK, where Trustees aim to help communities protect, maintain and improve areas of land and to support work aimed at improving rural conservation policy. The other main area of concentration is Women's Issues. Within this scheme the Trustees remain interested in domestic violence issues, particularly the promotion of inter-agency co-operation. To a lesser extent the Trustees will support local refuge services, women's self-help groups and organisations working with women offenders or ex-offenders with specific problems (including mental illness). There is also a General category of grant making which is able to support other charitable causes, which is often accomplished through the other Sainsbury Family Charitable Trusts. These grant making policies have not changed in recent years and no major changes are expected in the near future. The Trust does not replace statutory responsibility, nor will it fund in areas where there is corporate sponsorship or local funding available. The Trust does not generally become involved in organised partnership funding, although it may where there is a particular interest and personal knowledge or experience.

It is worth noting that the Sainsbury Family Charitable Trusts have a major policy in common – that most of them make few responses to unsolicited applications because they have Trustees who take a very pro-active stance and go out and find their own causes. In these cases the Trustees are often advised by consultants with relevant expertise. Unsolicited applications are discouraged and are unlikely to be successful, even if they fall within one of the above areas of interest. Grants are generally project based and may therefore be made over a number of years. Loans are not made, although some support can be given for infrastructure costs. Grants are not made to individuals.

The Trustees request progress reports from those who have received grants and also arrange periodic reviews of their major programmes, but do not have an assessment process whereby all organisations are visited

SAMPLE GRANTS

The top ten grants given in 1997 were:
£46,067 to African Medical and Research Foundation (AMREF) over three years towards the extension of an income-generation, health and family planning project in Kitui District, Eastern Province, Kenya
£40,000 to World Wide Fund for Nature (WWF) towards their work in gazetting and protecting the sacred coastal forests in Kwale and Kilifi, Kenya by developing workable programmes to prevent over-exploitation
£34,654 to CARE towards the Sanitation and Family Resource Project to support local Bangladeshi non-governmental organisations to implement high-quality hygiene education programmes
£33,551 to ActionAid towards a rural development programme in Cayambe, Equador
£33,000 to Population Concern for the Mobile Healthcare Services Unit project to provide family planning advice and education to rural populations in Bhopal, Gwalior, Kanpur and Madurai, India
£30,000 to Female Prisoners Welfare project over three years towards core costs
£30,000 to Women in Special Hospitals (WISH) over three years towards core costs
£25,000 to London Action Trust over two years towards the cost of employing a London co-ordinator for domestic violence issues
£23,464 to United Nations Association International Service over two years towards the costs of an agro-ecologist working to introduce appropriate technologies to the Gourma Province, South Burkina Faso
£22,750 to Plan International towards the

cost of energy conservation/agro-forestry training and materials in Kenya

■ The Hugh Stenhouse Foundation

WHAT IS FUNDED Nature reserves; woodlands; and bird sanctuaries

WHAT IS NOT FUNDED No grants for expeditions, etc

WHO CAN BENEFIT Organisations working in the areas outlined above

WHERE FUNDING CAN BE GIVEN West of Scotland

TYPE OF GRANT Recurring, one-off and core costs. Funding is available for more than three years

RANGE OF GRANTS £50–£24,000, typical grant £750

FINANCES
- Year 1997–98
- Income £28,500
- Grants £25,000

TRUSTEES Mrs P R H Irvine Robertson, M R L Stenhouse, P H A Stenhouse, R G T Stenhouse, Mrs R C L Stewart

HOW TO APPLY Applications should be made in writing to the address under Who To Apply To

WHO TO APPLY TO P D Bowman, Secretary and Treasurer, The Hugh Stenhouse Foundation, Lomynd, Knockbuckle Road, Kilmalcolm PA13 4JT
Tel 01505 872716

CC NO CR 40289   **ESTABLISHED** 1968

■ Will Trust of Edgar John Henry Stephenson (Deceased)

WHAT IS FUNDED Wildlife charities

WHAT IS NOT FUNDED No grants to individuals

WHO CAN BENEFIT Registered charities only, either national organisations or organisations local to Hampshire and Dorset

WHERE FUNDING CAN BE GIVEN UK, especially Hampshire and Dorset

RANGE OF GRANTS £5–£6,000

FINANCES
- Year 1996–97
- Income £33,786
- Grants £45,368

TRUSTEES A M B Butterworth, M T James

HOW TO APPLY To the address under Who To Apply To in writing

WHO TO APPLY TO A M B Butterworth, Will Trust of Edgar John Henry Stephenson, 48 High Street, Lymington, Hampshire SO41 9ZQ

CC NO 295065   **ESTABLISHED** 1985

■ The June Stevens Foundation

WHAT IS FUNDED Trustees have a particular interest in animals

WHAT IS NOT FUNDED Grants normally not paid to individuals

WHO CAN BENEFIT Charitable organisations benefiting animals

WHERE FUNDING CAN BE GIVEN UK, but with preference for Gloucestershire

TYPE OF GRANT At Trustees' discretion

RANGE OF GRANTS £200–£1,000

SAMPLE GRANTS £1,500 to National Canine Defence League
£1,500 to Brooke Hospital for Animals
£1,500 to Greek Animal Welfare Fund
£1,000 to World Society for Protection of Animals

FINANCES
- Year 1997–98
- Income £21,000
- Grants £21,800

TRUSTEES J D Stevens, A J Quinton, A R St C Tahourdin

HOW TO APPLY No formal applications procedure. Applications considered bi-annually, usually in June/July and November/December. Applications are not normally acknowledged

WHO TO APPLY TO A Tahourdin, The June Stevens Foundation, 13 Bedford Row, London WC1R 4BU

CC NO 327829   **ESTABLISHED** 1988

■ The Summerfield Charitable Trust (406)

WHAT IS FUNDED Environmental issues; landscapes; nature reserves; waterways; woodlands; agriculture; ecology; and organic food production. Causes in Gloucestershire attract the most attention: applicants from outside the county, where they are successful, are only likely to receive relatively small grants. Viewed especially favourably are: the needs of those living in rural areas; ventures which make a point of using volunteers (and which train volunteers); applicants who show clear indications that they have assessed the impact of their project upon the environment; joint appeals from groups working in similar areas, who wish to develop a partnership; and those who have a conscientious objection to applying for National Lottery funding. The

Summerfield

Trustees particularly welcome innovative ideas from small, voluntary groups

WHAT IS NOT FUNDED Donations are not usually given to: medical research; London-based projects; national charities, where the Trust has already supported a local branch; organisations working outside the UK; private education; animal welfare appeals; holiday appeals or students wishing to go abroad

WHO CAN BENEFIT Charities local to Gloucestershire. Private organisations and individuals are only very rarely supported, students being more likely to find favour than those with other needs. In any event, the Trustees urge individuals to use a specialist charity to sponsor their application

WHERE FUNDING CAN BE GIVEN It is increasingly rare for applicants outside Gloucestershire to receive a grant

TYPE OF GRANT Usually one-off. The Trustees prefer to award one-off grants to help fund specific projects rather than to make payments for revenue items. The Trustees will also consider start-up costs and grants for up to three years

RANGE OF GRANTS Average grant £2,000–£5,000

FINANCES
- Year 1997
- Income £341,341
- Grants £331,670

TRUSTEES Martin Davis, The Earl Fortescue, Dr The Hon Gilbert Greenall, Mrs Rosaleen Kaye, Mrs Rachel Managhan

HOW TO APPLY The Trustees meet quarterly, usually in January, April, July and October to consider all applications received prior to the end of the preceding month. Applicants should write to the administrator, Mrs Lavina Sidgwick, stating in their own words what is required, the purpose of the application, and giving a financial summary, including latest accounts, and a registered charity number. Further, it should state if and when the applicant has previously applied to the Trust. Applicants are asked to fill in an environmental questionnaire. It also helps if grantseekers say which other trusts they are approaching: they may be consulted (or members of an informal panel of advisers to the Trust) about any application received, unless applicants write to the Trust to request them not to do so. Applicants are informed of the Trustees' decisions as soon as possible after their meetings. All new applications are acknowledged; stamped addressed envelopes are welcomed

WHO TO APPLY TO Mrs Lavinia Sidgwick, Administrator, The Summerfield Charitable Trust, PO Box 4, Winchcombe, Cheltenham, Gloucestershire GL54 5ZD
Tel 01242 676774
Fax 01242 677120
E-mail admin@summerfield.org.uk
Web Site http://www.summerfield.org.uk

CC NO 802493   **ESTABLISHED** 1989

Commentary

The Summerfield Charitable Trust was established by the late Ronald Summerfield, a Cheltenham antique dealer, shortly before his death in 1989, for general charitable purposes. The Trustees have total discretion as to which charitable uses to apply the funds, but the three main areas that are supported are the elderly, the needy and the arts, all within the Gloucestershire area. Grants made fall into 11 categories: arts; churches, cathedrals, etc; conservation and environment; counselling; disabled, chronically sick; education; elderly; homeless; museums: recreation, community work and sport; and youth. Education receives approximately 16 per cent of the total grants made in 1997, which means it received the largest proportion of funding in that year. Within these broad headings, certain projects are particularly favoured. Viewed especially favourably are: the needs of those living in rural areas; ventures which make a point of using volunteers (and which train volunteers); applicants who show clear indications that they have assessed the impact of their project upon the environment; joint appeals from groups working in similar areas, who wish to develop a partnership; and those who have a conscientious objection to applying for National Lottery funding. The Trustees particularly welcome innovative ideas from small, voluntary groups. Funding policy is decided on by the Trustees, who have absolute discretion in this matter.

Applications from outside the Gloucestershire area are rarely successful, and if they do succeed, the grants awarded are usually very small. This reflects the fact that the Fund is very keen to support community work in the area in which the Founder lived.

The Fund funds statutory bodies in the sense that it will provide grants to schools, etc, but it prefers not to replace statutory funding. The Fund is not inflexible in this matter, because it likes to consider every project on its own merit, so it might be prepared to meet a shortfall in some statutory funding for a project, but this is not a hard and fast rule.

In general the Trustees prefer to award one-off grants to help fund specific projects, rather than to make payments for revenue items, but they are prepared to make particular one year or short-term grants to fund start-up salaries in promising local projects. Infrastructure costs may also be met. Loans are no longer made. Grants generally range between £500 and £5,000.

Summerfield

The Trustees meet quarterly, usually in January, April, July and October to consider all applications received prior to the end of the preceding month. Applicants should write to the Administrator, stating in their own words what is required, the purpose of the application, and giving a financial summary and a registered charity number. Furthermore, it should state if and when the applicant has previously applied to the Fund. It also helps if grantseekers say which other trusts they are approaching: these other trusts or members of an informal panel of advisers may be consulted about any application received, unless applicants write to the Trust to request them not to do so. Applicants are informed of the Trustees' decisions as soon as possible after their meetings. All new applications are acknowledged.

Applications are assessed according to the funding preferences of the Trust and approximately half of the total number of applications considered are visited by the Fund: either by the Administrator or one of 30 advisers to the Trust. Recipients are also visited, particularly if they receive a recurrent grant

SAMPLE GRANTS

The top ten grants made in 1997 were:
£16,000 to Forum for the Future for their work in identifying, developing and sharing solutions to today's environmental problems and galvanising progress towards a sustainable way of life: £7,500 for scholar's fees, £7,500 for Cheltenham Observatory for Sustainable Rural Initiatives and £1,000 for legal advice
£15,000 to Gloucestershire Historic Churches Trust as the last instalment of a £45,000 grant, so that Summerfield Trust can refer relevant applicants to them
£12,100 to Axiom Arts Centre: £10,000 for the first year salary of an education officer and £2,100 towards the purchase of office equipment
£12,000 to Everyman Theatre for its programme of arts initiatives for young people
£11,000 to Gloucester Dance Project for: Attic Dance Residency workshops in elderly residential homes; a training course for those who work with people with limited physical movement; and the Integrated Primary Project for developing dance activities in two primary schools, one of which has children with special needs
£10,000 to Gloucester Emergency Accommodation Resource as the last part of a three year commitment to help with running costs
£10,000 to Gloucestershire Resource Centre as a one-off grant towards the salary of a recently appointed development officer
£8,500 to Cheltenham and Gloucester College Development Trust Ltd: £7,500 as last instalment of a grant towards the salary of a lecturer in the 'Ethics of Imaging'; and £1,000 for Summerfield Rome Scholarship
£8,000 to Cheltenham Arts Festivals Ltd: £2,500 for Music Festival's access scheme; £5,000 for Literature Festival's education work and Summerfield Lecture; and £500 for an interpreter for the deaf
£6,000 to Cheltenham Open Door towards the refurbishment of its premises used for the provision of welfare services to the homeless

■ The Bernard Sunley Charitable Foundation (87)

WHAT IS FUNDED Endangered species; environmental issues; fauna and flora; nature reserves; waterways; woodlands; animal homes and welfare; and horses, stables and other facilities for horses. Also agriculture; animal breeding; botany; ecology; horticulture; and natural history

WHAT IS NOT FUNDED Registered charities only. No grants to individuals

WHO CAN BENEFIT Registered charities working in the areas outlined above

WHERE FUNDING CAN BE GIVEN Primarily UK, exceptionally overseas

TYPE OF GRANT One-off, capital and recurring, for up to a maximum of five years

RANGE OF GRANTS £100–£1,000,000; typical grant £5,000–£10,000

FINANCES
- Year 1998
- Income £3,576,000
- Grants £2,772,000

TRUSTEES John B Sunley, Mrs Joan M Tice, Mrs Bella Sunley, Sir Donald Gosling

HOW TO APPLY Applications in writing may be submitted at any time with a copy of the latest accounts. Unsolicited applications will not be acknowledged

WHO TO APPLY TO Duncan C Macdiarmid, CA, Director, The Bernard Sunley Charitable Foundation, 53 Grosvenor Street, London W1X 9FH

CC NO 213362   **ESTABLISHED** 1960

Commentary

The Bernard Sunley Charitable Foundation was set up in 1960 by Bernard Sunley using a parcel of shares from the Bernard Sunley Investment Trust valued at £400,000. When Bernard Sunley died in 1964 he left more shares to the Foundation in his Will. Soon after this the Investment Trust was taken over by Eagle Star Insurance who converted the shares into high interest loan notes. In 1979 Eagle Star was acquired by British American Tobacco and the loan notes were realised for cash, which was then spread widely in investments. At present the assets stand at £60 million.

The Trust deed is extremely broadly drawn, with the Foundation able to support any charitable cause worldwide. In practice though, recipients tend to be UK-based operational charities, though still right across the board.

The Foundation has always given a high proportion of its grants in four main areas: education, including schools, colleges and universities; medicine, including hospitals, medical schools, research institutes and care services; youth, including all manner of youth organisations; community aid and recreation, from helping the homeless and deprived, to drug rehabilitation and the support of community centres. The Foundation tends to place a regular and equal emphasis on the amounts it gives annually to the above categories, with each of the above receiving approximately 20 per cent of the grants total.

Outside of these main areas the Foundation has also funded churches, chapels and organisations concerned with wildlife, the elderly, the arts and museums, and service charities. No grants are ever made to individuals.

In most years, this wide range of grants can number over 300. In practice, the smallest grants given can be as little as £100, while the largest may be up to £1 million (however, this would be over a period of some years). The maximum time period for recurring grants would be likely to be only five years. Small annual grants are reviewed every year.

The Foundation has, in the past, involved itself in co-funding and has especially favoured community projects. It is also happy to co-fund on lottery backed projects. However, grants of this type are held ready for distribution until confirmation is received of the other funders' commitment. The Trustees will not replace statutory funding, or give capital funding unless they can be sure that revenue will continue after their initial involvement. They will not give funding for core and revenue costs. The Foundation does not consider giving loans instead of grants.

The process for deciding which applications are successful is relatively simple. There is initially a sorting through to get rid of unsuitable applications and those applications in an area of funding already heavily committed to in that year. Those asking for an unreasonably large amount will also be unsuccessful. The success of applications also depends heavily on their quality. Applications should be in writing to the Director, supported by a copy of the latest audited or independently examined accounts and the latest Annual Report. Applications should include the following details: what the charity is, what it does and what its objectives are; the project, what need there is for it and its purpose, who it will benefit and how; how much the project will cost and what size grant is requested; how much has already been raised and from whom; how the applicant will raise the shortfall; if applicable, how the on-going running costs of the project will be met once the project is established; and any other documentation that the applicant feels will support or explain their case.

Only successful applications are acknowledged, and an initial phone call to find out whether the Foundation is willing to fund in your particular area is welcome. The Foundation is keen to get the message across that they need sufficient time to consider grants, and that sending in an application, even a good one, a week before you need the money is of no use to anyone. The Trustees meet three times a year, generally in May, October and January/February – these dates may vary, however, as some of the Trustees live overseas. Applications must be received at least three to four weeks before the Trustees meet.

The Foundation has no formal grant-monitoring procedures, relying largely upon the grant recipient keeping the Foundation informed. A close eye is kept, however, on larger grants, especially if they are given in instalments. The Foundation has only three full-time members of staff, and so cannot actively seek projects to support, having to rely on unsolicited applications or upon Trustee-originated intelligence. By the same token the Foundation does not have the manpower to monitor all of its grants. The accounts of organisations which send in applications are very closely examined and are viewed more favourably if they are up-to-date

SAMPLE GRANTS

The top ten grants given in 1998 were:
£200,000 to the Purcell School
£125,000 to the National Council of the YMCA for their 150th Anniversary Homeless Appeal
£115,000 to McIntyre Housing Association, Herefordshire
£100,000 to Caldecott Community
£100,000 to the Almshouse Association
£100,000 to Barnardo's South City Project, Liverpool
£100,000 to Netherdall Educational Association, London
£100,000 to Extra Care Charitable Trust, Coventry
£60,000 to the National Gallery, London
£50,000 to Macmillan Cancer Relief, Guildford

■The Sutton Coldfield Municipal Charities (176)

WHAT IS FUNDED Rural conservation; animal facilities and services; and animal sciences in the former Borough of Sutton Coldfield

WHAT IS NOT FUNDED Grants are restricted to the former Borough of Sutton Coldfield

Sutton

WHO CAN BENEFIT Organisations working in the areas outlined above

WHERE FUNDING CAN BE GIVEN Sutton Coldfield

TYPE OF GRANT Buildings, capital, one-off and project. Funding may be given for up to three years

FINANCES
- Year 1998
- Income £1,237,661
- Grants £986,788

TRUSTEES S L Bailey, BEd, Dr N F D Cooper (Vice Chairman), Col A Fender, TD, DL, B K Fitton, FCA, J W Gray (Chairman), Cllr Suzanna McCorry, MSoc, BA, DipCM, J M Millington, A D Owen, OBE, MA(Cantab), Hon D.Sc(Aston), Cllr D C Roy, DMS, J Slater, Cllr J E Whorwood, MSc, CEng, MIEE, Cllr A York, BA, MEd

PUBLICATIONS Report and Financial Statement

NOTES The Sutton Coldfield Municipal Charities consists of: the General Charity and the Charity of Thomas Jesson for Apprenticing

WHO TO APPLY TO D J E Field, The Sutton Coldfield Municipal Charities, Lingard House, Fox Hollies Road, Sutton Coldfield B67 2RJ
Tel 0121-351 2262
Fax 0121-313 0651

CC NO 218627   **ESTABLISHED** 1898

Commentary

In 1528 John Harman, who was also known as Bishop Vesey, obtained a Charter for a Royal Town for Sutton Coldfield; this established a governing unit called the Warden and Society. Around the same time, John Harman donated some land for charitable purposes, and in 1831 more land was gained following the Enclosure Act. When Sutton Coldfield became a Borough in 1886 the elected Council replaced the Society, and later, in 1898, the Sutton Coldfield Municipal Charities were established. Today, the Municipal Charities consist of the General Charity and the Charity of Thomas Jesson for Apprenticing.

The Charities' objectives are the provision of almshouses, the distribution of funds and additional measures to alleviate poverty, and any additional needs of the inhabitants and organisations in the former Borough of Sutton Coldfield. There are no scales of preference and each application is considered on its merits. From recommendations made by the grants committee, funding policies are set by the Board and these are reviewed annually. The distribution of funds for community and individual purposes is calculated annually through the deduction of the estimated expenditure of running the almshouses; school clothing grants; grant support costs and other administrative costs. Reserve funds are held by the Trustees for any urgent requests. In addition, the extraordinary repair fund holds funds for major repairs, improvements or rebuilding of almshouses or other properties. Funding can only be given in the former Borough of Sutton Coldfield.

The governing scheme limits the extent to which the Charities can make grants where statutory funding should be responsible, although donations have been made to schools and hospitals. Grants have been made to organisations, providing them with the minimum sum required to apply for a Lottery Board award, although these are conditional on the application being successful.

Grants are not usually made for revenue funding and are not recurrent. However, there have been exceptions to this; for example, a grant was made to the Citizens Advice Bureau to enable them to establish two pilot projects with the grant specifically being used to pay salaries over a two-year period.

Application forms are available for personal grants and all applicants are visited. Similarly for students and those requesting sponsorship, application forms should be filled in; applicants are then required to attend an interview at the office. Groups have the opportunity to discuss their proposals with a member of staff and receive guidance about the information that is to be included in the final written appeal, as there are no formal application forms for group requests. When these procedures have been completed, a brief report is sent to the Grants Committee who meet nine times each year and a member of staff is available to respond to any queries. On the strength of the information provided, a decision is made. Any amount exceeding £20,000 must be ratified at a full Board meeting which are held on a quarterly basis.

Following the distribution of funds, the Charities maintain personal contact with recipients; it is not unusual for a member of the Charities to visit a project. Grants are rarely made in cash or cheques as the Charities prefer to address invoices or reimburse on sight of a receipt to ensure the grant is spent appropriately. Also, clothing grants are distributed by way of vouchers which are accepted at local stores

SAMPLE GRANTS
The top ten grants given in 1998 were:
£200,000 to Greenacres Cheshire Home
£90,000 to Paintsbrook School
£50,000 to Church of the Scared Heart of Jesus
£50,000 to Four Oaks Baptist Church
£50,000 to St Giles Hospice
£44,000 to St Peter's Church, Maney
£30,000 to Acorns Hospice
£28,000 to Emmanuel Parish Church, Wylde Green

£28,000 to St Nicholas' RC Church, Boldmere
£25,000 to Sutton Sailing Club

■The Swann-Morton Foundation

WHAT IS FUNDED Conservation and environment, and other charitable purposes

WHAT IS NOT FUNDED No grants are given for payment of household costs

WHO CAN BENEFIT Individuals and organisations working in the areas outlined above

WHERE FUNDING CAN BE GIVEN UK

RANGE OF GRANTS £50–£4,000. Average £750

FINANCES
- Year 1997
- Grants £68,381
- Income £66,364

TRUSTEES R Fell, M J McGinley, P B A Renshaw

HOW TO APPLY Applications in writing only to the address under Who To Apply To

WHO TO APPLY TO R Fell, Swann-Morton Foundation, Owlerton Green, Sheffield S6 2BJ
Tel 0114-234 4231
Fax 0114-231 4966

CC NO 271925   **ESTABLISHED** 1976

■The Charles Sykes Trust
(417) (known as The Charles and Elsie Sykes Trust)

WHAT IS FUNDED Animals and birds; and rural conservation

WHAT IS NOT FUNDED No grants to individuals or for their benefit. Preference for north of the country

WHO CAN BENEFIT Registered charities only

WHERE FUNDING CAN BE GIVEN Preference for North of England, occasionally overseas

TYPE OF GRANT Donations in cash, usually one-off for a specific project or part thereof. Also buildings, capital, core costs, feasibility studies, research, recurring and running costs, and start-up costs. Funding is given for one year or less. If on annual list, there is a requirement to submit accounts and report annually

RANGE OF GRANTS £250–£30,000. Typical size £1,000

FINANCES
- Year 1997
- Grants £313,115
- Income £434,890

TRUSTEES John Horrocks (Chairman), Mrs Anne E Brownlie, Mrs G Mary Dance, Michael G H Garnett, Dr M McEvoy, Dr Michael D Moore, John Ward

HOW TO APPLY To the Secretary in writing, with full details and audited or examined accounts. Acknowledgements given if sae supplied. No guidelines issued

WHO TO APPLY TO David J Reah, Secretary, The Charles Sykes Trust, 6 North Park Road, Harrogate, North Yorkshire HG1 5PA

CC NO 206926   **ESTABLISHED** 1954

Commentary

The Charles Sykes Trust was established in 1954 by an endowment. The Trust is also known as The Charles and Elsie Sykes Trust. The stated objects of the Trust are general charitable giving. However, donations are given in the following areas: animals and birds (which received 0.17 per cent of the Trust's donations in 1998); blind and partially sighted (4.62 per cent); children and youth (7.65 per cent); cultural and environmental heritage (15.19 per cent); deaf, hard of hearing and speech impaired (2.38 per cent); disabled and physically handicapped (4.93 per cent); education (0.58 per cent); hospices and hospitals (18.62 per cent); medical research (11.58 per cent); medical welfare (2.41 per cent); mental health and mentally handicapped (9.43 per cent); old people's welfare (2.05 per cent); overseas aid (5.72 per cent); services and ex-service (0.61 per cent); social and moral welfare (13.16 per cent); and trades and professions (0.90 per cent). There is an established list of organisations to whom the Trust gives regular annual donations, on receipt of satisfactory annual accounts, but provision is also made for special, ie one-off, grants. During 1998 a total of £324,600 special donations were given, ranging in size from £250 to £30,000, to a varied list of 128 organisations representing a wide area of interests. Funding will be given only to registered charities – individuals will not be considered.

Organisations throughout the UK can apply but the North of England is favoured for local projects. The co-funding of projects is not ruled out. Continuous funding in the form of annual donations and one-off payments for special projects are the types of support that the Trust favours. Loans are not considered. It was not apparent whether infrastructure costs would be funded.

Applicants should submit brief details of their project together with a copy of the organisation's most recent accounts. An sae will guarantee a reply. Telephone calls are not welcome.

Trustees meet periodically in subcommittees to advise the board on annual as well as special, or one-off, donations. There is no formal assessment procedure but Trustees may visit an organisation if they feel it would be beneficial to their decision-making process

Sylvanus

Alphabetical register of grant making trusts

SAMPLE GRANTS
The top ten grants made in 1998 were:
£30,000 to Yorkshire Dales Millennium Trust
£25,000 to Claro Enterprises, Harrogate
£25,000 to Royal Northern College of Music
£22,150 to Harrogate Health Care Cardiac Review
£20,500 to British Red Cross, re Central American Hurricane
£20,000 to Marie Curie Cancer Care, Bradford
£10,000 to Harrogate International Festival Ltd
£10,000 to Mencap Yorkshire Blue Sky Appeal
£10,000 to St Michael's Hospice, Harrogate
£10,000 to The Macmillan Harrogate and District Appeal

■ The Sylvanus Charitable Trust

WHAT IS FUNDED   Animal welfare, including wildlife sanctuaries

WHAT IS NOT FUNDED   The Trust does not give grants to expeditions, scholarships or individuals

WHO CAN BENEFIT   Organisation working in the areas outlined above

WHERE FUNDING CAN BE GIVEN   Overseas

TYPE OF GRANT   One-off and recurring

FINANCES
- Year 1997
- Income £63,000
- Grants £68,000

TRUSTEES   J C Vernor Miles, A D Gemmill

NOTES   The income of this Trust is normally fully committed

WHO TO APPLY TO   J C Vernor Miles, The Sylvanus Charitable Trust, Vernor Miles & Noble, 5 Raymond Buildings, Grays Inn, London WC1R 5DD

CC NO 259520   **ESTABLISHED** 1968

■ The Stella Symons Charitable Trust

WHAT IS FUNDED   To provide assistance to organisations operating in fields where specific identifiable needs can be shown and which are in the opinion of the Trustees not adequately catered for or likely to have large scale popular appeal. Charities working in the fields of: rural conservation; animal facilities and services; and environmental and animal sciences

WHAT IS NOT FUNDED   The Trustees do not normally favour projects which substitute the statutory obligations of the state or projects which in their opinion should be commercially viable operations per se. No grants to individuals or politically biased organisations

WHO CAN BENEFIT   Organisations working in the areas outlined above

WHERE FUNDING CAN BE GIVEN   UK and international projects with some funds reserved for projects and organisations local to Shipston on Stour

TYPE OF GRANT   Outright gifts and larger sums on loan on beneficial terms. Capital, core costs, feasibility studies, one-off, project, research, recurring and running costs, salaries, and start-up costs. Funding may be given for one year or less

RANGE OF GRANTS   £10–£5,000, average grant £200

FINANCES
- Year 1997
- Income £54,518
- Grants £55,600

TRUSTEES   M E Bosley, J S S Bosley, K A Willis

NOTES   The Trustees will consider all applications submitted but regrettably will not be able to support all that they might wish to

HOW TO APPLY   By post to address under Who To Apply To with no follow-up, please

WHO TO APPLY TO   J S S Bosley, The Stella Symons Charitable Trust, 20 Mill Street, Shipston on Stour, Warwickshire CV36 4AW

CC NO 259638   **ESTABLISHED** 1968

The Elsie Talbot Bridge Will Trust

WHAT IS FUNDED Rural conservation; animal facilities and services; and animal sciences

WHAT IS NOT FUNDED No grants to individuals. No grants for expeditions or scholarships

WHO CAN BENEFIT Local and regional organisations

WHERE FUNDING CAN BE GIVEN Sefton area only

TYPE OF GRANT One-off, buildings, capital and research. Funding is given for one year or less

RANGE OF GRANTS Smallest £50; normally £500–£1,000; largest £1,500

FINANCES
- Year 1996
- Income £20,145

TRUSTEES D T Bushell, J Kewley

HOW TO APPLY To the Trustees in writing at the address below

WHO TO APPLY TO The Elsie Talbot Bridge Will Trust, 11 St George's Place, Lord Street, Southport, Lancashire PR9 0AL

CC NO 279288   **ESTABLISHED** 1961

The Tay Charitable Trust

WHAT IS FUNDED Rural conservation

WHAT IS NOT FUNDED No grants to individuals

WHO CAN BENEFIT Registered charities only

WHERE FUNDING CAN BE GIVEN UK, particularly Scotland, with a preference for Tayside

TYPE OF GRANT Buildings, one-off and start-up costs

RANGE OF GRANTS £250–£10,000

SAMPLE GRANTS £2,000 to The National Trust for Scotland for Scottish heritage
£2,000 to John Muir Trust for Scottish Heritage

FINANCES
- Year 1997–98
- Income £116,554
- Grants £99,000

TRUSTEES Mrs E A Mussen, Ms Z C Mussen, G C Bonar

NOTES Recipients must be registered charities

HOW TO APPLY Applications should be made in writing to the address under Who To Apply To and must include full financial information. Initial telephone calls are not welcome. There are no application forms, guidelines, or application deadlines. Please enclose an sae

WHO TO APPLY TO Mrs Elizabeth A Mussen, The Tay Charitable Trust, 6 Douglas Terrace, Broughty Ferry, Dundee DD5 1EA
Tel 0132 779923

SC NO SCO 01004   **ESTABLISHED** 1951

The C P Thackray General Charitable Trust

WHAT IS FUNDED The Trustees areas of interest in Yorkshire include the protection of the local environment. International interests include ecology and conservation

WHAT IS NOT FUNDED Grants are not made for disaster appeals, appeals for medical or educational equipment, charities for domestic pets, politics, religion, the arts and heritage or unregistered charities. No grants to individuals

WHO CAN BENEFIT Organisations working in the areas outlined above

WHERE FUNDING CAN BE GIVEN Yorkshire and overseas

TYPE OF GRANT Recurrent grants are made, although this list is reviewed annually and capital projects are considered and allocated a small proportion of the total funds available. Unfortunately, this leaves little funding for new applicants

RANGE OF GRANTS £400–£18,750

FINANCES
- Year 1998
- Income £98,256
- Grants £48,150

TRUSTEES C P Thackray, Mrs L T Thackray, R C Gorospe, W M Wrigley, Mrs R L Lockie

HOW TO APPLY Administration is carried out voluntarily. For this reason no further guidance can be given to applicants and only successful applications are acknowledged, following the Trustees' annual meeting

WHO TO APPLY TO Mrs Ramona Lockie, The C P Thackray General Charitable Trust, PO Box 2002, Pulborough, West Sussex RH20 2FR

CC NO 328650   **ESTABLISHED** 1990

Loke Wan Tho Memorial Foundation

WHAT IS FUNDED Rural conservation; animal welfare; bird sanctuaries; wildlife sanctuaries; ornithology and zoology; and other charitable purposes

WHAT IS NOT FUNDED No grants to individuals

WHO CAN BENEFIT Registered charities only. Preference for Far East, ornithology and environment

WHERE FUNDING CAN BE GIVEN UK and Asia

TYPE OF GRANT Project and research. Funding can be given for up to one year

SAMPLE GRANTS £21,796 to Wetlands International
£10,000 to Birdlife International
£2,000 to World Society for the Protection of Animals

FINANCES
- Year 1997
- Grants £44,796
- Income £84,055

TRUSTEES Lady McNeice, Mr Tonkyn, Mrs Tonkyn

NOTES In writing to the Administrator at the address below

WHO TO APPLY TO The Administrator, Loke Wan Tho Memorial Foundation, 9 Greyfriars Road, Reading, Berkshire RG1 1JG
Tel 0118-959 7111

CC NO 264273   **ESTABLISHED** 1972

■Thoresby Charitable Trust

WHAT IS FUNDED Nottinghamshire based charities with the exception of a few national charities. Particularly those working in the fields of: environmental issues; nature reserves; waterways; woodlands; and agriculture. Other charitable purposes will be considered

WHAT IS NOT FUNDED No grants to individuals

WHO CAN BENEFIT Organisations, often local branches, usually well established, but innovatory appeals considered

WHERE FUNDING CAN BE GIVEN UK with preference to Nottinghamshire

TYPE OF GRANT One-off and project. Also buildings, research ands start-up costs. Funding for one year or less will be considered

RANGE OF GRANTS £100–£1,000

FINANCES
- Year 1998
- Grants £16,750
- Income £17,300

TRUSTEES Lady F R R Raynes, H P Matheson, I D P Thorne

HOW TO APPLY Donations decided in January of each year, for distribution in March. No application form, if acknowledgement required send sae

WHO TO APPLY TO Mrs R P H McFerran, Thoresby Charitable Trust, Century House, Thoresby Park, Newark, Nottinghamshire NG22 9EH

CC NO 277215   **ESTABLISHED** 1978

■The Tisbury Telegraph Trust

WHAT IS FUNDED Most distributions are to charities of which the Trustees have personal knowledge. Other applications are unlikely to be successful. Particularly charities working in the fields of: endangered species; environmental issues; flora and fauna; lakes; landscapes; waterways; and woodlands. Also animal welfare; wildlife parks and sanctuaries; zoos; and ornithology and zoology. Other charitable purposes will be considered

WHAT IS NOT FUNDED No grants to individuals

WHO CAN BENEFIT Registered charities only

WHERE FUNDING CAN BE GIVEN London, UK and the developing world

TYPE OF GRANT Capital, core costs, one-off, and research. Funding may be given for up to two years

RANGE OF GRANTS £100–£4,000. Any unsolicited applications will not receive more than about £200

SAMPLE GRANTS £1,120 to The National Trust

FINANCES
- Year 1997
- Grants £34,918
- Income £57,618

TRUSTEES J Davidson, A Davidson, E Orr, R Orr, S Phippard

HOW TO APPLY Applications only acknowledged if sae enclosed. No telephone applications please

WHO TO APPLY TO Mrs E Orr, The Tisbury Telegraph Trust, 35 Kitto Road, Telegraph Hill, London SE14 5TW
E-mail rogero@howzatt.demon.co.uk

CC NO 328595   **ESTABLISHED** 1990

■The Torrs Charitable Trust

WHAT IS FUNDED The conservation of wildlife, the environment and other charitable purposes as defined by the Trustees

WHAT IS NOT FUNDED No grants to individuals

WHO CAN BENEFIT Registered charities working in the areas outlined above

WHERE FUNDING CAN BE GIVEN UK and overseas

TYPE OF GRANT One-off, core costs and capital. Funding may be given for up to two years

SAMPLE GRANTS £2,000 to Rocha Trust for general funds for conservation in Lebanon

FINANCES
- Year 1997–98
- Income £20,872
- Grants £17,250

TRUSTEES Miss E G Dollar, Dr M T M Roberts, Dr E T Roberts, Mrs M V Roberts

HOW TO APPLY To the address below in writing. Not all applications can be acknowledged

WHO TO APPLY TO Dr E T Roberts, The Torrs Charitable Trust, 101 Havant Road, East Cosham, Portsmouth, Hampshire PO6 2JE

CC NO 1048219   **ESTABLISHED** 1995

■ The Town Lands (also known as The Utility Estate)

WHAT IS FUNDED Rural conservation; animal facilities and services; environmental and animal sciences; and other charitable purposes

WHO CAN BENEFIT Individuals and organisations

WHERE FUNDING CAN BE GIVEN Tysoe

FINANCES
- Year 1997
- Income £29,812

HOW TO APPLY To the address under Who To Apply To in writing

WHO TO APPLY TO Mrs J Walton, Secretary, The Town Lands, Lane End Farm, Lower Tysoe, Warwick, Warwickshire CV35 0BZ
Tel 01295 680289

CC NO 241493   **ESTABLISHED** 1965

■ The Trades House of Glasgow – Commonweal Fund (505)

WHAT IS FUNDED Charitable purposes benefiting the City of Glasgow and her citizens including: rural conservation; animal facilities and services; and animal sciences

WHAT IS NOT FUNDED No grants to individuals. No political, municipal and ecclesiastical appeals

WHO CAN BENEFIT Glasgow and its citizens

WHERE FUNDING CAN BE GIVEN Glasgow

TYPE OF GRANT Buildings, capital, core costs, feasibility studies, one-off, project, research, running costs, salaries and start-up costs. Funding is only given for one year or less

RANGE OF GRANTS £50–£5,000

FINANCES
- Year 1998
- Income £109,000
- Grants £122,000

TRUSTEES The Trustees are incorporated by Act of Parliament

PUBLICATIONS Annual Report and Accounts

HOW TO APPLY Contact the Clerk for further details, then make an application in writing

WHO TO APPLY TO Gordon M Wyllie, Clerk, The Trades House of Glasgow – Commonweal Fund, Dalmore House, 310 St Vincent Street, Glasgow G2 5QR
Tel 0141-228 8000

SC NO SCO 00618   **ESTABLISHED** 1920

Commentary

Established almost four centuries ago, in 1605, the Trades House of Glasgow consists of 64 representatives of the 14 ancient incorporated trades of Glasgow. It has various trusts under management – including the Corporate Funds of the House, W W and M Macfarlane Bequest and Drapers' Fund – of which the Commonweal Fund is the main one that is open to unreferred applications. Fund revenue is devoted to charitable projects that will benefit Glasgow and her citizens. In 1998 £122,000 was distributed from the Commonweal Fund for these purposes. Charities with national purposes will not usually be funded. Projects to be funded must be practical and businesslike. Funding policies basically remain the same from year to year. However, there is a new committee appointed each year, so funding policies may change slightly in reflection of members' personal interests.

The Trades House makes only one-off grants, so the policy is that projects that have received help one year will be refused the following year. Organisations can, however, reapply for a grant at a later date.

It is Trades House policy not to replace statutory funding, partly because of the likely volume of applications and partly because of a strong feeling in Scotland that the voluntary sector should not step in to pay for things that the government should be funding. Applications from statutory bodies will not be considered.

The Trades House will not fund political, municipal or ecclesiastical appeals. Nor will it normally help charities that duplicate rather than complement existing services or those with large running surpluses. Grants cannot be made to individuals.

There is no set application form. Applications should be summarised on a single A4 sheet, backed up as necessary by schedules, and accompanied by the applicant's latest accounts and/or business plan. Applications should include: (a) evidence of need; (b) evidence that client groups participate in decision-taking; (c) evidence that clients' quality of life and choice will be enhanced by the project; (d) details of current funding and the use being made of it; (e) evidence of charitable status; (f) where possible, a breakdown of costs and financial needs; (g) evidence of the difference a grant would make; and (h) details of other grants applied for, and the results so far.

Applications are considered twice a year. The last dates for receipt of applications for the spring and autumn meetings are mid-January and mid-August. Generally, only successful applications will be acknowledged.

All grant recipients must make a report on how the funds have been used. Grants not used for the purposes stated will have to be returned

SAMPLE GRANTS

The top ten grants made in 1997 were:
£15,000 to Child Psychotherapy Trust in Scotland for the cost of a room within conversion of premises
£6,000 to Glasgow 1999 towards the cost of a centre of architecture and design
£4,000 to Pollokshields Burgh Hall Trust towards the cost of developing a lower ground floor basement
£3,000 to Friends of Children of Middlefield School for the purchase of a computer, books for library, etc
£2,500 to Stepford Road Sports Trust towards the cost of a multi-sports complex in Easterhouse
£2,300 to Rotary Residential and Care Centres for fitting out a kitchen for disabled people
£2,000 to Cancer Research Campaign for a fundraising bicycling tour
£2,000 to Cornerstone Community Care towards the cost of accommodation for handicapped women
£2,000 to Accord Hospice towards the cost of beds
£1,650 to Glasgow Common Purpose towards their work of fostering a sense of civic responsibility among young members of the managerial class

■ The Twil Group Charitable Trust

WHAT IS FUNDED Environmental issues and nature reserves

WHAT IS NOT FUNDED Grants are not made for individuals

WHO CAN BENEFIT Organisations working in the areas outlined above

WHERE FUNDING CAN BE GIVEN Sheffield and Rotherham

FINANCES
- Year 1997
- Income £10,016

HOW TO APPLY To the address below in writing

WHO TO APPLY TO The Secretary, The Twil Group Charitable Trust, Twil Limited, PO Box 119, Shepcote Lane, Sheffield S9 1TY

CC NO 283212   **ESTABLISHED** 1981

V

■ Mrs Maud Van Norden's Charitable Foundation

WHAT IS FUNDED General charitable purposes in particular: endangered species; environmental issues; fauna; nature reserves; waterways; and animal facilities and services – with a preference for animal welfare. Annual review of list of donations with occasional additions and deletions at the discretion of the Trustees

WHAT IS NOT FUNDED No grants to individuals. Registered charities only

WHO CAN BENEFIT Registered charities working in the areas outlined above

WHERE FUNDING CAN BE GIVEN UK

TYPE OF GRANT Cash grants of £600 on an annual basis and of £600–£2,000 on a once only basis. Annual grants can be for running expenses: once only grants are more usually for capital projects and special appeals. Also research grants

FINANCES
- Year 1998
- Income £42,050
- Grants £38,200

TRUSTEES F C S Tufton, Mrs E M Dukler, A O Deas, Mrs E A Humphryes

NOTES Applications only considered if supported by a copy of the latest Report and Accounts

HOW TO APPLY In writing to the address under Who To Apply To. No acknowledgment or notification of result unless successful. If a reply is required sae should be sent. Appeals considered once a year in May or June

WHO TO APPLY TO Messrs Payne Hicks Beach, Mrs Maud Van Norden's Charitable Foundation, 10 New Square, Lincoln's Inn, London WC2A 3QG

CC NO 210844   **ESTABLISHED** 1960

■ The Vaux Group Foundation

WHAT IS FUNDED The Trust funds communities and organisations where the company operates. Particularly charities working in the fields of: rural conservation, and animal facilities and services

WHAT IS NOT FUNDED No grants to individuals. No grants to national appeals unless there is a local bias towards a Group trading

WHO CAN BENEFIT Small, local groups, local and regional charitable organisations and some national organisations working in the areas outlined above

WHERE FUNDING CAN BE GIVEN North East and North West England, and Yorkshire

FINANCES
- Year 1995–96
- Income £36,478
- Grants £127,000

TRUSTEES William P Catesby, Frank Nicholson, Sir Paul Nicholson, Christopher Storey, Neal Gossage

HOW TO APPLY To the address under Who To Apply To in writing

WHO TO APPLY TO Hilary Florek, Administrator, The Vaux Group Foundation, Vaux Group plc, The Brewery, Sunderland SR1 3AN
Tel 0191-567 6277
Fax 0191-514 2488
Web Site http://www.vaux.group.co.uk

CC NO 802636 **ESTABLISHED** 1988

■ The Verdon-Smith Family Charitable Settlement

WHAT IS FUNDED This Trust will consider funding: waterways, woodlands, agriculture and animal welfare. Quarterly review of regular donations with occasional addition of new donations at discretion of Trustees

WHAT IS NOT FUNDED No donations to individuals, no salaries or running costs

WHO CAN BENEFIT Registered charities with emphasis on local activity and needs

WHERE FUNDING CAN BE GIVEN South West England – new responses increasingly limited to Bristol, Somerset, South Gloucestershire, and Wiltshire

TYPE OF GRANT Recurrent, occasional one-off, buildings, capital, core costs, project and research. Funding is available for one year or less

RANGE OF GRANTS £50–£300, typical grant £140

FINANCES
- Year 1998
- Income £28,500
- Grants £22,625

TRUSTEES Lady Verdon-Smith, W G Verdon-Smith, Lady E J White, Mrs D N Verdon-Smith

PUBLICATIONS Annual Report

HOW TO APPLY In writing to the address under Who To Apply To. Applications will not be acknowledged unless successful. No telephone calls

WHO TO APPLY TO Lady White, The Verdon-Smith Family Charitable Settlement, Pypers, Rudgeway, Bristol BS35 3SQ

CC NO 284919 **ESTABLISHED** 1983

■ The Vodafone Group Charitable Trust

WHAT IS FUNDED Trustees favour applications from projects with a communications bias. They will give their support within the following areas: rural conservation and animal welfare

WHAT IS NOT FUNDED Funding is not generally given to overseas based charities. No grants to individuals or for individual studies

WHO CAN BENEFIT Registered charities working in the areas outlined above

WHERE FUNDING CAN BE GIVEN UK

TYPE OF GRANT Buildings, capital, one-off, project and research will be considered. Funding is available for up to three years

RANGE OF GRANTS £1,000–£20,000, typical grant £10,000

FINANCES
- Year 1998
- Income £359,938
- Grants £477,630

TRUSTEES P R Williams, T G Barwick, Sir Alec Broers

HOW TO APPLY Applications in writing with charity registration number. No application form required. Applications will be submitted to a quarterly Trustee meeting. Support is in cash only, no telecom equipment or prizes given. No third party applicants considered

WHO TO APPLY TO P R Williams, The Vodafone Group Charitable Trust, Vodafone Group plc, 2–4 London Road, Newbury, Berkshire RG14 1JX

CC NO 1013850 **ESTABLISHED** 1992

WWF UK (World Wide Fund for Nature)

WHAT IS FUNDED Projects which contribute to WWF UKs conservation programme which comprises targeted areas of activity within the broad headings of: living seas, forests, wetlands, species and habitats of special concern, future landscapes, climate change, toxics and sustainable resource use. Applicants should telephone to discuss whether projects would fall within the priority areas

WHAT IS NOT FUNDED No grants for expeditions, university courses, buildings, animal welfare, pure research or school/community conservation areas

WHO CAN BENEFIT Organisations working in the areas outlined above

WHERE FUNDING CAN BE GIVEN UK

TYPE OF GRANT Short or long-term grants (maximum usually three years). Interest free loans for 6–12 months. Core costs, one-off, project, research, running costs, salaries, feasibility studies and start-up costs will also be considered

RANGE OF GRANTS £1,000–£50,000, typical grant £10,000

SAMPLE GRANTS £22,000 to Bumblebee Working Group towards identifying the reasons for the decline of bumblebees in the general countryside and to develop strategies to restore these insects to their former range in the UK
£18,179 to The Wildlife Trusts for a Development Officer for Otters Plan to raise the funds required over the next three years to begin implementation of a long-term conservation plan for otters
£15,000 to Borders Forest Trust for Ettrick Floodplain Restoration - the ecological restoration of a habitat mosaic, including woodland, wetland, swamp and hay meadow, along a four kilometre stretch of the Upper Ettrick Valley, South Scotland
£14,000 to Wildfowl and Wetlands Trust for Barn Elms Project - Wetlands for the monitoring of the construction of a 100 acre mosaic of wetland habitats on the site of four redundant reservoir basins
£11,484 to Butterfly Conservation for Action for Butterflies - Planning and Implementation to enable Butterfly Conservation to implement action plans for 25 of the UK's most threatened butterflies
£11,400 to Wildlife Link for WCL Support to provide support for WCL which aims to help secure the conservation and protection of the UK's wildlife and countryside
£11,120 to Plantlife for a Species Action Co-ordinator Post to combine the existing 'Back from the Brink' and 'Action for Plants' projects to create a single overarching species conservation programme
£11,000 to Mammal Society for Look Out For Mammals Project which aims to involve local groups and volunteers in recording the distribution of British mammals
£10,000 to European Forum for Nature Conservation and Pastoralism for Nature Conservation and Pastoralism Project which aims to increase the recognition of the value of low-intensity agriculture to nature conservation, European biodiversity and more sustainable land management
£10,000 to Shark Trust for Development of Shark Trust and EEA which will result in a self-financing, active and influential non-government organisation

FINANCES
- Year 1997–98
- Income £22,998,000
- Grants £13,091,000

TRUSTEES Vice-Presidents: Rt Hon The Lord Buxton, MC, DL, Guy Mountfort, OBE, E Max Nicholson, CB, CVO, LLD. Trustees: Hon Mrs Sara Morrison (Chairman), Jeremy Edwards (Hon Treasurer), Mrs Pamela Castle, Sir Charles Fraser, KCVO, DL, John Laing, Prof Stephen Martin, Prof Adrian Phillips, CBE, Dr Anne Powell, Prof Sir David Smith, Sir Crispin Tickell, GCMG, KCVO, Prof Peter Toyne, DL, Christopher Ward, Charles Wilson

PUBLICATIONS *WWF-UK Catalogue of Conservation Projects and Report*

HOW TO APPLY By telephone prior to submitting a formal application. Two forms are available, one for the general category and one for land purchase, both include guidance notes. Applications should be completed by the end of each year to be considered for the following year's conservation programme. However, applications may be considered at any time for the uncommitted part of the budget set aside for innovative and urgent projects. It is expected that applicants will also be applying for grants to other bodies such as the Countryside Commission, Countryside Council for Wales, English Nature and Scottish Natural Heritage

WHO TO APPLY TO Bryony Chapman, UK Project Officer, WWF UK (World Wide Fund for Nature), Panda House, Weyside Park, Godalming, Surrey GU7 1XR
Tel 01483 426444
Fax 01483 426409
Web Site http://www.wwf-uk.org

CC NO 201707   **ESTABLISHED** 1961

The Charity of Thomas Wade & Others

WHAT IS FUNDED Lakes, landscapes, woodlands and open spaces

WHAT IS NOT FUNDED No grants to individuals. Tend not to support schools or medicine or health orientated bodies

WHO CAN BENEFIT Charities working in the areas outlined above

WHERE FUNDING CAN BE GIVEN Leeds (pre-1974 boundary of the City)

TYPE OF GRANT Usually one-off capital grants. Core costs, recurring costs, running costs and start-up costs. Funding for up to three years may be considered

RANGE OF GRANTS £200–£30,000, typical grant £1,000–£2,000

FINANCES
- Year 1997
- Income £187,488
- Grants £163,642

TRUSTEES Lord Mayor, Rector of Leeds, J Roberts, E M Arnold, J Horrocks, P J D Marshall, OBE, Dr A Cooke, M J Dodgson, I A Ziff, J Tinker, J M Barr, CBE, M S Wainwright, B T Braimah, MBE, J D M Stoddart-Scott, J Thorpe (+ three representatives of Leeds City Council)

HOW TO APPLY Trustees meet April, July and November. Applications should reach them at least three weeks before the meeting because applications are checked, applicants visited and the project discussed. Essential to submit accounts and contact telephone number with application. Reports are required from all successful applicants

WHO TO APPLY TO W M Wrigley, The Charity of Thomas Wade & Others, Wrigleys Solicitors, 5 Butts Court, Leeds LS1 5JS

CC NO 224939   **ESTABLISHED** 1530

The Prince of Wales's Charitable Foundation (506)

WHAT IS FUNDED Registered charities, particularly those in the field of environment

WHAT IS NOT FUNDED Applications for individuals, including students, will not be considered

WHO CAN BENEFIT Registered charities working in the area outlined above

WHERE FUNDING CAN BE GIVEN UK

TYPE OF GRANT One-off grants for capital or core expenditure

RANGE OF GRANTS £100–£15,000, typical grant £500

FINANCES
- Year 1997
- Income £168,230
- Grants £155,482

TRUSTEES Stephen M J Lamport, Sir Michael Peat, KCVO, Rt Hon Earl Peel, Fiona S Shackleton

HOW TO APPLY General appeals are unlikely to be supported. For any application, full details of the project, including financial data, should be provided in writing

WHO TO APPLY TO Stephen Lamport, Trustee, The Prince of Wales's Charitable Foundation, St James's Palace, London SW1A 1BS

CC NO 277540   **ESTABLISHED** 1979

Commentary

The Prince of Wales's Charitable Foundation, previously known as the Prince of Wales's Charities Trust, was established under a Trust Deed in February 1979, for general charitable purposes. It has two wholly owned subsidiaries – Duchy Originals Ltd and A G Carrick Ltd – from which most of its income is derived.

The Foundation supports general charitable purposes and charitable bodies, at the Trustees' discretion, especially those in which The Prince of Wales himself has particular interest. Favour is given to appeals from the following fields: environment; architecture; heritage; and health. In 1997, £155,482 was distributed to organisations within the following classifications: education received the largest amount, with 60.1 per cent of the total. United World Colleges (International) Ltd received 18.3 per cent; medical welfare received 7 per cent; environment received 5 per cent; restoration received 2.4 per cent; hospices and hospitals received 2 per cent; medical research received 1.9 per cent; overseas aid received 1.6 per cent; children and youth received 1 per cent; animals received 0.3 per cent; and social welfare received 0.3 per cent. It is not known whether the Foundation has any scales of preference within the areas that it supports.

The original funding policies of the Foundation were set out in the Trust Deed of 1979, but it is not known whether they have changed since. The Foundation makes grants to registered charities only, throughout the UK. It will not, therefore, fund statutory bodies. The Foundation's attitude to co-funding projects is not known.

The Foundation prefers to make one-off grants for capital or core expenditure and grants range between £100 and £15,000. The typical size of grant is £500. It is not known if loans are made or if infrastructure costs are supported.

Applications should be in writing, including full details of the project, and financial data. The assessment procedure is not known

SAMPLE GRANTS The top ten grants made in 1997 are not known

■ The Walker 597 Trust

WHAT IS FUNDED Animal welfare and the prevention of cruelty to animals. To make grants to relatively small organisations

WHAT IS NOT FUNDED None, but smaller organisations with low overheads preferred

WHO CAN BENEFIT Animal welfare organisations

WHERE FUNDING CAN BE GIVEN UK and overseas

TYPE OF GRANT Cash – generally not exceeding £200

SAMPLE GRANTS £200 to Animal Concern
£200 to Mare and Foal Sanctuary
£200 to Swan Lifeline
£200 to World Parrot Trust
£200 to Woodside Animal Welfare Centre
£200 to Donkey Sanctuary
£200 to Otter Trust
£200 to People's Trust for Endangered Species
£200 to Sebakwe Black Rhino Trust

FINANCES
- Year 1996
- Grants £18,600
- Income £25,740

TRUSTEES J C H Walker, Mrs J M Walker, N Q Grazebrook, Mrs R H Rowett

HOW TO APPLY To the address under Who To Apply To quoting Ref NQG, preferably in July or December

WHO TO APPLY TO The Walker 597 Trust, Messrs Shakespeares, Solicitors, 10 Bennetts Hill, Birmingham B2 5RS

CC NO 278582   **ESTABLISHED** 1979

■ The Anthony Walker Charitable Trust

WHAT IS FUNDED Environmental charities

WHAT IS NOT FUNDED No grants to individuals

WHO CAN BENEFIT Charities working in the areas outlined above

WHERE FUNDING CAN BE GIVEN UK

FINANCES
- Year 1996–97
- Income £3,100

HOW TO APPLY To the address below in writing

WHO TO APPLY TO The Clerk, The Anthony Walker Charitable Trust, Britannic House, Regent Street, Barnsley, South Yorkshire S70 2EQ

CC NO 326187   **ESTABLISHED** 1982

■ The Ruth Walker Charitable Trust

WHAT IS FUNDED Environmental charities

WHAT IS NOT FUNDED No grants to individuals

WHO CAN BENEFIT Registered charities only

WHERE FUNDING CAN BE GIVEN UK and overseas

FINANCES
- Year 1996–97
- Grants £13,115
- Income £9,435

TRUSTEES Michael J M Walker, Josephine R Lees, Helen E Porteous

HOW TO APPLY In writing to the address below

WHO TO APPLY TO Bury/Walkers with Smith/Ibberson (Trustees Solicitors), The Ruth Walker Charitable Trust, Britannic House, Regent Street, Barnsley, South Yorkshire S70 2EQ

CC NO 271910   **ESTABLISHED** 1976

■ The Isidore and David Walton Foundation

WHAT IS FUNDED Animal welfare charities will be considered

WHAT IS NOT FUNDED Grants are not awarded for political causes nor to individuals

WHO CAN BENEFIT Organisations benefiting animals

WHERE FUNDING CAN BE GIVEN West of Scotland, particularly Glasgow

FINANCES
- Year 1996
- Grants £40,000
- Income £100,000

TRUSTEES Prof L Blumgart, E Glen, Prof R A Lorimer, Mrs C Walton, D Walton, J R Walton, M Walton

PUBLICATIONS Accounts are available from Deloitte-Touche & Co Chartered Accountants, 39 St Vincent Place, Glasgow G1 2QQ

HOW TO APPLY Unsolicited applications are not invited

WHO TO APPLY TO David Walton, The Isidore and David Walton Foundation, Royal Exchange House, 100 Queen Street, Glasgow G1 3DL *Tel* 0141-248 7333

SC NO SCO 04005

■ Warrington Animal Welfare

WHAT IS FUNDED Dog owners in receipt of welfare benefits or who are on low income can be assisted with the veterinary treatment costs of neutering their pet dogs. Assistance may also be given towards the costs of other essential veterinary treatments (if there are sufficient charity funds available). Dog owners who can no longer keep their pet dogs (eg due to admission to a Residential or nursing home or hospital, or due to death and not having relatives who can take the dog) may be assisted by the Charity rehoming the dog

WHAT IS NOT FUNDED The Charity is concerned only with dogs (not other animals)

WHO CAN BENEFIT Dog owners in receipt of welfare benefits or low income; dogs' health and welfare; the environment by the prevention of the proliferation of unwanted/unplanned dogs

WHERE FUNDING CAN BE GIVEN The Borough of Warrington and immediate surrounding Districts

TYPE OF GRANT One-off grants towards veterinary treatment costs. (The grant payments are made direct to the veterinary surgeons undertaking the treatments authorised by the Charity on behalf of the dog owners)

RANGE OF GRANTS £30–£125. (The cost of neutering a dog costs approximately £30–£90; spaying a bitch costs approximately £60–£125 - depending on the size and condition of the dog)

FINANCES
- Year 1997–98
- Income £15,270
- Grants £15,030

TRUSTEES Joan M Rimmer, BEM, Pauline A Leigh, R Valerie Dabbs, Barbara Gilson, Jennifer Hindley, Joan James, Catherine Moore, Helen Potter

PUBLICATIONS Annual Report and Accounts; leaflet. Newsletter

NOTES Grantseekers contact the Co-ordinator who arranges for a visit to be made to the applicant to assess the need. If approved, the Charity arranges for the dog to be taken to one of the veterinary surgeries whose services are available to the Charity. When the veterinary treatment is completed the Charity pays the agreed grant to the veterinary surgery. Any excess payment required is met by the dog owner

HOW TO APPLY Contact should be made to the Co-ordinator by telephone or letter

WHO TO APPLY TO Joan M Rimmer, Co-ordinator, Warrington Animal Welfare, Flat 4, The Hill, Parkfield Road, Knutsford, Cheshire WA16 8NP
Tel 01565 634959

CC NO 1057149   **ESTABLISHED** 1982

■ Mrs Waterhouse Charitable Trust (440)

WHAT IS FUNDED General charitable purposes based in, or with branches in, Lancashire including: rural conservation; animal facilities and services; and environmental and animal sciences

WHAT IS NOT FUNDED No grants to individuals, or for expeditions or scholarships

WHO CAN BENEFIT Registered charities only

WHERE FUNDING CAN BE GIVEN UK, but preference for Lancashire

TYPE OF GRANT Cash grants, mostly recurring. Occasional large grants for capital purposes

RANGE OF GRANTS £1,000–£50,000; typical grant £2,000–£5,000

FINANCES
- Year 1998
- Income £288,936
- Grants £293,000

TRUSTEES D H Dunn, Mrs E Dunn

HOW TO APPLY In writing. See below for further details

WHO TO APPLY TO D H Dunn, Correspondent, Mrs Waterhouse Charitable Trust, 25 Clitheroe Road, Whalley, Clitheroe BB7 9AD

CC NO 261685   **ESTABLISHED** 1967

Commentary

In 1967 Mrs Elsbeth Waterhouse set up a family trust with the main objective of providing funds on a regular basis to augment the income of charities to enable them to maintain and improve their services. The Trust has continued to carry out these objectives since the death of Mrs Waterhouse in 1992, and the present Trustees are her nephew D H Dunn and his wife. A limited number of more substantial grants may be made in order that organisations can finance charitable projects of a capital nature. Donations are mainly given to organisations based in, or with branches in, the Lancashire area. However, applications from other parts of the UK may be considered.

Apart from favouring local projects, the Trustees place no restrictions on the types of project they are prepared to consider, except for those set out above. The accounts for the year 1997–98 show that 68 charities received a total of £293,000 in grants, the largest being £50,000 to BHRV Health Care NHS Trust. The grants list indicates that medical charities were favoured, particularly medical research, but many environmental organisations also benefited.

Most of the grants awarded are recurrent from year to year. Loans will not be considered.

There are no application forms or formal guidelines. Applicants are recommended to

Weatherby

Alphabetical register of grant making trusts

submit a brief description of their charity's aims and objects and, if available, a copy of their latest accounts. Applications can be made at any time during the year, but grants are normally made in March following a review during January/February. Telephone calls are discouraged. The Trustees usually award most of the grants towards the end of the financial year, in February and March, but money may be given throughout the year. The Trust does not have a formal assessment procedure

SAMPLE GRANTS
The top five grants made in 1998 were:
£50,000 to BHRV Health Care NHS Trust
£25,000 to National Trust Lake District Appeal
£10,000 to Royal Society for the Protection of Birds
£10,000 to Christie Hospital NHS Trust
£10,000 to Royal National Institution for the Blind

■The Weatherby Charity

WHAT IS FUNDED The International League for the Protection of Horses, the RSPCA and charitable organisations concerned with animal welfare at the discretion of the Trustees

WHO CAN BENEFIT Registered charities working in the areas outlined above

WHERE FUNDING CAN BE GIVEN UK

FINANCES
- Year 1995–96
- Income £9,122
- Grants £8,687

HOW TO APPLY In writing to the address below

WHO TO APPLY TO Peter A Williamson, The Weatherby Charity, Peachey & Co, Solicitors, 95 Aldwych, London WC2B 4JF

CC NO 803405   **ESTABLISHED** 1990

■Wensum Residents Association

WHAT IS FUNDED Animal facilities and services for the benefit of the inhabitants of the Wensum General Improvement Area and its surrounding areas

WHO CAN BENEFIT Individuals and institutions working in the areas outlined above

WHERE FUNDING CAN BE GIVEN Wensum General Improvement Area and surrounding areas

TYPE OF GRANT Recurring, project

FINANCES
- Year 1996
- Income £6,707

HOW TO APPLY In writing to the address below

WHO TO APPLY TO F A Dashwood, Wensum Residents Association, 28 Hotback Road, Norwich, Norfolk NR2 4HG

CC NO 272478   **ESTABLISHED** 1976

■Westcroft Trust

WHAT IS FUNDED Woodlands

WHAT IS NOT FUNDED Charitable bodies only. Applications from individuals are not accepted. No grants for medical electives, to sport, the arts (unless specifically for those in Shropshire with disabilities) or to armed forces charities. Requests for sponsorship not supported. Annual grants are withheld if recent accounts are not to hand or do not satisfy the Trustees as to continuing need

WHO CAN BENEFIT Organisations only

WHERE FUNDING CAN BE GIVEN Shropshire

TYPE OF GRANT Single or annual with or without specified time limit. Few grants for capital or endowment. One-off, research, recurring costs, running costs and start-up costs. Funding for up to and over three years will be considered

FINANCES
- Year 1997
- Income £81,329
- Grants £71,378

TRUSTEES Edward P Cadbury, Mary C Cadbury, Richard G Cadbury, James E Cadbury, Erica R Cadbury

PUBLICATIONS Annual Accounts and Report on file at the Charity Commission

NOTES The Trustees favour charities which carry low administrative overheads and which pursue clear policies of equal opportunity in meeting need. Printed letters signed by the great and good, and glossy literature are wasted on them

HOW TO APPLY In writing to the address under Who To Apply To. No telephone calls or fax. No application form or set format but applications should be restricted to a maximum of three sheets of paper, stating purpose, overall financial needs and resources, together with previous year's accounts if appropriate. No acknowledgement will be given. Applications are dealt with at about two month intervals. Relevant unsuccessful applicants will only be notified if a sae is enclosed with the application. Some annual grants are made by Bank Giro. Details of bank name, branch, sort code and account name and number are needed for these. Time and correspondence can be saved if these are sent

WHO TO APPLY TO Edward P Cadbury, Managing Trustee, Westcroft Trust, 32 Hampton Road, Oswestry, Shropshire SY11 1SJ

CC NO 212931 **ESTABLISHED** 1947

■ Garfield Weston Foundation (12)

WHAT IS FUNDED A broad range of activities including: rural conservation; bird sanctuaries; wildlife parks; wildlife sanctuaries; zoos; agriculture; and ornithology and zoology

WHAT IS NOT FUNDED No grants are made to individuals

WHO CAN BENEFIT UK registered charities working in the areas outlined above

WHERE FUNDING CAN BE GIVEN UK

TYPE OF GRANT Usually small contributions to a specific project or part of a project. Buildings, capital, core costs, endowments, one-off, research, recurring costs, running costs and start-up costs. Salaries are rarely considered. Funding is given for one year or less

RANGE OF GRANTS £100–£10,000,000

FINANCES
- Year 1998
- Income £39,347,000
- Grants £26,056,000

TRUSTEES Garfield H Weston (Chairman), Miriam L Burnett, Barbara E Mitchell, R Nancy Baron, Camilla H W Dalgleish, W G Galen Weston, Guy H Weston, Jana R Khayat, Anna C Hobhouse, George G Weston

HOW TO APPLY Applications may be made at any time and should include details of the need the intended project is designed to meet and an outline budget

WHO TO APPLY TO Fiona M Foster, Administrator, Garfield Weston Foundation, Weston Centre, Bowater House, 68 Knightsbridge, London SW1X 7LQ

CC NO 230260 **ESTABLISHED** 1958

Commentary

The Garfield Weston Foundation is a charity endowed in 1958 by the late W Garfield Weston and members of his family. Garfield Weston set up the Foundation because he wanted to give to charity and saw that setting up a trust would allow him to do so very effectively. As at 5 April 1996, the Foundation owned 79.2 per cent of Wittington Investments Limited, the ultimate holding company of Associated British Foods plc and Fortnum and Mason plc, and the backbone of the Weston family business.

The objects of the Foundation are widely drawn, and the Trustees have decided to continue the policy of supporting a broad range of activities in the fields of education; the arts; the environment; health (including research); religion; welfare and other areas of general benefit to the community.

Education received by far the largest amount of support from the Foundation in 1998, totalling £8,177,750. The health category of grants received grants totalling over £4 million. Much of this grant total was accounted for by capital grants to children's hospitals, with the rest distributed between other specialist hospitals such as the National Hospital for Neurology and Neurosurgery, also medical research activities, the provision of support for equipment, rehabilitation, hospices and nursing homes. Support for the arts category in 1998 totalled £6,758,300, with grants being made for both capital costs and revenue funding. There was a continued commitment to education in the arts, including endowment grants to organisations to provide scholarships in the fields of ballet, dance, music and drama. The Foundation is also keen to safeguard the fabric and quality of theatres for future generations and to nurture talent amongst young musicians, actors and designers. There is also an interest in helping quality productions to reach a variety of audiences around the UK.

Welfare projects received more grants than any other category in 1998, the category continuing to have a very high priority for the Foundation, with 220 appeals being supported, making a grant total for the category of £2,544,225. These grants focused upon charities working to benefit the elderly, disabled, the disadvantaged including the homeless, and the carers of these groups. Part of a common theme throughout the projects that the Foundation supports is the encouragement of healthy communities, and projects in this field have sought to help elderly people to regain their places within their own local communities. Under the Foundation's category of religion, there is continued support for the country's national heritage through the upkeep of its churches. In 1998 £987,000 was distributed to a total of 180 local parishes, mostly in donations of £5,000 or less. Mental health and mental handicap grants are made to organisations that deal with various aspects of mental disability, including support for the parents of disabled children as well as the provision of residential facilities for mentally handicapped adults. In 1998 a total of 31 appeals received £66,600, with many of the appeals coming from national charities or local branches of national charities.

The Foundation continues to be committed to its support of youth projects, giving 175 grants in the Youth category, totalling £477,800. Programmes supported include those concerned with personal development, especially those addressing problems of long-term unemployment, crime, drugs, abuse and anti-social behaviour. Those offering basic life and work skills coupled with knowledge and experience which enable disaffected young people to return to education and employment are especially favoured. The

Foundation also supports organisations taking young people who are at risk and providing them with opportunities to participate in community and environmental expeditions around the world. Other projects to receive support include facilities for disabled children, youth groups, youth drop-in centres, pre-school clubs, youth housing programmes, and holiday clubs. The Foundation seeks to provide a large number of small donations in the category of community projects, making 136 grants in 1998 totalling £624,450 to enable local projects to achieve improved facilities for a wide variety of sectors of the community. The Foundation is committed to supporting worthwhile environmental projects, and the £1,428,000 of grants given in the category in 1998 were directed at education programmes, conservation and restoration of the built environment, and conservation of the natural environment.

The areas of funding outlined above are reviewed by the Foundation on a regular basis, but to date there have been no major policy changes necessary, largely due to the broad remit that the Foundation has, and no major changes are expected in the near future.

Grants are almost entirely made to organisations in the UK. Sometimes (albeit rarely) the Foundation will give grants for overseas projects, but these must be through UK registered charities. The Foundation tries hard to spread its giving as widely as possible across the entire country.

The Foundation recognises that the replacement of state provision has become a more difficult area for grant making trusts. The view of the Trustees of the Garfield Weston Foundation is that, where there is a government responsibility to fund a project or an organisation, the Foundation will not become involved. However, where there is no clear indication of whether there is such a statutory responsibility the Foundation has in the past helped with funding – for example medical research and equipment may be supported in some cases. The Foundation does not have a set policy on any kind of partnership funding. If the Foundation is approached by another trust wishing to develop a funding partnership the approach would be examined in the same way as any other application, and looked at on its own merits.

Grants are given in the form most suitable to the project being supported, but are generally one-off. This can include capital and project grants, while core funding is generally not an area the Foundation would wish to become involved in. Grant commitments are only made for a year at a time, although at the end of a year it is possible for an organisation to re-apply. Loans are not made.

The Foundation has very broad guidelines for grant applications. There is no application form; applications should be by letter and should include details of the need the intended project is designed to meet, plus an outline budget and a copy of the latest Annual Report and Accounts. When an application is received, they are initially screened to see if there is any extra information required with the application. All applications are then logged onto the Foundation's database and separated into batches for the Trustees' consideration. The Trustees would usually expect to have considered an appeal and made a decision within ten weeks of it being received. This may take longer if the Trustees feel it is necessary to visit an applicant for appraisal purposes, in which case either the Administrator or one of the Trustees will arrange a visit. All applicants receive a reply.

After a grant has been made it is common practice for the Foundation to request updates on how a project has worked out, and visits to evaluate projects may also be made as part of the process of reviewing the effect that grants have made in practice

SAMPLE GRANTS

The top ten grants made in 1998 were:
£2,500,000 to Cambridge Foundation
£2,000,000 to Royal Shakespeare Company
£2,000,000 to Wales Millennium Centre Project
£1,000,000 to National Gallery
£1,000,000 to Royal Opera House Development Appeal
£1,000,000 to New College, Oxford
£1,000,000 to National Botanic Gardens of Wales
£1,000,000 to Marie Curie Cancer Care
£1,000,000 to Royal Shakespeare Company
£5,014,000 to NSPCC

■H Whitbread First Charitable Trust

WHAT IS FUNDED Localised charities working in the fields of rural conservation; animal homes; animal welfare; bird sanctuaries; wildlife sanctuaries; and environmental and animal sciences

WHAT IS NOT FUNDED No grants made to individuals or non-registered charities, except churches

WHO CAN BENEFIT Local organisations working in the areas outlined above

WHERE FUNDING CAN BE GIVEN UK and overseas, with a preference for the East of England and London

TYPE OF GRANT Many recurrent, including capital, one-off, project, recurring costs and research. Grants can be given for a period of up to two years

RANGE OF GRANTS £50–£5,000, average grant £250

FINANCES
- Year 1997
- Income £72,563

TRUSTEES H Whitbread, S C Whitbread, C R Skottowe

HOW TO APPLY To the address under Who To Apply To in writing

WHO TO APPLY TO Mrs Shirley Morrell, H Whitbread First Charitable Trust, Howards House, Cardington, Bedford MK44 3SR

CC NO 210089   **ESTABLISHED** 1949

■Whitley Animal Protection Trust (473)

WHAT IS FUNDED Animal welfare and protection

WHAT IS NOT FUNDED No grants to individuals

WHO CAN BENEFIT Registered charities only, working in the areas outlined above

WHERE FUNDING CAN BE GIVEN UK

FINANCES
- Year 1995
- Income £300,000
- Grants £267,000

TRUSTEES E Whitley, Mrs P A Whitley, E J Whitley, J Whitley

HOW TO APPLY No application form

WHO TO APPLY TO M T Gwynne, Secretary, Whitley Animal Protection Trust, Messrs R Gwynne & Sons, Solicitors, Edgbaston House, Walker Street, Wellington, Telford, Shropshire TF1 1HF
Tel 01952 641651
Fax 01952 247441

CC NO 236746   **ESTABLISHED** 1964

■The Whitlingham Charitable Trust

WHAT IS FUNDED (a) To acquire and maintain for the public benefit, land in the parishes of Trowse-with-Newton, Thorpe St Andrew and Kirby Bedon, particularly Trowse Marsh and the surrounding area (whether by acquisition of a freehold or leasehold interest in such land), and to conserve and make the same available as a Country Park for the recreation and enjoyment of members of the public who wish to enjoy its amenities for quiet and peaceful pursuits in a rural environment

WHO CAN BENEFIT The general public

WHERE FUNDING CAN BE GIVEN The parishes of Trowse-with-Newton, Thorpe St Andrew and Kirby Bedon

FINANCES
- Year 1997
- Income £27,456

HOW TO APPLY In writing to the address below

WHO TO APPLY TO R G Holman, The Whitlingham Charitable Trust, c/o Thomas Harvey House, 18 Colegate, Norwich, Norfolk NR3 1BQ
Tel 01603 610734
Fax 01603 765710
E-mail 100070,1364@compuserve.com

CC NO 802711   **ESTABLISHED** 1990

■The Wicksteed Village Trust

WHAT IS FUNDED The prevention of cruelty and unnecessary pain to animals

WHAT IS NOT FUNDED No grants to individuals

WHO CAN BENEFIT Organisation working in the areas outlined above. Favour is also given to local causes

WHERE FUNDING CAN BE GIVEN Mainly Kettering, but also elsewhere in the UK

TYPE OF GRANT Cash and kind

TRUSTEES R J Wicksteed (Chairman), J Brandon-Jones, Mrs C Joynson, Rev Canon F Pearce, J H Wicksteed, P J Wilson

NOTES The principal contribution is the support of our own Old People's Residential Establishment, Barton Memorial Trust, Barton Hall, Kettering

HOW TO APPLY A review of donations made, or to be made by the Trust, takes place annually

WHO TO APPLY TO R W Alderson, General Manager, Wicksteed Village Trust, Wicksteed Park, Kettering, Northamptonshire NN15 6NJ

CC NO 203662   **ESTABLISHED** 1916

■Wigan Town Relief in Need Charity

WHAT IS FUNDED Animal homes and animal welfare

WHO CAN BENEFIT Organisations and individuals within the Wigan boundary

WHERE FUNDING CAN BE GIVEN The former County Borough of Wigan

TYPE OF GRANT Core costs, recurring costs and one-off

FINANCES
- Year 1996
- Income £7,600

HOW TO APPLY To the address below in writing

WHO TO APPLY TO G Shepherd, Clerk, Wigan Town Relief in Need Charity, Moot Hall Chambers, 8 Wallgate, Wigan, Lancashire WN1 1JE

CC NO 248976 **ESTABLISHED** 1979

■ The Wild Flower Society

WHAT IS FUNDED To increase knowledge of field botany among the public and in particular young people. To advance knowledge and conservation of flora in Britain

WHAT IS NOT FUNDED No grants to individuals for research projects. No grants for expeditions, scholarships or capital equipment

WHO CAN BENEFIT Nature conservation trusts and educational institutions

WHERE FUNDING CAN BE GIVEN UK

TYPE OF GRANT One-off

RANGE OF GRANTS £50–£2,000; typical £50–£100 for eg: school wildflower work, or £400–£600 towards country flora publication

SAMPLE GRANTS £2,000 to Botanical Society of the British Isles for research on distribution of Scottish mountain flora
£560 to Workers Educational Association as a subsidy to wild flower study course in Liverpool

FINANCES
- Year 1998
- Grants £2,560
- Income £10,809

TRUSTEES R M Burton, D McClintock, R A Blades, Mrs P K Verrall, J Hawksford, Mrs G H Read, N Rumens, Mrs S Buckingham, G H Battershall, Mrs E Norman, A Gagg

HOW TO APPLY Apply in writing to General Secretary at the address below until November 1999, thereafter check Wild Flower Society Magazine for new General Secretary. No application form or guidelines available. Applications are considered by the Trustees at their executive meetings (twice yearly, usually March and September). Sae appreciated

WHO TO APPLY TO Mrs P K Verrall, Secretary, The Wild Flower Society, Woodpeckers, Hoe Lane, Abinger Hammer, Dorking, Surrey RH5 6RH
Tel 01306 730854

CC NO 271694 **ESTABLISHED** 1976

■ The H D H Wills 1965 Charitable Trust

WHAT IS FUNDED Funds are fully committed and donations can only be made to registered charities. Grants are given in seven year cycles to: 1st year Magdalen College, Oxford; 2nd year Rendcomb College Gloucestershire; 3rd and 4th years any registered charity dedicated or primarily dedicated to the conservation of wildlife; 5th year Ditchley Foundation (registered charity no 312911); 6th and 7th years such charitable institutions as the Trustees shall in their absolute discretion think fit

WHAT IS NOT FUNDED No grants to individuals

WHO CAN BENEFIT Organisations working in the areas outlined above

WHERE FUNDING CAN BE GIVEN UK including the Channel Islands, the Irish Republic, and Oxfordshire

RANGE OF GRANTS £100–£250

SAMPLE GRANTS £200,000 to Martin Wills Wildlife Maintenance Trust
£125,000 to Spey Research Trust
£25,000 to Farm Africa
£20,000 to Royal Botanic Gardens, Kew for Millennium Seed Bank
£20,000 to FWAG – Farming and Wildlife Advisory Group
£20,000 to Northumberland Wildlife Trust
£17,000 to TUSK
£14,000 to World Pheasant Association
£10,000 to University of Oxford, Botanical Gardens

FINANCES
- Year 1997
- Grants £920,109
- Income £1,086,917

TRUSTEES J S B Carson, Lord Killearn, Lady E H Wills, Dr C M H Wills, C P L Francklin

NOTES The above figures include the financial details for Knockando Church Fund and Martin Wills Fund

HOW TO APPLY No application form in use. No specific dates for making applications but at present few new applications can be considered

WHO TO APPLY TO Mrs I R Wootton, The H D H Wills 1965 Charitable Trust, 12 Tokenhouse Yard, London EC2R 7AN
Tel 0171-825 9483
Fax 0171-457 3348

CC NO 244610 **ESTABLISHED** 1965

■ J and J R Wilson Trust

WHAT IS FUNDED Grants are given to charitable bodies which are concerned with the care of both domestic and wild animals and birds

WHAT IS NOT FUNDED No grants to individuals

WHO CAN BENEFIT Organisations benefiting animals and birds

WHERE FUNDING CAN BE GIVEN Mainly Scotland, particularly Glasgow and the West of Scotland

HOW TO APPLY The Trustees decide which charitable bodies to support and how much funding should be allocated to each

WHO TO APPLY TO The Correspondent, J and J R Wilson Trust, Hugh Macfarlane, Keith Hopkins, Montgomerie & Co, Apsley House, 29 Wellington Street, Glasgow G2 6JA

SC NO SCO 07411

■The Kit Wilson Trust for Animal Welfare

WHAT IS FUNDED To aid and promote animal welfare

WHO CAN BENEFIT Those with limited income whose animals may breed unwanted litters, feral cat colonies, societies and individuals involved in animal rescue in need of assistance to spay/neuter cats/dogs

WHERE FUNDING CAN BE GIVEN UK, occasionally overseas

FINANCES
- Year 1996
- Income £131,981
- Grants £66,733

TRUSTEES Miss C H Marshall (Chair), Mrs M E Alexander (Hon Treasurer), Mrs C A Billings, Mrs S V Hill (Secretary)

PUBLICATIONS Newsletter – three times a year. Information and legacy leaflets

NOTES The purpose of the Trust is to promote the welfare of animals and especially to rescue abandoned, unwanted and ill treated and neglected animals; to care for these animals and provide them with any necessary veterinary attention until they can be rehomed; to spay/neuter animals in the Trust's care and to give financial help to people of limited means to spay/neuter their pets to reduce the number of unwanted animals. The figure under Grants in the Finances represents the amount spent on the various aspects of animal welfare and not donations to other organisations or individuals

HOW TO APPLY The Trustees meet every month. Possible grants would be considered at these meetings. Urgent applications are dealt with immediately on application to the Chairman

WHO TO APPLY TO The Kit Wilson Trust for Animal Welfare, Animal Rescue Centre, Stonehurst Lane, Hadlow Down, Uckfield, East Sussex TN22 4ED

CC NO 270419 **ESTABLISHED** 1975

■Wiltshire Gardens Trust

WHAT IS FUNDED The conservation or improvement of important and historic gardens in the area Where Funding Can Be Given; to improve schools gardens and develop children's interest in gardening

WHO CAN BENEFIT Primary schools to finance specific garden improvement; the provision of garden tools, greenhouses, paved areas and educational ponds; to provide advice on design, plantings and obtaining funds to owners of important gardens needing restoration; and to finance designs and feasibility studies. Practical help is occasionally given

WHERE FUNDING CAN BE GIVEN Wiltshire

TYPE OF GRANT Feasibility studies, project, start-up costs and the costs of the erection of small school gardens. Funding is given for one year or less

RANGE OF GRANTS Typical grant £200

SAMPLE GRANTS £2,400 in total to primary schools (ranging from £100 to £200 per school) for creating or improving the gardens surrounding the schools, or provision of plants, and garden tools, etc
£436 to Wiltshire Music Centre, Bradford-upon-Avon for the design and implementation of tree and other planting in the surrounding grounds

FINANCES
- Year 1998
- Income £12,400
- Grants £2,836

TRUSTEES Current members of the Wiltshire Gardens Trust Council

PUBLICATIONS *Wiltshire Gardens Trust Journal* (published every six months)

HOW TO APPLY Garden conservation items to the address below in writing. For school grants, apply for application form by telephone to Mrs J Wilmot, Tel:01380 850314

WHO TO APPLY TO Rear Admiral P Marrack, Hon Secretary, Wiltshire Gardens Trust, Treglisson, Crowe Lane, Freshford, Bath BA3 6EB

CC NO 292628 **ESTABLISHED** 1985

■Hyman Winstone Foundation

WHAT IS FUNDED General areas of interest – with emphasis on local charities. Particularly charities working in the field of: environmental issues; fauna; nature reserves; woodlands; bird sanctuaries; and wildlife sanctuaries

WHAT IS NOT FUNDED Registered charities only – no grants to individuals

WHO CAN BENEFIT Registered charities working in the areas outlined above

WHERE FUNDING CAN BE GIVEN Sheffield

TYPE OF GRANT One-off and project

FINANCES
- Year 1997
- Income £18,900
- Grants £17,500

TRUSTEES M H Elliott, R J Elliott, D H Gee

HOW TO APPLY In writing to the address below

WHO TO APPLY TO M H Elliott, Hyman Winstone Foundation, Benson Flint, Solicitors, 32 Wilkinson Street, Sheffield S10 2GB

CC NO 224442 **ESTABLISHED** 1956

■ Ruth Wolfe Charitable Settlement C

WHAT IS FUNDED General charitable purposes including lakes, landscapes, nature reserves and woodlands

WHAT IS NOT FUNDED No grants to animal charities or for educational purposes

WHO CAN BENEFIT Individuals and organisations working in the areas outlined above

WHERE FUNDING CAN BE GIVEN UK and overseas

TYPE OF GRANT One-off and project grants for one year or less

RANGE OF GRANTS £25–£2,000

TRUSTEES R J Wolfe, J A Atkinson

HOW TO APPLY In writing to the address below

WHO TO APPLY TO R J Wolfe, Ruth Wolfe Charitable Settlement C, 3 Rochester Terrace, London NW1 9JN

CC NO 259981 **ESTABLISHED** 1969

■ Woodlands Trust

WHAT IS FUNDED Preference to charities of which the Trust has special interest, knowledge or association. Particularly charities working in the fields of: woodlands and horticulture

WHAT IS NOT FUNDED No grants to individuals

WHO CAN BENEFIT Organisations working in the areas outlined above

WHERE FUNDING CAN BE GIVEN West Midlands

TYPE OF GRANT Core costs, one-off, project, research, running costs, recurring costs, salaries and start-up costs. Funding of up to three years will be considered

FINANCES
- Year 1996–97
- Income £73,369
- Grants £55,750

TRUSTEES J D W Field, J C Barratt, Miss J Steele, Mrs R M Bagshaw, Mrs J N Houston

HOW TO APPLY Six monthly. The Trust Administrator will only enter into correspondence if: (a) further information is required concerning the appeal, or (b) the appeal has been placed on the Trustees' next agenda. Notification will then be given as to the Trustees' decision

WHO TO APPLY TO The Trust Administrator, Woodlands Trust, Box W, White Horse Court, 25c North Street, Bishop's Stortford, Hertfordshire CM23 2LD

CC NO 259569 **ESTABLISHED** 1969

■ The Woodward Charitable Trust (285)

WHAT IS FUNDED Registered charities working in the field of environment. In 1997 four grants were made in this area, totalling £5,000

WHAT IS NOT FUNDED No grants to individuals, for educational fees or individuals joining exhibitions

WHO CAN BENEFIT Registered charities only

WHERE FUNDING CAN BE GIVEN Mainly UK, but a few grants are for overseas projects

TYPE OF GRANT One-off, recurring, capital, core, buildings, project, research and salaries. Funding may be given for up to three years

RANGE OF GRANTS £25–£10,000 for unsolicited appeals. Larger grants tend to be through personal contacts or are in areas in which the Trustees have a particular interest

FINANCES
- Year 1997
- Income £495,784
- Grants £553,509

TRUSTEES Mrs C D Woodward, S A Woodward, MP, Miss J S Portrait

NOTES The Woodwards Charitable Trust is one of the Sainsbury Family Charitable Trusts

HOW TO APPLY Application forms are available from the Secretary of the Trust and may be requested in writing or over the telephone

WHO TO APPLY TO Miss Karin MacLeod, Secretary to the Trust, The Woodward Charitable Trust, 9 Red Lion Court, London EC4A 3EF
Tel 0171-410 0330

CC NO 299963 **ESTABLISHED** 1988

Commentary

The Woodward Charitable Trust was founded in 1988 by S A Woodward, MP and Mrs C D

Woodward and is one of the group of charities known collectively as the Sainsbury Family Charitable Trusts. The Woodward Charitable Trust has extremely wide objectives, and primarily supports children's charities, youth organisations, medical and welfare charities, and arts organisations; although the Trustees sometimes make grants outside the fields to projects and organisations in areas in which they take a personal interest.

The Trust will fund anywhere within the UK. Any overseas grants are generally made through UK-registered charities or large international charitable bodies.

Grants may be made for the general support of an organisation, as well as for capital costs and for specific projects.

Although the Sainsbury Family Charitable Trusts make few responses to unsolicited applications because they tend to take a pro-active stance and go out and find their own causes, the Woodward Trustees consider all appeals in the categories listed above, and make a number of small grants to regional organisations.

Application forms are available upon request from the Secretary and when returned should include an Annual Report and set of Accounts. When an application is received, the Secretary of the Trust will assess whether it falls within the Trustees' current areas of interest before it can go forward to one of the Trustees' meetings.

Further communication will only be entered into if the application is being given serious consideration, although the Trustees emphasise that there is no obligation to fund; all grant makers having many more projects to support than they have grant making capability. The Trustees request reports from those who have received grants and also arrange periodic reviews of their major programmes, but do not have an assessment process whereby all organisations are visited

SAMPLE GRANTS
The top ten grants given in 1996 were:
£163,000 to English National Opera
£33,000 to Childline
£24,000 to the Royal Opera House, Covent Garden
£16,365 to Oxford Student Radio (Oxygen)
£12,000 to Working for a Charity
£10,000 to American Air Museum in Britain (Duxford)
£10,000 to Caldecott Community
£10,000 to Fairbridge
£10,000 to Kings Corner project
£6,500 to Northern Stage

■ The Worshipful Company of Gardeners of London Charity

WHAT IS FUNDED Charities connected with gardening and horticulture including: rural conservation and agriculture

WHAT IS NOT FUNDED No grants to individuals. No general funds

WHERE FUNDING CAN BE GIVEN UK

TYPE OF GRANT One-off and project. Funding may be given for one year or less

RANGE OF GRANTS £200–£1,500

SAMPLE GRANTS Horticultural Therapy
London Children Flowers Society
Flowers in the City
London in Bloom
Gardening for the Disabled
London Garden Society

TRUSTEES The Court of Associates

PUBLICATIONS *Root & Branch*

HOW TO APPLY In writing to the Clerk

WHO TO APPLY TO Colonel N G S Gray, Clerk, The Worshipful Company of Gardeners of London Charity, The Worshipful Company of Gardeners, 25 Luke Street, London EC2A 4AR
Tel 0171-739 8200
Fax 0171-613 3412

CC NO 222079   **ESTABLISHED** 1605

■ John William Wright Deceased Trust

WHAT IS FUNDED Charities working in the fields of rural conservation, bird sanctuaries and wildlife sanctuaries

WHAT IS NOT FUNDED No grants to individuals

WHO CAN BENEFIT Organisations working in the fields outlined above

WHERE FUNDING CAN BE GIVEN Preference to Lincoln and Lincolnshire, only very exceptionally are grants made outside this area

TYPE OF GRANT For capital expenditure of a non-recurring nature. The Trust has supported conservation and preservation projects. Buildings, one-off, project and funding for one year or less will be considered

RANGE OF GRANTS £100–£1,000

FINANCES
- Year 1998
- Grants £12,170
- Income £14,770

TRUSTEES R D Atkinson, P R Strange, Miss M Hall, Mrs G Harrison

Wyford

Alphabetical register of grant making trusts

HOW TO APPLY By letter with details of cost and applicants contribution and a copy of the accounts. Any application from outside Lincolnshire should telephone first to enquire if there is any probability their application will be considered. Applications from outside Lincolnshire will only receive a response if accompanied by an sae. They are most unlikely to be accepted

WHO TO APPLY TO Messrs Andrew & Co, (Ref JD), John William Wright Deceased Trust, St Swithin's Square, Lincoln, Lincolnshire LN2 1HB
Tel 01522 512123
Fax 01522 546713
E-mail andsol@enterprise.net

CC NO 249619   **ESTABLISHED** 1964

■ The Wyford Charitable Trust

WHAT IS FUNDED At Trustees' discretion – current emphasis on animal welfare and dogs, kennels and other facilities for dogs

WHAT IS NOT FUNDED No non-registered charities, no grants to individuals

WHO CAN BENEFIT Animal welfare organisations

WHERE FUNDING CAN BE GIVEN South East England and Switzerland

TYPE OF GRANT At the discretion of the Trustees. Core costs. Funding of one year or less will be considered

RANGE OF GRANTS £1,000–£5,000

SAMPLE GRANTS Grants given for core costs:
£2,000 to The Animal Welfare Trust
£2,000 to PDSA
£2,000 to Pine Ridge Dog Sanctuary
£1,500 to Societe Proectrice Des Animaux

FINANCES
- Year 1997–98
- Income £30,928
- Grants £30,000

TRUSTEES Robert Fleming Trustee Co Ltd, Roderick J Fleming, Nicholas R D Powell

HOW TO APPLY In writing to the address below. No application forms or guidelines issued

WHO TO APPLY TO The Trust Manager, The Wyford Charitable Trust, Robert Fleming Trustee Co Ltd, 25 Copthall Avenue, London EC2R 7DR

CC NO 298093   **ESTABLISHED** 1987

■ Wyre Animal Welfare

WHAT IS FUNDED The Trust supports the rehousing of homeless animals, and gives financial assistance to low income families to neuter and spay animals

WHO CAN BENEFIT Individuals or families, animal welfare organisations. All individuals and families must be on income support

WHERE FUNDING CAN BE GIVEN UK, with preferences to Lancashire and, if funds are sufficient, overseas

TYPE OF GRANT Very small grants, eg for OAP's vets fees, a few to animal charities, and medical fees for animal rescue. Running costs are considered

RANGE OF GRANTS £200–£250

FINANCES
- Year 1997
- Income £16,283
- Grants £650

TRUSTEES Mrs Evans, R A Dodd, Mrs Brown

NOTES Majority of income spent on running costs, ie pet food, veterinary fees, cleaning, etc

HOW TO APPLY In person at the Wyre Animal Welfare Shop, otherwise in writing to the address below

WHO TO APPLY TO R A Dodd, Wyre Animal Welfare, 87 Poulton Road, Fleetwood, Lancashire FY7 6TQ

CC NO 1025042   **ESTABLISHED** 1993

■ The Ash Yeo Trust

WHAT IS FUNDED Charities working in the following areas are supported: rural conservation particularly environmental issues; animal facilities and services, particularly animal welfare; and animal sciences

WHO CAN BENEFIT Animals, individuals and organisations

WHERE FUNDING CAN BE GIVEN Principally Devon

TYPE OF GRANT One-off grants

FINANCES
- Year 1996
- Grants £13,170
- Income £6,686

TRUSTEES Miss M E Yeo, J R Leigh

HOW TO APPLY To the address below in writing

WHO TO APPLY TO Barbara Pedersen, Secretary, The Ash Yeo Trust, Port of Liverpool Building, Pier Head, Liverpool L3 1NW

CC NO 252187   **ESTABLISHED** 1967

■ Yorkshire Agricultural Society

WHAT IS FUNDED (a) Promotion of agriculture and allied industries, related research and education. (b) Protection and safeguarding of the environment. (c) Holding of an annual agricultural show. (d) Appropriate charitable purposes. Priority is given to charities in Yorkshire and former Cleveland, with some activities extending into Durham and Northumberland. Environmental projects normally require relevance to agriculture to attract support

WHAT IS NOT FUNDED No grants are made for students' fees within higher or further education. Overseas projects are seldom supported

WHO CAN BENEFIT Primarily local individuals, activities and organisations in the farming industry and those living in rural areas

WHERE FUNDING CAN BE GIVEN North east England and in particular Yorkshire and (former) Cleveland

TYPE OF GRANT At discretion of Council/Executive Committee – most usually once only or starter/pump priming finance. Buildings, capital, core costs, feasibility studies, one-off, projects, research, and start-up costs will be considered. Funding may be given for up to three years

RANGE OF GRANTS £200–£10,000, typical grant £1,000

SAMPLE GRANTS £25,500 to nine universities for agriculturally related research
£7,661 for Nuffield Farming Scholarship
£5,995 for Nuffield Farming Scholarship
£5,000 to Schools Farm Challenge and Farm Project Competitions
£4,382 to Farm of the Year Competition
£3,809 to Universities Research Exhibit, Great Yorkshire Show to demonstrate up to ten agriculturally related projects
£2,500 each to two Agricultural Colleges in Yorkshire for student hardship
£2,000 each to four Farming and Wildlife Advisory Groups for administration costs
£2,000 to Wakefield 'Farmlink' for administration funding for school visits to farms
£2,000 to Yorkshire Federation of Young Farmers

FINANCES
- Year 1998
- Grants £126,390
- Income £2,568,442

TRUSTEES Council members of whom there are 38

PUBLICATIONS (a) Annual Report. (b) Quarterly Newsletter

HOW TO APPLY To Chief Executive in writing. Applications considered quarterly. Must include recent accounts (if applicable) and proposed budget together with confirmed and anticipated sources of funding. Details of ongoing management and costs also important

WHO TO APPLY TO R T Keigwin, Chief Executive, Yorkshire Agricultural Society, Great Yorkshire Showground, Harrogate HG2 8PW
Tel 01423 541000
Fax 01423 541414
E-mail info@yas.co.uk

CC NO 513238   **ESTABLISHED** 1837

■ The Elizabeth and Prince Zaiger Trust

WHAT IS FUNDED The care and protection of animals, and other charitable purposes

WHAT IS NOT FUNDED **This Trust will not respond to unsolicited applications**

WHO CAN BENEFIT Registered charities

WHERE FUNDING CAN BE GIVEN Somerset, UK

TYPE OF GRANT One-off and recurrent

RANGE OF GRANTS £25–£5,000

FINANCES
- Year 1998
- Income £124,351
- Grants £107,800

TRUSTEES P J Harvey, D G Long, D W Parry

HOW TO APPLY **This Trust states that it does not respond to unsolicited applications.** There is an on-going programme of supporting various charities, and this will not change in the foreseeable future

WHO TO APPLY TO D W Parry, The Elizabeth and Prince Zaiger Trust, 6 Alleyn Road, Dulwich, London SE21 8AL

CC NO 282096   **ESTABLISHED** 1981